The Victorian City

City

Images and Realities

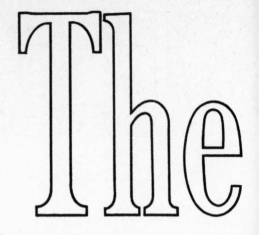

Edited by

H. J. Dyos and Michael Wolff

Routledge & Kegan Paul

London, Henley and Boston

Victorian City

Images and Realities

Volume II   **Shapes on the Ground**
and
A Change of Accent

To H. L. BEALES in his eighty-fifth year

Pioneer and Exponent of the Victorian World

The Victorian City: Images and Realities
first published in two volumes in 1973
Shapes on the Ground *and* A Change of Accent
first published as a paperback in 1978
by Routledge & Kegan Paul Ltd
39 Store Street,
London WC1E 7DD,
Broadway House, Newtown Road,
Henley-on-Thames, Oxon RG9 1EN and
9 Park Street, Boston, Mass. 02108, USA
Set in Monotype Modern Extended Series No. 7
with Gloucester Extra Condensed
Designed by Joseph J. Hart
Printed in Great Britain by
William Clowes & Sons Limited
Copyright 1973 H. J. Dyos and Michael Wolff

British Library Cataloguing in Publication Data

The Victorian city.

Vol. 2: Shapes on the ground; and, A change of accent.

1. City and town life — Great Britain
2. Great Britain — Social life and customs —
   19th century
I. Dyos, Harold James   II. Wolff, Michael
941'.00973'2   DA533   77–30334

ISBN 0 7100 8812 4

Contents

Illustrations

Plates

Maps

See also Plates 192–3, 229–35, 281–7

Acknowledgments

To the Editor of *Victorian Studies* for permission to reprint, in amended or developed form, material first published in its pages and now forming part of chapters 15 and 16; and to the Society of Authors, on behalf of the Bernard Shaw Estate, for the passage from *Widowers' Houses* in chapter 15.

To each of the following for their courteous permission to reproduce paintings, drawings, or photographs in their possession, as indicated: Aberdeen University Library (66, 70, 73, 74, 81, 116–18, 121–3, 128, 129, 139, 161–4, 176, 249, 255, 267); B. T. Batsford Ltd (277); the Trustees of the British Museum (253); Derby Museum & Art Gallery (250); Edinburgh Central Public Library (293, 295); the Provost and Fellows of Eton College (281–91); Mr David Francis (68, 74, 88, 90–2, 95–7, 99–101, 104–6, 115, 119, 126, 130, 134, 144, 151–3, 165, 166, 170, 172, 227); Greater London Council Photograph Library (67, 69, 72, 76, 135, 143, 155, 168); the Keeper of Prints and Pictures, Guildhall Library (93, 112, 120, 159); Kodak Museum (84, 89, 102, 103, 107, 109, 113, 124, 125, 127, 132, 133, 136–8, 140, 142, 147, 150, 154, 157, 177); Liverpool Public Libraries (94, 98, 110, 114, 131, 145, 146, 149, 156, 158, 169, 171, 173, 174); Mr Howarth Loomes (77–80, 83, 85, 160, 185); Mr Adam H. Malcolm (294); Manchester Public Libraries (108, 111, 141, 148, 167, 177–84, 186–226, 228); National Monuments Record (71, 256, 261, 266, 268–70, 275, 276, 278, 280); the Director-General, Ordnance Survey (229–35); Science Museum, London (245, 251); Scotsman Publications Ltd (292); Mr Timothy Summerson (259, 260, 279).

III Shapes on the Ground

9   The Camera's Eye

G. H. Martin and David Francis

Of all the cities of man, the Victorian city was the first to come under the camera's eye, the first to transmit the lights and shadows of its pattern directly to posterity. It lives for us, therefore, in its own image, as well as in the streets and buildings that we still inhabit. Just as the experiences and expedients of the Victorian age inform our own, so we share with that time a unique self-consciousness: a twofold vision. Study it as we may, the past must fall for us, as for Victorians, into the world before photography and the world that the camera has seen.

The nineteenth century's two great contributions to historical enquiry were a rigorous technique and the photograph. Both were products of a sophisticated industrial society, and both are with us still, though they are not as often found in conjunction as they might be. It was appropriate, and perhaps natural, that the century in which, above all others, the principles of historical criticism were refined, should also have passed on to posterity the first exact representations of the contemporary scene. We have drawings and paintings from the earliest ages of mankind, and the artist's vision still extends and intensifies our knowledge of the world. The early fear that the photographer would supplant the artist was never more than a misapprehension. The graphic arts and photography have come amicably to terms, but as a historical record the photograph stands alone. Only the camera enables us to see the past as though it were the present, to dwell upon an instant that is fixed for all time.

The camera is not a faultless instrument: its lenses distort, exaggerating some horizontal lines and depressing verticals, and it can be made to utter untruths. What matters most, however, is that its eye observes, but does not select. It has rather less capacity for deceit than we have ourselves, and each of its pictures offers us a unique record. At the same time, they share one important quality with the graphic artist's work, for every one is the consequence of a deliberate act. A photograph is a document, and the historian's first business is to ask of it, as he would of any other record, who made it, to whom it was addressed, and what it was meant to convey. Those questions imply others, and entail some reference to photographic techniques. A man may write what he will, within the bounds of his own skill and apprehension. He may photograph what he will, within the capacity of the camera. The first context of any photograph is the contemporary state of photography; the second, the intentions and assumptions of the photographer, so far as we can recover them. Those preliminaries established, there opens beyond them a world as wide as our curiosity.

The origin and the name of the camera lie in the *camera obscura*, an optical device which, in Leonardo da Vinci's time, consisted of a darkened room with a small hole in one wall through which a pencil of light passed to form on the opposite wall an inverted image of whatever lay outside.[1] In the seventeenth and eighteenth centuries a portable version fitted with a lens which transmitted an upright image on to a piece of translucent paper, by means of an inclined mirror, was used by painters to compose and draw landscapes, and it has a close connection with the iconography of the city. The brilliant paintings of Venice and London made by Antonio Canale (1697–1768), perhaps the most precisely observed records of the urban scene before the age of photography, rest on drawings made with the aid of the *camera obscura*.[2]

The illusory sense that those living images gave of commanding Nature, by setting a moment of reality aside for study and appraisal, excited artists and laymen alike. The *camera obscura* became a piece of picnic equipment, like the Claude-Lorraine glass, as well as, in its larger versions, a form of public entertainment which still survives in some towns. It was used as a surveyor's aid, and as the object of philosophical disquisitions upon art. The excitement of fixing its pictures by the power of their own light appealed to many of its users, but had to wait upon the ready availability of photo-sensitive chemicals. Science and art were beginning to separate, though learning was still nominally one, and the investigations upon which photography ultimately depended were the work of *savants* and industrialists rather than artists. The first report of successful photography came, appropriately enough, from the Wedgwoods, who could turn their talents to anything. Thomas Wedgwood (1771–1805), who took up scientific experiments when his health forced him to leave his father's firm, published an account of simple contact printing in 1802.[3] It was a modest triumph, because the prints, which were produced by the action of light on silver nitrate, could not be made permanent, but the salt eventually used as a fixative, sodium thiosulphate, had already been discovered by Chaussier in 1799.

It was a long step from these first principles to the photography of focused images, and the problems in the way were eventually overcome, as often happens, by several experimenters working independently. A French physicist, Joseph Nicéphore Niepce (1765–1833), already interested in the use of polished metal plates for lithography, began to copy etchings by allowing light to pass through an original made transparent with wax or oil, on to a plate sensitized with a preparation of bitumen. The idea occurred to him between 1813 and 1816; it was only a step beyond Wedgwood's technique, but by the 1820s he had devised ways of enhancing and fixing his images. In June or July 1827 he recorded a view from a bedroom window of his house at Gras with the aid of his camera. The faint lines and hazy shadows of that scene of roof-tops, *basse-cour*, and trees are our first authentic impression of time past.[4] News of Niepce's work reached Louis Jacques Mandé Daguerre (1789–1851), a scene-painter and the inventor of the diorama, whose own photographic experiments had followed the same course, though with less success. Daguerre proposed that they should work together, and after some hesitation Niepce agreed, with the result that the photographic image fixed upon a metal plate, which was substantially his work, is known to the world as the Daguerreotype.[5] We shall never know what neologism would have given Niepce his due.

Niepce and Daguerre had originally each worked with a solution of asphalt in oil, on both metal and glass plates. Their joint and perfected process used a polished silver plate made light-sensitive by iodine, and the image chemically developed and fixed, all by processes originally suggested by Niepce. Daguerre's principal contribution seems to have been the development of the latent image. In the meantime William Henry Fox Talbot (1800–77), Twelfth Wrangler in 1821, and a learned amateur of optical physics, had also begun to experiment with the images of the *camera obscura*, having pondered the idea of fixing its images by chemical means during an Italian tour in 1833. He also made contact prints of leaves and small objects. His work began with Wedgwood's process, but he worked out an elaborate technique for sensitizing a self-developing paper negative, on which the images were fixed with sodium hyposulphite. Fox Talbot eventually published his work in January 1839, a few weeks after Daguerre and Isidore, Niepce's son, had announced their own, but before they published details, and he patented his Calotype, or Talbotype, as a rival to the older process.[6] His method was overshadowed by the Daguerreotype, and his photographic printing-works at Reading were closed in 1847 as a result of the losses he suffered after agreeing to supply photographs to illustrate the magazine *Art Union*, but the calotype pointed to the future development of photography. Whereas Niepce and Daguerre envisaged and perfected a method that fixed a single image, Fox Talbot invented the photographic negative, from which any number of positive prints could be made. From its earliest days, therefore, the new technique held out the promise of unlimited exact reproductions of an exemplar: the very foundation of mechanical industry and the exacting society that it has to serve.

Although its inventors were all aware of its larger implications, especially for the graphic arts, the earliest achievements of photography were necessarily domestic in scale and relatively trifling in character. Their interest lay in their existence: cumbrously secured and limited in scope as these first reflections of life's patterns are, their appearance is a prodigy. If observation can change the character of the thing

229

observed, then photography changed the world that it recorded. We scan early photographs for the authentic detail of the past, yet their archaic features—costume, settings, ambience—are themselves a challenge to the imagination: a paradox. Though we prize those things because they are captured for us from the past, they partake of our own world, of modernity and even of contemporaneity, because they have been photographed. It was entirely proper that our earliest photographic views should include a French and an English country house. Niepce, the retired lieutenant of the engineers, *savant* and *fonctionnaire*, Fox Talbot at Lacock Abbey, the country gentleman with an aptitude for higher mathematics and a taste for physics and drawing, each photographed what was at hand and familiar, and in doing so presented what was traditionally characteristic of the societies in which they lived.[7] Yet at the same time they transformed what was traditional, and unified what was diverse: the camera, like the steam locomotive, makes all places one.

Of all the ingredients of the new world that mechanical industry was creating, and that now came under the camera's eye, none was more important than the city. Man could reach out further than ever before, but he was enabled to do so only by concentrating his resources and efforts in an unparalleled fashion. The forces so gathered bore equally hard upon the conventions of the pre-industrial town and the elegancies of the country house, and new patterns were inexorably imposed upon both. Everything had now to relate or respond to the needs and demands of industrial society: the capacity to do so was a condition of survival. The rule applied to the newcomer, photography, as it did to farming.

In the first decades of its existence, however, photography's debt to graphic art was more evident, and probably more anxiously discussed, than its debt to science and industry. The camera and its plate were still mere contrivances, and, though they called for ingredients unknown to Roger Bacon's pharmacopoeia, the ensuing recipes would not have been beyond his ingenuity. The product was another matter: here was the tantalizing promise of the *camera obscura* fulfilled, and Nature held captive. An early photograph could be compared only to a painting, and their familiarity with the principles of the camera gave artists the less reason to feel apprehensive about a new application of them. Hippolyte Delaroche (1797–1856), a robust executant of historical set-pieces, saw in Daguerre's pictures 'an easy means of collecting studies' which might otherwise have to be gathered 'over a long period of time, laboriously, and in a much less perfect way'.[8] It was an informed assessment, but the full effects of a world-wide repertory of styles upon artistic practice were not registered until the present century. In the meantime there were other interactions. Artists discovered that they had more than the techniques of other artists to learn from photography, but were driven ever further from representational work by photography's success. They also discovered that photography could satisfy demands which the graphic arts could never have met.

Photographers for their part were at first content with a role that implied subordination. Fox Talbot's first published collections of pictures were entitled *The Pencil of Nature* (1844–6)[9] and *Sun Pictures in Scotland* (1845), and he expounded his discoveries in a work called *The Process of Calotype. Photogenic Drawing.* It was not until the second half of the century that battle was joined between photographers themselves over the artistic and documentary attributes of their work, or that the public began seriously—and even then not always accurately—to distinguish the work and aims of the photographer and the graphic artist.

One reason for that slow differentiation lay in the practical difficulties of taking satisfactory photographs, and the consequent limitations of their scope. Early studies are either landscapes or portraits, and their majestically slow techniques greatly favoured portraiture. It took hours to expose a plate out of doors, and the finished scene was devoid of life. The intrinsic interest of the operation encouraged some photographers to persist with landscapes, and there are a few early pictures of towns, including a celebrated view of Trafalgar Square in *The Pencil of Nature*, but for the moment the results had only the appeal of novelty. The prospects for portrait photography were rather different. The daguerreotype technique was literally a painful one, and entailed the subject's sitting with unnatural stillness, restrained by iron clamps, but the result was a portrait-miniature in the most respectable tradition: personal, unique, and, by the standards of competent artistry, cheap. The number of miniatures exhibited at the Royal Academy fell dramatically, from some three hundred to sixty-four, between 1830 and 1860, and commentators took a despairing view of the future of the art, although established painters and their clients were glad to use photography to reduce the tedium of long sittings. One hard-wearing convention of portraiture, in which the sitter's chin rests on his hand, or one finger extends up the cheek while the others are doubled under the chin, seems to have spread from daguerreotype to painted portraits, and to have originated as an ingenious device to keep the face immobile before the camera.

Photography could afford to pay some dividends to painting, for the daguerreotype multiplied, not only amongst those who could have afforded to have their likenesses painted, but also, and more significantly, amongst those who could not. In the welter of domestic objects that distinguished the nineteenth-century house from its predecessors, the daguerreotype and its protective leather case or metal binding took a proud place. It was a marvel, and one of a solidly reassuring kind. In early years there were some disappointments. In 1847 *Punch* had a sketch called 'Photographic failures', with verses to point the moral that portraits 'taken by the cheap process' faded and vanished, like the affections that they were meant to commemorate.[10] Those properly prepared and developed, especially those intensified by a coating of gold, survived to grace the chimney-shelf or the occasional table. Soon daguerreotypes could be coloured or retouched to repair little blemishes in Nature: their advance was triumphant, and it prepared that mass-market for photographs of all kinds which grew up in the second half of the century.

One striking use of portrait photography in the 1840s was in a record of the 474 ministers who attended the signing of the Act of Separation by which the Free Church of Scotland seceded in 1843. The photographs were calotypes prepared by Robert Adamson, an Edinburgh chemist with a studio on Calton Hill, and David

Octavius Hill, who had been commissioned to paint a commemorative picture of the proceedings. The finished painting proved Hill to have been overwhelmed by his material, but the constituent photographs, both of individuals and of small groups, were of the highest order.[11] The series included some views of Edinburgh and St Andrews which are among the earliest photographs of Scottish towns.

Although each process was used for either purpose, the daguerreotype excelled in portraiture and in depicting the details of urban scenes—the shining surface of wet paving-stones was singled out as an impressive feature—whilst the calotype's softer tones lent themselves best to a classic portrayal of landscapes. Both could be finely handled by experts, but both processes were very slow. The deliberate ritual strengthened the analogy with painting, while its restrictions emphasized the photographer's subordination to the artist. Though photographs might be made to look like paintings, it was still possible to believe that their chief use was to collect material for the painter. The photographer's liberation depended upon improvements in his equipment.

The next major advance in technique came in 1851, displacing the calotype immediately, and the daguerreotype after a short rivalry. This was the wet-plate process, in which a glass negative coated with collodion, a solution of gun-cotton in ether, was charged with a solution of bromide or other photo-sensitive salts.[12] The method was not a simple one, but it cut the time of exposure from minutes to a matter of ten or fifteen seconds. The plate was not only more sensitive than anything used before, but also allowed substantial numbers of good positive prints to be taken. Its success established the photograph, as opposed to the photographic portrait, as a marketable commodity. Its disadvantages were a cumbrous apparatus, and a developing technique of which C. L. Dodgson made restrained fun in *Hiawatha's Photographing:*

> Secondly my Hiawatha
> Made with cunning hand a mixture
> Of the acid pyro-gallic
> And of glacial acetic
> And of alcohol and water:
> This developed all the picture.

There was no exaggeration in the satire: the plate had to be developed before the coating dried, and a rapid sequence of photographs demanded the presence of an assistant to deal with the exposed plates. The entire apparatus filled a trek-cart, and on occasion, a caravan: the camera, tripod, plate-holder, dark-tent, baths, and chemicals weighed eighty pounds or more. That was the paraphernalia that Roger Fenton took to the Crimea for his brilliant photographs of the camps and the detritus of the battles, and that Mathew Brady used even more adventurously in the American Civil War.[13]

The wet-plate process greatly broadened the scope of photography. It was still not possible to capture movement, but a great many kinds of activity could be temporarily stilled to allow the photographer to work with a full plate, and he could shorten the time of exposure even further by exposing only a part. The earliest photographs show outdoor scenes unpeopled, except when engravers were retained to copy and enliven daguerreotypes with a figure or two. Now the bystanders appear even on full plates, stiffly at first, not quite at ease for several decades: men in stove-pipe hats, ghostly figures of the impatient or the ill-at-ease, philosophical dogs. The camera could record formal occasions, like the opening of the Crystal Palace at Sydenham in 1854, when the event itself imposed constraints.[14] It could also depict ordinary scenes with a modicum of life. The wet plate did not make an immediate difference to portrait photography, although it removed much of the tedium in the sitting. Its most important applications were to the stereoscopic view-card and the *carte de visite*.

The principles of stereoscopic imagery were already well-understood; Sir David Brewster (1781–1868) exhibited a stereoscope at the Great Exhibition in 1851, and Negretti and Zambra produced for the occasion a fine series of stereoscopic daguerreotypes which were particularly admired by the Queen and the Prince Consort. Popular taste endorsed the commendation: the hand-stereoscope, invented by Oliver Wendell Holmes, was sold in large numbers in the 1850s and 1860s, and after a brief intermission enjoyed even greater esteem in the last two decades of the century. It was a device well suited to domestic use. The pleasure it afforded was private, but not exclusively so, as the viewer could be easily passed from hand to hand. The fascination of the illusion, so simply created and destroyed by moving the picture, was not even limited by the number of cards to hand.

Stereoscopic cards were published in large sets, many of which, like Francis Bedford's series on English counties and regions or G. Washington Wilson's *Scottish Scenery*, include striking views of town life.[15] Wilson's collection of negatives, a most valuable storehouse of topographical material drawn from all over Britain in the middle decades of the century, is now in Aberdeen University Library. Topography, however, though a usefully broad subject, was by no means the only theme for the stereoscope. The Manchester Art Treasures Exhibition of 1857 and the International Exhibition of 1862 were the subjects of elaborate sets. The former had a particular interest as the first public exhibition of works of art gathered nationally from private collections; as an art exhibition that included photographs; and as a token of Manchester's civic vitality and cultural eminence in the period. Other and less exalted matter can be found among the many series of comic cards, which range from the mildly lubricious—lovers surprised, girls washing clothes with their arms or legs bare—to the enigmatically dull. Even those pictures, however, have their own historical interest, not only as exemplars of taste, but also for the studio-contrived interior scenes that many of them portray. At a time when ordinary indoor photography was impracticable, a stage-set that was meant to carry some degree of conviction with contemporaries can also tell posterity something. The same is true of the photographic slides that multiplied from this time onward, and of much other superficially unpromising material.

233

The *carte de visite* was a trifling device, patented by André Disdéri in 1854. As its name implies, it was a small paste-down print, some $2\frac{1}{4}$ by $3\frac{1}{2}$ inches, that was originally designed as a cheap substitute for the conventional engraved card. Distributed as a keepsake with or without more elaborate mountings, it rapidly extended its range from personal portraits to views, and then to celebrities, to curios, and to any other theme acceptable to popular taste.[16] Like the stereoscopic card, the small print implied a small negative and therefore a short time of exposure. Photographs of that kind could capture some details of commonplace scenes more satisfactorily than full-plate studies, and it was from stereoscopic studies that painters now discovered that the human mode of walking, especially in the swing of the leg and foot, was markedly different from the established artistic convention. The motion of a galloping horse could not be analysed in the same way until Eadweard Muybridge began his ingenious experiments with a battery of cameras in 1872,[17] but in the meantime the cumulative experience of the camera's eye told upon the artist's practice and assumptions. The photographer's reactions were different, but the historical importance of these small glazed prints overrides their artistic and technical significance, even though many of them were of the highest quality. To the historian they speak of the mass-market that they commanded; their consequence lies in their numbers and diffusion. They are most literally the city-dweller's view of the world. They familiarized an urban public, avid for instruction, amusement, and discreet reassurance, with the wonders of the great exhibitions, with exotic scenery, with the triumphs of civil engineering, with the architecture and the living patterns of British and foreign towns. They showed a world complex and diverse, now subdued and even imprisoned, captured on pasteboard by the powerful devices of man. The photograph was a means of education, not just by virtue of what it depicted, but also in itself: it was part of the process by which men could persuade themselves of their mastery of material things.

One powerful extension of that process was waiting upon a further technical change: photographs could still not be reproduced with letterpress. The potential of photographic illustrations in books, periodicals, and newspapers was readily perceived, but only slowly realized. The magazine *Art Union* which ruined Fox Talbot's photographic firm was illustrated with calotypes; these were also used in the presentation copies of the catalogue of the Great Exhibition in 1851; the pasting-in was slow and expensive, but it was continued in works of limited editions to the end of the century. Some early daguerreotypes were copied by engraving, a process which, like colouring, allowed modifications to please the purchaser. As copying techniques improved, photographs were increasingly used as the basis of engraved illustrations. One notable example is Henry Mayhew's *London Life and the London Poor* (1851–62), a vivid and influential evocation of the city's street life, and an appropriate register of the camera's observations.

Work of that kind promoted in turn a general improvement in the accuracy of popular illustrations. The *Illustrated London News*, founded in 1842, had set new patterns in journalism and enjoyed a revolutionary success before any question of photogravure arose. It was itself an education in the uses of pictorial material, but its early methods were impressionistic and sometimes perfunctory. When Krook's fiery death in *Bleak House* brought men of science and philosophy to Cook's Court, Cursitor Street, it also brought, besides the ordinary journalist, 'the artist of a picture newspaper, with a foreground and figures ready drawn for anything, from a wreck on the Cornish coast to a review in Hyde Park, or a meeting in Manchester'. Afforded a seat in a neighbour's room, he proceeded to fill in his block with 'Mr Krook's house, as large as life; in fact, considerably larger', and for good measure he added the fatal chamber itself, showing it 'as three-quarters of a mile long, by fifty yards high', to the powerful gratification of his audience from the court. Historians value such evidence as they have, from any period, and they can only be grateful for early picture-newspapers and their versatile artists, even when they have to review them critically. What is remarkable is not so much that such works occasionally betrayed imaginative aberrations, as that the principles of photographic accuracy were established as early and as thoroughly as they were. Easy reference to an abundant pictorial journalism informed and improved public taste and its expectations. The fact is that artistic licence is something that can only be measured when there is a photographic standard to set against it; the historian of the Victorian city has to take a good deal less on trust than have some of his fellows.

The inevitably uneasy relationship of photography and graphic art had important effects upon both as the century advanced: an obvious one was to sharpen the professional pretensions of photographers. The notion that the photograph was a work of art as much as, and even more than, a mere record persisted, and caused much anguish both to those who entertained it and those who rejected it. The issue was complicated by the presence of painters who took up photography for its own sake, like the Swede, Oscar Rejlander (1813–75). Rejlander produced the first composite photographs, arranging and rephotographing more than thirty pictures for his moralistic study 'The Two Ways of Life' in 1857. Although Queen Victoria bought a copy of that photograph, it was subjected to some criticism because it depicted dissipation, and did so with painful realism. There was a similar reaction to a composite study of a deathbed scene by Henry Peach Robinson (1830–1901)— 'Fading Away'. It would have made an acceptable painting, but photography made verisimilitude intolerable.[18] The implication was that the public could not accept photography as an art; no matter what liberties the photographer might take with his material, its factual parts put an uncomfortable gloss of truth upon even the most imaginative whole. Some photographers were unconvinced, and the battle between the pictorialists—those who wished to create works of art with the camera— and the naturalists—who wished to record and define, though not necessarily without forethought and art—was joined noisily and repeatedly, dividing camera clubs and former friends all over the country.

Two results of the debate—at times a dispute—are particularly important to the historian. One is the emergence of a small but significant number of skilled photographic reporters: men such as Frank Sutcliffe,[19] whose studies of Whitby are among the finest we have of a nineteenth-century town, or the enthusiasts who first directed the Manchester Photographic Survey, a project of the 1880s still incomplete, but remarkable for the enlightenment and cogency of its original planning.[20] The other is more general, but not less considerable. Whichever side a dedicated photographer might choose to support, his professionalism was sharpened by the acrimony of the debate, as well as challenged by the difficulties of the medium. The wet-plate process was the salvation of photography: its elaboration helped the professional to establish himself, and paid a splendid dividend in the quality of his photographs. From the 1850s until the late 1870s amateur photographers were either deterred, or forced to take professional pains, by the patient skill and expensive care that a successful picture demanded. In the meantime the professionals were encouraged by the growing market for pictures of all kinds. The principles of dry-plate photography were discussed from the 1850s, but the sensitive emulsions and strong developers required took some years to perfect, and ready-coated plates were not generally available until the late 1870s. The dry plate needed only one-fifteenth of a second's exposure, and immediately made possible smaller cameras and rapid, informal photography. A new and splendid prospect opened before the amateur, but in the meantime a powerful tradition of deliberated and carefully executed pictures had been established.

The best town- and country-landscapes of the wet-plate camera are in many ways the most interesting of our graphic records. They did for the daily scene, or for some chosen aspect of it, what the portrait daguerreotype had done for the individual sitter, depicting its image as faithfully as the preceding formalities allowed. Their considered composition and subtle tones look to the long-established techniques of landscape and topographical painting: the calotype in its day had been esteemed in England because its soft outlines were reminiscent of brushwork. Their precision and searching detail, on the other hand, were rather material for the scientific observation in which the nineteenth century excelled. Except for the long-ranging shots exposing only a fraction of the plate, which were used for some stereoscopic pictures, they are all necessarily formal, but their formality comes not so much from the time that they took to expose as from the fact that the photographer was a conspicuous figure. His apparatus and ceremonial inspired respect, if not awe. With the notice that his preparations gave, the apprehensive and the naturally retiring could retire. Those who remained chose to be there, and their watchful gaze is not entirely a matter of muscular tension.

Professionalism assures its own satisfactions, but it also implies a sale for the skills entailed. The best prospects for the photographer of landscapes, in the widest sense, were the stereoscopic card, the lantern slide, and views of the picturesque— studies like the handsome sepia prints that the Abrahams of Keswick produced in the 1880s.[21] Although hand-drawn pictorial postcards appeared in the late 1860s, photographic printing on a large scale had to wait upon the half-tone process, which did not appear for another twenty years. Those considerations restricted commissioned and saleable work—even today photographs other than portraits are rarely bought for their own sake—and put a premium upon the picturesque, the celebrated, and the readily-assimilable among the subjects with which the camera could deal. Although the photographs of the third quarter of the century are an archive of high quality and interest, therefore, they still offer us only a selective view of the contemporary world. Rapid movement, indeed any movement, defeated the full-plate camera, and the small photographs from which stereographic cards were made, to which we owe the liveliest street scenes of that period, could not be effectively enlarged. Indoor photography was barely possible, and naturalistic work indoors out of the question. A crowd gathered and waiting for an event could be fairly taken, but anyone with business of his own, except of the most contemplative kind, was commonly beyond reach. The world of trade and manufacture, mines, factories, and moving trains, the whole strength of industrial society, were impracticable subjects in most ordinary conditions. The city itself could be captured only in moments of repose or formal excitement: in the camera's eye, the patterns of life were still or slow-moving.

Those conditions changed from the late 1870s onward, with the introduction of the dry plate and the miniature camera. The Kodak roll-film camera then appeared, in 1888, and was quickly refined, by the use first of celluloid film, and then of light-proof spools that allowed simple and rapid loading in daylight. With cameras that could lie in, and even be operated from, a coat pocket, and that could take scores of pictures in the time needed to expose and process a single wet plate, the whole concept of photography changed. The photograph as an instantaneous record came into its own.[22] Bustling streets, moving vehicles, men at work could all be taken at close range, unobtrusively and at the photographer's whim. The amateur and the casual photograph flourished, and popular interest and demand created a large photographic industry. Instantaneous photography and the flexible film made possible the invention of the cinematograph. Professional interest in the photographic analysis of rapid motion went back to the stereoscopic pictures of the mid-century, and beyond, to the optical toys of earlier decades. Muybridge's ingenious silhouettes of a galloping horse showed the most careful painters that they had entirely mistaken the sequence of movement entailed, and that in particular the rocking-horse posture, front and back legs simultaneously extended, in the best tradition of racing prints, was a crude illusion. Dry-plate photography allowed the physiologist Jules Étienne Marey to improve Muybridge's technique, and apply it to the flight of birds.[23] In 1896 the first paying audiences in London were regaled with pictures of people just like themselves, walking in the street, and other wonders of animation. The same year saw the *Illustrated London News* adopt half-tone blocks for its illustrations. The camera and its ancillaries were now the masters of all things.

Half-tone blocks had been used in the United States since 1880, but there were difficulties in adapting them to fast-running newspaper presses.[24] By the late 1890s, however, news-photographs were extensively used by the press, at least by popular and experimental papers, and they have survived in great numbers. Early cinematographic films are more rare; the nitrate stock of the oldest prints was extremely

237

unstable, and little thought was given to their historical interest until 1935, by which time much valuable material had been lost. Commercial films taken before the First World War are more common than those taken later in the century, because in the early days the copies were sold outright. After hiring was introduced, the distributors destroyed all copies when the film's commercial life was over. The National Film Archive's catalogue of news films from 1895 to 1933 naturally contains many records of formal events, and particularly of royal functions, but there are also a number of more casual and, therefore, more rewarding occasions.[25] Examples from the period 1896–9 range from pictures of rush-hour traffic on London Bridge or at the Mansion House—such popular subjects with photographers—to the turn-out of a fire-brigade, a bicycling rally, and the arrival at Henley railway station of visitors to the Regatta. The life that the illusion of motion lends to these pictures enhances their chief interest, which lies in the mere extension of photography to a new range of commonplace subjects. The camera had not long been able to freeze motion; now it was able to record it. The future of the cinematographic film as an art lay in the skilful use of the illusion: its historical interest lies largely, though not exclusively, in its individual frames.

Just as the cinematographic film as a work of art was long bound by the conventions of the theatre and still-photography, and television in its turn by cinematography, so the old uses of the camera bore upon those who experimented with its new devices at the end of the century. That was not a disadvantage. The snapshot—an expression borrowed from sporting slang and transformed by its association with the hand-camera—and the photographic analysis of rapid or confused motion could not entirely lose, in the nineteenth or even the early twentieth century, the formal touch that belonged to more deliberate studies. Amateur work, both good and bad, followed professional examples. The family photograph album, though it came to contain more photographs and less matrix than its predecessors—a change that has gone on more sluggishly in records of weddings—was informed by a continuing sense of ceremony. The restrictions upon indoor photography until the very end of the century diminish the social as opposed to the personal interest of such portraits, and in any case the accidents of time have reduced the number of albums available to us, but the rapid growth of amateur photography after the introduction of the flexible film greatly enlarged the repertory. It did so, however, without much immediate loss of formality. Even today the number of people who face a camera without some perfunctory gesture to decorum is very small. An age which hardly knew how to question the psychic value of ceremony (and which would certainly have accomplished much less if it had) was not likely to underplay formality in its most solemn, because most exact, records. The consequence was that the technical standards of most late-Victorian and Edwardian photography remained high; that the camera became ubiquitous without becoming entirely commonplace; and that those uses of photography which were aimed deliberately at enlarging its scope, by photographers who revelled in the techniques denied to earlier generations, are often most enviably good. The face of the Victorian city in its latest years is presented to us in admirable detail.

That face is there for us to study, making what allowance we can for the limitations imposed by occasion, circumstances, and above all, technique. The photographer's mind, its intentions and preoccupations, lie behind the photograph, removed from us, but not beyond our reach. The applications of photography are often more valuable objects of study, in that sense, than the prints themselves. The stereoscope provides one instructive example, and the lantern slide another. The stereoscope was a private amusement, though not necessarily a solitary one. The magic-lantern was widely used as a domestic toy, but was also an engine of public instruction. Before 1870 the ordinary choice was between small single-wick lanterns of low power, and oxy-hydrogen burners which demanded skilled handling. Then Walter Woodbury introduced the Sciopticon, an American-invented lantern with a brilliant oil-light, and with it a wide range of slides made from negatives of his own, exposed in the 1850s and 1860s. Woodburytypes, which were printed in sepia, are still recognized as outstandingly good slides, and they helped to promote a large domestic market for slides and magic-lanterns, besides encouraging amateurs to make slides, and showmen of all kinds to use the lantern as a popular attraction.[26]

The Victorians esteemed rational amusement highly, and were right to do so, because the elaborate structure of their society was threatened by what passed as the alternative. Public lectures combined instruction and diversion in an unexceptionable way, and lantern slides enlivened them, giving an attractive gloss to even the most unpromising subjects. Lantern shows were older than photography, and the technical improvements made in the last quarter of the century carried them through to the age of the cinematograph. Evangelists and temperance lecturers used lantern slides as intensively as anyone, although the catalogues of commercial distributors like Newton & Co. of Covent Garden reveal a public hungry for straightforward information of any kind, on subjects ranging from the evolution of the ironclad to the manufacture of looking-glasses or of chocolate. One of the most interesting sets of privately-commissioned slides was made for, and on occasions with the assistance of, Charles Spurgeon, the son of the celebrated evangelist, Charles Haddon Spurgeon, and himself the minister of a Baptist chapel in South Street, Greenwich. Between 1884 and 1887 Spurgeon secured a striking series of pictures of street life in the borough, to illustrate his evangelical lectures.[27] The collection includes some excellent individual studies of street-traders and bystanders, and offers us a valuable conspectus of outdoor life in the borough in the mid-1880s, but Spurgeon evidently directed the photographer carefully, and on occasion he took part in front of the camera himself. He was therefore dealing in symbols rather than exclusively in facts, and what we know of his pictures we may suspect of others.

Commercial undertakings like the Bamforth Company at Holmfirth, near Leeds, produced homiletic series of slides for the general market. The firm was founded in 1870 by James Bamforth, a local man, and specialized from its beginning in slides, although it turned to picture postcards, and especially comic cards, as soon as British postal regulations allowed the blank side of a card to be divided between address and correspondence.[28] The comic cards later bred their own ribald conventions, but in its early years the firm offered many temperance lessons, and its products include various photographic scenes of low life. Slides presented as 'Life Models', or 'Taken from Life' were universally popular, and a successful series called 'slum life in our great cities', though not exactly that, did include, like Spurgeon's pictures, some striking vignettes of life in the streets. Bamforth's slides, however, portrayed interior scenes photographed in studio sets. There was presumably some measure of verisimilitude in those productions, but for the most part it is not provided for a keenly critical audience. The unheated and ill-furnished garret in which the story called 'Dot and Her Treasures' is set will serve as an example of an unheated and ill-furnished garret, but even in the absence of authentic indoor scenes, it does not advance our knowledge of the poor and their houses to any degree. There is probably more to be gained from the representation of more prosperous households in other series, for there we have furnishings and bric-à-brac surviving against which the reconstructions can be checked. On the other hand, pictures of poverty, real and simulated, can tell us something about the interests, the experience, and the acumen of those classes of society that were instructed and admonished, perhaps, on occasion gratified or reassured, by such lantern slides in private shows and public lectures. There were, after all, physical dangers as well as technical difficulties in photographing low life, and the expedients that served instead are as informative on their own terms as the truest photographic reportage could be. So is the phenomenon of a respectable audience in a gas-lit Temperance Hall, or Railway Mission, moved to compassion, unease, or censure by the plight of the heathen abroad and the unfortunate or improvident at home.

There was even more to the lantern slides, however, than foreign travel, evangelism, and social reform. The ubiquity of the entertainment, and on particular occasions its imposing scale, tell their own story. Like Daguerre's dioramas in their day, it drew upon technical ingenuities to cater for a large audience, collectively a much larger audience than Daguerre was able to reach, and one which made very uneven demands upon the material that was presented. The captive audience is not a product of the twentieth century alone, and the lantern slide entrapped its admirers long before all images were expected to move and speak. Not that all showmen were content to accept uncritical tribute: D. W. Noakes of Greenwich, who was official lanternist at the Albert Hall, took his own slides for 'dioramic' projection, and built his own steam-launch for a photographic voyage through the Midlands from London. His illustrated lecture, 'England Bisected by a Steam Launch', was delivered to an audience of 1,500 at the Crystal Palace in 1891, and his set of 300 slides under that title constitutes one of the finest topographical records of the time. H. W. Taunt of Oxford, who also produced many slides of high quality, took an equally interesting series of pictures to illustrate a guide to the Thames Valley, preparing his prints in a floating photographic laboratory. The guide was illustrated with pasted-in photographs, an effective but expensive technique used for works in limited editions until the triumph of half-tone blocks and a commercially viable collotype.[29] Taunt's photographic collections include some excellent studies of the Thames and of shipping in its lower reaches, and a most valuable record of Oxford in the last decades of the century.

Photographers like Noakes and Taunt were able to experiment and perfect their work because the market for photographs of all kinds was expanding, and the growing amateur enthusiasm encouraged rather than hindered the professionals. The census returns show an increase in the number of professional photographers in Britain from a mere 51 in 1851 to 17,268 by 1901. By 1905 it was estimated that 4,000,000 amateurs, one-tenth of the whole population, were taking photographs, although the number of those willing and able to experiment effectively and to develop and print their own pictures, was comparatively small. In 1880 there were only fourteen photographic clubs in Britain, but their numbers increased sharply from that time, and by 1900 there were 256. Their membership was often riven by the debate between the champions of photography as a pictorial art and the photographic reporter, a debate re-opened and intensified by Peter Henry Emerson in 1886,[30] but the best work on either side showed the hollowness of the dispute. What matters to the student of the age is that technical improvement and high professional standards were maintained together. The great extension of photography as a popular pastime was bound in the long run to debase the quality of much that was done, but for some time the material available to us increases without any serious loss of interest. With the improvement of electric lighting and of flash photography, besides the constant refinement of lenses, by the beginning of the twentieth century the scope of photographic reportage had become almost as wide as it is today. The whole pattern of life, and especially of life in the city, which absorbed and displayed more and more of the sum of human energy, was depicted for the wonder of posterity.

The camera's eye, therefore, enables us to observe the Victorian city from almost its earliest years, and to catch all its nuances in its prime. What is more, what we can learn of it from its photographs goes back far beyond the mere details of the scenes that they display. The development of the camera itself is a comment upon the process by which the nineteenth century, like our own, exploited and refined ideas by popularizing devices. Photography both reflected and educated taste; its cumulative effect upon the popular mind was not less than its effect upon the graphic arts, or the part that it played in the elucidation of the natural sciences. The city was the natural setting for photography, and the photographer in quest of rustic idylls took the city with him in his uniform camera-box, machined-glass plates, and nicely-calculated solutions of salts. The progress of the city, and the formidably elaborate society that it housed and sustained, informs our assessment of every photograph, whatever appears in the print.

Some distinguished individual portraiture aside, our best photographic records are architectural; the camera has played on nothing with better effect or more consistently than on the forms, the details, and the setting of buildings. The value of such records is obviously great when rapid change is effacing traces of both the recent and the remote past in our towns, but even where buildings survive it is only the searching detail of photography that enables us to take a proper measure of change and continuity in the scene. What is less well represented in the towns is, in the first period, people, and for most of the time their work. We can deduce the processes by which wealth was created and applied, but for as long as photography was confined to the out-of-doors and the static scene it could take only a superficial account of human industry. Even when rapid and indoor photography became a commonplace, the complexity of industrial processes imposed their own barriers to analytical reporting. It has taken almost another century to establish an effective symbolism in cinematography, and to unlock some of the mysteries of social organization: the process is still far from complete.

A human figure gives scale and a sympathetic interest to a picture, and photographers have generally welcomed a bystander or two. Even the early daguerreotypes had figures added to them when they were copied by engravers. In the first decades of photography such human interest had to be contrived by one means or another; it is not until the small stereoscopic plates captured distant movement that the scene could be naturally peopled; the full tide of human existence could not be recorded until the coming of instantaneous photography. Individual figures stand out at all periods, many of them with their single claim to immortality in their presence, accidental or solicited, before the camera. For the rest, clothes and the manner of wearing them, stance, individual and collective style, all have their own story to tell. Only the record of activity is defective: what is represented is apt to be either withdrawn contemplation, or motion to some undisclosed end. Except when the celebrated are frozen in formality, those who emerge are usually, and not inappropriately, the middling sort. If they have no declared purpose, then their business is to people the scene. They do it well enough, and yield us an occasional bonus as well.

The scene itself has always two striking characteristics: it is by turns familiar and unfamiliar to us, and the familiarity is in some part the work of the camera itself. The photograph is part of our own world, and though we have apparently shed the primitive fear that what is captured in that way is lost to us, we have a lingering sense of community with what the camera's eye has seen. It is not so easy as it might seem to be, therefore, to take stock of the nineteenth century on its own terms; we are likely to be distracted by the emergence of our own context, and to delineate the wrong age. The temptation is the greater because one feature that the nineteenth century had in common with the twentieth was precisely the imposition of the town and its values upon the countryside: the substitution of road metal for mud and gravel, paint for vegetation, sewers for ditches, houses and streets for fields and farmyards. It is apparently a condition of man's social organization that he should replace what grows with what he has made; in the city the process is carried to its logical extreme. The change in the physical world that the camera observes is like the technical progress of the photographic print itself, from its shadowy beginnings to the instantaneous film; it is a progression from natural uncertainty to an unsettling precision, a progression from what is instinctive and self-renewing to what is contrived and temporary. Life is a product of change, but the pace and nature of social and physical change was radically altered in the nineteenth century. It was something more than the multiplication of people that we can observe coincidentally but significantly upon the photographic plates, and more, even, than the remorseless spread of the city itself. It affected every manifestation of organized life, including our own.

The Victorians were themselves aware of the peculiar qualities of the photograph. They grasped the significance of it as an impartially searching record and they appreciated its peculiar aesthetic very keenly. They saw it, quite properly, as one of their most remarkable achievements, distinctive and powerful, and they enriched their language with photographic metaphors in tribute to it. The connection between photography and other recording arts was obvious enough, and both authors and their critics invoked the comparison. Dickens, whose descriptive writing has the sharpness of personal experience, compared himself to a camera, and commentators upon his work both approved and reprobated what they took to be its photographic techniques.[31] For many purposes, and especially for works of social comment and criticism, the analogy had a useful uncertainty about it; to liken oneself to a camera might imply either an innocent impartiality or a superhuman power of comprehension. E. C. Grenville Murray's *Spendthrifts*, published in 1887, is subtitled 'and other social photographs'. As in other matters, popular allusion kept pace with technical change. W. D. Howells published a volume of essays in 1905 as an American observer of English life; he called it *London Films*, and began the first with the words, 'Whoever carries a mental Kodak with him (as I suspect I was in the habit of doing long before I knew it) must be aware of the uncertain value of different exposures.' He might reasonably count upon a sympathetic response from four million readers.

One passing but significant reference occurs in a work by Frederic William Maitland, the most felicitously gifted of English historians. Maitland's chief interest lay in the history of law, and especially the law of medieval England. In turning to those studies, he committed himself to one of the most rigorous techniques in historical science, and he showed himself always most perspicaciously aware of its strengths and limitations. In 1884, in the introduction to an edition of the plea roll for the county of Gloucester for 1221, he said of that document 'it is a picture, or rather, since little of imaginative art went into its making, a photograph of English life as it was in the early thirteenth century, and a photograph taken from a point of view at which chroniclers too seldom place themselves.' The reference to imaginative art cuts across the debate amongst photographers, but the metaphor was entirely a just one. Its appositeness lies not in the fact that judges and cameras might alike be supposed, or even hoped, to deal impartially with what is presented before them, but because written and photographic records alike are irrefutable upon their own terms. Both are documents, both are constructed with a purpose and an audience in mind. We use judicial and administrative records to explore the distant past because they are the most significant and informative evidence that we have from the society that made them. In its own age, and subject to like analyses, the photograph may have its rivals as a source of historical evidence, but it has no superiors. It offers us in its highlights and shadows the very pattern of the Victorian age.[32]

Notes

1 Helmut and Alison Gernsheim, *History of Photography, from the Camera Obscura to the Beginning of the Modern Era* (hereafter referred to as Gernsheim) (2nd edn, 1969), p. 19.

2 Aaron Scharf, *Art and Photography* (1968), p. 1.

3 His experiments were reported in a paper by Sir Humphry Davy in the *Journal of the Royal Institution*: Beaumont Newhall, *History of Photography from 1839 to the the Present Day* (2nd edn, New York, 1964), p. 12.

4 Gernsheim, plate 21.

5 Gernsheim, p. 62; Scharf, op. cit., pp. 5–6; Newhall, op. cit., pp. 13–16.

6 Gernsheim, pp. 76–7.

7 For one of Fox Talbot's 'photogenic drawings' of Lacock, see Newhall, op. cit., p. 33.

8 Scharf, op. cit., p. 17.

9 Scharf, op. cit., p. 9.

10 *Punch*, xii (1847), 143.

11 Scharf, op. cit., pp. 29–30.

12 Gernsheim, pp. 197–200.

13 Helmut and Alison Gernsheim, *Roger Fenton, Photographer of the Crimean War* (1945); Ray Meredith, *Mr. Lincoln's Cameraman: Mathew Brady* (New York, 1946).

14 Gernsheim, p. 266.

15 Gernsheim, p. 257. For a valuable account of the whole subject, and for dating stereo-cards, see William Culp Darrah, *Stereo Views: A history of stereographs in America and their collection* (Gettysburg, 1964).

16 On the *carte de visite* and photographic taste in the mid-century, see Helmut Gernsheim, *Julia Margaret Cameron, Her Life and Photographic Work* (1938), p. 39.

17 Gernsheim, pp. 435–7.

18 Gernsheim, pp. 246–9.

19 F. C. Lambert, *The Pictorial Work of Frank M. Sutcliffe* (1904).

20 See Harry Milligan, 'The Manchester Photographic Survey Record', *Manchester Review*, viii (1958), 193–204.

21 A selection of Abraham's work appears in A. P. Abraham, *Beautiful Lakeland* (Keswick, 1912), and in G. D. Abraham's books on rock-climbing, such as *British Mountain Climbs* (1909), but the firm is probably best known for its photographic prints, which provided images of wild nature for drawing-room walls.

22 One of the most talented photographic reporters to use a miniature camera was Paul Martin, whose vivid pictures of street life in London and elsewhere in the 1890s were published in 1939 under the title *Victorian Snapshots*.

23 Gernsheim, p. 440.

24 Gernsheim, p. 452.

25 British Film Institute, *Catalogue of the National Film Archive*, 2 parts (2nd edn, 1965). See also note 32.

26 Josef Maria Eder, *Ausführliches Handbuch der Photographie* (4th edn, Halle-an-der-Saale, 1926), *sub* 'Woodburydrück'.

27 See O. J. Morris, *Grandfather's London* (1956).

28 For a general account of Bamforth's work see Frederick Alderson, *The Comic Postcard in English Life* (Newton Abbot, 1970).

29 See, for example, H. W. Taunt, *Goring, Streatley, and the Neighbourhood* (Oxford, 1894).

30 Gernsheim, p. 457.

31 See, for example, Philip Collins, ed., *Dickens: The Critical Heritage* (1970), pp. 6, 190, 255.

32 The best bibliography of photography is Albert Boni, ed., *Photographic Literature: An international bibliographical guide* (New York, 1962). Its coverage of periodicals is particularly good, but as it is arranged in a continuous alphabetic sequence of authors and subjects the student in search of illustrative material needs either to know for what or for whom he is looking, or to use the work in conjunction with a comprehensive history of photography. There is a number of such studies which are concerned with the social and historical consequence of the subject, besides the development of techniques, and therefore valuable preliminary guides to the rich but ill-ordered fund of evidence that the camera has provided. Among the best examples are Josef Maria Eder's *History of Photography* (New York, 1945), Beaumont Newhall's *History of Photography from 1839 to the Present Day* (2nd edn, New York, 1964), and Helmut and Alison Gernsheim's *History of Photography, from the Camera Obscura to the Beginning of the Modern Era* (2nd edn, 1969). Aaron Scharf's *Art and Photography* (1968) is a perceptive study of the interplay of photography and the graphic arts, and essential reading for the historian who wishes to understand and use nineteenth-century photographs. Techniques and their bearing upon historical interpretations are also effectively discussed in Erich Stenger's *History of Photography: Its relation to civilization and practice* (Boston, Mass., 1939), and William Culp Darrah's *Stereo Views: A history of stereographs in America and their collection* (Gettysburg, 1964).

There is now a substantial literature of historical photographs, seeking either to evoke a particular period, or to illustrate a theme. Helmut and Alison Gernsheim's *Historic Events, 1839–1939* (1960), and Agnes Rogers, *The American Procession: American life since 1860 in photographs* (New York, 1933), are both of general application. Recent works on Britain include O. J. Morris's *Grandfather's London* (1956), Sir John Betjeman's *Victorian and Edwardian London from Old Photographs* (1969), and C. S. Minto's *Victorian and Edwardian Scotland from Old Photographs* (1970). The work of two distinguished photographers of urban life is recorded in Eugène Atget's *Photographe de Paris* (Paris and New York, 1930), and *Victorian Snapshots* (1939) by Paul Martin. There is a danger, even with work like that of Martin and Atget, that old photographs will be admired for their quaintness, and studied only superficially for their content. The best correctives are probably the writings of photographers themselves, particularly in the nineteenth century during the debate upon the documentary and artistic qualities of photography, and further study of the very extensive photographic archives that we possess, and upon which we have as yet drawn only lightly. Two guides to national collections, the British Film Institute's *Catalogue of the National Film Archive* (2nd edn, 1965) and D. B. Thomas's *The Science Museum Photography Collection* (1969), can stand here as exemplars, but there are still some notable collections, like that of the National Monuments Record, or the Wilson negatives in Aberdeen University Library, and the rather later collections of Henry Minn, in the Bodleian Library, which have been only inadequately discussed, or have passed unnoticed, in print. Local enquiries could well start with *The Camera as Historian: A handbook to photographic record works* (1916) by H. D. Gower, L. S. Fast, and W. W. Topley, which contains a useful list of county and other record collections. Thereafter only local enquiries will serve, until an effective national census is undertaken. There is no study of a British town to set against H. M. Mayer and R. C. Wade, eds, *Chicago: Study of a metropolis* (Chicago, 1969).

66 *preceding page* Temple Bar, a sagging relic of the old city, rescued and sentimentally mounted as a suburban conversation-piece, in a glade of Theobald's Park. The gateway, which marked the limits of the city's jurisdiction on the Strand was the true embodiment of early-modern London: it was designed by Sir Christopher Wren, and the room above the arch was rented for many years by Child's Bank, as a store for the ledgers.
Photo: G. W. Wilson
Aberdeen University Library

67 *left* St John's Gate, Clerkenwell, *c*.1890. The last relic of the Hospitallers' Priory of St John of Jerusalem, and a rare survival from the suburbs of medieval London. The gateway is also celebrated for having housed the publisher's office of the *Gentleman's Magazine*, and was preserved and restored by public subscription in 1845–6, at a time when the development of Clerkenwell might have swept it away.
Greater London Council

68 *below left* The Banqueting Hall, Whitehall, from a stereo card, *c*.1865. An early picture of the historic city in repose, with only kerbstones and gaslight intruded by the nineteenth century.
David Francis

69 *right* Butcher's Row, Aldgate, 1883: buildings in the tradition of the pre-industrial city tricked out with eclectic ornament and overshadowed by the cliff-like blocks of the nineteenth century. Note the pavement canopies, one with skylights, and the open counters of the shops. The City Bicycle School's advertisement offers a prospect of country lanes from a penny-farthing; the ghostly team of the dray stands for the restless movement in the streets that at this range the camera was still unable to arrest.
Greater London Council

70 *above* Butcher Row, Coventry. An undated but timeless scene: the stock of the second-hand furniture shop, fourth from the camera, suggests a date in the later decades of the century, but most of the detail belongs to the ages that escaped the camera's eye.
Photo: G. W. Wilson
Aberdeen University Library

71 *above right* A latterday inn yard: the Hotel Cecil decorated for the French president's visit to London, July 1903.
Photo: Bedford Lemere
National Monuments Record

72 *right* The Oxford Arms, Warwick Lane, Newgate, in 1875. The Oxford Arms was the chief Oxford carriers' inn in the seventeenth century, but was abandoned and turned into tenements in the nineteenth. The photograph is an effective study of a classic process of urban decay.
Greater London Council

73 *above* Whitehorse Close, Edinburgh, c.1890. The closes were a marked characteristic of old Edinburgh; this is a tolerably good one, with low ranges of buildings, archaic features in the outside staircases, and some marks of improvement. The cambered court covers what would once have been an open drain.
Photo: G. W. Wilson
Aberdeen University Library

74 *right* Sackville Street, now O'Connell Street, Dublin, c.1865: the Post Office and Nelson's column, a cab and an abstracted bystander. The condition of the roadway explains the persistence of the private crossing-sweeper.
David Francis

75 *above* The Old Town, Edinburgh, from the
Scott Monument. The eighteenth century drained
the Nor' Loch as a step towards developing the New
Town. The nineteenth century planted it, and then
filled it with the railway. This picture, taken with a
long enough exposure to blur the figures on the
bridge, emphasizes the harshness of the railway's
intrusion, both in the design of the metal bridge and
its booking office pavilions, and in the uncom-
promising ranks of the rolling stock.
Photo: G. W. Wilson
Aberdeen University Library

76 *left* The Victoria Embankment under construction, *c.*1865. The Embankment, built between
1864 and 1870, was a comparatively late addition to
London's public works, and really marks the end
of the river above the bridges as an important highway, and its acceptance as a nuisance that had to
be tamed into passivity. Large constructions were a
good subject for stereoscopic photography, especially
when work could be suspended to people the scene.
Greater London Council

77 *above far left* Leyton, the first Town Hall and Free Library. Leyton was an Essex forest village, long favoured as a retreat by London merchants, which became a town in the middle of the nineteenth century. The urban sanitary authority and a free library, an unusual amenity in a half-formed community, was housed in this Italianate building set down in the empty spaces of Leyton Road.
Howarth Loomes

78 *above left* The Sailors' Home, Great Yarmouth, from a stereo card, *c.*1860. A raw piece of the new urbanity, fronted by an unmade road, and with a windmill decaying behind.
Howarth Loomes

79 *above right* Bristol General Hospital, from a stereo card, *c.*1865. The hospital, raised in a characteristic mixture of the utilitarian and the ornamental, rises clean and new over the clutter of the quayside. Bristol's Royal Infirmary, opened in 1735, was the first provincial hospital,

in the modern sense of the word, and a measure of Bristol's early development. The General Hospital was built in 1862, after another century of urban growth.
Howarth Loomes

80 *above far right* The fifth Duke of Rutland, variously attended in Leicester market place, from a stereo card, *c.*1858. Not all the company stayed the course.
Howarth Loomes

81 *right* The Cobden Hotel, Corporation Street, Birmingham, *c.*1890: a bold marriage of Venetian Gothic with a Renaissance style, and an eloquent name. Corporation Street was vigorously promoted by Joseph Chamberlain: its objects were to improve and dignify the face of Birmingham, and to demonstrate the potentialities of municipal enterprise. It did both, though with more assurance than grace.
Photo: G. W. Wilson
Aberdeen University Library

82 *left* Queen Victoria and Prince Albert at the reopening of the Crystal Palace, 10 June 1854. An engraving from a photograph taken by P. H. Delamotte, generally accepted as the first news photograph. Engravings from photographs remained the mainstay of the *Illustrated London News* until the adaptation of the half-tone block to rotary printing.

83 *centre* A stereo card, showing a wet-plate photographer drying plates in his garden, in the late 1850s.
Howarth Loomes

84 *below* The Free Trade Hall, Manchester, *c.*1855, from a calotype negative by James Mudd. An appropriate subject for the early urban photographer, and massively apprehensible. The image has been retouched to strengthen detail, and it is now impossible to tell whether the figures once had a ghostly substance, or whether they are entirely the retoucher's work.
Photo: James Mudd
Kodak Museum

85 *right*   The Chain Pier, Brighton, from a stereo card, *c.*1865. The chain pier at Brighton has a special interest as the first seaside jetty which was formally used as a promenade. The card is an early one, and elaborately mounted.
Howarth Loomes

86 *centre*   An illustration from Mayhew's *London Labour and London Poor* (1851). The illustrations in the original edition were based upon daguerreotypes.

87 *far right*   An advertisement published in the *Illustrated London News* in 1856, depicting family life enhanced and beautified by the use of the stereoscope.

88 *below*   George Augustus Sala, from a *carte de visite*, *c.*1865. The photographic *carte de visite* was a vulgar device, but its real popularity was as a collector's novelty. It served as the mainstay of the popular photographer's business until the arrival of simple amateur photography. Sala was a London essayist, and a very appropriate subject for an urban fad. Members of the royal family, and celebrities such as Florence Nightingale, were other esteemed figures.
David Francis

89 *left* A stereo card workshop, c.1860, with blocks of cards drying, and a manual roller press. The picture is elaborately posed, but photographs of any manufacturing process are rare at that time.
Kodak Museum

90 *below* A late-nineteenth-century stereoscope, made in the 1890s, but essentially the instrument invented by Oliver Wendell Holmes in 1860. The card on this model is a transparency, to be viewed by transmitted light.
Howarth Loomes

91 *right Slum life in our great cities*, the title-slide of the series, 1890. The presentation of the title, to say nothing of the title itself, is a promise of sentimentally uncritical nonsense. The interest of the slides lies partly in their existence, and the implication of a market for them, and partly for what they offer in the way of direct observation. The subjects presumably earned silver for posing, but none of them seems to have been got up as a Respectable Pieman. *Life in the back streets* would have been a better name for most of the scenes depicted: the slums themselves are more secret places.
David Francis

92 *below* A group of children wearing straw bottle-wrappers, from *Slum life in our great cities.*
David Francis

93 *right* Street life in Seven Dials, *c.*1890
Guildhall Library

94 *below right* A municipal set-piece: a Liverpool fire engine, *c.*1890, with the brass burnished and the crew freshly brushed to face the camera. Even instantaneous photography cannot take the formality out of an occasion like this. For a snapshot on the street, see no. 110.
Photo: Thomas Burke
Liverpool Public Libraries

95 *below* An unidentified street trader, posed for *Slum life in our great cities*. The basket is a swill, made in Westmorland or Furness, and the scene is probably set in Manchester or Liverpool.
David Francis

96 *right* A patriarchal figure in a Jewish street in Liverpool, from *Slum life in our great cities*.
David Francis

97 *below right* A round game, c.1890. The children are being directed and have an adult audience, but there is no general awareness of the camera.
David Francis

98 *right* Jacks outside the barber's, Richmond Row, Liverpool, c.1890.
Photo: Thomas Burke
Liverpool Public Libraries

99 *below* Sweet vendor, from a lantern slide, c.1890. A scene from suburban life; the gravelled road, paved sidewalk, forbidding iron railing, and densely planted gardens imply a comfortable patronage for the Italian's sugar figures, if this was his ordinary beat.
David Francis

100 *left*   A hot chestnut man, from the series *Street life, or the people we meet*, 1890. The string of advertisements, the boys' collars, and the unswept roadway are so many comments upon an industrial society. The carnation in the vendor's buttonhole is a matter of taste.
David Francis

101 *below*   A second-hand shoe dealer, from *Slum life in our great cities*.
David Francis

102 *right* A bootblack at work, *c.*1900.
Kodak Museum

103 *below* A hokey-pokey ice-cream man, posed by his painted cart, London, *c.*1890. In Britain the baldacchino would more often serve to shelter than to shade the wares.
Kodak Museum

104 *left* Ice cream, the native product, from *Slum life in our great cities*. The original shows some signs of careless retouching, but the vignette of the vendor and his customer, the detail of the buildings, and the stridency of the written signs make it a telling picture.
David Francis

105 *below* A vendor of hot food, perhaps baked potatoes, with his donkey cart.
David Francis

106 *far left* Two boys from *Slum life in our great cities*. The authentic face of ragged poverty, although the photograph shows some signs of retouching to sharpen the picture.
David Francis

107 *left* A street-cleaner and his audience in Clerkenwell, *c.*1900. The drinking fountain, a fine specimen of its kind, was raised in 1868 by the Good Samaritan Temperance Society.
Kodak Museum

108 *below* Bricklayers posing, *c.*1890. The smallness of the fireplace suggests a bedroom; the walls are not cavity walls and are only casually bonded. Billycocks were entirely practical headgear, their comic dignity aside.
Manchester Public Libraries

109 *above left*   A London carthorse at his oats, *c.*1900. *Kodak Museum*

110 *below left*   A London & North-Western Railway Company's horse collapsed in South John Street, Liverpool, *c.*1890. The availability of the box camera and flexible film made drama of this kind an obvious subject for the roving photographer.
Photo: Charles Inston Liverpool Public Libraries

111 *above middle*   Selling a horse in the street, *c.*1900. *Manchester Public Libraries*

112 *below middle* Street life in
Kensington Park Gardens: the
Household Cavalry at exercise,
1889.
Guildhall Library

113 *above right* Laying Denver
blocks, 1900–2. Tar-coated
wooden blocks were first used in
Chicago in the 1870s. They
offered a reasonably quiet and
resilient surface to iron-tyred
wheels, but proved less satisfactory for heavy motor traffic.
Kodak Museum

114 *below right* Liverpool:
Herbert Campbell pressing
asphalt over cobbles, a street
scene of 1897.
Liverpool Public Libraries

115 *left*   The Rows, Chester, *c.*1860. A rare early view of a provincial town from a stereoscopic card. The Wild-West quality of such street scenes in the mid-century, which is a product of the superficially similar industrial development of England and the United States, is enhanced here by the wooden promenades of the rows.
David Francis

116 *right*   Borough High Street, Southwark: a splendid display of individualism in the shopfronts and roof-lines, of street furniture of all kinds, and of heavy commercial traffic.
Photo: G. W. Wilson
Aberdeen University Library

117 *below*   Lime Street, Liverpool, *c.*1890.
A thinly-populated but vigorous scene.
Photo: G. W. Wilson
Aberdeen University Library

118 *right*   Derby-Day traffic in the Clapham
Road, *c.*1895. The shop, a second-hand furniture
and piano dealer's built in the front garden of
the end house on the terrace, is a measure of the
road's decline into seedy commerciality.
Photo: G. W. Wilson
Aberdeen University Library

119 *above left* Whitehall in 1885, from a lantern slide. The patterns on the road are made by the water-cart at the right. *David Francis*

120 *left* Kennington turnpike gate, 1865. The gate, already an archaism among the stove-pipe hats, was swept away shortly after this photograph was taken. *Guildhall Library*

121 *above* Fleet Street and Ludgate Hill. A subtle and interesting contrast with the Borough High Street (no. 116), and a scene that betrays some awareness of the camera in the left foreground. *Photo: G. W. Wilson Aberdeen University Library*

122 *preceding page* Holborn in the 1890s. The open door of the omnibus shows a woman's skirts, but central London away from the shopping streets is a male preserve. The omnibus, with its spindly hand-rails and outside passengers perched like uneasy birds, makes no concessions to its passengers' dignity, but the photograph, which was probably taken with a camera concealed in a van, is a fine example of a snapshot, and has caught the whole scene off-guard.
Photo: G. W. Wilson
Aberdeen University Library

123 *above* The Trongate, Glasgow, *c.*1895, with horse-trams. As in Edinburgh and elsewhere in Scotland, the old buildings are taller than in English towns. The hand of the nineteenth century shows chiefly, the people apart, in the hard lines of the façades and in the sign-writing.
Photo: G. W. Wilson
Aberdeen University Library

124 A policeman on point-duty in the Euston
Road, *c*.1900.
Kodak Museum

125 *left*   Passengers boarding a
horse-bus, probably in the
Edgware Road, *c.*1900. The
intensive advertising is
noteworthy.
Kodak Museum

126 *above right*   A comic stereo
card of the 1860s, satirizing
competition between omnibus
companies.
David Francis

127 *below right*   A horse-tram
of the North Metropolitan line
in Graham Road, Dalston, 1895.
The horse-tram, which
provided a reasonably efficient
service between the inner
suburbs and the centre of the
city, was an important factor in
urban growth before the
development of mechanical
road transport.
Kodak Museum

128 Bristol, the swing-bridge, *c*.1890. A fine
photograph of the quays at the historic centre of
the town. Bristol was displaced in the course of
the nineteenth century by the growth of the
industrial north, from the first to the second rank
of cities. It had to change comparatively little to
maintain its size and essential functions, and the
difference between this and a view in the eighteenth century is a matter only of superficialities,
the steamer and horse-tram among them.
Photo: G. W. Wilson
Aberdeen University Library

129 West Hartlepool, the docks, *c.*1880.
Photo: G. W. Wilson
Aberdeen University Library

130 *above* Southampton,
the steamer pier, *c*.1895. An
atmospheric study, showing
the metabolism of the great
railway port at a low ebb.
David Francis

131 *above right* Passengers for
an emigrant ship, Liverpool,
c.1895
Photo: Thomas Burke
Liverpool Public Libraries

132 *right* London, the
Embankment in use, *c*.1895.
The water-trough, here refresh-
ing two cab-horses, is one of
those raised by the Metropolitan
Drinking Fountain and Cattle
Trough Association. It is the
equivalent of the motoring
accessories that now dot the
streets, but unlike them is
the product of philanthropic
enterprise.
Kodak Museum

133 *above* Kingsbury & Neasden station, Metropolitan Railway, *c.*1894. A snapshot of the journey to work, taken with a Kodak no. 2 camera.
Kodak Museum

134 *above right* A uniformed carrier and his son, from *Slum life in our great cities*. The association of this small, but carefully-caparisoned horse and his drivers and their painted cart with the slums is a useful reminder of the hazards that beset earnest but uncritical publicists.
David Francis

135 *right* The full tide of human existence: traffic on and below London Bridge in 1895–6. *Greater London Council*

136 *above* A picturesque study of St Paul's and the river from Wren's house, by a masterly photographer.
Photo: George Davison
Kodak Museum

137 *above right* Barges and a cargo of hay below Tower Bridge, *c.*1900. Victualling the Victorian city was a matter of providing fodder for horses as well as food for men.
Photo: George Davison
Kodak Museum

138 *right* The Thames, below Tower Bridge, *c.*1900. Another painterly photograph with its own value as an historical record: the successive changes in the current and temperature of the river effected by the removal of old London Bridge, the building of the Embankment, and the general growth of the city, have made its freezing an exceptionally rare occurrence in the present century.
Photo: George Davison
Kodak Museum

139 *above* Aberdeen at the close of the century. The tolbooth steeple and the mercat cross stand for continuity: the nineteenth century's peculiar contribution here is not so much the trams, which are eloquent enough, but in the numbers of people. Markets are traditionally thronged, but by this time densely-packed and disciplined crowds are ordinary and not extraordinary features of life.
Photo: G. W. Wilson
Aberdeen University Library

140 *above right* Provisioning the city: Covent Garden, with carts, baskets, and the Opera, in the late 1890s.
Kodak Museum

141 *right* Chapel Street, Salford: the edge of the Flat-Iron Market, 1894.
Photo: S. L. Coulthurst
Manchester Public Libraries

142 *left*   The enticements of
abundance: a butcher's shop,
c.1900.
Kodak Museum

143 *above right*   No. 1 Atley Road
and No. 700 Old Ford Road, in 1899.
A pawnbroker's, on hard times,
and an off-licence conveniently to
hand. The pawnshop was an
urban institution ranking with the
public-house, though in this
instance its general resemblance to
one is a matter of the fashion of
shop design.
Greater London Council

144 *right*   Children outside a
small provision shop: a slide from
Slum life in our great cities. The
battered panelling of the shop
front, the product of much aimless
scratching and kicking, is a
reminder that our present scruffy
habits have a long history.
David Francis

145 *above*   An ironmongers shop
in Athol Street, Liverpool, *c.*1890.
Photo: Charles Inston
Liverpool Public Libraries

146 *left*   Eggs, butter carefully
shaded, and fruit: a dairy shop off
Great Homer Street, Liverpool,
*c.*1890.
Photo: Thomas Burke
Liverpool Public Libraries

147 *above right* The Kodak Company's counting house, Clerkenwell Road, *c.*1902. The office of a vigorous and progressive company, with female clerks, typewriters, electric lighting, and pictures, albeit photographs, on the walls. Kodak's also appreciated the value of photography for advertising and recording; there would have been many obdurately old-fashioned offices at this time that escaped the camera's eye.
Kodak Museum

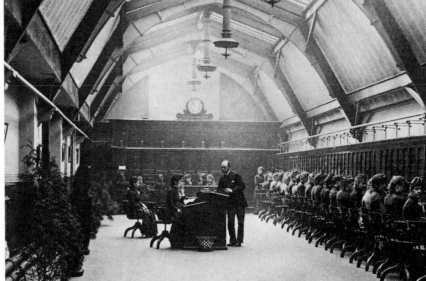

148 *middle right* A telephone exchange, *c.*1900. The room is an adaptation of a standard public hall, including institutional photographs and an ornamental dado. The potted shrubs are a concession to femininity, as indeed is the presence of a woman supervisor; the telephone service offered women one of the very few opportunities for advancement outside hospital nursing. The presence of the male manager marks the limits of enlightenment.
Photo: J. W. Wade
Manchester Public Libraries

149 *right* Exchange Buildings, Liverpool, 30 September 1881. A forest of silk hats at Cotton Corner.
Liverpool Public Libraries

150 *above left*   The Kodak Company's head office in Clerkenwell Road, *c.*1902, unobscured by false modesty. See also no. 147.
Kodak Museum

151 *middle left*   An advertising float, from *Street life, or the people we meet, c.*1890. Most societies have some addiction to the grotesque; the nineteenth century's came out strongly in its architecture, and in its advertisements.
David Francis

152 *below left*   A sandwich-board man in Bradford, from *Street life, or the people we meet.* With casual labour cheap, a sandwich-board offered an economical way of advertising widely, and Hepworth's sandwich-board, nothing if not eye-catching, was larger and therefore more economical than other people's.
David Francis

153 *above right*   The passing show: Hyde Park in the 1890s.
David Francis

154 *right*   Fun of the fair: a contortionist on Hampstead Heath, *c.*1900. The Heath was a popular Bank Holiday resort; the crowd shown here is socially mixed, but by that time casual gatherings of people away from their work are better and more individualistically dressed. The great revolution of the twentieth century is still to be accomplished, but it can be said to have begun by the last years of the nineteenth.
Kodak Museum

155 *above left* Surrey Gardens in the 1890s. A peep-show, becomingly brought up to date, and a cock-shy. *Greater London Council*

156 *left* A child reciting in a public-house, 1895. A photograph that at first glance is straightforwardly informative, and on closer inspection unsatisfactory in various ways. The group is obviously contrived, and so wooden as even to raise doubts about the assertively-explicit background. If the picture has any general purpose it fails to make it clear. The child cannot be said either to relish her situation or be distressed by it, and her audience is cataleptic. The object of the photograph may have been to immortalize a real Infant Phenomenon, but if so, it again fails for its lack of a title. *Photo: Thomas Burke Liverpool Public Libraries*

157 *above* Members of a bicycling club, *c.*1900. Group portraiture is a good deal older than photography, but a photograph is an ideal record of an association or meeting. This picture is reproduced from a lantern slide, an additional refinement of the original plate. The bicycle was an urban product that offered agreeable exercise and a sense of freedom; it has gradually been overborne by the motor car, but it has exercised a considerable social influence in its time.
Kodak Museum

158 *right* A tipster at Aintree, 1901, decked in the rags of Empire.
Photo: R. Eastham
Liverpool Public Libraries

159 *above left* *Urbs in rure*: Epsom on Derby Day, 1898.
Guildhall Library

160 *left* The pier, Greenwich, 1865. An early and rare picture of a Citizen Steamship Company's steamer at the pier, with a hulk among the river traffic in the background. The river was used intensively by Londoners, and the Margate wherries carried a heavy popular traffic to the coastal resorts of Kent before there were railways or steamers.
Howarth Loomes

161 *above* Brighton, launching the *Skylark*,
*c.*1890. Perhaps the original *Skylark*.
Photo: G. W. Wilson
Aberdeen University Library

162 *above left* Hastings, the beach, *c.*1890.
Pleasures taken soberly; the absence of anything
that might be called beachwear is notable.
Photo: G. W. Wilson
Aberdeen University Library

163 *left* The pier and the Grand Hotel, Hastings,
*c.*1895. The promenade is an aristocratic institution,
a place on which to stroll and be noticed. The pier
is an extension of the promenade, which also serves
as a landing place: pavilions and distractions are
extraneous to its real purpose. This photograph,
which includes one bathing machine boldly labelled
'For Gentlemen' shows how thin the veneer of
urbanity can be stretched on the sea-front, where
the visitor's and therefore the builder's first instinct
is to stay within sight of the sea. There are haystacks
and sheep on the open ground beyond.
Photo: G. W. Wilson
Aberdeen University Library

164 *above* The Grand Hotel and South Sands, Scarborough, *c.*1900. A fine photograph of the oldest of all seaside resorts in the high season. The seaside, as an institution, developed as it did because the mineral spring of Scarborough spa happened to flow out of the cliffs into the sea a little to the left of this picture. The nineteenth century's peculiar contribution was to make the seaside holiday a popular institution and one that mitigated some of the ills of an industrial society. Scarborough re-mained a fashionable resort (it is evident that Mr Walshaw's bathing machines bear no advertising of anything but his own business), but the orderly confusion of the beach here is at one with more simply popular places: it is informed by a gregarious individualism.
Photo: G. W. Wilson
Aberdeen University Library

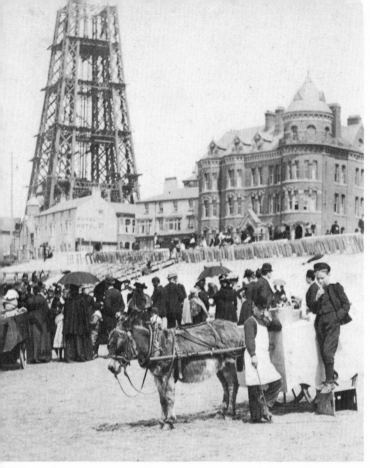

165 *left* Blackpool beach, from a stereo card, 1875. The huge legs of the Tower, an extra-ordinary construction, dwarf the Royal Hotel and contrast sharply with the casual contrivances of the promenade at this time. Blackpool has a long history as a resort, but its present face is a creation of the late-nineteenth and early-twentieth centuries. *David Francis*

166 *below* A band on a beach and a flotilla of bathing machines, from a lantern slide, c.1895. The bathing machine was concerned with bathing for health and with preserving modesty, not at all with pleasure. A study of this kind underlines the oddity of the institution. *David Francis*

167 *right*   The opening of the Manchester Ship
Canal, 1894. The triumphal arch is an ancient
institution; an arch of firemen and their
equipment over tramlines is the very essence of
municipality.
Manchester Public Libraries

168 *below*   The hustings: the declaration of the
poll for the coronership of Central Middlesex in
Lincoln's Inn Fields, 1884. The hustings was an
institution of high antiquity that survived long
enough to be photographed, although the early
difficulties of photographing crowds makes
pictures of it a comparative rarity. The
attendance on this occasion is predominantly
Respectable.
Greater London Council

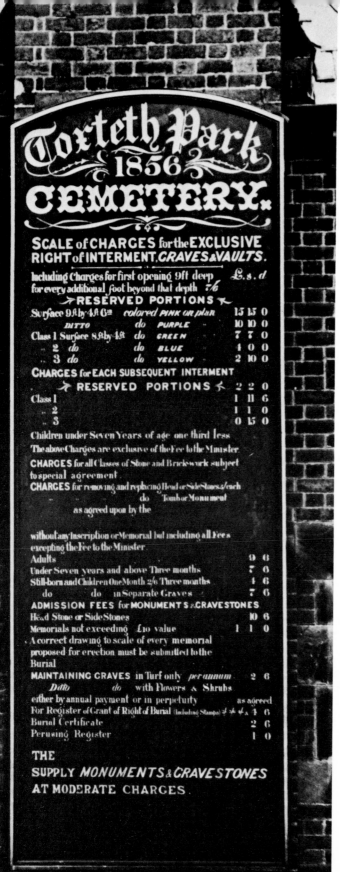

Toxteth Park
1856
CEMETERY.

SCALE of CHARGES for the EXCLUSIVE RIGHT of INTERMENT. GRAVES & VAULTS.

Including Charges for first opening 9ft deep   £. s. d
for every additional foot beyond that depth   7/6

RESERVED PORTIONS

				£	s	d
Surface 9ft by 4ft 6in	*colored*	PINK	*on plan*	15	15	0
DITTO	do	PURPLE		10	10	0
Class 1 Surface 8ft by 4ft	do	GREEN		7	7	0
2 do	do	BLUE		4	0	0
3 do	do	YELLOW		2	10	0

CHARGES for EACH SUBSEQUENT INTERMENT

	£	s	d
RESERVED PORTIONS	2	2	0
Class 1	1	11	6
2	1	1	0
3	0	15	0

Children under Seven Years of age one third less

The above Charges are exclusive of the Fee to the Minister.

CHARGES for all Classes of Stone and Brickwork subject to special agreement

CHARGES for removing and replacing Head or Side Stones   each
             do   Tomb or Monument
as agreed upon by the

without any Inscription or Memorial but including all Fees excepting the Fee to the Minister

	s	d
Adults	9	6
Under Seven years and above Three months	7	6
Still-born and Children One Month 2/6 Three months	4	6
do do in Separate Graves	7	6

ADMISSION FEES for MONUMENTS & GRAVESTONES

	£	s	d
Head Stone or Side Stones		10	6
Memorials not exceeding £10 value	1	1	0

A correct drawing to scale of every memorial proposed for erection must be submitted to the Burial

	s	d
MAINTAINING GRAVES in Turf only *per annum*	2	6

Ditto   do   with Flowers & Shrubs
either by annual payment or in perpetuity   as agreed

	s	d
For Register of Grant of Right of Burial (including Stamps)	3	6
Burial Certificate	2	6
Perusing Register	1	0

THE
SUPPLY MONUMENTS & GRAVESTONES
AT MODERATE CHARGES.

169 *left*   Board of charges at Toxteth Park Cemetery, Liverpool, photographed in 1907. The teeming city implied a populous cemetery, and the cemetery was a place to which people resorted not only to tend the family graves, but to walk soberly and reflectively among the evergreens. Heavy infant mortality, and a strong family tradition that observed the anniversaries of deaths for several generations, charged the cemetery with emotion. It was also a place in which proprietorial instincts were gratified, although as the board here shows, its business-like regulations were tempered by mercy.
Liverpool Public Libraries

170 *right*   Oakum-picking, *c.*1900, from a lantern slide. The setting is probably a workhouse. The parti-coloured brick walls have been familiar to later generations in other institutions.
David Francis

171 *above*   Rational amusement: a scene in Sefton
Park, *c.*1885.
Liverpool Public Libraries

172 *above right*   Brighton, municipal gardening,
*c.*1865, from a *carte de visite.*
David Francis

173 *right* Public benefaction: laying the foundation stone of the Brown Library, Liverpool, 15 April 1857. An early and striking photograph of a kind that becomes more accomplished and less interesting as time passes and municipal buildings multiply. The figures in front (from the left) are the Bishop of Chester (the Rt Revd Dr John Graham), Mr Brown himself, Dr Thomas Raffles (the leading Nonconformist minister in the town), the redoubtable Henry Picton, and Lord Stanley.
Liverpool Public Libraries

174 *above left*   The Brown Library, *c.*1890.
Photo: Frith's
Liverpool Public Libraries

175 *below*   Time to stand and stare: demolition on the Strand at Aldwych, when Kingsway was cut, photographed with a Kodak panoramic camera in 1901. The new street was to be called Queensway, but on Edward VII's accession its name was changed.
Kodak Museum

176 *right*   The high pitch of civic dignity: Sheffield Town Hall, *c.*1900. Sheffield was an untidy town with no particular architectural tradition, an important manufacturing centre, but not incorporated until 1838. By the end of the century it was a rich and powerful city, and felt that it owed itself a monumental town hall, which it raised in the years 1890–7. The architect was E. W. Mountford.
Photo: G. W. Wilson
Aberdeen University Library

177 The twentieth century inaugurated in Manchester: the departure of the first electric trams from Albert Square, 6 June 1901. *Manchester Public Libraries*

10   The Face of the Industrial City
Two looks at Manchester

G. F. Chadwick

To look again on the face of the industrial city of Victorian England as its own inhabitants saw it is an impossibility. The elements that compose the scene are too complex for that: complex around the edges where town becomes country, and rural villages and industrial colonies cohere with the larger mass; complex in the growing number of new paths being made through the city by new modes of transport; complex in the additions of new to traditional scales of buildings and spaces; complex in the changing scale of the city as a whole and of its related parts. These complexities were partly a function of new technologies and the economic motives from which they sprang, partly the product of historical inertia and the sheer durability of inherited structures and disposed space.

    Until the Industrial Revolution the major structures of most towns were their churches. The medieval town consisted principally of low-built houses—diverse in detail but consistent in height—accented visually by numerous period churches, but above all by the central church, the abbey or minster. This pattern can still be seen from the city walls of York, save where the monstrous bulk of the North Eastern Railway offices and more recent office blocks intrude: a huddle of rectangular red-brown roof planes meeting at many angles, but remarkably consistent in their general level, punctuated by pale white-grey limestone towers and spires of the minor churches, and presided over by the vast bulk of York Minster. In the Victorian industrial town, new economic pursuits reduced such dominants, replacing duomo and campanile by factory and chimney. The process was most pervasive in the textile towns of East Lancashire and the West Riding, where mill chimneys overshot church spires as the cotton and woollen industries grew and prospered. Multi-storeyed mills were compacted to conserve the energy generated by steam plants in vertical as well as horizontal transmission, to concentrate materials, skills, work people, and production in large volumes of space, either cheek by jowl with rows of workers' houses, or on new, level sites by watercourses or railways. Even today, when so many mill chimneys have been felled, those which are left dominate the skyline, as for example on that classic train ride from Manchester Victoria to Oldham Mumps: scores of cotton-mills riding at anchor on the plain near Failsworth, like the Review of the Grand Fleet of 1914, lighted at night: 'fabulous argosies, as romantic as if they were Venetian, and in the history of the world more important'.[1]

Other places, other shapes: as the metal trades grew, so primary extractive industry grew and its technology improved: pit-head gear, blast-furnace, rolling-mill, stamping-shop, gas-works, railway yards, specialized structures of every kind, even their indestructible debris and discarded apparatus, formed indelible outlines on the ground, with every technical improvement. The Welsh valleys, the Black Country of South Staffordshire, the shipyards of Tyneside or Merseyside, all became marked with characteristic local technologies, with characteristic structures, of a size and scale never seen before. The existence, from now on, of two scales within the industrial city is perhaps the most significant visual change of all: the human, in the continuing tradition of urban housing and life on the streets; and the super-human, not in the tradition of York, the daily reminder of God's omnipotence, but in terms of a temporal power, bursting out of industrial technology from hand- and water-power, to steam-power.

If we are to have any perception of these shapes on the ground we must visit specific spots and get the best focus we can through contemporary recordings of every kind, however fragmentary. In doing so, we should remember that the synthesis will inevitably be ours. We cannot resolve through our own imagination, for example, the nagging question whether the Victorian city was actually easier to grasp perceptually—whether one could get the feel of it more readily—than today's cities. We cannot know, in the terms of these volumes, the full reality of its image. Industrial steam and domestic smoke, factory hooters and horses' hooves, smelly people and stinking waterways, a wholly different catalogue of urban incident, preclude that. But we can for one place at a time get a *visual* focus.

Much of the early-Victorian city went unrecorded in photographs, and lithographs of street scenes were not common, being often related to specific occasions like royal visits. Manchester is no exception, and few photographs earlier than 1860 survive; however, there is the beautifully drawn and exceptionally complete Ordnance Survey of 1850 (surveyed in 1849), from which a very good picture of this city can be gleaned. The maps, to a scale of 5 feet to 1 statute mile (i.e., 1:1056), give a great deal of detailed information about the use of buildings and land, and the ground-floor plans of all public buildings are shown very completely. This survey and the prints and photographs from a range of dates make it possible to reconstruct the landscape as it might be experienced on a journey through the city.

If we begin our journey to the south of the city, in the Higher Ardwick area,* we find a mixture of the still-rural and the suburban. Fields are being tended, but small colonies of villas are being settled and the large grounds of Ardwick Hall are being invaded by new terraces of houses. To the east, mounds of spoil and hollows indicate the active presence of brick crofts, found all around the growing city, which can thus be said literally to rise out of the ground on which it stands. Here too is the junction of the Manchester, Sheffield & Lincolnshire Railway and the London & North-Western Railway, both marked by approach viaducts of dull red brick. Older routes are marked by toll-bars on the main approaches, and here is one guarding the turnpike leading over the Pennines to Sheffield. At Higher Ardwick, near the Green, are houses of different sizes, all with well laid-out gardens. South of it, the villas, in small groups or dispersed in their separate grounds, are mostly stuccoed and in the faintly classical styles which have been popular for some time; occupied by relatively wealthy merchants and professional men, they are in a green and pleasant land of trees and gardens whose arabesque beds would have been approved, no doubt, by the late Mr Loudon. Off the London Road, the group called the Polygon stands out, an arc of nine large houses set back from the long, lamp-lit approach from Stockport Road, behind a series of sweeping ovals of separate drives, and overlooking open country. The private gardens are furnished with summer houses, sundials, and ample water from private pumps and wells to nurture the products of their conservatories. The Polygon is dignified, solid, respectable: the outside world looks up the flights of its front steps to porticoes and solid front doors.

There are cemeteries near by at Ardwick and Rusholme Road, many of the headstones bearing pathetic witness to the high mortality of working-class children, and to the great epidemics of twenty years ago. The entrance to Ardwick Cemetery is flanked by a chapel on one side and the block of the registrar's and sexton's houses on the other, and its simple rectilinear pattern of paths and graves is already bearing testimony to changing taste—exotic stones for memorials, less restraint in feeling, bolder decoration and lettering.

In the developing parish of Chorlton-upon-Medlock the speculative builder is active everywhere. All classes are catered for, from those inhabiting the new, substantial villas along the wide, straight Oxford Road to the dwellers in mean rows of back-to-back houses a few yards behind them. But, as we move inwards towards the city centre, even the larger houses lack front gardens and few have rear ones. In regular terraces, the chequerboard pattern of new building estates south of the River Medlock is filling in: although small, skimpily built, and mean, these monotonous, red-brick rows are an improvement upon the courts and cellar dwellings in the centre of the city. For one thing, they are on the edge of the country, within sight, still, of green fields. Nevertheless, there are shops on corners and on the main thoroughfares,

* All place-names may be identified by reference to the sections of contemporary ordnance maps which have been included among the accompanying plates.

public-houses at frequent intervals, churches less often, and the apparatus of local government. Chapels and churches, indeed, form one of the main visual features of such suburbs, relieving the two-storeyed level of building by imposing stone façades, Classical or Gothic, porticoed, or towered: even the more nondescript Nonconformist chapels make some change in bulk and skyline, if not in materials. The city is still small enough for most of it to be reached on foot in fifteen or twenty minutes from any other part. The main streets, therefore, have their daily processions of people walking to work, with the middle classes patronizing the horse omnibuses or using their own traps or carriages: horses are a common sight, both at work on the streets, in fields or paddocks towards the edges of the city, and standing tethered in front of villas and coach-houses, or on cab-ranks.

If we take Oxford Street towards the centre of the city, we soon find ourselves, on crossing the Medlock, in an area almost completely given over to manufacturing, though pockets of small back-to-back houses and courts exist. This is industrial Manchester, by and large: the Atlas Ironworks, the Caledonia Foundry, cotton-mills, saw-mills. These manufactories are located near the wharves of the Rochdale Canal, which bisects the centre from north-east to south-west and joins the Bridge-water Canal at Castle Field. Eagle Quay and other wharves and basins penetrate deep on either side of Oxford Street, almost to St Peter's Square, once the edge of the urban area, offering large sites with water frontage. Now the water is largely hidden from the street, but there are numerous works entrances through which narrow boats and horse-drays, cranes and hoists, weighing-machines and chimneys, can be seen. Despite the new railways, the trade still passes over these quays—a canal port for the sea-going port of Liverpool, the coalfields of South Lancashire, the salt-fields of Cheshire.

The railways are already beginning to parcel out the city, to put a girdle of brick, stone, and iron around its vitals. By 1836 the Liverpool & Manchester and the Bolton & Manchester Railways have penetrated to within half-a-mile of the Royal Exchange; by 1849 Victoria station and London Road station are established, the former within a quarter of a mile of the Exchange, the latter half-a-mile away at the end of Piccadilly, whilst radial lines spread outwards from the beginnings of exten-sive yards and terminal facilities. The new railways, being almost exclusively on viaducts, are immediately visible and intrusive, and many houses have been knocked down to make way for them, causing great distress, with housing in short supply. The price Manchester paid for its progress fell heavily on the worst-paid and worst-housed, some of whom made homes of the undercrofts formed by the new viaducts. The new stations are now providing the city with a new class of public buildings, although (with the single exception later of the Central station train-shed) they are uninteresting structures. Around London Road station, to west and south-west, are large areas of crowded, back-to-back houses and narrow streets: minimal labouring-class housing on the slope down to the River Medlock's foul waters. In London Road itself is one of the many street-markets which characterized the inner parts of the city.

Between London Road station and Piccadilly, at this time, is another area of quays and basins: another part of the inland port. Here again is a great focus of industry and commerce, with bustling horse-wagons and boats arriving and leaving. A portent for the future, though, is the Manchester, Sheffield & Lincolnshire Railway's General Stores which have already taken up occupation and will eventually swallow up the entire Stockport basin and fill it in as a site for railway warehouses.

Piccadilly itself, in 1849, is a peripheral-centre area, not the major focus that it becomes much later. The Manchester Royal Infirmary and Lunatic Asylum, a solid, porticoed stone edifice, occupies what was later to be Piccadilly Gardens, flanked by the Infirmary Baths in George Street to the west. The pond in front of the Infirmary (a remnant, like the pond on Ardwick Green, of brick-pits?) is not incorporated into a formal promenade at this time, although for the Queen's visit in 1851 'The Manchester Fountains' were to be arranged there by Freeman Roe, Hydraulic Engineer. North of Piccadilly at this time is a great mixture: industry (including the very large Newton Street Cotton Mills near Stevenson Square), livery stables, chapels, public-houses, horse and carriage repositories, and private dwellings. Most buildings are rather domestic in scale, save for the cotton-mills, and many hotels line Piccadilly itself. South of here, towards Oxford Street, is another multiplicity of buildings in what is later to become the predominantly warehouse area of Portland Street—great Renaissance palaces to replace the mixture of back-to-back and terraced housing, courtyards, public-houses, schools, timber-yards, and mills.

The changes in this area of Manchester, north and south of Portland Street, are to be of great significance for the city: functionally, in the displacement of mixed uses, including manufacture, by warehousing and commerce; visually, in that many of the city's finest nineteenth-century buildings (including those shown in Ernst's 1857 map) are to arise here. Over a century later, however, some domestic structures still remain (now used as offices), and the basic street-pattern is unaltered.

The 'Main Street' of Manchester in 1849, as now, is Market Street, running from the River Irwell to Piccadilly, before falling again south-eastwards to the Medlock. The chief landmark in the city, by virtue of function and position rather than bulk, is the Exchange, one link in a sequence of buildings and open places which makes up the historic core of the city. Here are the remnants of a medieval street and building pattern: Cathedral, Market Place, Exchange, St Ann's Square, St Ann's Church, King Street, (Old) Town Hall. In 1849, of course, these replicate Renaissance ideas, but Long Millgate, Hanging Ditch, Withy Grove, and other streets around the Cathedral, with their many timber-framed houses, are indissolubly medieval. Thus around the Chetham Hospital and the Cathedral are courts and yards, long, narrow plots running back from street frontages, short vistas along curving streets, low 'black and white' buildings. There are many markets: the covered Victoria Market for meat; the Fish Market in the Old Shambles; the Flower, Fruit, Vegetable and Poultry Market in the Market Place; and Smithy Door Market for fruit and vegetables in Victoria Street. Crowded stalls stand on cobbled or sett-paved streets; numerous lamps on posts and stalls light the scene at night.

251

There are all kinds of juxtapositions in the city centre. We might well expect the Electric Telegraph Company's office to adjoin the Exchange, but be surprised that the nearby Cotton Finishing Works should so obviously point the moral of Manchester's main concern. The view along the Irwell, from one of its bridges, shows the Cathedral beset by at least half-a-dozen mill chimneys. The Old Town Hall and Cross Street Chapel are also cheek by jowl, with the Bank of England opposite, for good measure. The new commercial and public architecture is solid, even scholarly, in contrast to the sordid gimcrack aspect of the housing sandwiched in everywhere, between commerce and industry, inside the ring of railway viaducts. Little of what is to happen later is yet in evidence. Albert Square has not been contemplated, nor Waterhouse's Flemish-Gothic Town Hall, which is to rise twenty-five years later on the site of the Town's Yard, off Princess Street (the Yard's boundaries survive in the triangular site plan of the present building); and the Cross Street–Corporation Street route has not yet been pushed through. The unequal contest between living space and working space, which underlies the continuous process of rebuilding cities in a state of growth, is not yet evident. Apart from houses in the path of the railway, very little is being torn down to make room for something else. Manchester, it might almost be said, is still a coral island, growing largely by accretion, cell upon cell, haphazard, irregular, but terribly fast.

We now move forward fifty years. Manchester in the 1890s was photographed mainly in its central parts. Once again the Ordnance Survey is a great help, the 1:500 series of 1891 being most detailed and complete, though the very cartography speaks of a changing attitude, it would seem, since the series of 1849: a certain hardness and boldness of line, less elegance of lettering—but a profusion of accurate-looking detail.

The city now is much bigger, of course: it has spread inexorably outwards, especially along the railway lines. The diameter of the city has doubled, and so in the nineties it is fourfold the city of the fifties in spatial extent, whilst the population has increased by more than 300,000 in the same period. Manchester is no longer a city which can be covered on foot: transport has become more organized as the horse bus has given way to the street tramway, and suburban railway stations have begun to come into their own. The built-up area has yet to reach the flood plain of the Mersey in the south, for example, and many hamlets that are later to lose their geographical distinctness and become mere names in an urban mass are still identifiable, protected by open fields.

On the south, the city extends to Alexandra Park, newly laid out from farm land in 1867. To the south-east, it now engulfs Victoria Park, long isolated as a rural suburb; and there is an urban outlier at Birch, near Platt Hall. Eastwards, beyond the railway web, housing now creeps along the Hyde and Ashton Roads, to Beswick, and northwards towards Philips Park. To the north-east, Miles Platting and Harpurhey are unattached no longer, and a straggle of development goes northwards to Cheetham Hill. On this side of the city, buildings have now also sprung up along the Bury New Road to Broughton, and Salford, too, reaches into the great loop of the Irwell, and on its south bank north-westwards to Pendleton. West Salford reaches to Cross Lane, but Weaste and Eccles are still rural. To the south-west, Old Trafford is barely reached, whilst Trafford Park still has its deer and awaits the coming of the Manchester Ship Canal, and its later transformation into an industrial estate; Chorlton-cum-Hardy remains relatively remote.

Following again our journey of half a century earlier, we find Ardwick Green now laid out as a formal garden, with fountains in basins at either end, a ceremonial flagstaff, pavilions, and a urinal. There are tramlines now along the main roads to Hyde and Stockport, and a little more intensiveness in building. Ardwick Green is now more clearly a focus of local community services: Osborne House Institute (Young Ladies' Association) graces the north side of the Green next to Ardwick Town Hall. On its other side is the Industrial School, whilst nearby are the Post Office, Provident Dispensary, Nurses' Home, and St Thomas's Church. Such groups, such foci, are now to be found all around the parent city, representing an advance upon the formlessness of earlier dispositions of broadly similar facilities. At an equal distance north of Manchester, we find a similar situation at Cheetham Hill, with its fine Assembly Rooms, or—even more notably, because of its layout—the Chorlton complex around Grosvenor Square and All Saints' Church: Classical portico, Italianate twin towers and Corinthian columns, Gothic spire, Victorian-Georgian domestic façades. Even at Ardwick Green, though, there are still odd plots of land left vacant in the process of urbanization. The small, cramped courts of the 1830s are still there, the spectrum running through small back-to-back, tunnel-back, courtyard, terrace, substantial terrace, or semi-detached houses, in a haphazard and spasmodic arrangement.

The Polygon, to the south of Ardwick Green, is still large, spacious, and open—but now the Union Carriage Works seems perilously near, and the Baths behind Ardwick House have promoted a chimney which flagrantly overtops the suburban trees of this villa enclave. North and west of the Polygon are the very different ranks of terraced houses. These streets are exceedingly regular, with narrow back alleyways, tiny backyards, outdoor privies, and ashpits. Occasionally we meet a wider street—Brunswick Street, for example, running across the main south and south-west radial streets—but all are now paved, drained, lighted, and populated uniformly. The street-corners tend to be taken by churches and schools, counterpointing the red terraces and lopped forests of pale earthenware chimney-pots: St Paul's Church, with its school and segregated playgrounds and rectory; a Baptist Chapel (Particular); or the Balfour Club. (An alternative corner-marker, of course, is the public-house: the Salutation Inn—still standing in 1970—or the Wellington, both south of Cavendish Street.) In this area, too, is a wider spectrum of entertainment, industry, or out-of-worktime activity: a drill hall, a saw-mill, the Bridgewater Music Hall, the Ormond Hall (City Mission)—a further tier of community provision, mainly private rather than public, ranged behind the main grouping of Grosvenor

253

Square at a little distance. This area, developed well before 1835 in the main, has small, often short, terraces of tiny houses without gardens, whilst court-housing is quite common. Steps often lead up to front doors, so that there are basements, and coal-holes in the pavement, but local flavour may appear here and there in such things as street names, which appear occasionally carved in Pennine gritstone, like pathetic little Mahogany Street, off Oxford Road, only demolished in 1969 after about 140 years of mean life. Oxford Road itself, in the nineties, is a main artery, sett-paved, broad, and tramwayed. (It is interesting to speculate how much, in fact, of a late-Victorian city like Manchester was covered over by hard pavings or buildings or railway lines and other structures: little of the original ground surface can have been left uncovered, and streams like the Cornbrook were mercilessly culverted.) The shopping function of Oxford Road must have been considerable, complementing the many corner shops inside each housing area. Southwards along Oxford Road, the Gothic bulk of Waterhouse's Owens College is dominant on the right, its Flemish-roofed tower answering the calm, majestic statement of Holy Name Church a little further along to the left. The university atmosphere is limited as yet: there is no Whitworth Hall, though there is a Gymnasium, whilst a cab-rank and cabmen's shelter occupy the roadside. A suburban feeling is uppermost here: an increasing number of larger houses, like Arlington Place opposite Owens; broad approaches to substantial, stuccoed Classical-feeling villas; some of these are detached, some semi-detached, some large houses even in terraces, around Holy Name and Lime Grove. There is a High School on Dover Street, destined to survive as a university faculty building. The pattern continues southwards to Whitworth Park, and beyond to Victoria Park; more gardens to the houses, but a very mixed arrangement for most classes except the poorest, though the content of each area changes perceptibly as one moves away from the main street into quieter byways. There is, of course, still Victoria Park itself, its landscape maturing, its villas still protected by gate and lodge from the world without, but its atmosphere now sullied by the pall of urban smoke that cannot be dispersed.

Retracing our steps and moving north, rather than south, towards the city centre, we find that Oxford Street still has a partly industrial face, though commerce and other activities intrude increasingly. The Atlas Ironworks and the Eagle Foundry are still there, and the Eagle Mill (Smallwares), fronting or visible from Oxford Street; the canal wharves are still in use and teams of horses still draw ironshod carts across the granite carriageways; mills and timber-yards still flourish by the Rochdale Canal. Interspersed with the wharves and their travelling cranes are clusters of small houses: even the centre of the city still boasts a large resident population. But change is in the air already: northwards, major monuments like the Free Trade Hall in Peter Street have risen, flanked by the Theatre Royal, Y.M.C.A., Comedy Theatre, and Café Royal (all still identifiable in 1970). The Central station's great arched roof has been built (though not its attendant offices, which entirely failed to materialize); and the Cheshire Lines Railway goods station, of great bulk, raises its sombre brick walls behind the Florentine splendour of the Free Trade Hall.

The Midland Hotel has not yet arrived, but the St Peter's Square area, already distinguished in the image of the city by its intersection of streets at the front of the Church—a *tour de force* of civic design of long standing—is reinforced by these new additions, and, of course, by Waterhouse's masterpiece, the Town Hall, rising behind, its tower a majestic assertion of civic pride and financial irresponsibility. Albert Square is not fully laid out even in 1891, its ornaments then being the Albert Memorial, Bishop Fraser's statue, a urinal, and diagonal tramtracks.

The streets leading down to Deansgate from Albert Square are as mixed in their buildings and uses at this time as anywhere in the city: courts of small houses, pubs, clubs, and all manner of industry and public endeavour. For industry, there are the City Printing Works, the Albert Packing House, and the Gas Meter Testing Office; whilst the St Anne's Schools (Girls and Infants), the Fire Station, the Grand Circus, Manchester Technical School, St Mary's Chapel (Roman Catholic), and the High Court of Justice (Probate Division) represent different forms of public endeavour. But the subdued screen of warehouses and offices lining Albert Square itself must have produced an impression of greater uniformity, quite at odds with the circumstances behind them.

Passing from St Peter's Square again, Piccadilly-wards, we see many changes in the area south-eastwards, between Mosley and Portland Streets. Here are many of the newer, purpose-built warehouses for King Cotton: substantial, regular in plan, of masonry outside and framed structure inside, many of them with glazed internal courts and light-wells. Such structures are new, but some of the earlier buildings, like Watts's warehouse in Portland Street, remain the grandest of them all. Despite this, many of these façades will appear in the *Builder*'s pages, and be approved of generally, adding their little touches to an area distinguished already by Sir Charles Barry's Art Gallery, the Portico Library, and others portrayed by Mr Mennie's pencil in the frieze to Ernst's plan of the city in 1857.

In Piccadilly itself, the Hospital has gone, only the Dispensary for Outpatients remaining in its grounds. The formal layout of today has been completed along the north frontage, with the Queen's statue flanked by Dalton and Watt and Peel, and underground conveniences, but much of Parker Street and Piccadilly is given over to the tramcar. There are many hotels here and along Market Street or towards London Road: Mosley, White Bear, Albion, Royal; the Electric Hotel on Swan Court, off Market Street, particularly arouses the curiosity. Towards London Road station, the major hotel blocks complement the bulk and richness of the warehouses further west: the Grand, the Queen's, with lesser but loyally-named fellows nearer the station: Brunswick, Clarence, Waterloo, Imperial. Behind these, the Venetian-Gothic tower of the Police Courts in Minshull Street provides an unexpectedly rich vertical thrust to the dominantly horizontal canyon-like quality of most streets in the area (and a landmark from the railway). There are chapels, Sunday schools, and cotton-mills on the way across the Rochdale Canal back to London Road and its station, still jointly owned, but now rebuilt in a totally undistinguished fashion, and flanked to its north by the London & North-Western Railway's goods shed and the vast

Manchester, Sheffield & Lincolnshire Railway's Goods station near the Dale Street wharves of the Rochdale Canal.

Retracing our steps to Piccadilly, and down Market Street we might now let the photographs take over the story in greater detail—here in Market Street is the focus for the shopper newly arrived by tramcar or train from any point in south-east Lancashire; for the businessman at the Exchange lower down, or the warehouse near Piccadilly; for the roisterer in hotel, music-hall, or public-house near by. Here is the High Victorian City *par excellence*, hard and gritty, even proud, externally, but warm and human within.

Note

1   Keith Dewhurst, 'When Cotton was King', *Guardian*, 9 December 1967.

178 River Irwell, 1859: the Victoria Bridge, as seen from Blackfriars Bridge. The Cathedral is the only non-industrial building in sight. Industry hereabouts turns its back to the river and to neighbouring Salford. The stream itself is thickly polluted but is a traffic artery none the less. A small steam packet is moored between the wooden jetties on the right.
Photo: George Grundy
Manchester Public Libraries

179 *above* Victoria Fish Market in
Victoria Street, 1860. The classical style at
its most elemental for a public building
meeting a basic need. The cast-iron grilles
with their daisy-chain pattern admit the
necessary breath of air; skinned rabbits
hang outside; a restless knot of people
appear as ghosts. The haberdasher's shop
adjoining is a mongrel: Norman, Gothic,
Byzantine, and Classical influences.
Photo: George Wardley
Manchester Public Libraries

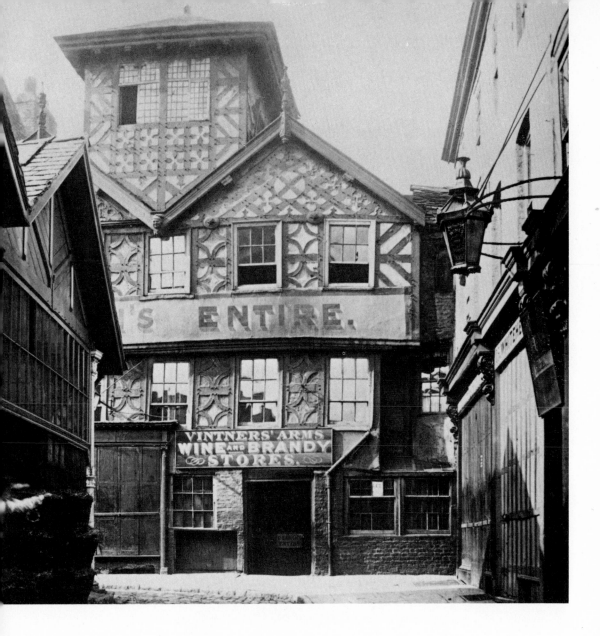

180 *left* The Wellington Inn, Old Shambles,
1865. A sixteenth-century building made
grotesque by Victorian commercial zeal and the
Florentine grace of the new watchmakers'
premises next door. The giant spectacles enable
us to read the date when the inn gave up its top
floor—1802. A man is sitting on the pavement.
This ancient place is a hub of impending change.
It survives still.
Photo: George Wardley
Manchester Public Libraries

181 *above* The Vintners' Arms, Smithy Door,
1865. A survival from the middle ages. The
shuttered shops and the Three Tuns pub on the
right are soon to disappear though the wine and
brandy stores will hang on.
Photo: George Wardley
Manchester Public Libraries

182 *above left* The Sun Inn, Long Millgate, 1866. Known locally as 'Poets Corner', this was the meeting-place of the group described in Chapter 31.
Photo: George Wardley
Manchester Public Libraries

183 *left* Free Trade Hall, Peter Street, 1861. A handsome symbol of Manchester's commercial ethos that overwhelms the lesser property downhill. The new Free Trade Hall, erected on the site of the original building of 1843, was opened in 1856. It was the forum for political agitation, temperance demonstrations, and religious revivalist meetings, rather than musical festivals—the great meeting-place of Manchester designed by Manchester's leading architect of the day, Edward Walters. It contained a pair of public halls and a foyer. In the spandrels between the nine arches are the arms of neighbouring towns—Liverpool, Rochdale, Oldham, Bolton, Stockport, Ashton-under-Lyne, and Wigan, grouped around Manchester and Salford in the centre. Free trade, the four continents, industry, commerce, agriculture, and the arts are garlanded above them. See also no. 84.
Photo: James Mudd
Manchester Public Libraries

184 *above* Newall's Buildings, Cross Street and Market Street, 1867. Boarded up and awaiting demolition for the new Royal Exchange.
Photo: James Mudd
Manchester Public Libraries

185 *above* Cotton warehouses, Portland Street, 1858. Such buildings had an almost swaggering confidence and completely dwarfed any people on the street. The more princely of this pair is Watts's warehouse, perhaps the finest building in Manchester at this time. Each of the four main storeys is in a different style, topped off by a prodigious attic. See also no. 327. *Howarth Loomes*

186 *above*   King Street, 1866. A good-class shopping street barricaded for the night. *Manchester Public Libraries*

187 *right*   Bank of England branch, King Street, 1866. A doorless neo-Classical façade with a daunting array of ironwork and blinkered windows, designed by C. R. Cockerell in 1845. The entrance is at the side. *Manchester Public Libraries*

188 *above* Royal Exchange, just before being demolished in 1868–9. It was founded in 1806 and replaced an earlier building demolished in 1790. A building of compact power by Thomas Harrison.
Manchester Public Libraries

189 *above right* Queen's Hotel, *c.*1866. A recently completed stucco building by Edward Walters, a symptom of commercial coming and going on a growing scale.
Manchester Public Libraries

190 *below right* Albert Memorial, 1866, by Thomas Worthington. A rather lonely outrider of the Gothic revival, placed in 1862 facing the site of the new town hall. The very similar design of the London monument by Scott was executed fifteen months later.
Manchester Public Libraries

191 *below far right* Manchester & Salford (later Williams Deacon's) Bank, on the corner of Marble Street and Mosley Street, 1866. The last of Walters's buildings, built six years earlier, and a rich celebration of Manchester's natural identification with the Renaissance, full of subtlety and power.

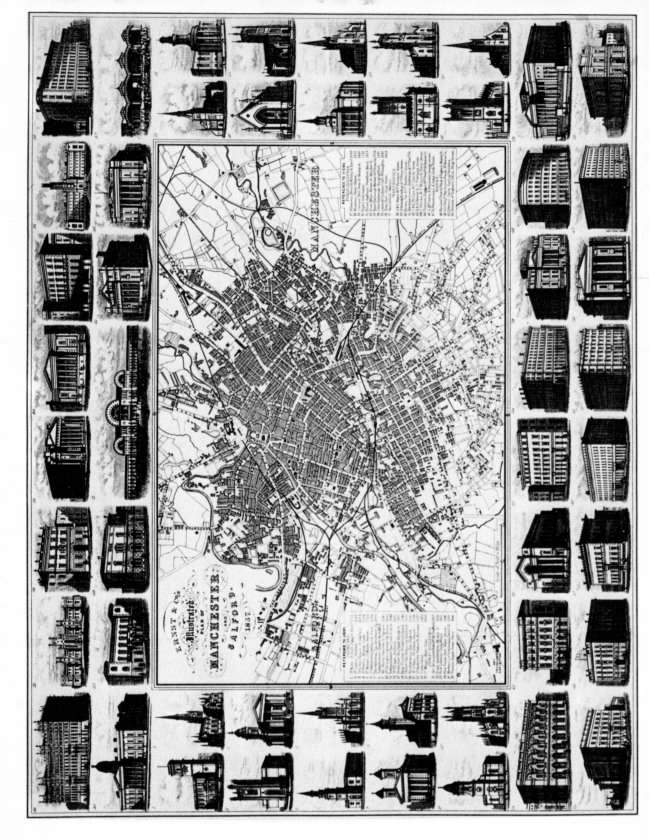

192 *above* Ernst & Co.'s *Illustrated Plan of Manchester and Salford*, 1857. The changing scale of the city centre is suggested by the frieze to this plan. The buildings differ stylistically but there is a feeling of solid uniformity about the way they are presented.

193 *below* The street plan of the High Victorian city: the central area around 1900. Seven railways converge on the city centre but do not pierce it; three rivers and four canals surround it; four major passenger stations and depots lie within a radius of just over two miles. The ancient centre of the city lay around the cathedral and the main axis of growth ran south and south-east. The more exclusive residential districts tended to be on this side, while those upwind of the gasworks along the Rochdale Road remained in possession of the working classes. For more detailed maps of parts of this area see nos 229–34.

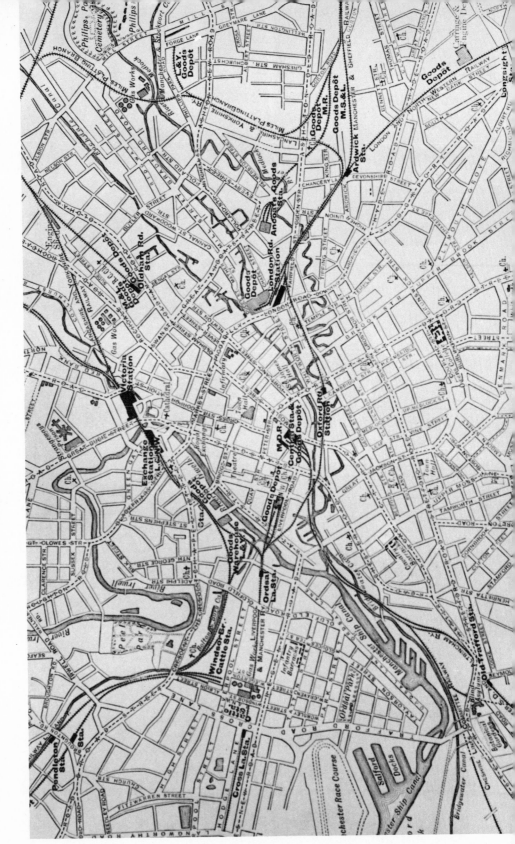

194 The Bridgewater Canal with the viaduct of the Manchester, South Junction & Altrincham Railway running alongside in the Knott Mill area. All the characteristic apparatus and signs of heavy wear and tear by industrial traffic. *Manchester Public Libraries*

195 River Irwell flowing under Regent Road. The last building in Salford on the left of the bridge is a brewery; the Hulme district of Manchester is on the right. This is part of the secret landscape of Manchester: its rivers functioned like sewers—out of sight and very largely out of mind.

Manchester Public Libraries

196 *below* London Road station, a place for loitering as well as dispatch. The rise to the station forecourt is steeper than it appears. A hotel surmounts the booking-hall.
Manchester Public Libraries

197 *above right* The southern approaches: Grosvenor Square on Oxford Road. The floor of the city was composed of acre upon acre of Penmaenmawr granite or Pennine gritstone.
Manchester Public Libraries

198 *below right* The London & North-Western Railway's Exchange Station. It overlooks the most ancient spot in Manchester. The Cathedral (so named in 1847) once stood on a mound sloping steeply to the Irwell, across which the station approach has since been thrown. The view of road and river on different levels below it is one of the grand sights of Victorian England, for the road into Salford is also concealed here. Cromwell did not arrive on the scene in the early seventies without a sectarian fight. The Greengate slum, which occupied much of this ground before the 1880s, did not go unresistingly.
Manchester Public Libraries

199 Market Street, from Piccadilly looking west, the aorta of Manchester. It is early morning and the shops are still shut. The tallest buildings in the city line this street and comprise a veneer of commercialism uniformly undistinguished and graceless, except for the slender stems of the gaslamps (which have had to be protected from the traffic by wooden gaiters).
Manchester Public Libraries

200 *below* Market Street in full use, accumulating litter and loiterers.
Manchester Public Libraries

201 Market Street, looking
towards Piccadilly: gritstone
pavements, granite kerbs,
setts laid at right-angles to
the movement of traffic,
ornate gaslamps, everything
made to last.
Manchester Public Libraries

202 *below* The Town Hall,
c.1885: Alfred Waterhouse's
masterpiece erected between
1868 and 1877, in which
economy and light were more
telling in the public competition than in the elevation.
Its outside walls blackened
rapidly but the interior
remained an archive of
municipal images and
architectural taste.
Photo: Valentine
Manchester Public Libraries

203 St Ann's Square, 1894. Here was the apotheosis of rich, comfortable, fashionable Manchester behind the Exchange. Richard Cobden is looking the other way. *Manchester Public Libraries*

204 *below* Smithy Door market, *c.*1885. Places that have developed over many generations tend to have more human eccentricity than those laid out on a large scale. Manchester contained many irregular clusters of streets in the central areas, and many different aspects. This view is looking in the reverse direction to no. 205. *Photo: Valentine Manchester Public Libraries*

105 Smithy Door, 1875.
The Royal Exchange is still
being completed; the
Vintners' Arms is being
nibbled away.
Photo: George Wardley
Manchester Public Libraries

106 *below* The Shambles,
1885. Twenty years on from
no. 180.
Photo: Valentine
Manchester Public Libraries

207 *left* The Royal Exchange, Market Street, *c.*1885. A self-important rather than distinguished building, this was the very heart of late-Victorian Manchester: every important firm in the city was represented here, and three-quarters of Britain's cotton yarn and woven cloth was marketed in it. The telephone, though catching on fast, had not yet made such human contacts a luxury.
Photo: Valentine
Manchester Public Libraries

208 *below left* Victoria Buildings, between Victoria Street, Deansgate, and St Mary's Gate, designed by William Dawes, a local architect, and erected in 1877. It contained 28 shops, 88 offices, and a hotel. The capitals to the columns at ground floor level are surmounted by carvings from Aesop's Fables.
Photo: Valentine
Manchester Public Libraries

209 *right* Daniel Lee & Company's warehouse, 1885. Here was an expression of commercial achievement and personal aspiration. Mr Lee was the most prominent Roman Catholic layman in the city in the fifties and sixties.
Photo: Valentine
Manchester Public Libraries

210 *left* Piccadilly, 1900: a succession of horse-trams. The trams were a major cause of traffic jams, especially on the narrower streets. Hackney carriages were much less conspicuous than in London at this time.
Photo: Valentine
Manchester Public Libraries

211 *below left* Shudehill Poultry Market. Such institutions tended to persist whatever changes occurred in the physical environment. Livestock are still sold on this spot.
Manchester Public Libraries

212 *right* Market Street. The social mix is striking, as is the filthy condition of the roadway. Shop windows were commonly clamorous.
Manchester Public Libraries

213 *below right* Between Cross Street and Princess Street.
Manchester Public Libraries

214-17 Rochdale Road. Life for the working classes was a matter as much of the street as of the home. This was a major thoroughfare but it suffered the penalty of containing the gasworks. The shops lining the road almost continuously from the city centre outwards were designed as such, and contained two storeys of accommodation over. The area round about was streaked by poverty and contained much housing built before by-laws became stringent regarding cellar dwellings.

218 *left* Police and Sessions Court, Minshull Street, *c*.1877. The architect was a local man, Thomas Worthington, who liked to think that Manchester was the Florence of the nineteenth century. His Italian Gothic exercise of 1868 in red brick was too hemmed in by other brick-built warehouses and narrow streets to allow that to happen here, but the fine profusion of pointed arches and detailing round the entrances made it a proper seat of law. *Manchester Public Libraries*

219 *below* Assize Courts, Great Ducie Street, *c*.1885. One of Waterhouse's earliest commissions, discharged under the influence of Ruskin in 1859, and reputedly the one building in the Venetian Gothic style that Ruskin approved of. Waterhouse went on to design Strangeways Gaol just beyond this site. *Photo: Valentine* *Manchester Public Libraries*

220 *right* Belle Vue Gaol, Hyde Road, 1890. An awesome pile that did not have a very long existence and was superseded by Strangeways. *Manchester Public Libraries*

221   Palace of Varieties, Oxford Street. An
aspect of urban enrichment largely unsuspected
from the street. Electric lighting has been
installed.
Manchester Public Libraries

222 Reference Library, Old Town Hall, King Street, *c.*1890. This building belongs to the Classical Revival, having been built in 1819 to the designs of Francis Goodwin. It was demolished about 1911 and its portico re-erected in Heaton Park. The adaptation of the main suite of rooms to the needs of a library was fittingly skilful though the original decorations had to give way to books. Contrary to the impression of studied indifference given here, the reference library was normally in heavy use. Before the present Central Reference Library was opened in 1934 readers had to use a series of temporary huts on Piccadilly.
Manchester Public Libraries

223 The Folly Theatre of Varieties, Peter Street, *c.*1890. A place for a sixpenny treat next door to the Free Trade Hall.
Photo: S. L. Coulthurst
Manchester Public Libraries

224 *above* Jersey Dwellings, Ancoats, 1897. The visitors to these model dwellings are ladies of the Manchester & Salford Methodist Mission, which was formed for such purposes in 1886.
Manchester Public Libraries

225 *above right* Strangeways Gaol entrance, 1900. Another activity of the Methodist Mission, performed daily. Prisons were places of private punishment and public admonishment. This was another of Waterhouse's designs.
Manchester Public Libraries

226 *right* The Whit Walk, Portland Street. Each denomination held its own on a different day of Whit week, the great festival that rivalled even Christmas in the nineteenth century. These were days for the throng, one's Sunday best, and protection against the rain.
Manchester Public Libraries

227   Botanical Gardens, Old Trafford. A place of
beauty and recreation a tram-ride from the
centre.
David Francis

228 The crematorium, three years after its
erection in 1892. Only 138 hearses arrived here
in the first ten years of its existence. The
Romanesque design was by Edward Salomons.
Photo: J. O. Pickard
Manchester Public Libraries

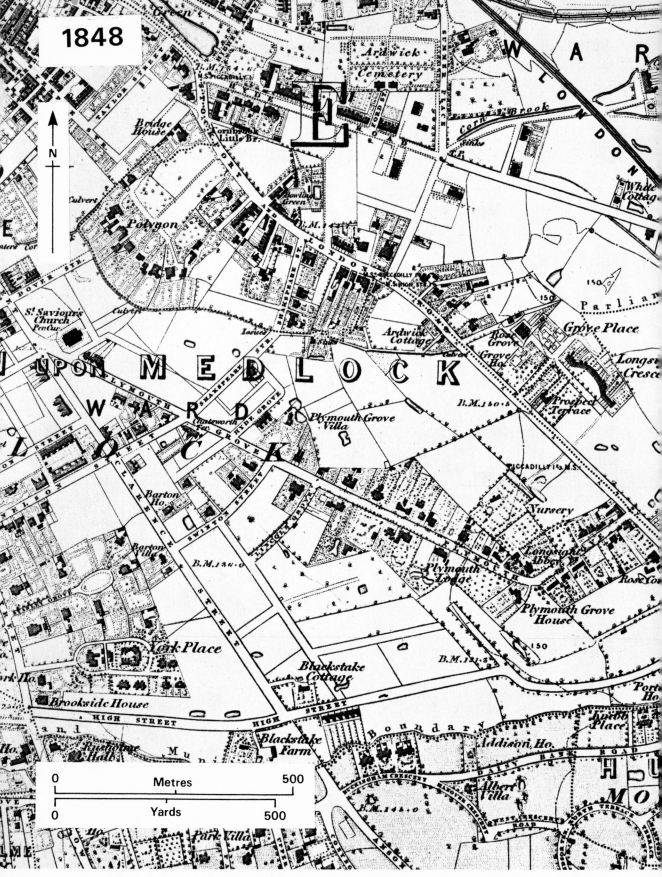

229–30 The south-eastern suburbs. Taken from the Ordnance Survey maps 1:10,560 of 1848 and 1895.

1895

ARDWICK CEMETERY

231-2 The central area. Taken from the Ordnance Survey maps 1:10,560 of 1848 and 1895.

1895

233–4   The environs of the Exchange. Taken from the Ordnance Survey maps 1:1,056 of 1850 and 1:500 of 1890.

1890

N

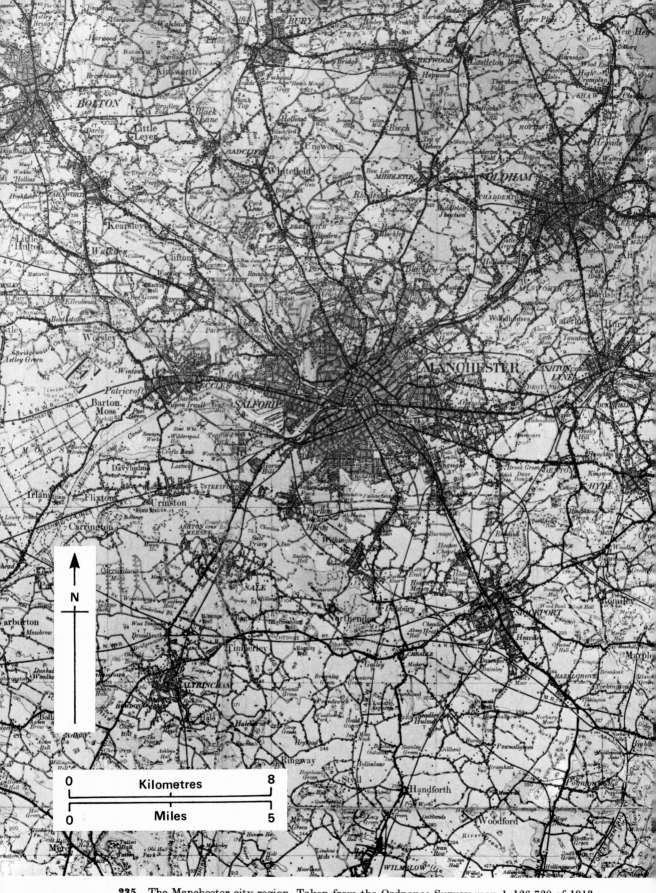

235 The Manchester city region. Taken from the Ordnance Survey map 1:126,720 of 1913, based on a survey of 1904.

11 Reading the Illegible

Steven Marcus

One of the chief components of the distress commonly felt by many people in modern cities is their sense that the city is unintelligible and illegible. The city is experienced as estrangement because it is not perceived as a coherent system of signs, as an environment communicating to us in a language that we know. After London, Manchester was the central site of that experience in Great Britain in the early nineteenth century, as Carlyle and Disraeli, Cooke Taylor and Kay-Shuttleworth, Faucher and de Tocqueville, among many others, have testified.[1] The discontinuities and obscurities, the apparent absence of large, visibly related structures, the disorganizations and disarticulations, seem to compose the structure of a chaos, a landscape whose human, social, and natural parts may be related simply by accidents, a random agglomeration of mere appearances.

It was into this prototypical anxiety-creating modern scene that Friedrich Engels, a young man sent by his father in Barmen to complete his business training in the family cotton-mills in Manchester, precipitated himself.[2] He arrived in Manchester at the very end of 1842 and remained twenty months. In that time he shunned polite circles and gave virtually all his spare time to 'intercourse with plain Working Men.' He wanted, he said in the dedication he wrote (in English) to 'the Working Classes of Great-Britain' in the original German edition of 1845 of his *The Condition of the Working Class in England in 1844*, 'to see you in your own homes, to observe you in your every-day life, to chat with you in your condition and grievances, to witness your struggles against the social and political power of your oppressors.' He wanted above all 'more than a mere *abstract* knowledge of my subject.'

In the event, he learned to read Manchester with his eyes, ears, nose, and feet. Long before Ruskin declared that one has to read a building, he demonstrated that one had to read a city. He learned to read it with his senses, the chief inlets, if it is permissible to adapt Blake, of mind in the present age. What he experienced he also perceived as a total intellectual and imaginative structure. It was a vision sustained by applying and adapting the systematic, coherent, consequent, Hegelian style of analysis to a complex, apparently unsystematic, and possibly incoherent massive aggregate of experiences and materials of disparate orders; to an English social reality notorious for its capacity to withstand theoretical incursions. The result was an account of Manchester which became a central part of what I take to be the best single thing he ever wrote, the chapter on 'The Great Towns' in *The Condition of the Working Class in England in 1844*. His first words about the town itself, composed in a single paragraph that runs to almost three pages in length, remain one of the most enduring and important statements ever written about the modern city.[3]

> The town itself is peculiarly built, so that someone can live in it for years and travel into it and out of it daily without ever coming into contact with a working-class quarter or even with workers—so long, that is to say, as one confines himself to his business affairs or to strolling about for pleasure.
> This comes about mainly in the circumstances that through an unconscious, tacit agreement as much as through conscious, explicit intention the working-class districts are most sharply separated from the parts of the city reserved for the middle class. Or, if this does not succeed, they are concealed with the cloak of charity. [*Oder, wo dies nicht geht, mit dem Mantel der Liebe verhüllt werden.*]

If this is so, how then does the city work? Engels turns at once to a description which is simultaneously an explanation and analysis:

> In the center of Manchester there is a fairly extensive commercial district, which is about a half-mile long and a half-mile broad. This district consists almost entirely of offices and warehouses. Nearly the whole of this district is without permanent residents, and is forsaken and deserted at night, when only policemen on duty patrol its narrow, dark lanes with their bull's eye lanterns. This district is intersected by certain main thoroughfares in which an enormous volume of traffic is concentrated. The ground floors of the buildings along these streets are occupied by shops of dazzling splendor. Here and there the upper stories of such premises are occupied as residences, and these streets present a relatively lively appearance until late at night. With the exception of this commercial district, all Manchester proper, all Salford and Hulme, an important part of Pendleton and Chorlton, two-thirds of Ardwick, and certain stretches of Cheetham Hill and Broughton—all of these comprise a pure working-class district. This area [or district] extends around [or surrounds] the commercial quarter in a

belt that is on the average one and a half miles in width. Outside, beyond this belt, live the upper and middle classes. The latter are to be found in regularly laid out streets near the working class quarter, in Chorlton and the lower-lying regions of Cheetham Hill. The upper middle class has situated itself in the remoter parts of Chorlton and Ardwick, or on the breezy heights of Cheetham Hill, Broughton, and Pendleton, where they live in villa-like houses surrounded by gardens.

And so on. There is the organization. What remains is to set it in motion. This is done in the first instance by the system of transport, the omnibuses which run every fifteen or thirty minutes and connect these outlying areas with the center of Manchester. And the beauty of it all, Engels continues,[4] is that the members of Manchester's monied aristocracy can now travel from their houses

> to their places of business in the center of town by the shortest routes,
> which run right through all the working class districts, without even noticing
> how close they are to the most squalid misery which lies immediately about
> them on both sides of the road. This is because the main streets which
> run from the Exchange in all directions out of the city are occupied almost
> uninterruptedly on both sides by shops, which are kept by members of the
> middle and lower-middle classes. In their own interests these shopkeepers
> should keep up their shops in an outward appearance of cleanliness and
> respectability; and in fact they do so. To be sure, these shops have none the
> less a concordant relation with those regions that lay stretched out behind
> them. Those shops which are situated in the commercial quarter or in the
> vicinity of the middle class residential districts are more elegant than those
> which serve to cover up [or as a facade for] the workers' grimy cottages.
> Nevertheless, even these latter adequately serve the purpose of hiding from
> the eyes of wealthy gentlemen and ladies with strong stomachs and weak
> nerves the misery and squalor that form the completing counterpart,
> the indivisible complement, of their riches and luxury.

He then proceeds to a concrete demonstration, and conducts the reader along a number of the main streets and simply and irrefutably shows how the changes in character of the buildings that front the street indicate what is to be found behind them. He is in fact charting one series of connected and stratified variables within the social ecology of the city.

By this means, Engels continues, 'it is possible for someone who knows Manchester to infer the social character of a district from the appearance of the main street that it adjoins. At the same time, however, it is almost impossible to get from these main streets a *real* view of the working class districts themselves.' He then moves towards his conclusion:

> I know perfectly well that this deceitful manner of building is more or less
> common to all big cities. I know as well that shopkeepers must in the nature

259

of their business take premises on the main thoroughfares. I know that in such streets there are more good houses than bad ones, and that the value of land is higher in their immediate vicinity than in neighborhoods that lie at a distance from them. But at the same time I have never come across so systematic a seclusion of the working-class from the main streets as in Manchester. I have never elsewhere seen a concealment of such fine sensibility of everything that might offend the eyes and nerves of the middle classes. And yet it is precisely Manchester that has been built less according to a plan and less within the limitations of official regulations—and indeed more through accident—than any other town. Still when I consider in this connection the eager assurances of the middle classes that things are going splendidly for the working classes, I cannot help feeling that the liberal industrialists, the Manchester 'bigwigs,'[5] are not so altogether innocent of this bashful structural style.

In Manchester, as others had observed, the separation of classes had been driven to new extremes. What Engels added to this observation is that the separation had been built into the very structure of the city, and that this actual fabric both perpetuated such a condition and visibly expressed it. Even more, it had virtually effected the disappearance of one of the segregated classes, and the invisible poor of the mid-twentieth century was a reinvention of the invisible working classes of the mid-nineteenth. Yet how has this extraordinary phenomenon come about? In part, Engels says, it is through unconscious and unstated agreement, in part through deliberate intention—both of these, he intimates, applying to both groups, though not necessarily in equal proportions. The point to be taken is that this astonishing and outrageous arrangement cannot be fully understood as the result of a plot, or even a deliberate design, although those in whose interests it works also control it. It is indeed too huge and too complex a state of organized affairs ever to have been *thought up* in advance, ever to have preexisted as an idea.[6]

The city is a recognizably contemporary institution in other respects. It has already constructed for itself a central or inner core that is packed by day and deserted at night. This radical discrimination of function is equally borne out in the circumstances that those who during the day direct the city's workings from the center have moved away from there—where their homes originally were as well—and redistributed themselves as far from the center as the current means of transportation allow, on suburban heights. That is to say, as the city has rapidly and enormously expanded as an organization of production and a concentrated center of power and wealth, it has also deteriorated as a place in which to conduct other human and civilized activities. As the wealthier population have fled the center, they have leap-frogged over the vast working class and left them there massed, as it were, about that dense yet hollow core, in an immense unbroken belt in which they work and live. It is impossible at this point in history to disperse them, since they have to live within close walking-distance of their places of work. Despite all these sudden shiftings and evolutions—the fearful concentration of the working class, the flight from the center to the periphery—things have worked themselves out in what is apparently tidy and orderly detail. Indeed, the city reveals its social or class structure in each of its important spatial arrangements. These are most notable in those zones where the two extremes approach each other, or—to put the same idea in another way—at their lines of division, which is where the middle-middle and lower-middle classes come in. Their houses lie outside of the working-class belt, and between that belt and the more favorably situated suburban estates of the upper-middle class. And their shops and small businesses are located along the main thoroughfares—acting so to speak as insulators for the city's system of communication. Their location in space, therefore, is at both critical junctures an intermediate one, and their intermediary position is not merely structural but functional as well. They are acting as buffers between the antagonistic extremes.[7]

These streets, then, are Manchester's Potemkin villages. Yet behind the facades there lies not the nothingness of trans-Altaic wastes but a negative existence that is paradoxically a positive fullness, the indispensable creative source of all that positive wealth that lies beyond it. As Engels describes and analyzes them, those streets represent a collective effort of isolation, distancing, and denial, and work socially to the same ends as the same unconscious defensive processes work towards in individual persons. All he has neglected to add is that, when these symbolic aids were not available, it was possible to take to literal avoidance—the recourse adopted, for example, by the heroine of *North and South*:

> The side of the town [i.e., Manchester] on which Crampton lay was especially a thoroughfare for the factory people. In the back streets around them there were many mills, out of which poured streams of men and women two or three times a day. Until Margaret had learnt the times of their ingress and egress, she was very unfortunate in constantly falling in with them. (ch. 8)

These ways of dealing with experience were not confined to Manchester or the industrial towns or even to London. Some years earlier, in his essay 'Civilization,' John Stuart Mill had illuminated this subject from another point of view. 'One of the effects of civilization (not to say one of the ingredients in it),' he wrote, 'is, that the spectacle, and even the very idea of pain, is kept more and more out of the sight of those classes who enjoy in their fullness the benefits of civilization.' In the old cruel and heroic ages of Greece and Rome and of feudal Europe, this was not so. Today, however, all this has changed.[8]

> All those necessary portions of the business of society which oblige any person to be the immediate agent or ocular witness of the infliction of pain, are delegated by common consent to peculiar and narrow classes: to the judge, the soldier, the surgeon, the butcher, and the executioner. To most people in easy circumstances, any pain, except that inflicted upon the body by accident or disease, and the more delicate and refined griefs of the

imagination and the affections, is rather a thing known of than actually
experienced. This is much more emphatically true in the more refined classes,
and as refinement advances: for it is in keeping as far as possible out of
sight, not only actual pain, but all that can be offensive or disagreeable to
the most sensitive person, that refinement exists. We may remark too,
that this is possible only by a perfection of mechanical arrangements
impracticable in any but a high state of civilization.

It is a wonderfully intelligent passage and provides a useful context for Engels's
remarks, as those remarks do in turn for Mill's. Both are aware that they are dis-
cussing a special modern development, and both regard this development with an
equally critical, not to say jaundiced, eye. What is striking about Mill's statement is
that, although it is written with the intention of the highest generality, the one
thing that it fails to include is precisely the content of Engels's passage—the every-
day world of labor and industry and the conditions of life in which it was sustained.[9]
Furthermore, although Mill certainly sees the reciprocal and necessary connection
between civilization or refinement and the concealment of pain, he does not press
upon that connection with the same degree of force as does Engels. For what Engels
is saying is that the riches and luxury are not only connected with the hidden
suffering and squalor. They are connected in such a way as to be integral components
of a unified-diversified phenomenon, whose very separation is the clue to their
unity, both of these manifestly made visible in the structure of Manchester's streets.

Engels had demonstrated that a city could indeed be read. And yet, Engels says,
doubling back upon himself, reading is *all* one can do from the main streets themselves. Those rows of shops, commercial buildings, pubs, warehouses, and factories,
different and discriminable as they are, are still ultimately coverings. They function,
depending upon the context in which we regard them, as appearances, symbols, or
symptoms. They are the visible parts of a larger reality; they both reveal and conceal
that reality; they are formations made up of displacements of and compromises
between antagonistic forces and agencies. In order to get at the real things one has to
go behind such appearances—no nineteenth-century novelist could have put his
theoretical case more distinctly.[10]

But before he does this, Engels doubles back upon himself once more. He is
aware of the fact that this kind of thing can be found in other cities, and he is
acquainted with such innocuous 'explanations' of these arrangements as those that
argue that the main streets are simply the places where shops and stores have to
locate themselves, although there is some truth in these observations as well.
Nevertheless, he has observed what he can only describe as the systematic exclusion
of the working classes from the main streets of the city; at least, what he is describing
—the informal ghettoization of the working classes—seems to act with systematic
thoroughness and consistency, although the ghetto is itself the largest part of the
town. But he knows, as well, that Manchester has been built up without plan, without explicit designs, and largely even through accident. Indeed, as he remarks later

on: 'The big cities have sprung up spontaneously and people have moved into them wholly of their own free will' (p. 135). It is at the same time impossible to observe how this entire set of arrangements works to the advantage of the controlling class of industrialists, and to hear them speak of how the lives of the working class are improving—lives which have been in effect excluded from their sight—without suspecting that these industrialists are not so entirely innocent of it all as they appear; innocent in the sense of knowledge, of interest and implication, and of responsibility for behavior undertaken in the past, continued in the present, and projected into the future.

It is an invincible conclusion. It dramatizes the triumph of the intellect and experience of a single young man, but it represents as well the coming to fruition in him of a sovereign mode of thought, in the secularized application of its method to a new field of experience. What Engels has perceived and created is a general structure; its form is that of a coherent totality, a concrete, complex, and systematic whole, each of whose parts has a meaning, and more than one meaning, in relation to all the others. These meanings begin to come into view when we realize that this total whole is, naturally, more than the sum of its parts, that it is made of its parts and their histories, and that the entire elaborated and coordinated structure is in motion. For Engels is describing a process whose properties are unique. As I have remarked before, this process is neither mechanical nor organic; it partakes of both and yet is neither and something other as well. The only names we can assign to it are the human or the social, or, what is the same thing, the human-social, since the two cannot in fact or theory be held apart. It was this singular process that Hegel's style of thinking explicitly and preeminently dramatized. And yet there is something oddly moving and appropriate in the fact that this, one of the early successful adaptations of the method of this most difficult and obscure of all philosophers, should fall to the lot of a young man who considered himself to be a virtual auto-didact, who was the son of a factory owner, and that it should of all places have happened on the streets of Manchester.

Having thus constructively made out the macro-structure of the city, Engels girds himself to go behind those main street frontages, to enter that dark, dense belt formed by Manchester's working class and their dwellings, and to examine it. In this examination he has two purposes in mind: to describe it literally as it is, and to determine whether he can discover in it some kind of corresponding micro-structure. Before we follow him on this expedition, we may be prompted to ask ourselves a question. This question may appear superfluous and otiose in the very asking, and it may still seem so after we have tried to answer it. Why should Engels have followed this procedure? Why should he have begun with the buildings along the main streets of Manchester and then gone on to discuss the buildings in which the working class lived? The reader may be warranted in feeling that I have put the matter in this way because, like the character in the Talmudic story, I have an answer for which the question has to be invented; and he might very well reply, Why should he not have? He began with what was most strikingly evident to the senses; to begin anywhere else would have been tantamount to obscurantism. And moreover he was following the practice of other investigators, from Kay-Shuttleworth to Chadwick, who regularly opened their reports with an account of the conditions of the 'residences' of the laboring classes.[11] Still, the old saw—that children learn about the necessaries of life—runs 'food,' 'clothing,' and 'shelter,' in that order, at least in English. Is this only because that is the order of priorities for children, or is there some other meaning in the inversion practised by the investigators? In short, is there some unstated, perhaps unconscious, theoretical meaning at work? It seems hardly necessary to say that I think there is.[12]

In the houses men build for themselves they are expressing a behavior which binds them in common with other living creatures and species. The nests and burrows of animals represent efforts at altering the environment; they introduce something utterly new to it, something that did not exist before, but belongs to the creature who has made it. The purpose of this behavior is to create a surrounding suitable to the particular creature: shelter, protection, a stable micro-climate, a site for breeding, etc. These structures tend to be specifically characteristic, and scientists can distinguish between closely-related species, and even sub-species, of animals by examining these products of behavior that are in addition extensions of the creatures who made them. These structures are aboriginal artifacts; they are morphological embodiments of behavior, and represent in part the way in which particular creatures relate themselves to the world about them. In other species this behavior is genetically controlled or preprogrammed; in man it is not. It still holds, however, that in this fundamental artifact of a house or dwelling-place men express a good deal of how they relate themselves—or of how they are related—to the world in which they live. And in the collective human artifact—the settlement, town, or city—men as a group are expressing historically the character and quality of their existence, of the arrangements they have made, on the one hand, with the natural world, and, on the other, with one another. Engels is thus on sound theoretical grounds, when he remarks that the manner 'in which the need for shelter is satisfied furnishes a measure for the manner in which all other necessities are supplied' (p. 78).[13]

Engels takes the plunge. But where in this essentially doughnut-shaped belt is he to enter, and how is he to survey it with any coherence? His solution to this problem is as simple as it is sensible. At the northern limits of the commercial district— at about twelve on an imaginary clock— lying between that limit and the confluence of the rivers Irk and Irwell, and extending east along the banks of the Irk, is the Old Town, 'a remnant of the old, pre-industrial Manchester. The original inhabitants and their children have moved to districts that are better built, and have left these houses, which were not good enough for them, to a tribe of workers containing a strong admixture of Irish' (p. 57). Beginning with this section, which is conventionally, cartographically, and historically an admirable place for starting out, Engels proceeds to box the compass, to traverse the belt of working-class districts in a clockwise direction, describing what he has seen as he goes along. What he has seen and what he describes vary from section to section, but these variations fall within a uniform context of mass immiseration, degradation, brutalization, and inhumanization, the like of which had never before been seen upon the face of the earth.[14] We cannot follow him here in any detail but must select several of the more telling moments of his descriptive analysis.

As he stands in Long Millgate, one of the 'better' streets of the Old Town, Engels sees himself surrounded by houses that are old, dirty, and tumbledown; many are not even standing upright. Here, he says, one is 'in an almost undisguised working-class quarter,' since the keepers of the shops and pubs on such a street 'make no effort to give their premises even a semblance of cleanliness.' Yet these, too, are in a sense only facades, for they are as nothing compared to the alleys and courts that lie behind them, 'to which access can only be gained by covered passages so narrow that two people cannot pass' (p. 57). It is as if one were really penetrating into the heart of darkness. And once he is there, all Engels can do at first is to mutter 'the horror, the horror.' It is literally, he says, 'impossible to imagine for oneself'— or to represent—the chaos, confusion, density, cramming, and packing that exist in these spaces. Every available inch of ground has been built over, and the blame for this almost inconceivable overcrowding 'is not only to be ascribed to the old buildings surviving from Manchester's earlier periods.' It is in fact only quite recently, in modern times, that the practice has been followed of filling up every scrap of space that the old style of building had left. To prove his point, Engels then reproduces a 'small section of a plan of Manchester'—it is the subdistrict he has just been writing about—and adds 'it is by no means the worst spot and does not cover one-tenth of the Old Town.' It is a pretty enough section, but at least to my unpractised eye more or less unhelpful.[15]

But Engels is not to be stymied by the indescribable, and he takes us out of this set from an earlier version of *The Cabinet of Dr. Caligari* and into some other courts that branch off Long Millgate and are reached by covered passages that run down toward the banks of the Irk. On reaching these courts, he finds himself met with an assault of 'dirt and revolting filth, the like of which is not to be found . . .[and] without qualification the most horrible dwellings I have until now beheld.' He is going to say this more than once; he has run out of superlatives before he has barely begun; the language itself is giving out on him. In none of these inadequacies was he alone; indeed it may be suggested that one of the saving functions of language honestly used is that it should collapse before such realities, that it should refuse to domesticate these actualities with syntax and imagery, that it should compel writer and reader to at least a momentary extra-linguistic confrontation with such unspeakable man-made terrors, from which our man-made speech ordinarily protects us. In such a predicament, however, what is a writer to do? There is one course open, and Engels promptly takes it. He begins to specify. 'In one of these courts, right at the entrance where the covered passage ends is a privy without a door. This privy is so dirty that the inhabitants can only enter or leave the court by wading through puddles of stale urine and excrement (p. 58). This is the first of many such passages, and it will have to do service for almost all the others. It is at the same time difficult to know how and at what pitch of discourse literary criticism enters into such a scene. This difficulty has to do in the first place with what the intelligent student of literature can be expected to know. He may, I rashly speculate, be expected to know something about Swift and about Freud; he may have heard of Norman O. Brown's excremental vision, and will probably have read *Our Mutual Friend*; if he is a hard-working graduate student he will recall a scene in chapter six of *Mary Barton* that vividly, if gingerly, rehearses this material. That is, I believe, about it. The difficulty is further compounded by certain limitations that may be inherent in the historical imagination. How in fact does one reconstruct and apprehend the existential quality of such a situation? It may not be possible to do so. Or perhaps we ought to alter our terms, and recall Wallace Stevens's remark that 'in the presence of extraordinary actuality, consciousness takes the place of imagination.'[16]

What seems to have happened is that at about this moment in history, advanced middle-class consciousness—in which consciousness Engels may be regarded as representing the radical wing—began to undergo one of its characteristic changes. This consciousness was abruptly disturbed by the realization that, to put it as mildly as possible, millions of English men, women, and children were living in shit. The immediate question seems to have been whether they were not drowning in it. The catastrophe was worst in the great industrial towns where density and overcrowding went hand in hand with the interests of speculative builders, medieval administrative procedures and regulations—where they in fact existed—and produced a situation in which millions of grown people and their children were compelled to live in houses and neighborhoods that were without drains and often without sewers—and where sewers existed they took the run-off of street water and not waste from houses—without running water—sometimes not even in an entire neighborhood—and with one privy shared by who knows how many people: in some parts of Manchester over two hundred people shared a single privy. Such privies filled up rapidly and were cleaned out on an average of once every two years or so, which was as good as not at all. Streets were often unpaved, and where they were paved often no provision existed for their cleansing. Large numbers of people lived in cellars, below the level of the street and below the level of the waterline. Thus generations of human beings, out of whose lives the wealth of England was produced, were compelled to live in wealth's symbolic, negative counterpart. And that substance which suffused their existence was also a virtual objectification of their social condition, their place in society: that was what they were. We must recall that this was no Freudian obsessive neurosis or anxiety dream; but it is as if the contents of such a neurosis had been produced on a wholesale scale in social actuality. We can, then, understand rather better how those main-street palisades were functioning—they were defensive-adaptive measures of confinement and control. And we can understand what they were concealing: plenty.[17]

Engels tells the reader exactly where this court is, in case he is interested in confirming the truth of this account, and then takes us out of there and up onto Ducie Bridge, which spans the Irk at this point. Here he pauses to take a view, and composes a formal landscape in a style one wants to call authentic urban-picturesque:

> The view from this bridge—mercifully concealed from smaller mortals by a parapet as high as a man—is quite characteristic of the entire district. At the bottom the Irk flows, or rather stagnates. It is a narrow, coal-black stinking river full of filfth and garbage which it deposits on the lower-lying right bank. In dry weather, an extended series of the most revolting blackish green pools of slime remain standing on this bank, out of whose depths bubbles of miasmatic gases constantly rise and give forth a stench that is unbearable even on the bridge forty or fifty feet above the level of the water. . . . Above Ducie Bridge there are tall tannery buildings, and further up are dye-works, bone mills and gasworks. The total entirety of the liquid wastes and solid offscourings of these works finds its way into the River Irk, which receives as well the contents of the adjacent sewers and privies. One can therefore imagine what kind of residues the stream deposits. Below Ducie Bridge, on the left, one looks into piles of rubbish, the refuse, filth, and decaying matter of the courts on the steep left bank of the river. Here one house is packed very closely upon another, and because of the steep pitch of the bank a part of every house is visible. All of them are blackened with smoke, crumbling, old, with broken window panes and window frames. The background is formed by old factory buildings, which resemble barracks. On the right, low-lying bank stands a long row of houses and factories. The second house is a roofless ruin, filled with rubble, and the third stands in such a low situation that the ground floor is uninhabitable and is as a result without windows and doors. The background here is formed by the paupers' cemetery and the stations of the railways to Liverpool and Leeds. Behind these is the workhouse, Manchester's 'Poor Law Bastille.' It is built on a hill, like a citadel, and from behind its high walls and battlements looks down threateningly upon the working-class quarter that lies below. (p. 60)

It is Tintern Abbey forty-five years hence, with the further exception that these ruins are densely inhabited.[18] Right up to the end, the representation is unusually telling. It sticks unwaveringly to the point, and, in the presence of catastrophe, consciousness, observation, *becomes* itself imagination. The juxtaposition of the paupers' cemetery and the railway stations is very good; but, it should be added, the work of synthesis is being selectively noted by Engels—it is already there. There is no evidence, in so far as I am aware, that Engels knew anything of Pugin, but this is *Contrasts* and more, and by a much more complex and civilized mind.[19] With the workhouse, Engels introduces some imagery and along with it a note of equivocation. The description of its situation and architectural style is accurate, and in so far as it is, communicates its own symbolic weight. But the representation is a trifle too 'medieval' in its suggestive associations and tones, and these do not really work well with the idea of the Poor Law Bastille. The current power of the phrase was contained in the threat implied, and that threat is the reverse of the one indicated by Engels. What the phrase brought to mind in these years of turmoil, protest, and crisis was less how the Bastille functioned in seventeenth- and eighteenth-century France than the fate it met in 1789. Still, on any reading, this is a very small falling-off on Engels's part.[20]

He moves back into Long Millgate and up along the Irk. If one turns left off the street here, he writes, 'he is lost. He wanders from one court to another. He turns countless corners, through innumerable narrow, befouled pockets and passageways, until after only a few minutes he has lost all direction and does not know which way to turn' (p. 61). This is certainly a sufficiently familiar report; to which we may add that it is also Todgers's without the fun and games.[21] Wherever one turns, Engels continues, there is filth—'heaps of rubbish, garbage, and offal.' Instead of gutters, there are stagnating pools, and the entire region is pervaded with 'a stench that would alone make it unbearable for any human being who was in some degree civilized to live in such a district.' The ambiguity pivots evenly and is going to take considerable working-out. Either those who live there are uncivilized, or those who live there do so under conditions which cannot be borne. If it is the latter, then a further series of contradictory alternatives come into play. Engels does not pursue these at this point. Instead, he continues to produce these large analytical observations.

> The recently constructed extension of the Leeds railway which crosses the Irk at this point has swept away some of these courts and alleys, laying others in turn, and for the first time, completely open to view. Thus, immediately under the railway bridge there exists a court that in point of filth and horror far surpasses all the others [there he goes again]—just because it was formerly so shut up, so hidden and secluded that it could not be reached without considerable difficulty. I thought I knew this entire district thoroughly, but even I would never have found it myself without the breach made here by the railway viaduct.

Readers will recall the epic passages in *Dombey and Son* (1846–8) to which this condensed and miniaturized passage has useful applications. Great projects like the railways led, among their many other inadvertent effects, to large-scale slum removal and clearance.[22] In addition, if one follows Engels in thinking of the city as a systematic, dynamic whole, the inherent course of its development brings that which has been pressed away and hidden into sight; it exposes itself by its own movement, the exposure being understood in a double sense. And the disarming, self-confident admission is in no way extraneous to the systematic effort of mind: self-moving intellect, self-realizing intention of will could never have made these discoveries by themselves. They are not victories of the study, wrested by rigor of method from the philosopher's teeming brain. Nor are they immediately victories of language, since social reality, on this side, expresses itself first in the concrete language of the nose, the eyes, and the feet. It is this developing group of signs that the young investigator must meet and follow and transform into the language of conceptualization. These are axioms of philosophy being proved upon the pulses, and elsewhere. It only remains to add what Engels could not then have known: that each of these new railway lines became itself the source of new divisions and demarcations; that for every slum destroyed in their construction a new one came into existence around them; that they became the new dialect lines of social distinction, having each of them a right and a wrong side, and serving in their finished state to restrict and confine as much as in their building they cleared out and exposed.[23]

Engels thereupon leads the reader into this micro-section of previously inaccessible slum.[24]

> Passing along a rough path on the river bank, in between posts and washing lines, one penetrates into this chaos of little one-storied, one-roomed huts. Most of them have earth floors; cooking, living and sleeping all take place in one room. In such a hole, barely six feet long and five feet wide, I saw two beds—and what beds and bedding—that filled the room, except for the doorstep and fireplace. In several others I found *absolutely nothing*, although the door was wide open and the inhabitants were leaning against it. Everywhere in front of the doors were rubbish and refuse. It was impossible to see whether any sort of pavement lay under this, but here and there I felt it out with my feet. This whole pile of cattle-sheds inhabited by human beings was surrounded on two sides by houses and a factory and on a third side by the river . . . a narrow gateway led out of it into an almost equally miserably-built and miserably-kept labyrinth of dwellings. (p. 63)

He has gotten almost to the center and the bottom, and what he finds there is that something has happened to the species. Men have gone back to living in holes (those thousands who dwelled in cellars were literally doing so). These nests or dens are virtual emptinesses, whose evacuated spaces are the counterpart of the densely packed humanity with which such absences are filled. The transformation may be taken one step further. Just as the pavement has disappeared beneath the accumulated wastes of the natural social life of the species, so too is man himself tending to vanish in certain of his distinguishing attributes. He has taken to living in cattle-sheds, or, what is the same thing, in shelters that cannot be told apart from them. It is quite impossible to know whether this is an image or a reality; that is its point.

The filth inside these hovels is in keeping with what is outside of them. Engels describes the condition of these interiors, which can only be compared to the pigsties that were frequently to be found in such quarters. Indeed, he remarks, it is impossible to keep such places clean or to keep oneself clean in them. The facilities for getting rid of wastes have already been mentioned; the only water available was from the

Irk itself, in which washing would only be a further form of pollution. It is at some such point in this account that the modern reader begins to realize that what Engels is embarked upon is a description of what has been called the Culture of Poverty, and that this is historically the first full-scale attempt at the representation.[25] Engels himself seems to have been struck by this awareness, and by the immensity and difficulty of the task he had undertaken. After conducting the reader through a number of other subsections of the Old Town, he pulls up, brings his account of this quarter to a close, and then turns to address the reader.

> This then is the Old Town of Manchester. On re-reading my description
> once more, I must admit that, instead of being exaggerated, it is by far not
> nearly strong enough. It is not strong enough to convey vividly the filth,
> ruination, and uninhabitableness, the defiance of every consideration of
> cleanliness, ventilation, and health that characterise the construction of this
> district, which contains at least twenty to thirty thousand inhabitants.
> And such a district exists in the very center of the second city of England,
> the most important factory town in the world. (p. 63)

Of all the characteristic utterances that issue from the humane consciousness of the middle classes—whether this consciousness be beleaguered, on the attack, or simply thunderstruck—during the decades around the middle of the century, this remains among the most poignant, the most authentic, and the most recognizably modern. One could compose an anthology of some decent size of such remarks and exclamations, whose authors represented every variety of political opinion and every substratum of middle-class life. Manchester itself, as we have seen, was often the source of such comments, but in this it was only hypertypical. The occasions were legion; among them were conditions that prevailed in all kinds of industrial work, in child labor, in agriculture, and everywhere in Ireland from 1846 onwards. And of course the twentieth century has been prodigal in the creation of such mind-stunning spectacles, mass events of such inhuman extremity that the only response to them is no response.[26] Out of all the responses from the earlier period, we can select only one more to represent the rest. After Lord Normanby accompanied Dr Southwood Smith on a tour through Bethnal Green, he wrote: 'So far from any exaggeration having crept into the descriptions which had been given, they had not conveyed to my mind an adequate idea of the truth.'[27]

In confessing that he was unable to represent the phenomenological quality of this reality, Engels was in effect coming very close to revealing its inner form. It was the dissolved and negated analogue of the unexampled transformation wrought by the industrial middle class upon the world.[28]

> The bourgeoisie . . . has been the first to show what man's activity can
> bring about. It has accomplished wonders far surpassing Egyptian pyramids,
> Roman aqueducts, and Gothic cathedrals; it has conducted expeditions
> that put in the shade all former Exoduses of nations and crusades . . . The

bourgeoisie, during its rule of scarce one hundred years, has created more massive and more colossal productive forces than have all preceding generations together.

Another part of that hegemony was revealed in the location of these working-class districts. They were at the very center of things, yet out of sight. To say that they were at once central and peripheral is to describe their contradictory existence in the structure of social consciousness of the time. It is also to define them in a rigorous and classical way as the hidden ground of things, a substructure. Nevertheless, to be at once central and peripheral is to occupy a place in society that is ordinarily relegated to crime and its attendant institutions—criminal sections, prisons, police-courts and police-stations. The wealth of contradictions implied in such relations did not escape Engels or other writers at the time.[29]

Engels proceeds to conduct the reader on a methodical survey of the other working-class sections. Beginning with the New Town, which is adjacent on the south and east to the Old Town, and then moving on around the compass to Ancoats and the area south of it, he analyzes the structural composition of each of the districts. These areas were built up later than the Old Town, and as he describes each section, Engels also describes the three different kinds of working-class cottages (all of them built in connected blocks or rows) that were to be found. Each style of building came into existence at a certain point in the Industrial Revolution and the expansion of Manchester, so that although sometimes the different methods of construction exist side by side, they are usually located in different parts of town and make it possible to 'distinguish the relative age' (p. 67) of each district. That is to say, even these working-class districts have their history, their industrial archaeology, their discernible meaning. Conditions in these districts are pretty much on a par with those already described. Some of the reasons for this have already been given, and include the want of public facilities for drainage and cleansing. Others have to do with methods of building and terms of land-holding and tenure, into all of which Engels goes in convincing detail. The outcome of this number of converging circumstances has been the building of working-class houses that last for about forty years: the houses themselves have their own life-cycle, which is on average only slightly longer than that of the industrial working people who inhabited them. This is another part of the structural composition of Manchester that signifies and not of Manchester or nineteenth-century cities alone.

As he systematically passes along this great circle, Engels drops pertinent observations about the ecological relations of the various parts of the district to the rivers, streams, and flats amid which they are situated; to the factories that surround them; and to the middle-class residential districts that begin at their outskirts. He takes us south of Great Ancoats Street, along the area crossed by the Birmingham railway, and through which the Medlock twists and turns. He then stops to represent in some detail the enclave of Little Ireland that lies in a bend of the Medlock.[30] This slum was described by Kay (later Kay-Shuttleworth) in 1831, and Engels remarks that in 1844 it is in a virtually unaltered state. It is surrounded by factories and embankments and is below the level of the river. Four thousand people live in it, most of them Irish; or, rather, they wallow in it, along with the pigs that thrive upon the garbage and offal in the streets. Large numbers live in porous cellars, and the density of habitation is ten persons per room. He moves on next to Hulme, to Deansgate and its rookeries, and finally to Salford, which faces Manchester in a bend in the Irwell. Conditions here in this district of some 80,000 people resemble those in the Old Town again, and Engels closes his discussion of this district and his entire survey of the belt of working-class quarters with the following observation:

> It was here that I found a man, who appeared to be about sixty years of age, living in a cow-shed. He had constructed a sort of chimney for his square-shaped pen, which had no flooring, no plaster on the walls, and no windows. He had brought in a bed, and here he lived, although the rain came through the miserable, ruined roof. The man was too old and too weak for regular work, and sustained himself by removing dung, etc. with his handcart. Puddles of excrement lay close about his stable. (p. 75)

We have at length reached the bottom, the bottom of the heap. The image has been actualized and become the literal reality—that is to say, in such an actualization the structure is openly disclosed. It is *Our Mutual Friend* without the Golden Dustman. And it is our urban pastoral again, but it also catches up another side of the micro-structure. The old man has been productively used up and discarded as refuse; accordingly in his old age he sustains himself from refuse. Yet he, too, is part of the life of the city and his life has a meaning, although the terms in which that meaning may be assessed will give comfort and peace of mind to almost no-one.[31]

Engels has brought to a close his first examination of what lies behind and between the network of main streets. It is Manchester itself in its negated and estranged existence. This chaos of alleys, courts, hovels, filth—and human beings— is not a chaos at all. Every fragment of disarray, every inconvenience, every scrap of human suffering has a meaning. Each of these is inversely and ineradicably related to the life led by the middle classes, to the work performed in the factories, and to the structure of the city as a whole. The twenty-four-year-old Engels has achieved a *tour de force*. I know of no representation of an industrial city before this that achieves such an intimate, creative hold upon its living subject. For anything that stands with it or surpasses it one has to go to the later Dickens, to *Bleak House, Hard Times, Little Dorrit,* and *Our Mutual Friend.*[32] But even to mention *The Condition of the Working Class* in the same sentence with such masterpieces suggests the quality of critical neglect which it has suffered and the misuses to which it has been put. And, one may add, in this last section it has *not* been Hegel's system that has been primarily instrumental in the creative achievement, but the courage and intelligence of a young foreign intellectual—and a businessman at that—who, during a twenty months' stay in Manchester, opened himself to its great and terrible realities and was not afraid of allowing himself to be overborne by them. He read the city well.

Notes

1 I have in mind, respectively: *Chartism* (1840) and *Past and Present* (1843); *Coningsby* (1844) and *Sybil* (1845); *Notes of a Tour in the Manufacturing Districts of Lancashire* (1842); *The Moral and Philosophical Condition of the Working Classes Employed in the Cotton Manufacture in Manchester* (1832); *Manchester in 1844* (1845); *Journeys to England and Ireland* (New York, 1968 edn).

2 I have considered the antecedents and meaning of this episode in his life and work in a book to be published under the title *Engels, Manchester, and the Working Classes*.

3 This last clause is given in Mrs Wischnewetzky's rendering, which retains the obscure referential character of the German. Since Engels read through and made revisions in her translation, it is to be presumed that he let this sentence pass as perspicuous. It is indeed highly suggestive and one could associate out from it in all directions, but it remains not exactly perspicuous. Henderson and Chaloner invent a sentence in its place: 'In those areas where the two social groups happen to come into contact with each other the middle classes sanctimoniously ignore the existence of their less fortunate neighbours' (Engels, *The Condition of the Working Class in England*, trans. and ed. W. O. Henderson and W. H. Chaloner (Oxford, 1958), p. 54). The references to this work in the present chapter follow the Henderson and Chaloner edition, though at certain points I offer an alternative translation.

4 'Das ergänzende Moment' is what the old or former young Hegelian wrote. A beautiful illustration of Engels's thesis is to be found in the *English Note-Books* of Hawthorne, who came to Manchester in 1856 and then returned in 1857 for the Exhibition, rented a house first at Old Trafford and then on Chorlton Road, used the omnibuses exactly as Engels described, saw 'many handsome shops,' many fine paintings, and very little else—except for a sensational scene in Manchester cathedral. *Works* (Boston 1894), VIII, pp. 285ff, 517–45; also *Our Old Home, Works*, VII, pp. 169, 359ff.

5 In the original German edition Engels wrote 'big Whigs'; he later corrected this to read 'big Wigs,' a feeble enough pun in either form.

6 'The first glance at history convinces us that the actions of men spring from their needs, their passions, their interests, their characters, and their talents . . . Passions, private aims, and the satisfaction of selfish desires are . . . tremendous springs of action. Their power lies in the fact that they respect none of the limitations which law and morality would impose on them . . . [At the same time] human actions in history produce additional results, beyond their immediate purpose and attainment, beyond their immediate knowledge and desire. They gratify their own interests; but something more is thereby accomplished, which is latent in the action though not present in their consciousness and not included in their design.' G. W. F. Hegel, *Reason in History*, trans. Robert S. Hartman (Indianapolis, 1953), pp. 26, 35. (This is an augmented version of the Introduction to *The Philosophy of History*; an earlier translation of the whole work by J. Sibree remains widely available.)

7 Compare, with appropriate allowances, this passage from George Orwell: 'I was born into what you might describe as the lower-upper-middle-class . . . a sort of mound of wreckage left behind when the tide of Victorian prosperity receded . . . the layer of society lying between £2,000 and £300 a year: my own family was not far from the

bottom . . . In the kind of shabby-genteel family that I am talking about there is far more *consciousness* of poverty than in any working-class family above the level of the dole . . . Practically the whole family income goes in keeping up appearances . . . But the real importance of this class is that they are the shock-absorbers of the bourgeoisie. The real bourgeoisie, those in the £2,000 a year class and over, have their money as a thick layer of padding between themselves and the class they plunder; in so far as they are aware of the Lower Orders at all they are aware of them as employees, servants and tradesmen. But it is quite different for the poor devils lower down who are struggling to live genteel lives on what are virtually working-class incomes. These last are forced into close, and in a sense, intimate contact with the working class, and I suspect it is from them that the traditional upper-class attitude towards "common" people is derived.' *The Road to Wigan Pier* (New York, 1958 edn), pp. 153ff., 156.

8 *Essays on Politics and Culture*, ed. Gertrude Himmelfarb (New York, 1963), pp. 64f. See also the study of the development of the mechanism of death in the slaughtering and meat-packing industries in Siegfried Giedion, *Mechanization Takes Command* (New York, 1948), pp. 209–45.

9 I do not mean by this that the statements are opposed or contradictory of one another; they are not.

10 And no twentieth-century one, for that matter. See *L'Emploi du Temps* (Paris, 1957), trans. *Passing Time* (1960) by Michel Butor. Butor systematically uses the city in ways that are strongly reminiscent of Engels. He even provides a map that in its details resembles the maps supplied by Engels, and he traverses his northern English industrial town with the intention of finding the center of its 'complex net-work.' The main difference between the two is that Engels believes that through systematic study one can get to know the essence of the city, or of its reality, while Butor, one hundred and twenty years later, does not.

11 The first section of Chadwick's Report was titled 'General Conditions of the Residences of the Labouring Classes where Disease is Found to be most Prevalent.'

12 It may be noted in anticipation that for Rousseau's natural man, the three necessaries were 'nourishment, a female, and repose,' in *that* significant order: *The First and Second Discourses*, ed. Roger D. Masters (New York, 1964), p. 116.

13 In this paragraph I have summarized and drawn heavily on the writings of a number of behavioral scientists, such as N. Tinbergen, J. Calhoun, and J. Ralph Audy. I am in particular indebted to Audy's paper 'The Environment in Human Ecology: Artifacts—the Significance of Modified Environment,' in *Environmental Determinants of Community Well-Being*, Pan American Health Organization Scientific Publications No. 123 (Washington, 1965), pp. 5–16. The sense in which 'artifact' in this context is used is very close to a reversal of the usage of the eighteenth-century social and political theorists, who conceived of society as an artifact in the sense of a mechanical model. See J. H. Burrow, *Evolution and Society* (Cambridge, 1966), pp. 10ff., 26, and *passim*.

14 Immiseration is Schumpeter's apt translation of Marx's powerful coinage 'Verelendung.' The historical derivation of this word connects it inwardly with Marx's earlier, explicit writings about alienation, or 'Entfremdung,' and demonstrates, in terms of language, a genuine continuity in his thinking.

15 In *A Child of the Jago* (1896), Arthur Morrison tries to do the same thing for a small section of the East End, with relatively greater success—as far as the map is concerned.

16 *Opus Posthumous*, ed. Samuel Morse French (New York, 1957), p. 165.

17 The *locus classicus* for this subject is of course Edwin Chadwick's *The Sanitary Condition of the Labouring Population of Great Britain* (1842); two secondary works of interest and importance may be mentioned: S. E. Finer, *The Life and Times of Sir Edwin Chadwick* (1952); and R. A. Lewis, *Edwin Chadwick and the Public Health Movement, 1832–1854* (1952).

18 After Engels had visited Ireland in 1856, he wrote to Marx that ruins were characteristic of Ireland, 'the oldest dating from the fifth and sixth centuries, the latest from the nineteenth, with every intervening period included': *Werke*, XXIX, p. 56. Beginning in the eighteenth century, when artificial ruins were first constructed for taste and pleasure, civilization moved on in the nineteenth century to create instant, modern ruins—of which Ireland is a rural and Manchester an urban instance. The twentieth century has, in America at least, kept up the record.

19 Engels has in part introduced the cemetery and the railway stations in order to use them again, and to considerable effect, later on.

20 This does not of course mean that people did not feel threatened by the new Poor Law. They did in overwhelming numbers, even and particularly in places like Manchester where its most odious provisions were irrelevant and could not be enforced. For an account of how it was resisted in the North, see Cecil Driver, *Tory Radical: The Life of Richard Oastler* (New York, 1946), pp. 331–77.

21 See also *Oliver Twist*, ch. 50, for Dickens's similar description of Jacob's Island.

22 Further along, Engels notes that Liverpool railway has led to such a result in Salford (p. 74). In *Dombey and Son*, the pertinent subpassage in ch. 20 reads:

> Everything around is blackened. There are dark pools of water, muddy lanes, and miserable habitations far below. There are jagged walls and falling houses close at hand, and through the battered roofs and broken windows, wretched rooms are seen, where want and fever hide themselves in many distorted chimneys, and deformity of brick and mortar penning up deformity of mind and body, choke the murky distance. As Mr. Dombey looks out of his carriage window, it is never in his thoughts that the monster who has brought him there has let the light of day in on these things: not made or caused them. It was the journey's fitting end, and might have been the end of everything; it was so ruinous and dreary.

23 It was just such an experience that proved momentous in the career of Dickens's brother-in-law, Henry Austin. While working at surveying for the construction of the new Blackwall railroad, Austin first caught sight of what it was that the railway was clearing away and building through. The effect on him was to turn his interests permanently toward working for the alleviation of the living conditions of the laboring classes. See K. J. Fielding and A. W. Brice, 'Bleak House and the Graveyard,' in *Dickens the Craftsman*, ed. R. B. Partlow (Carbondale, Ill., 1970), pp. 115–39; 196–200.

24 The reader will recollect to what use Dickens put such properties of poor urban life as the posts and washing lines of the opening sentence. In *Little Dorrit* they become part of John Chivery's pastoral 'groves.'

25 See Oscar Lewis, *La Vida* (New York, 1968), pp. xlii–lii for a summary discussion.

26 The literature on this subject is enormous. One may, however, point to the work of Robert S. Lifton, who has made a special study of responses to extremity. See in particular *Death in Life* (New York, 1967). The discussion of the relation of changing consciousness to such events is exceptionally tricky. It is certain that natural and social catastrophes on a mass scale existed before the nineteenth century; it is also certain that consciousness responded to these catastrophes differently before and after that time. Something happened to consciousness, but something was happening to society as well, to stimulate that consciousness and legitimize it. The tracing out of such intricately connected reciprocal developments is a study in itself.

27 Quoted in S. E. Finer, *The Life and Times of Sir Edwin Chadwick*, p. 161.

28 *The Communist Manifesto* (Penguin edn, 1967), pp. 82–5.

29 See J. J. Tobias, *Crime and Industrial Society in the Nineteenth Century* (1967), for an extensive discussion of this subject.

30 By this juncture, however, not quite willingly. 'If I were to describe all these separate parts in detail,' he conceded, 'I would never get to the end' (p. 71).

31 One makes wide exception for such sociological theorists as Edward Shils, in whose way of thinking such phenomena are part of the positive functioning of any society, and serve to accentuate its blessings. 'The humanitarian element in Marxism— its alleged concern for the poor—' he feelingly observes, 'can have no appeal where there are still many very poor people in Communist countries, and the poor in capitalist countries can now be seen not to be poor, not to be miserable, not to be noble—but to be as comfortable and as vulgar as, if not more vulgar, than the middle classes.' And again, 'Every society has its outcasts, its wretched, and its damned, who cannot fit into the routine requirements of social life at any level of authority and achievement. . . Those who are constricted, who find life as it is lived too hard, are prone to the acceptance of the ideological outlook on life.' Where would we be without such wisdom? 'Ideology and Civility: on the politics of the intellectual,' *Sewanee Review*, lxvi (1958), 450–80.

32 Mrs Gaskell's representations of Manchester in *Mary Barton* and *North and South* are very good—and, as has been mentioned earlier, are in accord with Engels's— but they do not have the generalizing and organizing power of Engels's account.

12   The Power of the Railway

Jack Simmons

'I perceive', wrote Carlyle in 1850,[1] 'railways have set all the Towns of Britain a-dancing. Reading is coming up to London, Basingstoke is going down to Gosport or Southampton, Dumfries to Liverpool and Glasgow; while at Crewe, and other points, I see new ganglions of human population establishing themselves, and the prophecy of metallurgic cities which were not heard of before. Reading, Basingstoke, and the rest, the unfortunate Towns, subscribed money to get railways; and it proves to be for cutting their own throats. Their business has gone elsewhither; and they—cannot stay behind their business! They are set a-dancing, as I said; confusedly waltzing, in a state of progressive dissolution, towards the four winds; and know not where the end of the death-dance will be for them, in which point of space they will be allowed to rebuild themselves. That is their sad case.'

As it often happened, what Carlyle saw was a quarter of the truth, or less; but his grasp of it was firm, and he expressed it with a memorable pungency. We are accustomed to think of the development of the railway as a potent force in the towns' growth and development. Carlyle, watching it at the very moment when it burst on the scene, saw only confusion: loss to the old-established towns, gain to the 'ganglions' he disliked, the Liverpools and Londons, the Crewes it had brought to birth. And in this he was wrong only in understatement: for the confusion, in the second half of the century, was greater than he foresaw.

With the proliferation of railways, Reading, Basingstoke, and Dumfries recovered themselves, to reach a new prosperity, founded largely on their position as junctions on the system.* It was not in the long run they, but towns of another kind, that lost. Nor did the ganglions gain, automatically or in equal measure. For those towns too, as they peered into the future, the railway could bring perplexity, the extremes of gloom and optimism. Here are two simple instances from Liverpool. Shortly before the opening of the Liverpool & Manchester Railway a correspondent of a local newspaper argued that if railway communication were extended to Birmingham and London, London would suck up Liverpool's trade. He assumed that when transport between two towns of unequal power was improved, the effect was to strengthen the stronger of the two; and he adduced the decline of Lancaster in relation to Liverpool, since the canal had been opened between them, as an example.[2] Five years later a much more sophisticated observer, de Tocqueville, prophesied that the development of railways would make Liverpool commercially more powerful than London.[3] Neither of these opposite forecasts turned out to be right. But there was some force in the reasoning behind both of them; and they illustrate very well the uncertainty that people felt as they tried to assess the effect of the railway on the towns they knew.

By the time Carlyle wrote those words the railway had arrived in every large town in the United Kingdom. The biggest that were not yet served by it were Worcester and Hereford.† In every town it touched it had begun its upheaval. It had all been the work of just twenty years. Before 1830 no major town in Britain had felt the impact of the railway to any significant extent. Primitive lines for the carriage of coal touched the fringes of a few of them—Newcastle, for example, and Edinburgh; the citizens of Swansea could make a jaunt along the shores of their Bay by coach on the Oystermouth Railway: but tiny developments like these were quite

---

* The elements of truth and error in Carlyle's assertions can be illustrated simply from the history of Reading. The railway arrived there in 1840, and in the succeeding decade the population of the town increased at a much slower rate than in any other of the nineteenth century. These are the percentage figures for the years 1821–81 (after which there was an alteration of boundaries):

1821–31 increase of	24·0
1831–41	19·6
1841–51	12·5
1851–61	20·6
1861–71	24·9
1871–81	30·1

At the same time it is worth noting that the critical expansion of the town's industries immediately followed the arrival of the railway. An 'extensive silk manufactory' appeared in 1841; the business of Messrs Huntley & Palmer dates from the same year. Sutton's emerged as seed-growers in the 1840s, conducting their trade largely with distant customers, by post and railway. W. M. Childs, *The Town of Reading during the Early Part of the Nineteenth Century* (Reading, 1910), pp. 23–4; idem., *The Story of the Town of Reading* (Reading, 1905), pp. 209–12, 228; *Victoria County History of Berkshire* (1906–27), I, p. 411; II, p. 243 (census figures). Reading was just over twice the size of any of the other Berkshire towns in 1801; by 1881 it was four times as big as Windsor, which stood second. It was the only town in the whole county that was placed on a main line of railway.

† Worcester got its first railway very shortly afterwards, on 5 October 1850; Hereford not until 1853.

marginal to the life of such places. Only two pairs of towns had yet been linked by rail: Gloucester and Cheltenham by a line authorized in 1809, which remained modest in scope, useful as a conveyor of coal from Gloucester Quay but otherwise barely perceptible as a factor in the economy of either town; Stockton and Darlington since 1825, but they were both towns of minor importance.

The Liverpool & Manchester Railway, however, opened up a new world. When its public traffic started on 15 September 1830 the railway began to exercise, for the first time, its full impact upon two of the great cities of Europe.* The railway was immediately successful, most conspicuously in the carriage of passengers. The number travelling between Liverpool and Manchester was at least twice as many as the coaches had conveyed before the railway was opened.[4] Nor was this a flash in the pan. The figure fell in 1832, when the novelty of railway travelling had worn off, but thereafter it rose steadily, to stand at 474,000 in 1835 and 609,000 in 1838.

Even before the railway was built, some landowners feared the effects it might have on their urban property, and with good reason. To the west of Deansgate in Manchester, for example, Henry Atherton had recently laid out a residential estate, in which trades and manufactures were prohibited. When the railway was first projected in 1825 his successors petitioned against it, on the ground that the locomotives would alarm the inhabitants, impair their comforts, and drive them away. This opposition was unavailing. When the Liverpool Road terminus was built, still more when it was extended in 1836, it exactly fulfilled the petitioners' fears, destroying the amenities of the Atherton estate, with the result that 'the establishment of the [station] . . . and the cushion of mean housing which surrounded it, tended to provide a westward barrier to the expansion of the business district.'[5]

The effect of the railway on the trade of Manchester and Liverpool can be inferred, though not precisely demonstrated. The railway was peculiarly well adapted to handling the commerce of Manchester, which was the metropolis of a large group of manufacturing towns, each playing its own part in the complicated production of textiles and some of the raw materials, like coal, that were consumed in it. The textiles were bulky to store, and subject in a high degree to the volatility of fashion. The railways at once speeded their concentration in Manchester and their distribution to clamorous customers, at the same time drastically reducing the space required for warehousing them.[6] For Liverpool the railways provided, what water communication could not, a system of rapid transit from the greatest English port facing out towards the Atlantic to the whole of the United Kingdom. 'There is now no town of any consequence in Great Britain', wrote Thomas Baines in 1852, 'with which the port of Liverpool has not constant communication by means of railway, and scarcely one which does not add something to the commercial prosperity of the port.'[7]

The physical impact made by the railway, both on Liverpool and on Manchester, was slight at first. The early passenger stations were placed at the very edge of the

* The Lyons–St Étienne line of 1829 made, by comparison, a trifling impact on Lyons.

built-up area. The inconvenience of this arrangement soon showed itself, and in Liverpool the passenger line was extended to a much better situated terminus in Lime Street, by the Haymarket. No such development occurred in Manchester, which came to be ringed round with a series of stations—Victoria and Exchange, London Road, Central—linked with one another by a series of not very convenient junction lines.

The system of unrestricted private ownership on which the British railways were constructed did much to determine the provision of major stations in the towns, which took on a pattern different from that usually found in Europe. The centre of London was encircled by a series of terminal stations unparalleled in number anywhere else in the world; the last of them—Marylebone, opened in 1899—was the fifteenth. The only other European capital with a similar multiplicity of stations was Paris, and that had no more than eight. By the end of the century the characteristic pattern in Continental cities was that of the single great station, the *Hauptbahnhof*. It was usually a terminus, and gathered to itself all the incoming lines, from whatever quarter they ran. It achieved its classic expression in Germany with the *Hauptbahnhof* of Frankfurt, built in 1879–88. By the end of the century almost all the great European cities had a station like this—Copenhagen, Amsterdam, Dresden, Marseilles, Milan, Rome—paralleled by the Union stations in North America.

In the comparable towns of Britain there are only three examples of this kind. Newcastle, Stoke-on-Trent, and Aberdeen alone concentrated the whole of their passenger traffic into one station. The single central station appeared also in Bristol, Hull, and Norwich; but in each of those towns there was also a small second terminus, belonging to a different company from that which owned the main one. In all the towns just mentioned, except Aberdeen, the central station was built by a railway company that enjoyed a preponderant share of the traffic in the district and could therefore mould the system, with comparative ease, so as to concentrate all its incoming lines at a single point. Elsewhere, each main company built its own station; and though sometimes, as in Leeds and Manchester, two or more companies might share a station between them, this still left a multiplicity everywhere: two in Birmingham, Sheffield, Edinburgh, Bradford, and Leeds;* three in Leicester,† Liverpool, and Belfast; three or four in Manchester;‡ four in Glasgow; five in Dublin. Aberdeen stood alone among all the large towns of Britain in the possession of a single central station, served by three companies.

The inconvenience of arrangements of this kind, in the passenger's eyes, does not need to be pointed out. The practice was even more tiresome for the trader and the manufacturer, for it was usual for each company to maintain at least one goods station of its own, sometimes more than one—those gaunt, austere brick buildings, many of which continue in use even under a unified railway system today.

* Three in Leeds if the New and Wellington stations, which were adjacent, are reckoned separately.
† Strictly speaking four, if the minor West Bridge terminus is included.
‡ According to whether Victoria and Exchange stations are reckoned as one, because they adjoined and were linked, or two.

Stations were usually placed well away from the centre. There were a few exceptions: the Central station in Glasgow, for example, was truly named. Only Birmingham, however, succeeded in getting the whole of its railway passenger traffic into the heart of the city. Its original stations, in Curzon Street and Lawley Street, were some distance out, and this was immediately complained of as a disadvantage.[8] In the 1850s the lines of all the three main railway companies were brought into two central stations (for a time it looked like being one,[9] but narrow gauge and broad gauge could not happily coalesce in this way); and the physical configuration of the town allowed both of them to be placed below the level of the ground, approached at each end through tunnels. In London there were eventually six terminal stations within the City proper;* but looking at the town as a whole, only Charing Cross could fairly be called central. The rest were all built on the perimeter. They have now been thoroughly engulfed by the spread of London; yet it should be remembered that the distance between Paddington and London Bridge is not far short of five miles.

There were those who advocated the construction of a *Hauptbahnhof* for London; they urged it again and again from the forties to the eighties. The most imaginative of them was Charles Pearson, the most persistent the *Builder*.[10] The more the termini multiplied, the more attractive the idea became: for the congestion of traffic in the streets rendered the transference from one station to another with each decade slower and more uncertain. The decisive arguments against any such proposal, however, were the still greater increase in street congestion that it would produce, concentrating the passengers on arrival and departure at one point rather than keeping them dispersed at a dozen, and the enormous capital cost of the land and construction. In the provinces, moreover, notorious difficulties of management had arisen in the big stations into which two or more companies ran their trains. London Road at Manchester provided perhaps the worst example.[11] But there were others: in Manchester, again, Victoria station,[12] Chester,[13] London Bridge, and King's Cross.[14] There were, it is true, other stations where sharing gave rise to few troubles: Carlisle (Citadel), for example, which eventually served as many as seven companies; Leeds (New);[15] those like Victoria in London, or Bristol (Temple Meads) in which the traffic of one of the sharing companies could be largely segregated from that of its partner. But one must admit that the chance of achieving the smooth joint management of a London station used by perhaps half-a-dozen companies was remote, and that the idea was, for this reason, rightly rejected. The *Hauptbahnhof* was more easily achieved on the Continent. There the cities were smaller, and the great stations were either under the management of a single company, as at Lille or Toulouse, or constructed under State control, as at Basle and Zürich and in Germany.

In London the alternative, adumbrated in 1846 and realized from 1863 onwards, was to allow multiple termini to develop, outside the centre, and to assist the movement between them by the building of urban railways. The first—and the most

* Broad Street, Liverpool Street, Fenchurch Street, Cannon Street, Holborn Viaduct, Blackfriars.

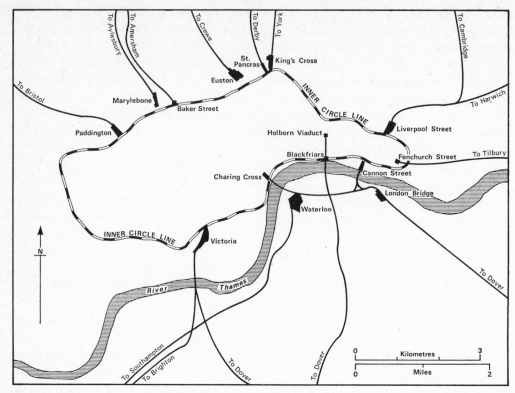

VII   London terminal stations and Inner Circle line

important urban railway ever built anywhere, when one considers the consequences that sprang from it—was the Metropolitan Railway, opened from Paddington to Farringdon Street on 10 January 1863. In this too the far-sighted Charles Pearson had a hand. Its champions hoped that it would, at a stroke, solve the whole problem of urban congestion in the district through which it passed. They were too optimistic. Its immediate effect was to hit the buses and cabs very hard; but, once the novelty of travelling on it had worn off, the buses and cabs recovered their passengers. There seemed to be almost as much congestion as ever on the New Road, though the railway was *also* carrying over nine million passengers in its first year of operation.[16] The truth was that, here as elsewhere, the opening of the new railway had simply increased the number of travellers.[17]

The Metropolitan Railway was to be carried on eastwards to Moorgate, and under powers conceded in 1864 extensions were built to make the line into a complete circle. The circle (not completed for twenty years) developed in a way different from that originally intended. It remained primarily an urban railway, throwing out offshoots of its own—to St John's Wood and Harrow, to Ealing and Hounslow, to Whitechapel and Bow. It conveyed passengers between most of the main-line termini; only three—London Bridge, Waterloo, and Holborn Viaduct—lay off its route. But it did little to carry passengers through London without changing. Although trains from the Midland and the Great Northern lines ran on to it, they were mostly suburban trains, terminating at Moorgate. The London Chatham & Dover company, thrusting across the Thames by Blackfriars, linked up with the Metropolitan at Farringdon Street and thus gave central London in 1864 its solitary link from south to north. In the long run the greatest importance of this line was in the conveyance of freight; but it also carried a strange variety of passenger services, including some main-line trains from the Midlands and the North to the Kent coast. None of them was very successful. Nor were the outer suburban services: from St Pancras via Willesden to Earls Court; from the Great Western line—even, for a time, from Birmingham—to Victoria; from Croydon to Liverpool Street.

The truth was that the passenger in transit across London, from the north to the south coast, obstinately preferred to travel by the streets. Through services to the Channel ports, for the Continental steamers, were often discussed and occasionally provided.[18] But travellers generally chose, if they were passing through London, to stay at least a night there.[19]

The underground railways never made their shareholders' fortunes. The dividends of 5 percent that were usually paid by the Metropolitan Railway were derived in part from the Company's profitable surplus lands; the District had a struggle to keep up payment of any dividend at all, even on its Preference stocks.[20] These difficulties were partly due to the folly of the companies themselves in quarrelling rather than collaborating. But their chief cause lay in the conditions imposed upon them by landowners and local authorities, anxious to profit by the needs of the companies that arose from the special form the railways took. They were shallow lines, built directly below the surface. They interfered with sewerage; they required ventilating shafts, emitting fumes and smoke; even though they ran, as far as possible, underneath streets, their building involved the demolition of many houses; the Metropolitan Board of Works was determined to make them pay for a substantial part of the very expensive programme of street improvements that it rightly deemed necessary in London.

All these considerations are exemplified in the Metropolitan District Company's first Act.[21] There were to be no ventilating shafts on Lord Harrington's estate in South Kensington; special protection was accorded to the Duke of Norfolk and the Strand Estate when the Temple station was erected; no part of the Tallow Chandlers' Hall in Dowgate Hill was to be taken unless that Company gave its consent. Where the railway ran through the Inner and Middle Temple it was to be entirely covered in; and, except in emergency, 'the steam whistle of any locomotive engine . . . shall never be sounded within the prescribed limits', nor was steam ever to be blown off there. The District Company had to pay for enlarging Tothill Street to a width of 60 feet, and to construct, if so requested by the Metropolitan Board of Works, a low-level sewer, in the same trench with the railway, from Cannon Street to Trinity Square. And finally, on every weekday it had to provide a workmen's train in each direction at a maximum fare of a penny a journey.[22]

The last is an early example of an obligation that was placed on most London railways from 1860 onwards.[23] These workmen's services became numerous as time went on. In 1883 the number of trains required to be run by Act of Parliament was eleven; the number actually running was 107.[24] They were not always a cause of gratitude to the men who used them. In 1871, for example, a working man wrote to the *Builder* to complain of the overcrowding on the Metropolitan trains, which drove him to walk instead of using them, adding that he and his fellows would be great supporters of the new tramways as they were extended.[25] But Parliament kept the horse tramways out of the centre of London, and none of them ever provided an alternative to the Metropolitan Railway.[26]

The cost of building railways in the heart of London began to become prohibitive in the sixties. The Charing Cross and Cannon Street lines cost £4 million—that is, £2 million a mile, 'the most expensive piece of railway construction in the world'.[27] The rate for the Dover Company's Metropolitan Extension was £1½ million a mile.[28] When the Great Eastern first planned its line to Liverpool Street in 1862, the Company's Engineer, Robert Sinclair, estimated the cost at a little over £400,000;[29] the line was at last completed in 1875, and the price of it was in fact over £2 million.[30] A substantial proportion of this expenditure was attributable to large terminal stations. But the underground railways, which were not burdened in that way, were costing much the same. The bill for the first section of the District line, from South Kensington to Westminster, a little over two miles long, was £3 million.[31]

No wonder that the Circle line remained unique. Schemes for similar railways had burst out in profusion in 1863–4. All had failed, including the one for a line from Euston to Charing Cross, associated with a badly-needed new street, running southwards from the Tottenham Court Road. That project was authorized twice, in 1864 and 1871; but it was never realized. If more urban railways were to be built, it seemed that they must either be raised above ground level or tunnel much deeper in the earth. The first solution was adopted with success in New York and other American cities. It had supporters in this country,[32] and in the 1890s it was realized in Liverpool.[33] But that was a special case, the line running not through the centre of the city but along by the docks. Even then, the scheme was criticized for its unsightliness. It would have been much worse—indeed unthinkable, in terms of noise, dirt, and disfigurement—in the middle of London.[34]

The first experiments with tube railways, built at a deep level underground, and operated by 'atmospheric' (pneumatic) or cable power, had begun in the 1860s.[35] They failed; but when the Germans and Americans demonstrated the capabilities of electric traction, they were resumed, with much greater hope of success. The upshot was the City & South London Railway, the first electrically-operated underground railway in the world, opened to the public on 18 November 1890. A second line of the same sort—the Central London, running due east and west from the Bank to Shepherd's Bush—was sanctioned in 1891. In the following year half a dozen fresh projects for tube railways in London, to be worked by electricity or cable traction, were brought forward. Parliament referred them all to the consideration of a Committee of both Houses. Its report examined them from many different points of view—technical, commercial, economic. Some of the witnesses who appeared before it, looking far ahead into the twentieth century, considered these underground railways as agents of social change, an instrument of town-planning. The Committee accepted the necessity that these lines should be worked by electricity or cable power, that they should not be extensions of existing railways but independent, and that they should be constructed in tunnels of small bore, which excluded normal rolling stock. Parliament took the Committee's advice, and the London tube system, realized slowly and painfully in 1898–1912 and only slightly extended since that time, was the result.[36]

While that work was in progress the transport system of London came under the exhaustive scrutiny of the Royal Commission on London Traffic appointed in 1903. In its report it passed under review the whole course of legislation concerning railways in the capital, which it saw as a catalogue of almost uninterrupted error. The critical decision of the sixties, to keep railways out of the centre of London, had been wrong.[37] The tube railways then under construction were a grave extravagance; the provision of lifts had alone added 8 percent to the cost of building the Central London line. Shallow underground lines of the Metropolitan type (which required no such lifts) could by this time be built with comparatively little disturbance of the streets, as the Metro in Paris—then brand new—had demonstrated.[38] Lines of this sort should be preferred to deep-level tubes wherever possible. Almost the only point on which the Commissioners found themselves in agreement with current railway policy was in the tendency to favour electric traction.[39] (While their report was in preparation, the finishing touches were being put to the electrification of the Inner Circle, and the Brighton Company had begun the work of electrifying the South London line.) Yet though they were so much disturbed by the great expense of building tube railways, they ignored the financial problems that confronted some companies as soon as they began to contemplate electrification. The densest of the London suburban systems was that of the Great Eastern Railway, which was competently managed but indigent. Capital expenditure on the scale required for electrifying the lines out of Liverpool Street lay quite beyond its scope, without the benefit of State aid.

The Commission did a splendid work. The eight volumes of its report, evidence, appendices, and maps, constitute the most intelligent and thorough analysis of the problems of urban transport in the early twentieth century that any country can show, and they were studied with close attention on the Continent and in America. But the new Liberal government, which took office in December 1905, showed scant interest in the Commission's recommendations and implemented none of them. In the years that followed, the railways fought the electric trams and the motor buses all over London. It was a battle from which the State stood aside.

In considering the development of railways in London, one must be struck by the relatively small part that was played in it by the government of the city itself. This was in part because, at least until 1888, that government was dispersed among a large number of separate authorities—the Common Council of the City, the parish vestries, the Metropolitan Board of Works. In part, too, it was a consequence of the very size of London, of the inevitable difficulty of bringing public opinion to bear on matters of this kind. Something of the same sort can be seen in the biggest provincial cities too; but in those that were a little smaller the attitudes of the citizens could express themselves and might have a strong influence on the course of railway development. Let us consider two such towns: Sheffield and Nottingham.

Sheffield kept a particularly close eye on railway development. When the North Midland line, from Derby to Leeds, was projected in 1835–6, with George Stephenson for its engineer, it adopted a route from Chesterfield northwards that took it well to the east of Sheffield. Stephenson's stated reason for this choice was that he was thus

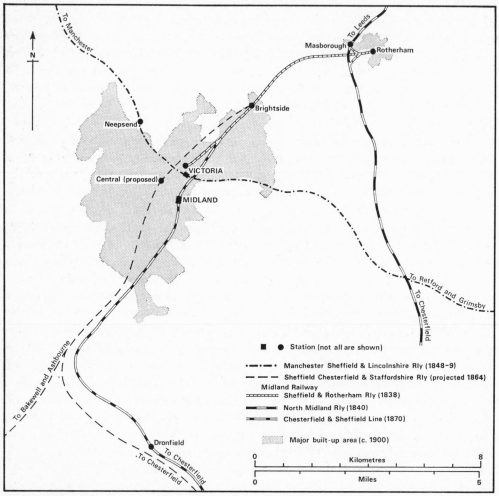

VIII Sheffield railway connections

enabled to keep to the high ground and avoid the heavy engineering works that would be necessary if the line took the direct route through the town, tunnelling at Dronfield and then running down the steep valley of the Sheaf. There was more to it than that, however. The Sheffield Coal Company and its landlord the Duke of Norfolk did not wish to stimulate the development of the competing Dronfield coal. When Stephenson came down to Sheffield to defend his plan his behaviour was arrogant and disingenuous. At one point he even went so far as to threaten the townspeople that if they succeeded in delaying the passage of the North Midland's Bill through Parliament 'Sheffield would be for ever deprived of any line whatever'. His performance gave great offence; but in the end, through apathy, the opposition to the Bill in the town collapsed.[40] In consequence, the line came no nearer to Sheffield than Masborough, five miles away to the north-east, whence a branch was built by a separate undertaking, the Sheffield & Rotherham Railway. Both projects were authorized by Parliament in 1836; they were in operation by 1840.

It quickly became clear that Sheffield had been wrong to acquiesce in Stephenson's plan. It was soon placed on what promised to be the chief east–west trunk line, from Manchester to Grimsby; but that accentuated the other failure, which prevented Sheffield from becoming one of the principal railway junctions of the North of England. During the 'railway mania' a succession of projects was brought forward with frantic insistence, aimed at giving Sheffield a direct route to the south: the Gainsborough Sheffield & Chesterfield, the Manchester Sheffield & Midland Junction, the Sheffield & Newark, the Boston Newark & Sheffield—all were launched in 1844–6, and all failed.[41] For fifteen years Sheffield then sank back into a tame acceptance of the existing situation, improved only, as far as passengers were concerned, by the opening of the Great Northern Railway and, after 1857, the running of a relatively brisk service via Retford to King's Cross.[42]

The Midland Railway built up for itself a large company of enemies in Sheffield. Its station, inherited from the Sheffield & Rotherham Company, was deplorable. Even Allport, the Company's General Manager, admitted that 'great inconvenience had arisen from [its] insufficiency';[43] at a meeting of the Sheffield Town Council a member observed that it was 'of such a character that even decent cattle might take offence at it'.[44] The coal and minerals of the Dronfield district remained inadequately exploited.[45] It was asserted by a Town Councillor—and he was not contradicted—that the price of coal in Sheffield was higher than it had been before the first railway arrived.[46] Iron and steel manufacturers were loud in their complaints against the Midland Company.[47]

The possibility of a new line to the south, joining the Midland main line at Chesterfield, reappeared in the autumn of 1861, and the Town Council appointed a committee to confer with the Midland directors. But the project moved forward at a snail's pace, and it began to be hinted that the Great Northern Company, one of the Midland's chief rivals, might interest itself in the matter. Next year the Midland revived its plans, and a new project also came forward, at first bearing the compendious title of the Sheffield Chesterfield Bakewell Ashbourne & Stafford & Uttoxeter

Junction Railway, later shortened to Sheffield Chesterfield & Staffordshire.[48] The chairmanship of the Company was accepted by the Mayor of Sheffield, the iron and steel manufacturer John Brown. In the Parliamentary session of 1864 it did battle with the Midland.

It seemed strong in its chairman and in the support of the Town Council, which petitioned in its favour. Yet it collapsed ignominiously. The chief promoter of this venture appears to have been William Field, one of the great railway contractors of the day, who had no local interest in it at all. He undertook to find £800,000 of the cost if a further £300,000 were forthcoming from Sheffield. Of that £300,000 the amount actually subscribed was rather less than £10,000.[49] So much for the urgent anxiety of Sheffield for the new railway. Worse still, the deposit required by the Standing Orders of the House of Commons was irregularly raised, not in the form of personal investment but through a loan from the General Insurance Company. When this came to light, the project was held to have evaded Standing Orders; and that settled its fate.[50] It was an interesting scheme. The line would have been very expensive to build and operate,* but from Sheffield's point of view it had important merits: it gave direct access to Chesterfield and the south, serving the intervening coalfield; it provided a valuable route to Staffordshire and South Wales; it offered a centrally-placed station in Sheffield;† and—a particularly interesting feature—it proposed to build six other stations within the borough boundary, linking them by a frequent service at fixed intervals, on the model of that run by the North Staffordshire Company in the Potteries.[51] Nevertheless, the Midland prevailed, securing powers in this session to build the line through Dronfield to Chesterfield.[52]

It was in no hurry, however, to exercise them. The Company was over-extended in many directions at the time, and hard hit by the Overend, Gurney crisis of 1866. The new Sheffield line took a low priority among its commitments. It was not opened until 1 February 1870.[53]

Sheffield had now at last achieved the objectives for which some of its citizens had been contending for thirty years: direct railway access to an under-exploited mineral field on its doorstep, a place on a trunk route from north to south, and a new railway station above the contempt of cattle. With this achievement it rested content —though the train service provided by the Midland and Great Northern Companies exhibited for a time the most laughable features of English railway competition.‡ But the Town Council still kept its eye closely on railway matters. In 1881 it gave

---

* The deposited plans (there is a copy of them in the Sheffield Central Library) show that, of the thirty-six miles of main line, thirty were graded at one in 130 or steeper, and over seven miles were in tunnel.

† This was to be at the junction of Townhead Street, Tenter Street, and Broad Lane (there is a roundabout there today), much closer to the middle of the town than any other railway station, then existing or subsequently built. It could not have been a satisfactory station, however, for it would have had to be crammed into a space of only 900 ft between a viaduct and a tunnel.

‡ Consider the down service provided by the two companies eighteen months after the opening of the Midland main line (*Bradshaw*, July 1871) as shown at foot of page 289.

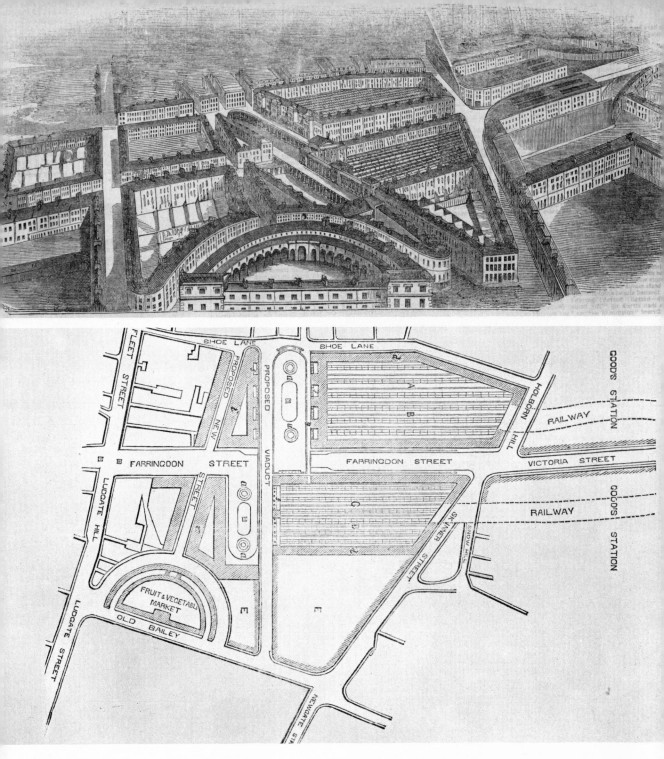

236–7 Charles Pearson's proposed Central Railway Terminus in London. The separate stations, for passengers and goods, to be used by a number of companies, appear in the upper part of the picture to the right with colonnaded entrances and forecourts. The plan shows the new streets he proposed, in conjunction with them, as a further London improvement. It shows stations for four companies (marked A, B, C, and D), and vacant sites (marked E) for one more. From *Illustrated London News*, viii (1846), 333–4.

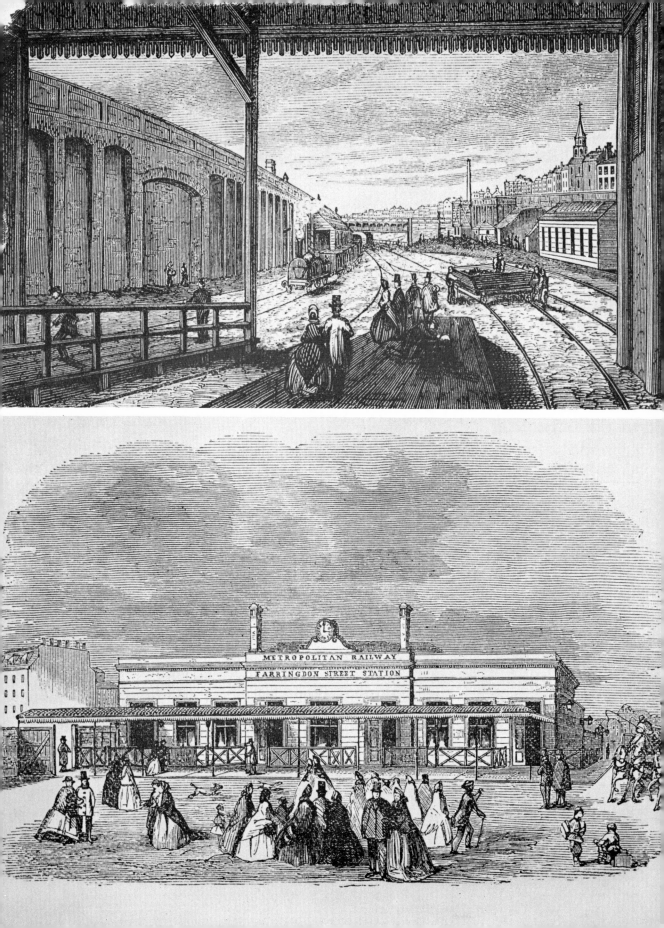

238–9 *left*   Metropolitan Railway: Farringdon
Street station. The interior view looks east and
shows the 'widened lines' to the Great Northern
and Midland Railways on the left. From W. J.
Pinks, *History of Clerkenwell* (2nd edn, 1880),
pp. 357, 359.

240 *above*   The Metropolitan Railway crosses the
line coming in to join it from the Great Northern
west of Farringdon Street station. The Metropolitan train is entering the Clerkenwell tunnel.
The crossing was known as 'the gridiron'. This
picture appeared immediately after the Great
Northern passenger service on the line began, on
17 February 1868. From *Illustrated Times*, xii
(1868), 137.

241 *above* The construction of a shallow underground railway: making the junction, close to Baker Street station, between the Metropolitan and Metropolitan & St John's Wood Railways. From *Illustrated Times*, xii (1868), 216.

242 *above right* The Thames Embankment under construction at Charing Cross. On the left the Metropolitan District Railway is seen in its tunnel; in the centre the sewers and a proposed 'pneumatic' railway intended to run from Charing Cross under the river to Waterloo, but never in fact built. From *Illustrated London News*, l (1867), 632.

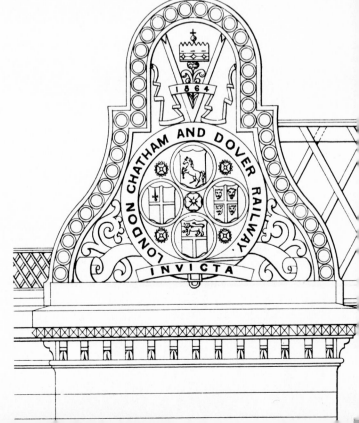

243 *right* Blackfriars Bridge, London Chatham & Dover Railway: detail of the decoration. 'The entire invention of the designer [Joseph Cubitt] seems to have exhausted itself in exaggerating to an enormous size a weak form of iron nut, and in conveying the information upon it, in large letters, that it belongs to the London Chatham & Dover Railway': Ruskin, *Works* (ed. Cook and Wedderburn), XIX, p. 26. Engraving from W. Humber, *Record of the Progress of Modern Engineering, 1864* (1865), plate 27.

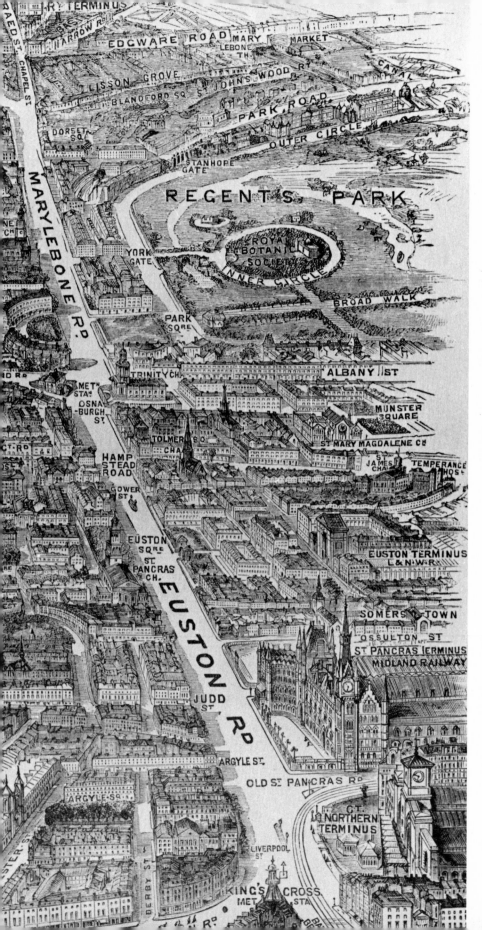

244 *left* Bird's-eye view of the Euston and Marylebone Roads, showing the four chief northern termini: King's Cross, at the foot, followed by St Pancras, Euston, and at the top of the picture Paddington. A fifth, Marylebone, was later to be built between Dorset Square and Lisson Grove. King's Cross station of the Metropolitan Railway is to be seen at the bottom; the line followed the course of the Euston and Marylebone Roads and Praed Street. Its Portland Road station, on an island site, has been exactly replaced by the modern Great Portland Street. From Herbert Fry, *London in 1885* (1885), plate xiv.

245 *above right* Bird's-eye view of the London & Greenwich Railway, rising above the houses on its continuous viaduct. The conspicuous church with an Ionic column for its spire is St John's, Horsleydown (now a ruin). The railway terminus is at Tooley Street—the nucleus of the modern London Bridge Station. From a lithograph by G. F. Bragg.
Photo: Science Museum, London

246 *right* St Pancras station under construction, 1868. The outer brick wall on the east side is nearly complete. Three of the spans of the roof have been erected, with the aid of the movable timber scaffolding that stands beneath them. In the foreground is an arch of the tunnel being built to contain the Fleet Ditch. From *Illustrated Times*, xii (1868), 149.

247 *above left* Hawkshaw's bridge and station at Cannon Street; London Bridge in the background.
below left The station roof under construction. From *Illustrated Times*, vi (1865), 99, 241.

248 *above right* The last fragment of the old Fleet Prison, on the east side of Farringdon Street close to Ludgate Circus; the London Chatham & Dover Railway above. From *Illustrated London News*, lii (1868), 261.
below right Ludgate Hill station. From *Illustrated Times*, vi (1865), 41.

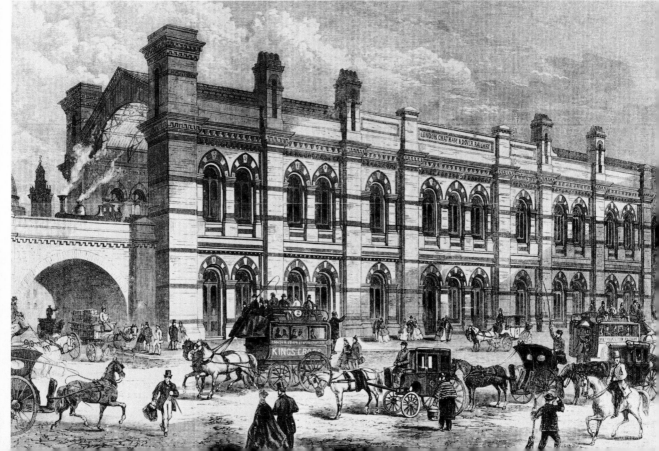

249 *left* The bridge over Ludgate Hill.
Photo: G. W. Wilson
Aberdeen University Library

250 *below* The Great Northern Railway bridge
over Friargate, Derby.
Derby Museum & Art Gallery

251 The North London Railway bridge over
Church Street (now Mare Street). From a litho-
graph by C. J. Greenwood.
Photo: Science Museum, London

252 The Great Western Railway's entrance
into Bath through Sydney Gardens, 1841.
From a lithograph by J. C. Bourne.

253 *left* Stoke-on-Trent station. Drawing by George Buckler: British Museum, Add. MS. 36387, fol. 232.

254 *below left* Birmingham, New Street station at the time of its opening. Its iron and glass roof, designed by E. A. Cooper, then claimed to be the largest single span in a station anywhere; its greatest width was 211 ft. From *Illustrated London News*, xxiv (1854), 505.

255 *below* Bristol, Temple Meads joint station (1871–8). The architect was Sir Matthew Digby Wyatt.
Photo: G. W. Wilson
Aberdeen University Library

256 *above* North end of the Royal Border Bridge, Berwick-on-Tweed. The railway cuts straight through the Castle. *National Monuments Record*

257 *below* The Great Central Railway striding across the Old Town of Leicester, on a viaduct ¾ mile long, built at the close of the railway age (1899). The road running across the lower part of the picture is aligned on the Roman Fosse Way; the Norman castle and its collegiate church stand towards the top left-hand corner of the picture. In the centre foreground is the yard of the Leicester & Swannington Railway, built in 1832 on the site of the Augustinian Friary. This photograph was taken in 1936. *Aerofilms Ltd* evidence in the Parliamentary enquiry into railway rates; it petitioned the House of Commons in favour of the Railway & Canal Traffic Bill of 1888; two years later it urged the directors of the railway companies serving the town to provide a single central station.[54] Nor did it confine its attention to such large issues of general policy. It wrestled with the Manchester Sheffield & Lincolnshire Company for thirty years to secure a station to serve the populous north-western part of the town at Neepsend. Its pertinacity triumphed at last when the station was opened on 1 July 1888.[55]

Here was an attempt to improve transport to and from the suburbs, before the age of the mechanized road vehicle had arrived. So far as Sheffield was concerned it stood in isolation. But in Nottingham the Town Council took that matter seriously. It became interested in railways at an early date: chiefly because Nottingham, too, found itself placed on branch lines and feared the loss of its trade, in consequence, to its more happily-situated neighbours, Derby and Leicester. When the 'mania' came in 1845 the Council set up a special Railway Committee to examine proposals affecting the town. It looked into thirty-five in all.[56] The strongest support appeared for plans to build a line to link the Great Northern at Grantham, through Nottingham, with Manchester and Liverpool. This line eventually emerged in the hands of the Great Northern Company, which took the traffic east of Nottingham, and the Midland, which took it over to the west. Nottingham remained the focus of a series of branch lines until 1875–80, when the Midland Company at last opened a new trunk line to the north by Radford and to the south by Melton Mowbray and Kettering.

The interest taken by the Nottingham Council in railway development did not cease when the town had at last been placed on a main line. It had long had a particularly onerous and difficult task in promoting the development of inner suburbs, in order to relieve the dreadful overcrowding in the slums near the centre of the town.[57] That development could not begin until the common fields were enclosed, under an Act of 1845; and it was only in 1877, with a rational extension of boundaries, that the Council could grapple with Nottingham's urban and suburban problems as a whole. When, in 1885, local businessmen promoted a Nottingham Suburban Railway, the Corporation adopted an attitude of positive benevolence towards the scheme that was highly unusual among Victorian local authorities. The plan provided for a line 3¾ miles long, skirting the north-eastern side of the town, into which a large population was then moving. Its principal sponsor was Edward Gripper, who had established very large brickworks at Mapperley, in the district which the railway was

		a.m.					p.m.				
King's Cross (via Retford)	dep.	7.40		10.00			12.00	2.45		5.00	
St Pancras	dep.		8.45		10.00	11.45			3.00		5.00
Sheffield	arr.	12.25	12.42	1.53	1.53	4.11	4.35	6.30	7.40	8.53	8.53

Thus of these ten trains, two pairs departed from adjacent stations in London and arrived in Sheffield at identically the same times, two other pairs left London within a quarter of an hour of each other. The responsibility for this farce rested with the Midland Company, for the Great Northern's timetable had been unchanged since before the Midland line opened.

designed to serve.[58] The Council came forward with a grant towards the preliminary costs of promoting the scheme, and when Parliamentary sanction was granted in 1886 it was specially authorized to accept payment for land taken for the railway in the form of shares in the Company; this on the ground that the construction of the line would be 'of special benefit to the inhabitants of the town and borough of Nottingham'.[59] The line was opened in 1889.

The Council's efforts continued. When the Manchester Sheffield & Lincolnshire Company announced the plans for its London extension in 1890 it saw a fresh oppor-

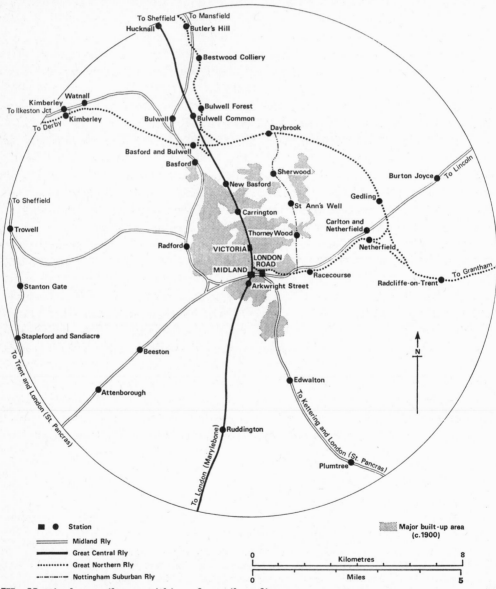

IX Nottingham railways within a five-mile radius

tunity. The Council was determined that this line too should help to solve the problems of suburban transport. It therefore insisted, successfully, that the railway company should be obliged to open four stations, in addition to the main one, within the limits of the borough. Their location was indicated in the Act of 1893, which required the provision of 'a reasonably effective service of local trains', stopping at each of these stations.[60]

By the time this railway was opened in 1899, the Nottingham Council had taken another decision, which diminished the value of such suburban railway services.

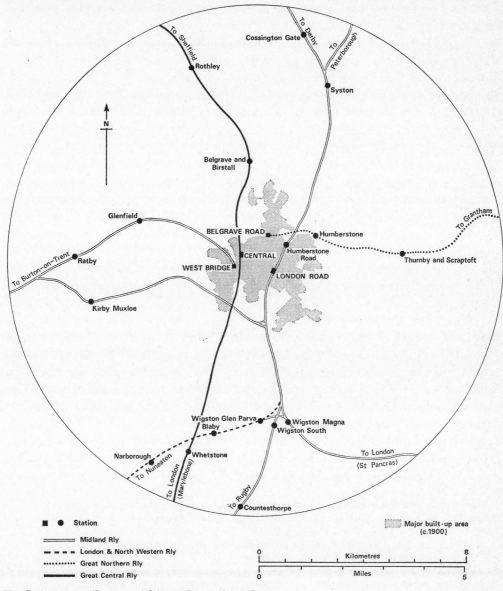

X Leicester railways within a five-mile radius

In 1897 it had bought out the privately-owned Nottingham Tramway Company, and in the following year it had decided to electrify the system.[61]

In Sheffield and Nottingham, then, the cities themselves were actively involved in railway development.* Though this book is concerned with the Victorian city, that is the large town, it is useful to glance briefly at what happened in small towns too: magnified as it were under a microscope. One can also see something of the power which the railway wielded in shaping its own course, regardless of the pleas or the hatred of the communities by which it passed. These towns had been there long before railways were thought of—prosperous markets, even centres of industry. How did they fare when the railway came?

Very variously. Some were fortunate or far-sighted enough to associate themselves with the railway: like Peterborough, which turned itself into a railway town, or Swindon, which found itself hitched up to a railway town adjoining it. Some, which were prospering before the railway developed, went on growing for a little and then stagnated, perhaps because they lay off a main line. Look at Kendal and Frome: two towns that were important enough to secure the right to separate parliamentary representation in 1832, and were deprived of it in 1885. Kendal was by-passed by the West Coast main line to Scotland—the two-mile branch from Oxenholme was a poor substitute. Frome's railway history was truly ironical. Placed on the meandering Wiltshire Somerset & Weymouth line, it found itself on a trunk route in 1906, when the Great Western inaugurated its new main line through Westbury—only to be relegated once more to a loop when a by-pass, running south of the town, was opened in 1921. Neither of these towns ceased to be industrial centres: K Shoes still come from the one, the high-class printing of Butler & Tanner from the other. But both have remained small, and for that their position on the railway system is in part responsible.

We can see the matter more clearly, however, if we look at towns smaller than these. Let us use Tewkesbury as an illustration. When Mr Pickwick stopped to dine there at the Hop Pole, it was a comfortable town of about 5,800 people, with a few small industries, profiting handsomely from its position on the great highway from the North to the West. Twenty-six coaches a day went from Tewkesbury to Worcester, twenty to Gloucester, besides others for Hereford and Malvern.[62] When the Birmingham & Gloucester Railway was first promoted, the Tewkesbury people complacently assumed it must pass through their town; but Cheltenham—a rapidly-growing place, already four times as large—insisted that the line should run by Ashchurch instead, two miles away to the east.† A public meeting of protest was held

---

* Other Corporations showed a no less anxious and long-continued concern in the matter. Railways took up a large part of the time of the standing Commerce of the Port Committee in Southampton; the Corporation subscribed to the Didcot Newbury & Southampton Railway in 1881 and gave it the most explicit and public support: Southampton Record Office, SC2/3/11, pp. 86, 96–7, 99, 112.

† Cheltenham's fear, no doubt, was that the line might follow the Severn valley closely through Tewkesbury (which would give a shorter route to Gloucester), serving Cheltenham by a branch. The line by Ashchurch was, however, superior from the engineers' point of view.

and two petitions submitted to Parliament. In vain. The railway company would only agree to build the line 'as close to Tewkesbury as practicable' and to throw off a branch running through the town to the Quay on the Severn.[63] After a little shilly-shallying on the Company's part, this was achieved. When the branch was opened in 1840 it was worked by horses; locomotives were not regularly used on it until 1844.[64] The trade of the town was now stagnant; drained away, one may fairly infer, by the railway to Cheltenham and Gloucester. The population rose, it is true, in 1851 to 5,878. But that was its peak. Thirty years later it was only a little over 5,000; it was 5,400 in 1901.[65] 'Whatever may be the ultimate effect of railroads', a local journalist remarked in 1841, 'it is evident that their introduction has hitherto been one of almost unmixed evil to the inhabitants of Tewkesbury.'[66]

This case stands by no means alone. There are many other examples of English towns like Tewkesbury: ancient urban centres in a rural society, which attained the limit of their growth in 1841–61 and then fell back for the rest of the century.[67] Such towns did not always stand on branch railways. Wellington had a station on the Bristol & Exeter line from its opening in 1843; but it reached its maximum size in 1851 and thereafter declined for forty years. Though Moreton-in-the-Marsh got its station on the Oxford–Worcester line in 1853, it was a smaller place in 1901 than it had been in 1851. It is, however, fair to say that the majority of the towns that went this way in the second half of the nineteenth century suffered from inferior railway communication or the total want of it.*

The railway had two outstanding duties to the towns it served: to promote their trade and industry and to make them more satisfactory places to live in. How did it perform them?

Nobody would dispute that railways literally created Crewe or New Swindon; or that they made substantial and old-established towns, like Doncaster and Darlington, into major centres of industry; or that they added a new element to places that were already industrial centres, by siting large works there, as at Derby and Wolverhampton. The equipment they needed was at first supplied almost wholly by private firms. The most successful of these firms grew steadily, to become important elements in the economic life of the towns in which they were situated. For some time they were on a relatively small scale. Robert Stephenson & Co. in Newcastle were employing only about 500 men in the late 1830s; they were building some thirty locomotives a year, and their turnover was about £60,000.[68] In the forties, however, the scale of operations was transformed. The rapid development of

---

* They are particularly numerous in the south-western counties, where the clothing trade was declining in these years in favour of Lancashire and Yorkshire. Wiltshire, for example, can show at least eight: Great Bedwyn, Highworth, Malmesbury, Market Lavington, Marlborough, Melksham, Ramsbury, and Warminster. Of these, Highworth and Malmesbury stood on branch lines; Great Bedwyn, Marlborough, Melksham, and Warminster on secondary cross-country routes; Market Lavington was not served by a railway until 1900; Ramsbury never at all.

the railway system set up a demand for plant of all kinds, from Britain and overseas. The railway manufacturing firms grew much bigger, partly as a consequence of amalgamations. At the same time the railway companies, competing with one another for the equipment they needed, often found it difficult to secure punctual delivery and began manufacturing on their own account. The companies' locomotive works at Crewe and Swindon were both established in 1843 and turned out their first engines two or three years later.[69] The Sheffield Ashton-under-Lyne & Manchester Railway* set up its works at Gorton in 1846–8. The choice fell on Gorton because it was far enough from the centre of Manchester 'to be clear of the heavy local taxes with which all such establishments in large towns are burdened'.[70] Those words were used by Richard Peacock, the Company's Locomotive Superintendent, and when he left the railway to set up in business on his own, in partnership with Charles Frederick Beyer, he selected a site for the new works just opposite those he had established in 1846. The relationship between the two companies was perfectly friendly; there was work enough for both of them. With Ashbury's carriage and wagon factory near by, the Lancashire & Yorkshire Company's works at Miles Platting, and other private locomotive builders such as Sharp Bros, Manchester became an important centre of railway manufacture. So did Glasgow. When the North British Locomotive Company had absorbed all its chief rivals, it was employing 8,000 men and building 700 locomotives a year.[71] The two biggest Scottish railway companies also had their works in Glasgow: the North British at Cowlairs, the Caledonian at St Rollox. Sheffield too, in spite of the unsatisfactory railway communication of which it had cause to complain, became a producer of railway goods—springs, rails, tyres, and axles—for almost the whole world.[72] The vast business of John Brown was founded largely on his invention and development of the conical steel spring for railway buffers in 1848.

The big railway companies' works were big indeed. In 1877 those at Crewe were employing 6,000 hands;[73] 14,000 were employed in 1905 at Swindon—it has been suggested that this was 'the largest undertaking in British industry at the end of the century, if not in Europe'.[74]

The influence of the railway is writ large in the history of commercial and industrial development in all Victorian cities. The part it played in assembling the raw materials of manufacture and in distributing the finished product was as evidently vital for West Riding woollens or Macclesfield silk or Birmingham guns as it was for the cottons of Manchester. Some of the evidence for this process is still plainly visible in the siting of factories by the side of the line: in the Lea Valley of north-east London, for example, by either route between Birmingham and Wolverhampton, or by the Midland line in Leicester and Nottingham.

The part played by the railway in transforming the economic life of cities is seen nowhere more clearly than in some of the great ports. Cardiff is a striking example. It grew into a great industrial city in the course of the mid-Victorian age. In the early nineteenth century it had been no bigger than its neighbour Newport, and much

* Later the Manchester Sheffield & Lincolnshire Railway, later still the Great Central.

smaller than Swansea. It decisively outpaced Newport in the fifties and Swansea in the seventies.[75] Its growth and prosperity were then so impressive that it seemed 'likely, at some future day, to outstrip Bristol'.[76]

It was the railway that made Cardiff into a coal-shipping port of world-wide fame. The work of bringing the coal down had been begun by the Glamorganshire Canal (completed in 1798) and the tramroads built in connection with it. In 1835 they were carrying 100,000 tons of coal annually into Cardiff; fifteen years later the Taff Vale Railway (opened in 1841) was carrying six times as much.[77] The opening of this railway gave Cardiff the advantage over Newport, which did not get a corresponding line for another ten years.[78]

The pre-eminent suitability of Welsh coal for use in steamships was now being demonstrated, in the thorough tests made at the instance of the Admiralty in 1847–51.[79] Henceforward, for the rest of the century, both supply and demand seemed boundless; the only limiting factor was transport. A virtual monopoly was exercised here for a long time by the Taff Vale Railway and its ally the Bute Docks Company. This brought great benefit to Cardiff, which became the one port of shipment for the unimaginable quantities of steam coal that poured out of the Rhondda in the seventies.[80] But the railway and the dock company overplayed their hand. Between 1874 and 1882, though the export of coal through Cardiff and Penarth rose by 170 percent, nothing was done to increase the facilities for handling it beyond the construction of one new dock. Congestion, both on the railway and at the docks, became intolerable. Having given repeated warnings, the coalowners took the sole measure open to them. They promoted new railways, providing alternative routes to the sea: first the Barry Railway, then others that connected the Rhondda to all Cardiff's rivals, Port Talbot, Swansea, and Newport. Cardiff therefore had to share with others in a trade that might have remained her own. But that trade was prodigiously valuable, and Cardiff's growth and prosperity continued uninterruptedly down to 1914. It was on the transport of coal that Cardiff emerged as the chief city of Wales.

The enduring symbol of that emergence is Cathays Park, laid out from 1899 onwards with imagination and a true civic pride. If the city fathers and their architects had had one touch more of imagination and piety, surely they would have mounted at its very centre, on a handsome plinth, a tank engine from the Taff Vale Railway.

Some of the benefits that accrued to the citizens of towns like Cardiff from these operations are plain enough. They brought in business to shopkeepers and bankers, to builders and professional men; they created much employment in the railways and docks. But how did they affect the whole lives of these people—not just their economic activities, the working day?

They unquestionably made things better for the comfortable classes. Indeed, they made possible a new kind of life—a life that could be lived in two quite different places at once. Almost as soon as the London & Brighton Railway was opened in 1841, it became practicable to live by the sea and work in London. The 8.45 express up from Brighton, and the 5 o'clock down from London Bridge at night, were already running in 1851, in an hour and a quarter each way.[81] They became a great institution, dignified with Edwardian pomposity by the name 'City Limited' in 1907, and still running at the same times (though to a faster schedule) even now. In the Victorian age they admitted first-class passengers only, the large majority of them holding season tickets, which cost about two shillings a day.[82] A similar express began to run to and from Southend in 1856.[83] In the North the merchants of Liverpool (more than their fellows of Manchester) were inclined to live a long way from their work;[84] and before the end of the century both Manchester and Liverpool men were building themselves 'palatial villas . . . on the shores of Windermere',[85] on the strength of business trains like those of Brighton and Southend.

When they took their families for a long journey, or visited a distant town, they might owe the railway more than rapid and easy conveyance. Many railway companies saw the need to provide hotel accommodation for their passengers and built hotels adjoining their stations, usually managed by lessees. The first in London was at Euston, followed by others at many termini, though not all. These hotels proved to be profitable ventures—so profitable that the railway companies themselves presently went into the business of management. The London & North Western Company, for instance, bought the Crewe Arms in 1876, took into its own hands the hotels at Liverpool and Birmingham in 1879 and 1882, and built a new Euston Hotel in 1881.[86] The Manchester Sheffield & Lincolnshire Company did likewise at Sheffield and Grimsby in 1885–90.[87]

The best of these hotels were very good indeed,[88] a real addition to the high-class amenities of London and the bigger provincial towns. Their contributions to urban commercial and social life were important, with the facilities they offered for public functions, for board and shareholders' meetings (it would be hard to calculate the number of those held in the Cannon Street Hotel alone in the course of a single year), for private discussions and family parties. Though they varied in merit, in most of the cities in which they were established—in Liverpool and Preston, in Hull, in Edinburgh and Glasgow—they set a new standard of comfort, solid, efficient, and dependable.

Such services benefited only the well-to-do. Except in so far as they created new employment, they were of no interest to the working classes or the poor. The railway, however, affected these people intimately, both for good and ill. At first the main thing it did for them was to help to lower prices, and especially the price of coal. The opening of the Leicester & Swannington Railway reduced the price of coal in Leicester at a stroke by 60 percent;[89] when the Great Northern Railway began to carry coal into London in 1851, in competition with that brought by sea, the price fell from thirty shillings to seventeen shillings a ton.[90]

Since in London (with the exception of the Blackwall line) the early railways stopped at the edge of the built-up area, or out in suburbs like Paddington, they did not ordinarily need to displace much of the population. The first notorious problems of that kind arose in provincial cities. The construction of the High Level Bridge in

Newcastle (opened in 1849) involved the removal of nearly 800 families;[91] more than 500 houses were pulled down to allow the erection of Tithebarn Street (later Exchange) station in Liverpool, which was completed in 1850.[92] When the plans for New Street station in Birmingham were first announced, it was remarked that with the completion of the undertaking 'the whole face of the present destitute-looking and filthy place will be changed'.[93] The building of the station (which was finished in 1854) was indeed historic, for it 'began the task of slum clearance in central Birmingham'.[94]

In London, while King's Cross station was being built in 1851, it involved the demolition of much of 'the awful rookery at the back of St Pancras Road'.[95] A lull then followed, for nearly all the rest of that decade, when no important railway construction was going on within the central mass of London; the lull was broken from 1859 onwards when the Metropolitan, North London, South Eastern, Dover, and Midland companies were engaged in fighting their way into the city. By this time a few consciences had been aroused by the suffering that evictions of this kind entailed. In 1853 Lord Shaftesbury persuaded the House of Lords to accept a Standing Order requiring the promoters of any scheme involving the demolition of thirty houses or more in the same parish to state the number and the occupants of them, and the steps they proposed to take to meet the consequent 'inconvenience'.[96] This did no more than oblige the promoters to supply information. The information was defective; but at least it provided some evidence, which could be well used by those who thought that the process should be regulated further. They were confronted by a phalanx of powerful opponents: not only the directors, managers, and shareholders of the railway companies, but *Punch* and *The Times*—with that insufferably sanctimonious devotion to *laissez-faire* which roused Matthew Arnold to a most noble wrath. It was only slowly that they battled through to reveal the full extent of the problem and to propound workable remedies for it.

The Demolition Statements tell us that between 1853 and 1901 sixty-nine schemes were put forward in London, requiring the displacement of more than 76,000 people. Nearly half these displacements were attributable to the great rush of metropolitan railway construction between 1859 and 1867.[97] The requirement to provide this information was only a step towards the re-housing of the displaced at the expense of the promoters. That notion made headway very slowly. It was not until 1874 that any provision of the kind was adopted, and then in a form that was totally ineffective. Even after numerous loopholes had been stopped up in 1885, this compulsion remained imperfectly enforceable. When the Great Central Railway built its London Extension at the end of the century, it did indeed re-house those who were displaced by its progress through Nottingham and Leicester and north-west London.[98] But 1,750 people, who lived on the site of Marylebone station, were not provided for, and they had to move out into the already overcrowded Lisson Grove.[99]

The Times and its supporters in the sixties, with a wilful ignorance, argued that those who were displaced would simply move further away from the centre of London, and that would be a gain all round. 'Thousands of cottages', the newspaper remarked, 'are springing up yearly in the suburbs.'[100] But of course this was airy and irresponsible nonsense. Of those who were losing their houses, the great majority walked to and from their work. Could they now suddenly afford substantial railway fares instead? And what of the casual labourers? Their chance of work depended first of all on their ability to be on the spot when work was going.

The first of these questions had already found its answer. (The second was never satisfactorily answered at all.) The requirement that was imposed on the London Chatham & Dover Company in 1860, to offer special fares to workmen, was rapidly extended to most of the railways that were building new lines into London.* In 1883 the Board of Trade was given a general power to compel companies to introduce workmen's fares wherever it considered them desirable.

This policy achieved its objective in part. It certainly facilitated the huge migration away from the centre of London that occurred in the last quarter of the nineteenth century. It contributed positively to the growth of working-class settlement within reach of the South London line[101] and, on a bigger scale, in north-east London and Essex, the preserve of the Great Eastern Railway, which was characterized in a report of a committee of the L.C.C. in 1892 as 'especially the workmen's London railway'.[102]

We have just looked at two extreme examples of suburban development: the growth of Brighton, Southend, and Windermere as settlements for the wealthy commuter, and of south and north-east London for the working man. But suburban development as a whole was not determined by people of either of these kinds. It was predominantly an affair of the middle classes—using that term in a broad sense. That is clear enough to any one today who walks round a suburb that was created in the Victorian age, using his eyes—in the way in which H. J. Dyos has taught us to use our eyes in south London.[103] The middle-class character of the suburb may well have changed since; it may have begun to fall into working-class occupation before the end of the nineteenth century. But most Victorian suburbs were originally intended to provide an airy, quiet, economical residence for middle-class family men. And for all of them alike it was an essential condition of living there that the suburb should be within easy travelling time of the man's place of work in the city.

That travelling might be performed in a number of different ways: on foot,† by bus or tram or bicycle or private carriage, as well as by railway. The railway's part

---

* But not to all. No such obligation was laid on the Midland Company in the Acts authorizing its London Extension in 1863–4.

† It was not only the very poor who walked to work. The middle-class family man who was economically minded did so too. My grandfather was appointed to a clerkship in the Admiralty in 1860. He lived in Stockwell, and for many years he walked to and from Whitehall daily, either at no expense at all or at the cost of a penny for tolls if he took the shortest route, over Hungerford Bridge, and back again. The practice of walking was noted as already on the decline when he began. 'The habit of walking is becoming less the rule; and the habit of riding less the exception,' said John Thwaites, Chairman of the Metropolitan Board of Works, in 1863. 'We find that parties instead of walking ride to the railway stations for the purpose of travelling by the line' (*P.P.*, 1863, VIII, S.C. on Met. Rly Comm., Q.1026). On the relation between different forms of suburban transport see G. A. Sekon, *Locomotion in Victorian London* (1938).

in suburban development varied greatly in importance. In some cities it was vital: in others it seems hardly to have mattered. The extremes are well represented by two neighbours, Nottingham and Leicester: towns closely comparable in size and not dissimilar in economic character. We have already seen an example in Nottingham of a railway built specifically to serve a new suburban area, and another of a burden laid upon a railway company to provide suburban stations with a satisfactory service. Nothing remotely like this occurred in Leicester. There the true suburban station was represented by two examples only, both on the Humberstone Road. Within a six-mile radius from the centre, there were thirty-two stations* in Nottingham, sixteen in Leicester. The Victorian expansion of Leicester was almost entirely independent of the railway. It followed the lines of the old main roads, and from the seventies onwards it was promoted by a service of horse trams. At the end of the century, when Leicester had become a city of 200,000 people, the Great Central Railway could sweep through it, opening only two suburban stations in a stretch of seven miles.

The railways themselves differed greatly in their willingness to provide suburban services. Such services were much less profitable than those running through on a main line, and some railways were frankly reluctant to provide them at all: the two earliest trunk lines opened into London, the London & Birmingham and the Great Western, for example.[104] The Great Northern began with a similar attitude and found itself thrust, step by step, protesting loudly, into the business of expanding its suburban services, ultimately in conjunction with tube railways running south-east and south-west from Finsbury Park.[105] The companies south of the Thames, on the other hand, with shorter main lines and much smaller freight traffic, were more interested in promoting suburban services, which became the life-blood of them all.

The pattern of development was not always like this, from shy beginnings into reluctant growth. Suburban services appeared in some cities that were in advance of their needs and had to be discontinued: in Hull, for example, one that made almost a complete circle was put on in 1853, and withdrawn for lack of patronage less than eighteen months later.[106] Here was an intelligent venture that failed. We are apt to overlook the tentative, experimental character of much of the railways' early work. They were feeling their way forward, and sometimes having to retract, with little experience to guide them and many local circumstances to be delicately appreciated and taken into account.

The expansion of the suburban railway system in the great cities is usually discussed in impersonal terms: the promotion of companies, the purchase of land, house-building, the train services provided. If we try to penetrate behind these large matters, to discover how the men and women who went to live in these suburbs felt, we are confronted with a great difficulty. The new suburban dwellers were the subject of no political or sociological investigations, nor did any important novelist except George Gissing take much interest in them. Yet by the seventies the railways had brought a whole new suburban world into being—or rather, two worlds: that of the closely built-up suburb, comprising miles of two-storeyed houses, mainly in terraces,

* Excluding the terminal or principal station on each line.

like Camberwell, Hornsey, or Kilburn, the world we associate with Mr Pooter; and the outer suburbs where the houses spread themselves out with sizeable gardens—which came to represent, for many of those they belonged to, the most passionate attachment of their lives. It was now possible for people of modest means to live in the country (an urban-dweller's country, at least) and to work in the heart of the city. 'Railways, and the untiring enterprise of suburban builders', said a writer in the *Cornhill* in 1874, 'have made it easy for them to do so if they like ... As regards getting to business in the morning and home again in the afternoon, the train puts the dwellers in them nearly on a level with the inhabitants of Tyburnia or South Kensington.'[107] We can watch the process at work, almost photographically, in James Thorne's indispensable book *The Environs of London*, published in 1876.[108] But to Thorne, as a rule, it was just uglification.* Drab enough those houses may be to us now. To many of their first occupants they represented a Paradise. And yet, widespread though the experience was, where does it find expression? Very rarely, and more rarely still in terms of gratitude to the railway, which alone had made a life of this kind possible. Here is one of the rarities:[109]

Our Suburb

He leaned upon the narrow wall
That set the limit to his ground,
And marvelled, thinking of it all,
That he such happiness had found.

He had no word for it but bliss;
He smoked his pipe; he thanked his stars;
And, what more wonderful than this?
He blessed the groaning, stinking cars†

That made it doubly sweet to win
The respite of the hours apart
From all the broil and sin and din
Of London's damnèd money-mart.

The railway did not ordinarily present a handsome appearance as it made its way into the city. The passenger's usual view of it was well characterized by an American,

---

* Of New Barnet, for example, he says (p. 31): 'About the Barnet Stat. has sprung up, within the last few years, one of those new, half-finished rly. villages which we have come to look on as almost a necessary adjunct to every stat. within a moderate distance of London.' Of Buckhurst Hill (p. 64): 'The Stat. is at the foot of the hill, and about it a number of ugly houses have been awkwardly disposed.' In Redhill he sees (p. 481) 'a populous railway town of hideous brick shops and habitations, and around it a belt of ostentatious villas, comfortable looking mansions, and tasteful and ornate dwellings of many varieties, with a super-abundance of builders' detached and semi-detached malformations.' Cf. also his accounts of Croydon (p. 128) and Penge (p. 467).
† Underground; old style. (Author's note)

familiar with England, in the sixties: 'You enter the town as you would a farmer's house, if you first passed through the pig-stye into the kitchen. Every respectable house in the city turns its back upon you; and often a very brick and dirty back, too, though it may show an elegant front of Bath or Portland stone to the street it faces.'[110] And when the traveller emerged on to the street, if he looked back at the station he would seldom see anything very impressive.

The railway gave London a few major architectural monuments—the Arch and the Great Hall at Euston, the stations at King's Cross and St Pancras, the engineers' triumphs at Paddington and Charing Cross; some finely-treated works on the London & Birmingham line in masonry and iron, in the Camden Round-house and the portals of the tunnel under Primrose Hill; good brickwork on a vast scale, vermilion on the Midland line, Staffordshire blue on the Great Central. The provinces also had their imposing monuments. There were the great stations, at Bristol, Chester, Huddersfield, Newcastle; formidable displays of engineering skill at Birmingham, Liverpool, York, and Glasgow; the spacious and convenient stations built at the turn of the century, at Nottingham for example and Sheffield; some magnificent viaducts, striding over scores of houses, at Truro, Brighton, Folkestone, Mansfield, Stockport, Durham, Berwick.

In a few towns the railway showed pride in its achievement. When it approached a town of elegance, it often tried to make its works harmonize with the spirit of the place—at Bath, for instance (where the section through Sydney Gardens still shows something of its original charm), and at Tunbridge Wells. Yet not one major Victorian city used its railway station as a focal point in town-planning, as it was often used so handsomely on the Continent, at Geneva and Amsterdam, in Paris at the Gare de l'Est. The nearest approach to anything of the kind in Britain is to be found at Stoke-on-Trent. There the North Staffordshire Railway laid out its station in 1848 and opposite it, across a square, an hotel,[111] all in a Jacobean style, of red brick diapered with the local blue: a pleasing composition little altered today and still perhaps in the 1970s the most agreeable piece of coherent urban planning in the whole modern city.

Railway companies rarely collaborated with municipal authorities to make their stations into civic embellishments. The Town Council of Liverpool set an interesting precedent when it lent the services of its architect, John Foster the second, to the Liverpool & Manchester Company to design a stone screen to run in front of Lime Street station, facing across to St George's Hall, and contributed £2,000 towards the cost of erecting it.[112] But that example was not followed. The railways did indeed sometimes employ well-known architects of their time to design the façades of stations and their hotels: Tite, Dobson, E. M. Barry, Waterhouse, Gilbert Scott. But they rarely held any competitions for their buildings, even when that practice was fashionable.[113] They occasionally engaged other architects of merit, though no great fame: like Francis Thompson, who endowed Derby and Chester with stations of a true grandeur; David Mocatta, on the London & Brighton line;[114] Sancton Wood, who worked for the Eastern Counties Company in London and

Ipswich;[115] G. T. Andrews, the designer of the first stations in York and Hull;[116] J. T. Mulvany, and again Sancton Wood, who gave railway stations to the city of Dublin that worthily maintained its noble architectural tradition.[117]

In visual terms, however, it must be allowed that the railway generally damaged the city. There could be no doubt on the matter in London—certainly the Victorians themselves had none. Ruskin's denunciations of the railway bridges over the Thames[118] were not merely the raging of an affronted aesthete. On this matter he was at one with his middle-class contemporaries. 'The aggregate disfigurement of the metropolis by the London Chatham & Dover Railway, particularly by its viaducts and its bridges, is very great,' we read in an outspoken gazetteer of the late sixties. It goes on to characterize the newly-built line from London Bridge to Charing Cross in these terms:[119]

> A huge iron bridge goes over the roadway from the station [at London Bridge]: an enormous iron tube, long, high, and most ungainly, goes across Wellington Street, with severe injury to its formerly fine views; a struggling course follows, past the church of St. Mary Overy, across the Borough Market, and through dense back streets; another ungainly tube crosses the fine new street from Blackfriars into Southwark, utterly spoiling its handsome aspect; two more unsightly tubes cross Blackfriars Road, at awkward angles to each other and to the lines of houses; and another intersecting struggle through dense back streets goes onward to the site of the quondam beautiful Hungerford suspension bridge.

The *Builder* summed it all up in 1876 in a terse judgment on railways: 'No rural district we know of has suffered so much disfiguration from the structures connected with them as we have to complain of in London itself.'*

Nor were the visual disasters wrought by the railway in central London offset by the street improvements they brought with them; for here expectation far outran performance. The early underground railways made some contributions to this end: the Metropolitan to the widening of the New Road, the District to the Thames Embankment and to Queen Victoria Street. But the urgently-needed new street to run north and south, from Tottenham Court Road to Charing Cross, was delayed for years through the collapse of the Euston St Pancras & Charing Cross Railway

---

* *Builder*, xxxiv (1876), 847. Not all these bridges were universally condemned at the time. The Blackfriars railway bridge was pronounced 'successful' by William Humber: *Record of the Progress of Modern Engineering* (1864), p. 42. Hawkshaw, who was responsible for the bridges on the Charing Cross line, while admitting that they were 'ugly enough', went out of his way to explain to the Committee of 1863 that the conditions imposed by Parliament on their design precluded their being anything else (*P.P.*, 1863, VIII, S.C. on Met. Rly Comm., Q. 1105).

It is particularly unfortunate that all the railway bridges over the Thames in central London should have dated from the 1860s: a moment when structures of such exceptional strength could be produced only in cast iron in its heaviest and coarsest forms. The recent rebuilding of the bridge that carries the railway from Victoria to Battersea shows how simple and unobtrusive such a structure can now be, using the techniques of the mid-twentieth century.

project of 1871.[120] The Charing Cross Road was completed only in 1887, and then in complete dissociation from any railway.

The most fiercely hated of the London railway bridges, that across Ludgate Hill, exemplified all these matters to perfection. It was a means of street improvement: it afforded a pedestrian crossing over one of the busiest streets in London—for those who were willing to toil up it and down the other side; it made possible the construction of Ludgate Circus; and it was associated with the enlargement of Ludgate Hill to a width of 60 ft. But no one could regard it as anything other than an eyesore, a blow right across the face for St Paul's. Listen again to the gazetteer's judgment: 'That viaduct has utterly spoiled one of the finest street views in the metropolis; and is one of the most unsightly objects ever constructed, in any such situation, anywhere in the world.'[121]

If London suffered outstanding damage from railways in this sense, it did not suffer alone. A valiant battle had been waged in Edinburgh in 1838–42 to prevent the Edinburgh & Glasgow Company from extending its line from the Haymarket to the North Bridge through the Princes Street Gardens. At the end of the battle the honours were even. The railway got the powers it sought, but it agreed to disguise itself in a deep cutting, topped off by a high wall, made seemly to the residents of Princes Street by 'a profuse use of ivy, evergreens, and trees'.[122] The general convenience of the city demanded the extension of the railway from its western terminus. To put it wholly in tunnel would have been impracticable without a lavish provision of ventilators, which would have belched smoke like factory chimneys. In the course of time the traffic along the line grew, and it became the one offensive feature in the whole of that noble valley—until, with the disappearance of the steam locomotive in the 1960s, it has relapsed into an unobtrusive element in the townscape.

There were other railway bridges in provincial towns nearly as frightful as that over Ludgate Hill: the one erected by the Great Northern Company over Friargate in Derby in 1878, for example. Friargate is lined with exceptionally large brick houses: in its satisfying amplitude it is one of the grandest Georgian streets in England. The railway mauled it beyond repair, the bridge pinching in the street line to its own span and drawing attention to itself with gaudy paintwork and fussy decoration. It was a thoroughly offensive piece of commercial vulgarity, bawling away at the aristocratic company it kept. The harm the bridge has done is irreparable to the shape of the street and to the character it once bore as a residence.

The railway was, indeed, at many points in Britain, a vandal. It displaced medieval castles to establish stations and goods yards, at Berwick, Northampton, and Clare. It injured the castle and medieval walls of Conway—though here an enlightened architectural historian can recognize a 'skilful and considerate handling' of the problem which the railway builders faced.[123] It swept away Trinity Chapel in Edinburgh in favour of Waverley station.[124] It drove straight through the ruins of the Priory of St Pancras at Lewes.* At times its ambitions soared higher. A central

* This outrage provoked its response. It was directly responsible for the foundation of the Sussex Archaeological Society.

station was projected for Dublin in 1876 near College Green. It was to be reached by continuing the Kingstown line from Westland Row station on a viaduct across Trinity College Park and the Fellows' Garden, incidentally demolishing the Provost's House. The advocates of this scheme believed that the compensation money payable to the College would silence its opposition, by enabling it to solve 'the vexed question of a fund for retiring pensions for Senior Fellows'.[125] But the Senior Fellows were denied their pensions. The railway was not built.

Sometimes railway companies were forced to accept a deviation, to avoid doing damage of this kind. The London & South Western Railway intended to cut through Maumbury Rings at Dorchester, but it was frustrated by a local antiquary, Charles Warne.[126] At Leicester a long battle was fought in the 1890s, chiefly by the Leicestershire Archaeological Society, to stop the Manchester Sheffield & Lincolnshire Railway, first from driving its London Extension through the Jewry Wall (one of the largest pieces of Roman masonry in England) and the medieval castle, and then from destroying a Roman pavement that had impertinently placed itself underneath the intended site of the station.[127] With the backing of the Town Council the battle was won. The pavement survives *in situ*, in a chamber of white glazed brick beneath the platform. And the Jewry Wall and the Castle laugh last, for the railway is now entirely closed.

Such battles had their effect. Protection was sometimes accorded to notable antiquities and historic buildings. Special arrangements for tunnelling within 200 feet of Westminster Abbey were among the financial burdens placed on the District Railway in 1864.[128] The Central London Railway was required in 1891 to preserve 'all objects of geological or antiquarian interest discovered by them in the execution of their works', and to deposit them in the Guildhall Museum.[129]

The railway obliterated the past as relentlessly as new roads, airports, and reservoirs obliterate it now. That is not to deny the improvement in life that the railway often brought. There is a proverb about omelettes and the breaking of eggs. But the steam locomotive, now passing into dim recollection, was a noisy machine[130] and could be a grave nuisance from the smoke it emitted. The railway offered new amenities to those who lived in the city. It also killed, or seriously impaired, a number of those they had enjoyed in the past.

And so we end, as we began, in a measure of confusion. For the country as a whole the building of railways in the Victorian age meant growth, progress at least in an economic sense, increasing power. Within cities it sometimes meant just that: the expansion and diversification of industry, the improvement of economic opportunity for most of the people living there. At other times it meant uncertainty or loss —the sudden removal of works elsewhere, to some more favoured site. In quality of life its effects were equally various. It offered access to recreation, to beauty and quiet, with undreamt-of ease. It also did much to destroy beauty and quiet within the city itself; and yet, on the other side again, it sometimes displayed a ruthless magnificence that was—and has remained—all its own. Anybody born about the time of the Battle of Waterloo, who grew up with the railway and watched its development closely, must have seen it as a complex and puzzling spectacle. Nowhere was it more complex, or harder to understand rightly, than in urban life. The railway did indeed set the towns of Britain a-dancing when it came. They were dancing to it still, though the tunes were different, when Queen Victoria died.

Notes

1   *Latter-day Pamphlets* (1858), p. 229.
2   *Liverpool Albion*, 26 April 1830.
3   *Journeys to England and Ireland*, ed. J. P. Mayer (1958), p. 112.
4   At the time of its opening it was reckoned that the greatest number of people who could be conveyed by the coaches between Liverpool and Manchester was 700 a day. If every coach had been filled to capacity, Sundays included (an impossible supposition), 255,000 passengers could thus have been carried in a year. In the course of 1831 the railway actually carried just over 445,000. J. Wheeler, *Manchester: Its political, social and commercial history* (Manchester, 1836), pp. 293–4.
5   J. R. Kellett, *The Impact of Railways on Victorian Cities* (1969), pp. 154–5, 164. This book, based on a comparative study of London, Birmingham, Manchester, Liverpool, and Glasgow, is by far the most important study of the subject. It is especially valuable for its analysis of the dealings between the railway companies and the landowners in these five cities and the relations between the companies themselves.
6   Ibid., p. 173.
7   T. Baines, *History of the Commerce and Town of Liverpool* (1852), p. 828. Cf. Braithwaite Poole's statement of the goods traffic in and out of Liverpool by the London & North Western Railway in 1851, analysed by towns and districts (ibid., p. 829).
8   J. A. Langford, ed., *A Century of Birmingham Life* (1868), II, p. 580.
9   *A Pictorial Guide to Birmingham* (1849), p. 162.
10 Pearson, who was Solicitor to the City of London, put forward two versions of his scheme. One was examined by the Commission on London Termini of 1846 (*Parliamentary Papers* (*P.P.*), 1846, XVII, QQ.2289–351, 2821–53), the other by the Select Committee (S.C.) on Metropolitan Communications in 1855 (*P.P.*, 1854–5, X, QQ. 1337–78). The *Builder* argued that the need for a great central terminus in London was 'obvious' as late as 1881: xli (1881), 195.
11 See Kellett, op. cit., pp. 161–3.
12 Ibid., p. 171.
13 E. T. MacDermot, *History of the Great Western Railway* (1927–31), I, pp. 356–7.
14 Kellett, op. cit., pp. 264, 266; J. Simmons, *St Pancras Station* (1968), pp. 16–17.
15 For the remarkable complexity of the railway system here see E. L. Ahrons, *Locomotive and Train Working in the Latter Part of the Nineteenth Century* (1951–4), I, pp. 59–61.
16 T. C. Barker and Michael Robbins, *A History of London Transport* (1963), I, p. 125.

17 *P.P.*, 1863, VIII, S.C. (H. of L.) on Metropolitan Railway Communications: Minutes of Evidence (500–II), 239.

18 A bizarre example is that which ran in 1899 from Liverpool (Central) to Folkestone, via the Mersey Tunnel, Birkenhead, and Reading—Liverpool dep. 8 a.m., Paris arr. 10.50 p.m.: G. W. Parkin, *The Mersey Railway* (n.d.), pp. 16–17.

19 It must moreover be remembered that until late in the Victorian Age all the express services for the Continent, except the night mails, left in the morning, too early to take passengers who had travelled any substantial distance from the North. See C. W. Eborall, Manager of the South Eastern Railway, in his evidence to the Committee of 1863: *P.P.*, 1863, VIII, S.C. on Met. Rly Comm., Q. 677.

20 Barker and Robbins, op.cit., I, pp. 74–5, 237, 271–2.

21 Local and Personal Act, 27 & 28 Vict., cap. cccxxii.

22 Sects 28, 45, 55, 36, 33, 76, 90.

23 Cf. C. E. Lee, *Passenger Class Distinctions* (1946), and H. J. Dyos, 'Workmen's Fares in South London, 1860–1914', *Journal of Transport History* (*J.T.H.*), i (1953–4), 3–19.

24 *P.P.*, 1883, LXI, Report to Board of Trade upon . . . Workmen's Trains, etc., 466.

25 *Builder*, xxix (1871), 16–17. Overcrowding on these trains was frequent: see, e.g., *P.P.*, 1883, LXI, Report on Workmen's Trains, 449, 451, 453; 1894, LXXV, Notes of Conference held at Board of Trade, etc., 836–7.

26 See the map in Barker and Robbins, op. cit., I, p. 185.

27 *Builder*, xxxiii (1875), 315.

28 Ibid.

29 British Transport Historical Records, GE1/1, 53–4.

30 C. J. Allen, *The Great Eastern Railway*, 1955, p. 58. No statement of the final cost was ever given to the shareholders; surprisingly, none of them seems to have demanded it.

31 Barker and Robbins, op. cit., I, p. 153.

32 Three of them spoke in favour of it to the Lords Committee of 1863 (long before the New York Elevated railway had appeared)—G. P. Bidder, John Parson, and William Baker—though the last two recognized that its unsightliness was a grave objection. (*P.P.*, 1863, VIII, S.C. on Met. Rly Comm., 88, 106, 154: QQ. 614, 802, 1139–41.)

33 The origins of this line go back to 1877, when the Mersey Docks & Harbour Board, having investigated the Elevated system in New York, determined to build such a line in Liverpool. They secured Acts for this purpose in 1878 and 1882, but did not carry out the work. The railway was eventually built by a separate company, incorporated in 1888; it was opened in 1893–1905. In one important respect it was an advance on all its American prototypes. It was the first such line to be electrically operated. C. E. Box, *The Liverpool Overhead Railway 1893–1956* (1962 edn), pp. 15, 18–19, 33.

34 The *Builder*, as early as 1881, was prepared to believe that electric traction might make the railway clean and relatively quiet, and in that case would perhaps have been prepared to accept the disfigurement (xli (1881), 196); but when the Liverpool

Overhead Railway got its second Act in the following year its comment was: 'These new works will, doubtless, afford many facilities, but will greatly damage the appearance of important parts of Liverpool. Everything is sacrificed nowadays to making money and "getting along"'' (xlii (1882), 750).

35 For the pneumatic lines see H. Clayton, *The Atmospheric Railways* (1966), pp. 124–8; for the cable-operated Tower Subway see Barker and Robbins, op. cit., I, pp. 301–3.

36 The Committee's report and the minutes of evidence given before it are in *P.P.*, 1892, XII, Joint S.C. on Electric and Cable Railways (215–I), 1–172.
Cf. J. Simmons, 'The Pattern of Tube Railways in London', *J.T.H.*, vii (1965–6), 234–40.

37 *P.P.*, 1905, XXX, R.C. on the Means of Locomotion and Transport in London (Cd. 2597), 609.

38 Ibid., 621–2. The Metro had been the subject of a special investigation in 1902 by Lt-Col. H. A. Yorke, Chief Inspecting Officer of Railways at the Board of Trade: *P.P.*, 1902, XXIII, 479–93.

39 Ibid., 1905, XXX, R.C. on London Traffic, 623, 630.

40 The *Sheffield Mercury* (which was opposed to the North Midland's plan) gives the fullest account of these events: see especially the issues of 16 January, 19 and 26 March, and 9 April 1836. Its Whig rival the *Iris* supported the Sheffield & Rotherham Railway and paid little attention to the North Midland debates.

41 *Transactions of the Hunter Archaeological Society*, ix (1964), 16–19.

42 C. H. Grinling, *History of the Great Northern Railway* (1966 edn), pp. 162–3.

43 *Sheffield Daily Telegraph (S.D.T.)*, 2 July 1864.

44 Ibid., 12 May 1864.

45 See, for example, the evidence of William Rangeley of Unstone before the Parliamentary Committee of 1864: *S.D.T.*, 2 July 1864.

46 *S.D.T.*, 10 October 1861. To be fair to the Midland Company, if this was true the blame rested also with the Manchester Sheffield & Lincolnshire and its ally the South Yorkshire.

47 Cf. Charles Cammell's evidence: *S.D.T.*, 1 July 1864.

48 *S.D.T.*, 10 October 1861, 13 November 1862, 10 September 1863.

49 Ibid., 6 July 1864.

50 The report of the Committee that enquired into the Company's promotion, and the evidence given before it, are in *P.P.*, 1864, X, S.C. on Standing Orders (510–I), 903–21.

51 *S.D.T.*, 16 October 1863.

52 For a clear account of the Midland Company's contest with its rival, from the Midland's side, see F. S. Williams, *The Midland Railway* (5th edn, 1886), pp. 135–43.

53 *S.D.T.*, 2 February 1870.

54 J. M. Furness, *Record of Municipal Affairs in Sheffield* (Sheffield, 1893), pp. 257, 409, 447.

55 Ibid., pp. 110, 119, 204, 253. Cf. *S.D.T.*, 13 December 1860, 13 June 1861, 12 March 1863.

56 Nottingham's place on the early railway system is discussed in R. A. Church, *Economic and Social Change in a Midland Town* (1966), pp. 170–4.

57 Church, op. cit., ch. 8.

58 For Gripper see Church, op. cit., pp. 229, 372, and Simmons, *St Pancras Station*, p. 53.

59 Local and Personal Act, 49 & 50 Vict., ch. xciv, sect. 34.

60 Local and Personal Act, 56 Vict., ch. i, sect. 21.

61 Church, op. cit., pp. 349–50.

62 *Tewkesbury Yearly Register and Magazine*, ii (1850), 45.

63 Ibid., i (1840), 289–91.

64 Ibid., ii (1850), 29, 157.

65 *Victoria County History (V.C.H.) of Gloucestershire* (1907), II, p. 187.

66 *Tewkesbury Register*, ii, 45.

67 Cf. *V.C.H. Essex* (1907), II, p. 137.

68 J. G. H. Warren, *A Century of Locomotive Building by Robert Stephenson and Co., 1823–1923* (1923), pp. 91, 93.

69 These were not the first locomotives to be built by a railway company in its own works. The Stockton & Darlington's Company's works at Shildon had turned out the *Royal George* in 1827: W. W. Tomlinson, *The North Eastern Railway* [Newcastle, 1915], p. 143.

70 G. Dow, *Great Central* (1959–65), I, pp. 106, 211.

71 *Murray's Handbook for Scotland* (8th edn, 1903), p. 148.

72 A. Gatty, *Sheffield Past and Present* (Sheffield, 1873), p. 311.

73 W. H. Chaloner, *The Social and Economic Development of Crewe 1780–1923* (Manchester, 1950), p. 74. The whole population of Crewe was then rather more than 20,000.

74 D. E. C. Eversley in *V.C.H. Wiltshire* (1959), IV, p. 215. Swindon's population was then about 47,000.

75 In 1840 the port of Swansea (including Neath) shipped 493,000 tons of coal, Newport almost exactly the same (489,000), Cardiff 166,000. By 1874 the corresponding figures were 1,043,000; 1,066,000; 3,780,000. (J. H. Morris and L. J. Williams, *The South Wales Coal Industry, 1841–75* (1958), p. 91.) In 1841 Cardiff and Newport both had populations (in round figures) of 10,000, as against Swansea's 25,000; by 1881 Cardiff had 83,000, Swansea 66,000, Newport 35,000.

76 *Murray's Handbook for South Wales* (1877 edn), p. 14.

77 D. S. Barrie, *The Taff Vale Railway* (2nd edn, 1950), pp. 6, 14.

78 Morris and Williams, op. cit., pp. 100–1.

79 Ibid., pp. 34–6. The North-country coalowners repeatedly tried to controvert this demonstration in subsequent years, but without success: pp. 36–41.

80 E. D. Lewis, *The Rhondda Valleys* (1959), p. 121. The increase was from 2,886,000 to 7,775,000 tons a year.

81 C. F. D. Marshall, *History of the Southern Railway* (1963 edn), p. 209.

82 Ahrons, op. cit., V, p. 28.

83 H. D. Welch, *The London Tilbury & Southend Railway* (1951), p. 25.

84 *Murray's Handbook for Lancashire* (1880 edn), pp. 115–16.

85 R. S. Ferguson, *History of Westmorland* (1894), p. 286.

86 W. L. Steel, *History of the London & North Western Railway* (1914), pp. 364–5, 375, 385, 388.

87 Dow, op. cit., II, p. 219.

88 Cf. Simmons, *St Pancras Station*, pp. 80–1.

89 A. T. Patterson, *Radical Leicester* (1954), p. 262.

90 Grinling, op. cit., p. 103.

91 J. Sykes and T. Fordyce, *Local Records* (Newcastle, 1867), III, p. 246.

92 *Builder*, viii (1850), 185.

93 *Birmingham Journal*, 9 January 1847, quoted in *Modern Birmingham*, ed.
    J. A. Langford (1873), I, pp. 5–6.

94 *V.C.H. Warwickshire* (1969), VIII, p. 10.

95 *London and its Vicinity Exhibited in 1851*, ed. J. Weale [1851], p. 811.

96 H. J. Dyos, 'Railways and Housing in Victorian London', *J.T.H.*, ii (1955–6), 13.
    This paper gives a very clear account of the problem and the remedies proposed and
    tried for it. See also Kellett, op. cit., pp. 325–36.

97 Dyos, ibid., p. 14. All these figures are certainly too low: see H. J. Dyos,
    'Some Social Costs of Railway Building in London', *J.T.H.*, iii (1957–8), 23–5.

98 Dow, op. cit., II, pp. 244, 279, 287.

99 Dyos, 'Railways and Housing', 19.

100 Quoted in ibid., 14.

101 Dyos, 'Workmen's Fares', 15.

102 *Report of the Public Health and Housing Committee on Workmen's Trains* (1892).

103 H. J. Dyos, *Victorian Suburb: A study of the growth of Camberwell* (1961). See his
     remarks on the social character of suburbs, pp. 22–6.

104 M. Robbins, *Middlesex* (1953), pp. 78–80.

105 Grinling's *History of the Great Northern Railway* treats the suburban problem
     markedly better than any other history of a large railway company running into
     London.

106 K. Hoole, *Regional History of the Railways of Great Britain: North East England*
     (Newton Abbot, 1966), pp. 45–6.

107 *Cornhill Magazine*, xxix (1874), 603.

108 Reprinted by Adams & Dart in 1970.

109 Ernest Radford, *A Collection of Poems* (1906), p. 60.

110 Elihu Burritt, *A Walk from London to John o' Groats* (New York, 2nd edn, 1864), p. 2.

111 The architect was H. A. Hunt, of Parliament Street, London (not the 'otherwise
     unknown R. A. Stent'—H.-R. Hitchcock, *Early Victorian Architecture in Britain*
     (1954), p. 523), and he put the cost of the whole complex of buildings, including
     the passenger and goods stations, engine shed, workshops, and hotel, at £127,000:
     Staffordshire Advertiser, 4 August 1849. For accounts of the station when it was new
     see ibid., 14, 21 October 1848.

112 Hitchcock, op. cit., p. 497; J. A. Picton, *Memorials of Liverpool* (2nd edn, 1907),
     II, p. 187.

113 The most famous exception is the St Pancras Hotel, for which the competition was
     won by Scott in 1866: Simmons, *St Pancras Station*, pp. 48–9. Others include:
     the first station at Ipswich in 1846 where Sancton Wood was the successful
     competitor (*Builder*, iv (1846), 140; see also British Transport Historical Records,
     EUR 1/3, ff. 37–8, 41, 56); the Park Hotel at Preston, erected by the London &
     North Western and Lancashire & Yorkshire companies (competition won by

T. Mitchell of Oldham—*Building News*, xxxviii (1880), 248, 269); and
Exchange Station, Liverpool (John West of Manchester—*Builder*, xli (1881), 222).

114 See *J.T.H.*, iii (1957–8), 149–57.

115 He designed for the Eastern Counties Company its second Shoreditch terminus in 1849 (Hitchcock, op. cit., p. 524); for Ipswich see note 113 above.

116 See *J.T.H.*, vii (1965–6), 44–53.

117 Mulvany was responsible for Broadstone station, for the Midland Great Western Railway; Wood for Kingsbridge (now Heuston), for the Great Southern & Western.

118 *Works*, ed. E. T. Cook and A. Wedderburn (1903–12), XVII, pp. 389–90; XIX, pp. 25–6.

119 J. M. Wilson, *The Imperial Gazetteer of England and Wales* [Edinburgh, 1866–9], II, pp. 167–8.

120 See the plan in the *Builder*, xxix (1871), 205.

121 Wilson, *Imperial Gazetteer*, II, p. 167.

122 D. Robertson, *The Princes Street Proprietors* (1953), pp. 37–46.

123 A. J. Taylor, *Conway Castle and Town Walls* (1956), p. 43.

124 The strange story of this demolition and its sequel is summarized in J. Grant, *Cassell's Old and New Edinburgh* [1884], I, p. 290.

125 *Builder*, xxxiv (1876), 1202. Dublin had long been interested in plans for linking its five terminal stations. Twelve years earlier the Dublin Trunk Railway Connecting Act had been passed, which authorized the construction of a tunnel under the Liffey. But it had a fatal drawback: it prohibited altogether the use of steam, atmospheric, and cable power on the line. (Local and Personal Act, 27 & 28 Vict., ch. cccxxi, sect. 19.)

126 *Murray's Handbook for Wilts. and Dorset* (1899 edn), p. 524.

127 For this struggle see *Transactions of the Leicestershire Archaeological Society*, vii (1893), 222, 273; viii (1899), 133, 134, 205, 375; ix (1904–5), 6, 15, 68, 114, 152. Public access to the pavement *in situ* was guaranteed under the Company's Act: Local and Personal Act, 56 Vict., ch. i, sect. 29 (17).

128 Local and Personal Act, 27 & 28 Vict., ch. cccxii, sect. 34.

129 Local and Personal Act, 54 & 55 Vict., ch. cxcvi, sect. 69.

130 Cf. for instance the agonized complaints of a correspondent of the *Builder* concerning the use of the steam whistle on the North London Railway near Dalston Junction: xxix (1871), 291.

13   London, the Artifact

John Summerson

It must be admitted that architecture in the nineteenth-century city is a somewhat abstruse agency of emotional effect. In any age, the 'language' of architecture is an almost exclusively professional affair; in the nineteenth century, when many architectural languages came to be spoken simultaneously, often in archaic dialects, with broken accents and much rhetorical improvisation, the situation is the equivalent of an exclusive babel, architects making speeches to each other or mumbling to themselves. Nevertheless, the babel makes itself felt. It has a telling effect within the mental image of the city. Anyone calling up an image of Victorian London will have a strong sense of this obscure and complicated dialogue.

Victorian London developed through sixty-four years, undergoing striking qualitative as well as quantitative changes in its fabric. With the quantitative changes we are here less concerned than with the qualitative. The enormous increment of suburbia will not be our concern at all. We shall deal only with those questions of architectural style and taste which so conspicuously transformed the central mass of the capital. These changes are not exclusively of an aesthetic kind. They are linked with economic considerations, such as increase of height on expensive land; socioeconomic considerations like the arrival and increase of flats and office blocks; purely social considerations like the incidence of churches, schools, and infirmaries; and technological considerations, such as the exploitation of iron-frame construction, lifts, and plate-glass. All these helped to change the appearance and 'character' of

311

London between 1837 and 1901, but it is only in combination with factors of style and taste that the changes powerfully affect the image.*

In this process of change there are certain clearly marked phases of stylistic usage and they can be diagrammatically spaced at twenty-year intervals. Thus, from 1837 to 1857 there is post-Georgian eclecticism, characterized mainly by ornate Italian stucco streets, stone-built Italian club-houses, and Gothic churches. From 1857 to 1877 there is a phase of intense conflict between Italian and Gothic, accompanied by attempts to combine the two into a style appropriate to the age; stucco nearly disappears, brick, stone, and polished granite are the prevailing materials with some polychromy in tile and terracotta; street architecture becomes and remains chaotic. By 1877, the conflicts have relaxed and the next twenty years see a variety of stylistic enterprises, mostly based on English, French, Flemish, or other Renaissance schools; red brick is in high fashion, liberally combined with terracotta and a wide choice of stones. By 1897 a new phase is beginning, with the re-establishment of formal classicism on the one hand and new attempts at modernity of treatment on the other.[1]

These are some of the superficial indications of change. Before we pursue their meaning more deeply, however, there is one consideration requiring the utmost emphasis. *Victorian London was, to a very great physical extent, Georgian London*. That it was also, morphologically, Stuart and Tudor and medieval London is obvious. The point is that, whereas the buildings of those periods had mostly vanished or become curiosities, the buildings of the Georgian age survived in enormous bulk and in full use, to the extent that little of Georgian London was actually destroyed before the eighties. The only part of it which the Victorians did blot out was the City, where a steep rise in land-values made redevelopment pay. But the City was not in any case very extensively Georgian; much of it still dated from the rebuilding after the Great Fire. Further west, the great estates built up in the eighteenth and early nineteenth centuries preserved their integrity. The leasehold system put a brake on redevelopment and when ninety-nine-year leases did fall in they tended to be renewed. Only in streets where business interests strongly asserted themselves (Bond Street and Oxford Street, for instance) or where the raffish margin of an affluent estate stirred the interest of an ambitious landlord (as in Mount Street) did Georgian walls crumble,

---

* Advances in building technology made almost no visible difference to the London street-scene. The undivided plate-glass shop-window, increasingly common after 1870, was probably the most striking departure. Iron, although extensively used as an empirical substitute for brick or timber, and facilitating large uninterrupted floor-spaces, had little external effect. Building legislation consistently reflects a bricks-and-mortar mentality. The Metropolitan Building Act, 1855, insisted that openings and recesses in the fronts of buildings should not account for more than one-half the total area of the front above first floor level. This provision was carried over to the Act of 1894, thus perpetuating the idea of the solid masonry front. Iron buildings required special consent. On height, there was no restriction in the Acts of 1844 and 1855, the human capacity to mount stairs imposing a natural limitation. This being disposed of by the advent of lifts, the Act of 1894 imposed a height of eighty feet with two additional storeys in the roof and some liberty in respect of ornamental features.

and then only in the last three decades of the century. Victorian London *was* Georgian London: vastly extended, carved into by new highways, lanced by railways, elevated from its river by embankments, and sprigged with buildings new in scale and style. It was a city in which the ideas and products of one age were imposed upon and inserted into those of another.[2]

The Victorian attitude to the left-over Georgian environment needs to be defined. It was mostly and for most of the time one of utter disgust. The 'hole-in-the-wall' architecture of uniform eighteenth-century streets seemed to touch the very lowest architectural level conceivable and any opportunity of displacing some part of it was greeted with glee. Since it was rarely economic to do so, attempts were made to redeem these eyesores with adventitious ornaments. On the Bedford estate, Great Russell Street was richly stuccoed in the sixties[3] and the hated Gower Street was given heavy cement doorcases as leases fell in in the eighties.[4] When the leases of Adam's Adelphi Terrace fell in, around 1870, the opportunity was taken to add the coarsest kind of window-dressings and a gross pediment.[5] Some degree of kindness towards the earliest Georgian houses (usually identified as 'Queen Anne') does emerge with the new tide of taste in the seventies, and the cosmetic enrichment of Russell Square with terracotta dressings in 1900 is not entirely unsympathetic to the original structure. The objections to Georgian streets were their meanness, poverty of scale, and lack of 'character'. They were a standing incitement to be big, bold, and picturesque.

Notwithstanding the hatred of the Georgian, the principles of Georgian estate-development, planning, and design were for long inescapable. In fact, the whole architectural development of London from 1837 to 1857 shows so little radical change that it is more natural to think of it as a final chapter in Georgian urban history than as a period of innovation. The whole of Bayswater, from Marble Arch to Notting Hill and beyond to Shepherd's Bush; the whole of North Kensington, of South Kensington, Brompton, and Earls Court; the whole of Pimlico—all this is an overgrowth of late Georgian developed on the same leasehold system in big units and built by builders in the tradition of James Burton and of Thomas Cubitt (himself a major participant) or by ruthless captains in the building world like Sir Charles James Freake, William Jackson, and Charles Aldin, the creators of South Kensington.[6]

The Victorian houses are bigger than their Georgian equivalents but not bigger than those of Nash's Carlton House Terrace, the evident model for extreme affluence. Their layout in squares and streets and mews is no advance on eighteenth-century practice nor, in the relation of houses to their communal gardens, on what Nash had done in the grander Regent's Park terraces (Sussex or Cumberland, for instance). The ornaments, certainly, are different; they follow Sir Charles Barry's lead from severe neo-classicism to *cinquecento* revival. The fenestration of Barry's Reform Club echoes through Bayswater; the garden front of the Travellers' inspires terraces in the Ladbroke area. More lavish in the use of ornament than Barry's work ever was, these houses have nothing of his quality; with their serried ranks of windows and their ambitious height they betray too readily the builders' anxiety to exploit.[7]

Turning from estate development to 'street improvement', the impetus again is Georgian, and so indeed is the administration. Up to 1855 new streets were planned and their execution conducted by Her Majesty's Office of Works, just as Regent Street had been planned and administered by the Woods and Forests which the Office incorporated. James Pennethorne, Nash's protégé and professional legatee, was in charge. The façades in Cranbourne Street and New Oxford Street are a little different: there are fewer columns and more fancy window-dressings and sometimes a little Louis XV, even Elizabethan. But in principle they are the same.[8]

Even the railways started their careers in full sympathy with the Georgian framework. The Euston portico and lodges were nothing but an enlarged version of a type familiar as a park entrance. More than that, the portico was triumphantly placed on the great Bloomsbury axis established by an Earl of Southampton around 1660. Paddington, too, was carefully sited in 1838 in relation to the plans being prepared for the Bishop of London's estate in Bayswater. King's Cross, less happily sited, is Georgian at least to the extent that its frontispiece (sometimes mistaken for a piece of pure engineering) derives from a design in a French academic treatise.[9]

Lastly, churches. Here, certainly, there was an important displacement of Georgian practice by the new willingness to supersede state-aided church building by voluntary effort. But Bishop Blomfield, the pioneer of 'church extension', thought in statistical and political terms much as the old Commissioners had done; he even considered 'fifty new churches' as a goal, echoing a famous Act of Queen Anne.[10] Churches of the forties and fifties differ from churches of the twenties and thirties only in that the choice of style is always, instead of only sometimes, Gothic, and that the Gothic of the fifties has more of archaeology in it. The churches mostly stand on sites as well prepared for them on estate-development plans as any Commissioners' church by Nash, Smirke, or Soane.[11]

All this merely emphasizes the truth that early-Victorian London was a city which not only had a completely built-up Georgian body but also proceeded to expand from that body in a way which differed only in its superficial affluence from the practice of previous generations. Architectural innovation was in the air but scarcely yet on the ground. Architects talked of a new style but had little to show—nothing to compare in novelty with the Crystal Palace, which was not quite architecture. A few buildings, strange in style or structure, did make their appearance. In a cul-de-sac off Endell Street an obscure architect, James Wild, built a parish school in a severe version of Italian Gothic in 1849.[12] In the same year Butterfield started All Saints, Margaret Street, in red and black brick Gothic, strangely proportioned.[13] In 1851, the year of the Crystal Palace, I. K. Brunel and M. D. Wyatt tried consciously to evolve a new style for the sheds of Paddington Station.[14] There were other prophetic enterprises, but they were mere straws in the wind and London in the late fifties was still Georgian London—over-grown, over-ripe, over-rich in trite ornament. The Palace of Westminster, just approaching completion, was its great new symbol, but it was a symbol standing at the end, not the beginning, of an epoch. To despise it for its Palladian symmetry and multiplicity of corrupt ornament was a mark of sophistication. For a new epoch was already present in thought and word and in the years between 1857 and 1877 it exploded into architectural effect. The causes and nature of this explosion it is now our business to investigate.

The *causes* relate directly to the types of building on which people were prepared to spend and the opportunities available for siting such buildings. The *nature* of the explosion has more to do with architectural styles and the philosophies behind them. To draw a proper picture of Victorian London, it will not do to separate these issues. They must be taken together wherever the activities of investors, architects, and builders converge.

For concentrated redevelopment in the Victorian age there is nothing more striking than the virtual rebuilding of the central area of the City between 1857 and 1877. The transformation had indeed begun much earlier, the chief agents being the great banking-houses and, still more, the competing insurance companies, but it was around 1857 that the scramble for sites began. These businesses all required much the same sort of accommodation—and it was not very much. Vital, however, was that they should be well sited, and so the formula was quickly evolved of a large building on an important site (the sites, perhaps, of two or more old houses) in which the ground and first floor only would be occupied by the building-owner and the upper floors be profitably lettable for offices; there would be a housekeeper's flat in the roof, and boiler-room and strong-rooms or a lunch-room in the basement. The street front would be a lavish piece of Italian architecture, dedicated to the building-owner's sense of status. The interiors would comprise a handsome public hall and board-room and nothing else except space, to be subdivided at will. The formula combined convenience, prestige, and sound investment in a way which is still perfectly familiar. There still stand in the City buildings of the 1850s which differ little in type and style from their successors of the 1930s.

City architecture thus became a matter of competing, prestige-bearing façades. Many of the earlier buildings were architecture of the highest quality, like C. R. Cockerell's two works near the Bank of England.[15] Later, however, in the boom period, the City streets became a jungle of classical ornamentalism with all sorts of architects playing the Italian game with more gusto than sense. Barry's club style was the most commonly accepted basis, but devices from modern France, Sansovinesque essays in rustication, and extra flourishes of symbolic sculpture gave the City an aspect very different from that of serene Pall Mall.

Nor was the game always Italian. The new Gothic sophistication made a modest but not unnoticed entry when the Crown Life Office employed the Ruskinian partnership, Deane & Woodward, to design its headquarters in Bridge Street, Blackfriars, in 1859.[16] The lead was not immediately followed, but by 1868 the General Credit company was building in Lothbury, right opposite the Bank of England, a Venetian façade reflecting unambiguously Ruskin's plates in *The Stones of Venice*.[17]

Banks, insurance offices, and discount houses tended mostly to adhere to conventional Italian, accepted symbol of the aristocratic and secure. More latitude is noticeable in buildings put up by land-investment companies for the sole purpose of letting as offices. The 'office block' in this sense had emerged as early as 1823.[18] In 1844–5 came Royal Exchange Chambers whose architect, Edward I'Anson, was a leader in this field.[19] This was conventional enough, but he experimented with a nearly all-glass front in Fenchurch Street in 1857,[20] a fifteenth-century palazzo type in Seething Lane in 1859,[21] and a Venetian Gothic front in Cornhill in 1871.[22] Some daringly novel office blocks were built in Mark Lane in the mid-sixties, notably a smooth round-arched affair, with an all-iron interior, designed by George Aitchison, a future R.A.[23] Warehouses, too, sometimes ran to stylistic extravagance. The drapers and fancy warehousemen off Cheapside tended to prefer Italian of the most ornate kind.[24] A coarser type prevailed elsewhere, but in Thames Street, an old warehouse was re-fronted by the dedicated medievalist, William Burges, in 1866,[25] producing a type of warehouse imitated far and wide; while in Eastcheap, R. L. Roumieu built for a firm of vinegar manufacturers in 1867 a Gothic pile of extravagant absurdity and no little skill.[26]

It will be seen that from 1857 the stylistic character of City architecture began to change very fast. Before 1857 it could be said that there was scarcely a building in London which could not be accounted for by reference to some accepted school or tradition of architectural design. Within seven or eight years the whole tendency had changed. In 1864, George Gilbert Scott, surveying the scene with the lofty detachment of a Gothic master, delivered himself of the following:[27]

> There has . . . been no end to the oddities introduced. Ruskinism, such as would make Ruskin's very hair stand on end; Butterfieldism, gone mad with its endless stripings of red and black bricks; architecture so French that a Frenchman would not know it . . . Byzantine in all forms but those used by the Byzantians; mixtures of all or some of these; 'original' varieties founded upon knowledge of old styles, or ignorance of them, as the case may be; violent strainings after a something very strange, and great successes in producing something very weak; attempts at beauty resulting in ugliness, and attempts at ugliness attended with unhoped-for success.

Scott did not direct this diatribe especially towards the City, but for each of his gibes some City building, built before 1864, could be found to fit—not, perhaps, among the more costly buildings, in one of the better streets, or under the name of a known architect. An important aspect of Victorian architecture is the development of a class of architect with a temperamental reluctance to attach himself to any stylistic school and a certain aptitude for improvisation. There were a great many architects in this class, for which the politest name is the 'latitudinarian'.[28] They were not all bad architects, and their works constitute a very large proportion of the building product of the capital.

The boom period in the City's rebuilding tailed off in the late seventies and in its last years there was a slackening of stylistic competitiveness and a general acceptance of any style which any architect cared to bring along. This was partly due to the shock administered by one particular building—an office block in Leadenhall Street called New Zealand Chambers, designed by Richard Norman Shaw in 1873.[29] Here, for the first time, the turn of taste characteristic of the seventies intruded into the City. New Zealand Chambers went back to the rude vernacular of the early seventeenth century, with red-brick piers, peasant ornaments, and huge, luminous bay-windows. The architectural profession was shocked, but the well-lit floor-space let instantly at high rents, and Shaw's artistry soon reconciled the younger generation of architects to a brilliantly perverse choice of style.

New Zealand Chambers marks a turning-point in City architecture, and indeed in business architecture generally, because of its lack of stylistic seriousness; it was totally disloyal both to the Italian school and to the Gothic. Also, it came at a moment when classical banks and insurance offices were in sharp decline and City building consisted almost entirely of 'business premises' either for private firms or investment companies, mostly in the smaller streets. After Shaw, and in this context, all liberties could be taken. In 1878 gabled Flemish warehouses arrived in Wood Street[30] and in 1882 Ernest George & Peto were much praised for some brick buildings in Cheapside which would not have looked out of place in Bruges.[31] The *style François 1er* appeared in London Wall in 1880,[32] in Cornhill in 1881,[33] and was found extremely practical by the type of architect who believed that in City offices light was the biggest selling factor—which it obviously was.

In reviewing the rebuilding of the City we have been looking at the one really concentrated episode in the making of Victorian London—concentrated within a small area and within a period of no more than twenty years. There was no other concentration quite of this kind. To observe the progress of architecture outside the City the best course is to follow the formation of new highways. New highways necessarily brought new building-sites into the market and these sites were an invitation to business and residential projects of new kinds. The development of London architecture, both as to types and styles, is thus bound up with and richly illustrated by the buildings which these new thoroughfares attracted.

Victoria Street, Westminster, was the first new street created outside the control of the Office of Works.[34] It was formed by Commissioners under a series of Acts, the first of which was passed in 1845. Among the earliest buildings was a block of flats—the first middle-class flats in London—built by Henry Ashton for a Scottish developer and completed in 1853.[35] This pioneer block is, as one would expect from the date, much in the style of Bayswater or South Kensington and not bad of its kind. Unsuccessful at first in attracting tenants, it did succeed in planting the notion of flat-building firmly in the Victoria area of London; and there the idea grew. Belgrave Mansions, in a smart Parisian style, came in 1867,[36] with Albert Mansions rushed up alongside by 1870, in 'latitudinarian' Italian.[37] Hankey's shameless ten-storey enterprise, Queen Anne's Mansions, stood itself up in no style at all in 1874,[38] and from then on till the end of the century one block of flats followed another along the length of the street and in its lateral connections.

A characteristic of Victoria Street was the availability of sites of uncommonly long frontage. This facilitated economies of scale in various types of project. Thus, at the east end of the street a monster hotel and a monster block of offices were undertaken. The Westminster Palace Hotel[39]—the first of its size not projected by a railway company—was an immediate success; technically in advance of anything of its kind, its elevations were in a scraggy French style which the architect hoped 'would possess at least some indication of "high art"'. The long and monotonous office block—Westminster Chambers[40]—was financed by a tontine; though designed by one of Sir Charles Barry's sons, it displayed little more 'high art' than the hotel. Indeed, 'high art' was conspicuously absent from Victoria Street, a street of undertakings too anxiously calculated on the economic plane to admit serious thought about aesthetics.

The formation of new highways was vigorously pursued when, in 1855, the Metropolitan Board of Works took over from the Office of Works the responsibility for street improvements.[41] The responsibility was limited, for the Metropolitan Board of Works was never a planning body, nor did it ever assume more than a very superficial control of architectural design. So, as the new streets emerged and the lots of surplus land were taken up, strange assortments of façade architecture came upon the scene. In Garrick Street we have the Garrick Club,[42] in ponderous Italian, on one side of the street (1861) and, on the other side, a quaint Gothic stained-glass factory by A. W. Blomfield (1861).[43] In Southwark Street, cut through the poor district west of the Borough, we have the sensationally mannered Hop Exchange at the east end (designed by an architect who was one of the shareholders) followed by a long succession of warehouses, some very well designed, illustrating the whole gamut of brick polychromy.[44]

The M.B.W.'s most majestic achievement in the creation of new thoroughfares was, of course, the Thames Embankment.[45] This was not only a monumental achievement in itself but also the container for one of the cross sewers in Bazalgette's drainage system and the carrier of a major new highway. Furthermore, it led immediately to the construction of two other highways—one, linking the embankment to the Mansion House, called Queen Victoria Street; the other, linking the embankment to Charing Cross, called Northumberland Avenue. These three highways created together a new route from the City to the West End and, in the process, made available an amplitude of building sites, nearly all of which were occupied by the mid-eighties. The whole sequence, from Mansion House to Charing Cross, was, up to 1935, a continuously representative parade of Victorian architectural performance. The contents of the three highways are functionally very different. Queen Victoria Street, cutting through the City, necessarily attracted speculators in office accommodation. At the other end, Northumberland Avenue became almost entirely occupied by hotels and clubs. The Victoria Embankment developed miscellaneously. Here, the M.B.W. had no surplus land to dispose of, but by vastly enhancing the value of the land adjacent, it set the scene for a long riverside succession of expensive building enterprises.

If we glance down the lengths of these three connecting thoroughfares we get a pretty strong impression of what was going on in metropolitan architecture between 1870 (when the first buildings went up in Queen Victoria Street) and 1885 (the approximate date of completion of Northumberland Avenue). At the City end, in Queen Victoria Street, we find a few solidly competent blocks, characteristic of the sixties, alongside wildly experimental works, conditioned by a determination to combine optimum fenestration with vigorous stylistic exercises, both Gothic and Italian.[46]

The Victoria Embankment gives us a succession of monuments of wonderfully diverse sizes, shapes, and styles. No two of them seem to have anything in common. There are the academic French of the City of London School;[47] the English Perpendicular of Sion College;[48] the Elizabethan of the Astor Estate Office;[49] the Tudor of the houses on the Norfolk estate;[50] and, further west, the French Renaissance of Whitehall Court and the National Liberal Club;[51] the more or less pure François 1er of the St Stephen's Club;[52] and the French-Dutch-English mixture of New Scotland Yard.[53] All these are still standing. Missing are the School Board Offices (François 1er)[54] and the Hotel Cecil (modern Parisian).[55] These two, as it happens, were the earliest and latest in date (1875 and 1895 respectively). The whole assemblage is strangely unconvincing and raises all sorts of questions about the types of architects at large in London at this period and the nature of their stylistic persuasions and philosophies. When we come to Northumberland Avenue the same questions intrude themselves. The Society for the Promotion of Christian Knowledge building belongs to Italianism of the City type,[56] but next to it is a monster hotel in a very smart Parisian style.[57] Opposite, there stood until recently a large club in a felicitous blend of Jacobean and Flemish Renaissance.

If we go further in pursuit of new architecture in new streets we come to Shaftesbury Avenue, built up between 1879 and 1886. Here is a mixture of Renaissance improvisations in red brick, terracotta, and stone, exhibiting marked incompetence. The reasons for this are readily accessible. The M.B.W.'s policy of buying as little marginal land as possible had the effect of creating wholly inadequate sites; these were taken by wholly inadequate developers employing wholly inadequate architects. Before Shaftesbury Avenue was finished, the inadequacy of the M.B.W. itself had been exposed and it sank in a morass of scandal, to be superseded by the L.C.C.[58]

From Shaftesbury Avenue we may proceed to Charing Cross Road. Here we witness the effects of a crisis brought about by a statutory injunction on the M.B.W. to rehouse the victims of 'improvement' near the sites of their homes. The street was thus channelled for part of its course through meanly fenestrated cliffs of cheap working-class tenements. The remaining parts, shambling along into the nineties, are little improvement upon Shaftesbury Avenue.[59]

Much discredit attaches to the 'improvements' conducted by the M.B.W., an inadequate and, in its last phase, corrupt body. In contrast, the City Corporation conducted a series of operations within, and also without, its own boundaries which contributed honourably to the changing character of London. Within the City, King William Street and Moorgate were already appearing in well-dressed stucco at the

319

beginning of the reign. Between 1846 and 1854 Cannon Street was extended westward. In 1847–9 came the Coal Exchange,[60] in 1850–3 Billingsgate Market[61] (rebuilt 1874), in 1867–8 Smithfield Meat Market[62] and, outside the City, in 1851–5, the Metropolitan Cattle Market.[63] All these were buildings of picturesque Italianate monumentality, the creation of the City's architects, J. B. Bunning and, after him, (Sir) Horace Jones. Other imposing City improvements were the construction, under the engineer to the Commissioners of Sewers, of Holborn Viaduct[64] and, concurrently, the rebuilding of Blackfriars Bridge by Joseph Cubitt.[65] Both were opened in 1869. Like so much Victorian engineering they were architecturally adorned by anonymous hands, the pillared piers of the bridge paying rich tribute to *The Stones of Venice*. Twelve years later the City was to sponsor Tower Bridge, magnificently if perversely engineered and clothed in absurd and outdated Gothic.[66]

The fact must be accepted that much of the architectural product of Victorian London was at a desperately low level. But whether the level of performance be low or high there is still the problem of the appearance and effect of these buildings—the styles they adopted, their sources, their varieties, and idioms. What are they and whence do they issue?

The answers must be sought in the new attitudes emerging in the architectural profession in the early seventies. These are attitudes both towards style and towards opportunity—attitudes adopted at first among the artistic élite of the profession and then spreading outwards towards its more or less illiterate fringes. Style and opportunity are of necessity closely linked. The Gothic Revival would not have succeeded to any extent had it not been linked with the High Church movement and with a widespread social and philanthropic drive towards the architectural rehabilitation of the established church. The momentum in this field was much reduced by 1870 and with it the chief incentives towards Gothic designing. Intelligent young architects of the 1870s saw ahead of them a widening range of opportunities in which churches played a diminishing part. The problem of Gothic for modern secular purposes was one which had never been happily solved; the competition for the new Law Courts in 1866–7 merely underlined the anomalies it involved, and the indirect outcome of that competition, Street's great Gothic composition in the Strand, was considered, even before it was finished, as the swan-song of the Revival.

The shift towards new stylistic attitudes is first observable in a particular sector of the domestic field—the house of the well-to-do artist, architect, or art-patron. We can witness the whole development in houses which are still for the most part standing, in Kensington and Hampstead. The house built for Val Prinsep by Philip Webb in Holland Park in 1864—a little brick house like a country vicarage—is said to have started the series.[67] Webb's house for George Howard in Palace Green (1868) still stands[68] but J. J. Stevenson's clever and important vulgarization of the same theme in Bayswater Road has gone.[69] Norman Shaw comes into the series with Lowther Lodge, Kensington Gore, in 1873, and from that date he is unquestionably the leading architect of the movement. His houses for artists in Melbury Road, Kensington, and Fitzjohn's Avenue, Hampstead, in Queen's Gate, Kensington, and on the

258 Threadneedle Street. On left, Imperial
Insurance Office (John Gibson, 1848); in the
centre, Bank of Australia (P. C. Hardwick, 1854).
From *Illustrated London News*, xxvi (1855), 144.

259 National Discount Company,
Cornhill (Francis Bros, 1858).
Photo: Timothy Summerson

260 City Bank, Threadneedle Street (Moseley,
1857).
Photo: Timothy Summerson

261 Nos 59–61 Mark Lane (George Aitchison,
1864).
National Monuments Record

262 Design for General Credit Company, Lothbury (G. Somers Clarke, 1868), from *Building News*, xv (1868), 11.

STAIRCASE WINDOWS.

UPPER STAIRCASE WINDOWS AND CORNICE.

PLAN.

ONE STORY DIVIDED INTO TWO SEPARATE DWELLINGS.

263 Flats, Victoria Street (Henry Ashton, 1853), from *Builder*, xi (1853), 722.

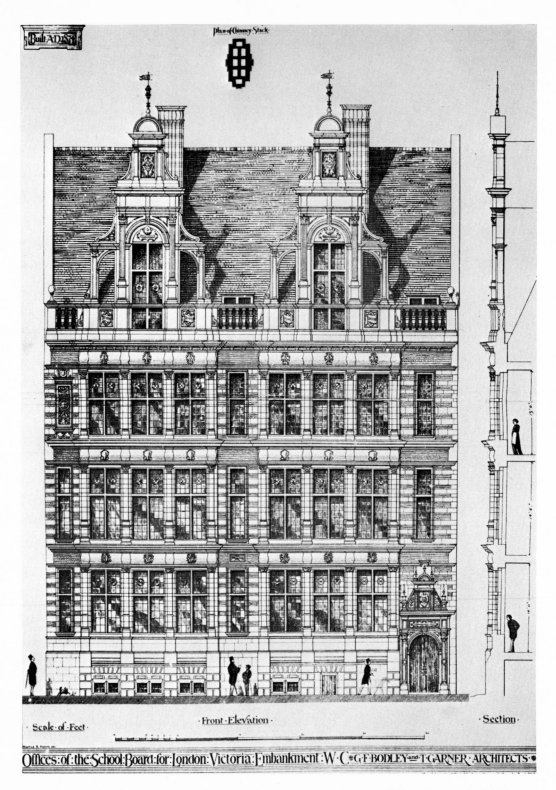

Built A.D. 1874

Plan of Chimney Stack

· Scale of Feet ·   · Front · Elevation ·   · Section ·

Offices: of: the: School: Board: for: London: Victoria: Embankment: W.C. & G.F.BODLEY and T.GARNER ARCHITECTS

264 The London School Board Offices (G. F. Bodley, 1874), from *Building News*, xxix (1875), 14–15.

SAUNTERINGS IN SOUTHWARK STREET.

AN impartial observer, a "looker-on in Vienna," if called on to choose a field for the display of collective architectural talent, would unhesitatingly select Southwark-street. The *tabula rasa* produced by the demolition of obsolete buildings, and the construction of the noble thoroughfare from Blackfriars Bridge to the Borough has offered a "fair occasion" for various architects to show their metal. That the metal should have, in all cases, the genuine ring is scarcely to be expected. There is alloy in all of the specimens, and pure pinchbeck, if the term be allowable, in too many. Asmodeus did not accompany us; nothing beyond the general appearance of the elevations can therefore be described in these notes. Crossing Blackfriars, and passing under the railway bridge, leaving the quaint old almshouses of good Charles Hopton on the left, the first building encountered is the immense store of Messrs. Tait and Co., army contractors. This building was illustrated in the BUILDING NEWS, No. 589, and will therefore be but cursorily noticed at present. The architect was Mr. R. P. Pope. It is distinguished by a liberal use of colour, and even gilding, but the effect is peculiar. Over the ground and first-floor windows are about eight courses of pseudo-reticulated glazed red and green bricks, and it is needless to say that the contrast is too violent for a building of otherwise sober

FIG. 1.

colour. Again, the use of black—or, rather, artificially blackened—brick in the form of labels to windows and doors is most objectionable. In the present instance it makes the building appear as if in mourning, and the too free introduction of black tiles in the frieze of the cornice heightens the indications of woe. What connection there can be be-

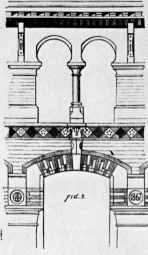

FIG. 2.

tween an army contractor's establishment and a family mourning depôt we cannot see. It is true that a pursuit of reputation in the career of arms may occasionally be effectively checked, but from the time when the Venetians furnished supplies to the Crusaders to the days of Cloncurry—or, for that matter, to this year of grace—army contractors have had little occasion to make a moan. Why, then, this "suit of sables?" From the south-

east a good view is obtained of the tower over the staircase, and from this point the building is seen to the greatest advantage, the management of the tower being really artistic. The material is, for the most part, yellow brick, with a little red Mansfield stone in the form

FIG. 3.

1867

of dressing. There is, however, an unreasonable mixture of noble with mean material. Common yellow bricks, Mansfield stone, glazed bricks, gilding, white stone—either Portland, white Mansfield, or some similar stone—encaustic tiles, polished granite shafts, elaborately carved caps, and a dismal bordering of black brick, a bordering such as the well-dowered widow orders to be put on her writing paper (see fig. 1), which shows one of the window heads.

The next building on the same side of the

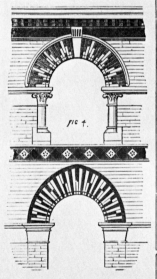

FIG 4.

street is the warehouse of Messrs. Causton and Sons, stationers. The utilitarian character of this building is so plainly indicated by its external appearance that criticism would be

disarmed were it not that a display of festivity, in the guise of carving, has been attempted over the first-floor windows. Carving, if attempted, should be good of its kind. This is bad of its kind. Ill-designed and coarsely executed, it disfigures a building which should

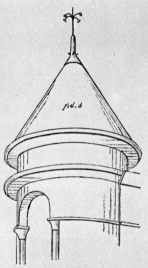

FIG. 5.

certainly not court attention. The jointing of the basement window heads is what we have ever protested against. A joint in the centre of a segmental or circular arch is neither conformable to recondite theory nor rule of thumb practice. The balcony over the entrance door, not yet fixed, may do something for the building, but the

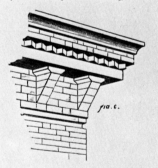

FIG. 6.

trusses already in place are of very uncouth form. The frontage is about 108 feet. Mr. Saunders, Finsbury Pavement, is the architect. On the same side of the way a warehouse is in course of erection for Messrs. Lawson and Co., seed merchants; Mr. J. Wimble, No. 2, Walbrook, being architect. So little progress has been made that beyond recording the fact that the first-floor joists are laid, nothing need be said at present. Immediately opposite, and in an unfinished state, is a warehouse for Messrs. Waite, Barnett, and Co., also seed merchants; Mr. Edis, architect. It is of yellow brick, and very plain in its present state, as the ornamentation is to be in stucco. The third-floor joists are not yet laid, so that it is not easy to say what will be its appearance when finished. It has a frontage of about 65ft., and a height of 50ft., enough for the display of a good deal of architectural skill. The contractors are Messrs. Sandon

266 *left*   New Zealand
Chambers (R. Norman Shaw,
1873).
National Monuments Record

267 *above right*   Northumber-
land Avenue. The S.P.C.K.
building between the Hotel
Metropole (left) and the
Northumberland Avenue (later,
Victoria) Hotel, 1883–4.
Photo: G. W. Wilson
Aberdeen University Library

268 *below right*   Albert Build-
ings, Queen Victoria Street
(F. J. Ward, 1871).
National Monuments Record

269 *left* The Hotel Cecil,
designed by Perry & Reed
and opened in 1886.
*Photo: Bedford Lemere
National Monuments Record*

270 *right* The Red House,
Bayswater Road
(J. J. Stevenson, 1871).
National Monuments Record

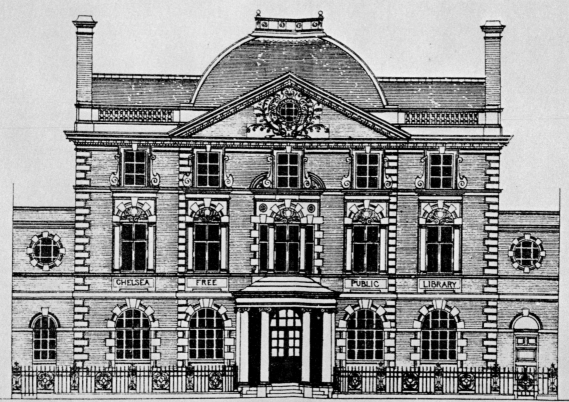

CHELSEA FREE PUBLIC LIBRARY

271 *above left* Lowther Lodge, Kensington Gore (R. Norman Shaw, 1873), from *Building News*, xxviii (1875), following 716.

272 *left* Design for Chelsea Public Library (J. M. Brydon), from *Building News*, lvi (1889), 802–3.

273 *above* British Museum of Natural History (Alfred Waterhouse, 1873–80), from *Builder*, xxxi (1873), 10–11.

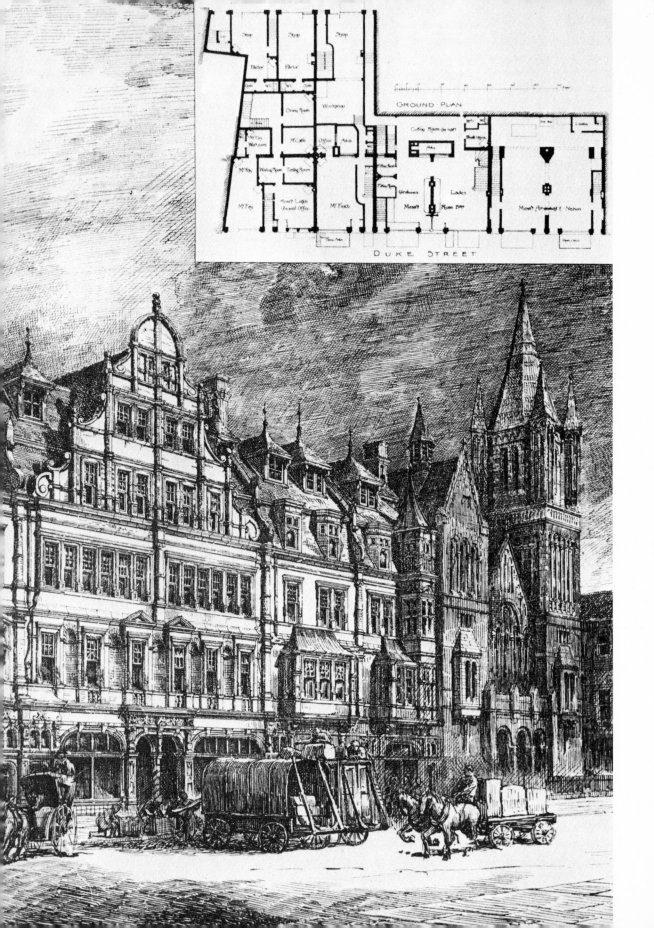

274 *left* Business premises, Duke Street (W. D. Caröe, 1891), from *Building News*, lx (1891), 238–9.

275 *right* No. 1 Old Bond Street (Alfred Waterhouse, 1881).
National Monuments Record

276 *below right* Grosvenor Hotel (James Knowles, 1860–1).
National Monuments Record

277 *above left*   Albert Hall
Mansions (R. Norman Shaw,
1881).
B. T. Batsford Ltd

278 *left*   Palace Theatre,
formerly British Opera House
(T. E. Collcutt, 1891).
Photo: Bedford Lemere
National Monuments Record

279 *above*   Royal Albert Hall
(Capt. Fowke and General
Scott, 1867–71).
Photo: Timothy Summerson

280 Imperial Institute, South Kensington
(T. E. Collcutt, 1887–91).
National Monuments Record

Chelsea Embankment; his block of flats (Albert Hall Mansions); his famous office block in the City (New Zealand Chambers); his insurance office in Pall Mall—all these established him as by far the most influential architect of the last quarter of the century.[70] Just as Sir Charles Barry's Italian was the source of so much in the stylistic flavour of London of the forties, fifties and sixties, so the Renaissance of Norman Shaw pervades the London street-scenes of the later period.

What exactly was the nature of this revolution in taste emerging from the affluent circles of artists and art-patrons around 1870? It was a revolution away from the Gothic Revival and the 'battle of the styles'; away from church architecture as the central theme in architectural practice and towards domestic and social programmes; away from scholarly reference in design and towards complete freedom of handling. The new attachments to history were neither to textbook Gothic nor textbook Classical, but to the in-between vernaculars which had no textbooks. Indeed, a quite distinct new vernacular was created and given the curiously misleading title of 'Queen Anne'. From the early seventies 'Queen Anne' signified buildings usually of common brown and special red brick ornamented in the bourgeois style of the English seventeenth century and with gables and dormers moving in a Flemish direction. It was really a Renaissance revival—indeed, the term 're-renaissance' was suggested at the time as a more accurate designation than 'Queen Anne'—as indeed it would have been.[71] The metamorphoses of 'Queen Anne' are the clue to nearly all the architecture of London from the seventies to the nineties. The style incited no real antagonisms and the only architects who held away from it were those who felt a greater security (often for business reasons) in conventional Italianism and 'modern French'.

This revolution in taste coincides with changes in the responsibilities and opportunities open to architects brought about by the increased wealth of the professional classes and the tendency of the second generation of successful families to bring the arts into their lives and homes. It coincides also with a new proliferation of building types. Alfred Waterhouse, in a speech of 1883, observed that, whereas a few years earlier an architect's practice would embrace simply town and country houses, City buildings, churches, and the occasional public building, now, at the date at which he was speaking, it would embrace a whole multiplicity of types.[72] He gives a list, reflecting his own wide field of activity, but it falls far short of the reality as reflected, for instance, in the building journals of the time. Waterhouse very perceptively related the proliferation of types to the change in style which we have just been considering. He said that *style* (in the abstract sense associated with personal artistry) was now the thing, not *styles*. In other words, choice of this or that style from the past was less important than the way in which any style or mixture of styles was handled. Complexity of types demanded flexibility and richness in the architect's vocabulary, not rhetorical statement. Flexibility and richness are what the architecture of late Victorian London unambiguously reflects.

It was not only that building types were proliferating. The planning of each type was becoming more complex and so was the structure; so was the provision of

services. Structural ironwork; lifts; fire-proofing the high buildings which lifts facilitated; the improvement and elaboration of sanitary equipment; heating and ventilation; and, latterly, electric lighting: the architect had to deal with all these, and in
doing so saw himself as a different sort of professional from the man who built only
churches, vicarages, and village schools, building them in the way in which they
would have been built fifty or a hundred years before, and worrying mainly about
pillar mullions and plate-tracery, symmetry, or the picturesque. .

The proliferation of building types must not be taken to imply the introduction
of positively new building-functions so much as the assumption by various classes of
building of a new typological importance. Here, one of the most striking instances is
that of the schools built by the London School Board after the Education Act of
1870. Schools of various kinds had been built in London for many years, mainly in
association with churches. Their accommodation was primitive, their architectural
style often picturesque. Until the School Board came into being it had been nobody's
business to study the school as a type and to consider what principles were involved
in, for instance, daylighting, heating, hygiene, and educational equipment. E. R.
Robson, the Board's first architect, undertook to study these things and produced an
admirable book on the subject in 1872.[73] He was also the designer, with his partner,
J. J. Stevenson, of many of the early Board Schools. For these, the style of Stevenson's own Red House, in the Bayswater Road, was adopted. It was, of course, the
'Queen Anne' style, and the style characterized London Board Schools till near the
end of the century. A 'Robson School' with its great windows, high Flemish gables,
and dainty brickwork is still a familiarly repetitive London landmark. It was a new
and exciting accent in the London sky-line of the seventies.

The Board Schools were immediate products of social legislation and in that
respect are symptomatic of a tendency which is increasingly reflected in the London
architecture of the eighties and nineties. The Metropolitan Poor Act of 1867 engen-
dered grim, grey, towered infirmaries and led, in due course, to the great suburban
hospital layouts for which the Sick Asylums Boards were responsible in the nineties.
Architecturally and typologically more important are some of the building enterprises of the vestries. The vestries were not overloaded with building responsibilities,
but there were buildings for which they had statutory powers to borrow money if
prodded into doing so by their electors. From 1846 they had, like every authority in
the country, powers to build public baths and wash-houses. The idea of public baths
had been to raise the standard of hygiene among the grubbier sections of the population, but the notion that swimming could be a healthy recreation for all had reached
England by the eighties. Lewisham built an establishment with first- and second-
class swimming baths in 1885;[74] other vestries followed in rapid succession. They got
bigger and bigger, and the Lambeth establishment of 1897, with four swimming-
baths, ninety-six slipper-baths and provision for sixty-four washers was reckoned to
be the biggest in Europe.[75] There was some fumbling with architectural style as the
new type emerged. Lewisham's building was in the *démodé* Gothic of the seventies,
Hampstead's was Queen Anne in front with a hammer-beam roof over the bath.[76]

But a handful of specialists soon evolved a satisfactory compromise between style and efficiency, just as Robson and his colleagues had done in the case of schools. And the style was always more or less 'Queen Anne'.

From 1850, the vestries could build free libraries, but built very few indeed until the nineties, when the new literacy of the first Board School generation required them and they came with a rush. Unlike public baths, they could not be made to pay and the reluctant vestries rarely proceeded without philanthropic subventions from such men as Henry Tate and John Passmore Edwards.[77] Architectural performance was variable but sometimes ran high, as in E. W. Mountford's library in Battersea,[78] J. M. Brydon's in Chelsea,[79] a neo-Georgian pioneer, and Henry Wilson's sensational free Gothic escapade in Paddington.[80]

The rising importance of architecture in the public sector is one of the significant features of the period after 1870. Its products are necessarily less conspicuous, however, than building in certain other sectors, especially those in which investment was the main incentive. What we may broadly call the investment sector includes a wide range of types: business premises of all kinds, blocks of flats, hotels, theatres and music-halls, restaurants, and public-houses. The religious and philanthropic sector is scarcely less important, with a vast production of churches and chapels on the one hand and the extensive development of philanthropic or semi-philanthropic industrial housing on the other, to which should be added a certain number of hospitals. Finally, the institutional sector includes clubs, the headquarters of professional bodies, and privately or corporately owned schools and colleges; the products of the Polytechnic movement of the nineties may appropriately be placed in this category.

Each of these many types has its own architectural history and its own peculiar engagement with the question of style. Rarely indeed is there any consistent association of type and style such as we found in the case of the Board Schools and such as we should find again if we were to look at London churches after 1870. On the other hand the general stylistic character of London advances with the development of the more important types, and to some of these we may give cursory attention before proceeding to general conclusions.

Clearly, it is in the investment sector that the ubiquitous and most manifest changes occur, blocks of flats, business premises, and hotels being of outstanding effect. Of flats and their adolescence in and around Victoria Street something has already been said. The first architecturally original block of flats was Norman Shaw's brilliant, but perhaps extravagant, Albert Hall Mansions of 1881, with its great Dutch gables and recessed balconies, and dwellings ingeniously planned on two levels.[81] Thereafter, flats were rarely placed in the hands of architects of major talent and reputation. The first large block after Shaw's was Whitehall Court (1884) where the firm of Archer & Green looked to early French Renaissance (the lost Château de Madrid in particular) for a way of controlling a huge cellular mass and giving it animation and a silhouette.[82] But the later monster blocks are, for the most part, either mechanical solutions made more or less acceptable by a conventional distribution of cornices, or vulgar concoctions by architects of a very low type working with builders who were often themselves the developers. Stylistic improvisations based on 'Queen Anne' with strong infusions from Norman Shaw's private vocabulary are the typical product. One trouble about flats was that they depended for success on a good address. Suburban flats were unknown, except in Battersea, till after 1900.[83] So investment in flats meant the grabbing of central sites and the piling on to them of as much as the Building Acts would permit. In the nineties, Cavendish Square, Hanover Square, Berkeley Square, and Kensington Square were all broken into by blocks of flats. The destruction of Georgian London had begun.

'Business premises', that vague denomination which usually signifies a combination of lettable offices and shops, but may also include flats or multi-storey show-rooms, began to change the character of the West End in the seventies. Successful shopkeepers, content before with show-windows in an old house or a clutch of old houses, now tended to rebuild their entire premises with ample provision for office- or flat-letting as an investment and, very naturally, in as fashionable a style as possible. Marshall and Snelgrove rebuilt a large block in Oxford Street for their drapery business as early as 1878, but drearily, in bad French;[84] 'Queen Anne' and the gay red of Farnham bricks had not yet arrived. Oxford Street only changed colour in the eighties. In Bond Street, the quaint windows of Norman Shaw's New Zealand Chambers found a ready imitator in 1876,[85] and in the same year Robert Edis rebuilt a shop at the corner of Brook Street with a tile-hung gable, the first of its kind in Central London.[86] Here were country manners coming shockingly into the smart West End. In Piccadilly, which up to the seventies had had a soberly institutional character, Waterhouse's shop at the corner of Bond Street[87] must have dazzled in 1881 with its cheerfully decorative terracotta. Wigmore Street was transformed by Collcutt, Ernest George, and others;[88] while on the Grosvenor estate 'Renaissance' flourished as nowhere else, with Ernest George's François 1er, Robert Edis's Dutch, and 'Queen Anne' mixtures by Thomas Verity, Wimperis, and others making a regular gallery of re-births in Mount Street,[89] while in Duke Street the blocks flanking Waterhouse's King's Weighhouse Chapel show W. D. Caröe at work with what is perhaps Danish Renaissance (1891).[90] The quality architecture of the Victorian West End cannot be better appraised than by probing this concentrated collection.

Among the most substantial and visually prominent enterprises in Victorian London were the hotels. The large hotel was the creation of the railways, and Paddington was the first (1852–3).[91] Incorporating some French ideas in the programme, the architect gave it a stucco front on the lines of a *hôtel de ville*. The next monster was the French-styled Westminster Palace Hotel, already mentioned as an important component of the new Victoria Street.[92] This was followed in 1860–1 by the London Chatham & Dover Railway's Grosvenor Hotel at the other end of the street. By this date the railway hotel was seen to have become a portent; it was 'one of those striking conceptions which distinctively mark the civilization of the age' and the Grosvenor with its bigness of scale and liberality of ornament (with busts of the Queen's prime ministers) played this role with conscious success.[93] In the early sixties came two more railway hotels, at Charing Cross[94] and Cannon Street,[95] and also the Langham, on the site of an old house and grounds in Langham Place.[96] The emerging type was a massive and ornate brick-and-stone block with high French roofs (for staff accommodation) and corner pavilions. At St Pancras (1865–72)[97] the Midland departed into something different at the Gothic hands of Sir Gilbert Scott, but the Holborn Viaduct Hotel strongly re-established the 'modern French' idea in 1874.[98] The same architects (Isaacs & Florence, the latter Paris-trained) designed the best of the three great hotels in Northumberland Avenue.[99] Again, in the Carlton[100] and the Cecil (1895)[101] the French idea prevailed, but the last years of Victoria's reign saw free Renaissance at the Great Central[102] and, in Russell Square, two exuberant Renaissance outbursts—the Russell and the Imperial, the latter a Baltic fantasy with a strong infusion of *art nouveau*.[103]

Among types in what may broadly be called the investment sector none had anything like the size or architectural effrontery of the hotels. The creation of 'theatre-land', by the exploitation of sites offering themselves during the formation of Shaftesbury Avenue and Charing Cross Road, is a phenomenon more striking socially than visually. Theatre designing was in the hands of a few specialist architects (notably C. J. Phipps and Walter Emden) who contributed little to the street-scene beyond weakly conventional 'modern French' or commercial 'Queen Anne'. The one remarkable late Victorian theatre is Collcutt's British Opera House (now the Palace Theatre) in Cambridge Circus (1891), a Plateresque study in brick and terracotta;[104] but Collcutt did not plan the theatre—merely overlaid the structure with his idiosyncratic art. Restaurants make a number of sharply accented contributions without developing a type. There is Pimm's Restaurant (now no longer such), a ludicrously mannered front in Poultry[105]—the first rationalized City chop-house (1870); and in Piccadilly still stands the Criterion (1874), a highly elaborate enterprise of Spiers and Pond where Thomas Verity enclosed behind his *cinquecento* façade a whole world of dining-halls, grills, bars and buffets, dives and saloons, with an art gallery at the top and a theatre in the basement.[106] The great restaurants of the eighties and nineties—the Holborn, Romano's, Frascati's, and the Trocadero—never quite competed with this, though each had its stylistic singularity. Descending from restaurants to public-houses, we can observe departures in various directions from the pre-1870 convention that a public-house was simply an over-decorated version of a common London house, preferably on a street corner. The pubs which today are regarded as being enjoyable by reason of their uninhibited vulgarity mostly belong to the eighties and nineties; their exteriors are, in fact, largely made up of assorted thefts from Norman Shaw and 'modern French'.

This almost entirely random inspection of types within the investment sector alone is perhaps sufficient to indicate the kind of complexity with which an analyst of late Victorian London's visual image has to deal. The question now arises whether the apparent chaos of the stylistic scene can be reduced to some coherent order. If it can, the main clue to it is to be found in the study of the architectural profession. From being a fairly small body in the 1830s, numbering probably fewer than a hundred, the profession in London was said to number 1,114 in the census of 1851 and had reached nearly 2,000 by 1871. At this date it was a grossly inflated, ill-defined, and badly under-educated professional category, dependent for leadership on a few brilliant men who formed that élite to whose reforming agency reference has already been made. The élite was a constellation rather than a group, and from the major figures there was constant devolution to lesser men and lesser constellations. Furthermore, there were architects who stood away from the main sources of influence, holding to old-fashioned ideas and bringing them out in new guises. And there was always the rabble of hacks, ghosts, and incompetents of all sorts, cribbing and corrupting the performances of their betters.

Philip Webb,[107] J. J. Stevenson, Norman Shaw, and Waterhouse were the rising constellation of the seventies. All born in 1830 or 1831, they powerfully changed the face of London. They changed its style through their new attitudes to the past. They changed its colour by changing its materials: from brown brick to brown and red, then to red; from Portland stone to granite or Mansfield or to red or buff terracotta. A second constellation followed when men born around 1840 came into full practice in the eighties. In the hands of Ernest George, R. W. Edis, and T. E. Collcutt, the 'Queen Anne' liberalism was diffused into a variety of northern Renaissances—French, Flemish, and Dutch, and even Spanish Plateresque, while J. M. Brydon turned 'Queen Anne' into a truly historical George I, thus promoting the return to Wrennian and Gibbsian classicism which was one of the directions taken at the end of the century.

An analysis of the whole architectural content of London as it stood in 1901 would show an overwhelming indebtedness to these names. Furthermore, if the work and influence of the 'constellations' could be detached from its context and considered in isolation, we should have before us an entirely consistent pattern of stylistic growth and performance. London, however, gave room and opportunity for much else. Conspicuously, there is the 'modern French' school allied with the Italian conservatism of Barry's time (mainly represented in the work of his sons, Charles and Edward M.), operating at a somewhat conventional, though usually affluent level. And in the church-building world there are still the protagonists of Gothic, like G. F. Bodley and A. W. Blomfield and, later, J. P. Sedding and J. F. Bentley, running parallel with our two constellations and, in their secular works, showing no aversion to 'Queen Anne' and her progeny. Indeed, Bodley's headquarters for the London School Board, an early and well-informed interpretation of François 1er, was instanced by J. J. Stevenson, in a lecture of 1874, as a good example of the 'Queen Anne' school!

At this stage, it may well have occurred to the reader that in the course of a fairly lengthy discussion of London types and styles not a single building of national status, built by the central government or built to incorporate national sentiment, has received more than passing mention. The omission is natural and reflects an important truth about Victorian London. Whatever may have been the case in provincial towns, where vast town-halls and exchanges arose amid general applause, in the capital the history of major public buildings is, to an astonishing extent, a history of governmental parsimony, ill-conducted competitions, and results which were either roundly condemned or soon forgotten. The loss of esteem of the Palace of Westminster was noted earlier. In 1856 came the fiasco of the Government Offices competition, and if, in the outcome, a reasonably good work of the Italian school emerged at the hands of Gilbert Scott, it is not one that counts for much in the history of English architecture. The Law Courts competition was a notorious administrative disaster and Street's eventual building, cramped in site and cost, makes a sad cadence to the Gothic adventure.[108] The Admiralty competition of 1884 was badly assessed, the award going to architects of slight calibre and a design outside the main creative currents of the time.[109] Meanwhile, the Government did achieve an important architectural result when it directly commissioned Waterhouse to design the British Museum of Natural History in South Kensington.

South Kensington, rather than Whitehall, is the district where one must look for the expression of Victorian architectural ideas at a national level. The particular area is that between Kensington Gore and the Cromwell Road, bought with the surplus arising from the Great Exhibition of 1851.[110] The first buildings to be put on the site were arcades and a conservatory for the Horticultural Society, which leased part of the ground: slight buildings, but already, in 1861, announcing that the South Kensington site would be no place for the normal Italian or Gothic convention.[111] The Albert Hall, promoted by a private company to honour the memory of Prince Albert, was built on the northern part of the site in 1867–71[112] and, on another part, the nucleus of the museum later to become the Victoria and Albert was begun in 1865.[113] Under the influence of Henry Cole these buildings were placed in the hands of military engineers.[114] The Albert Hall, based on a Roman theme and daringly contrived, was decorated by an architect in a north Italian Renaissance style, appropriate to brick and terracotta. The north court of the Museum, in the same materials, wears the same dress. The results are a special South Kensington product, rather outside the general stylistic flow.

The British Museum of Natural History is another matter. The Government commissioned Waterhouse directly, without competition, and the building was begun in 1873.[115] At a moment when his contemporaries were moving forward from Gothic to early Renaissance vernaculars, Waterhouse moved dramatically backward to a hard, rhythmical, Germanic Romanesque. The colossal emphasis of Waterhouse's building posed a problem for the next comer to the South Kensington site. T. E. Collcutt won the competition for the Imperial Institute in 1887.[116] It was to be on a site to the north of the museum (the old Horticultural Garden) and on the same axis. It must either agree with or protest against Waterhouse. It did, in fact, agree in its general disposition but disagreed in the stylistic handling. If Waterhouse's building is rooted in hard mid-Victorianism, Collcutt's was rooted in the gentler 'Queen Anne' movement of the seventies and owed much to the compositional devices of Norman Shaw. Its extreme elegance of detail and subtle combinations of brick and stone were the exact contrary of Waterhouse's tough, positive handling in terracotta.

It is sad that we have lost the Imperial Institute (except for its slim Sevillian tower) because that building and the Natural History Museum together represented, as no other London buildings do or did, the power of expression of mid-Victorian and late-Victorian architecture at the level of national monumentality.

South Kensington is a good point at which to leave the subject of Victorian London as artifact. From Scott's Albert Memorial some of the most significant phenomena are within easy range—the stucco terraces of the fifties; the rich houses of Webb, Stevenson, and Shaw; and the monumental museums, with the steeples of Kensington and Lancaster Gate peering over the trees. But, having said that, it becomes obvious that to consider London as a visual entity is to entertain a plurality of images. Many suggest themselves, but perhaps five have crucial relevance: the rebuilt City; the trail of new buildings in new streets; the products of domestic affluence; the products of religion, philanthropy, and social progress; and South Kensington. From sixty-four years of prodigious expansion and energetic innovation no unique totality, no single architectural image emerged to typify the London of Victoria. To the twentieth century, the London legacy was incomprehensible chaos. Only today, with architectural horizons stretching to irredeemable monotony, does the Victorian city, by the very virtue of its complexity, once again strike the imagination.

Notes

1 The history of style in early Victorian architecture is admirably expounded in H.-R. Hitchcock, *Early Victorian Architecture in Britain* (New Haven, 1954). There is no comparable study for the later decades, but on a small scale the English sections of the same author's *Architecture: Nineteenth and Twentieth Centuries* (1958) are valuable.

2 Dickens's London is essentially Georgian London, even when he sets his scene in the railway age. The new London of his time was 'Stucconia' where the Veneerings resided (*Our Mutual Friend*, ch. 10) and that was perhaps Belgravia or Tyburnia.

3 The houses on the corners of Great Russell Street and Museum Street were rebuilt or remodelled by an architect called Trehearne in 1862 (*Builder* (*B*), xx (1862), 416).

4 This was part of an endeavour on the part of the Bedford estate to preserve Bloomsbury from 'lodging-house dry-rot'. See D. J. Olsen, *Town Planning in London: The eighteenth and nineteenth centuries* (New Haven, 1964), pp. 174–7.

5 London County Council, *Survey of London*, XVIII: The Strand (1937), p. 103, plate 71b.

6 There are, as yet, few studies of Victorian estate development in London. The following are important: Dorothy Stroud, *The Thurloe Estate, South Kensington* (published for Thurloe Estates Ltd by Country Life Ltd, 1965); I. Scouloudi and K. P. Hands, 'The Ownership and Development of Fifteen Acres at Kensington Gravel Pits', *London Topographical Record*, xxii (1965), 77–125; D. A. Reeder,

'A Theatre of Suburbs: Some Patterns of Development in West London, 1801–1911', in *The Study of Urban History*, ed. H. J. Dyos (1968). For the Radcliffe Estate, Brompton, see *B*, xxvi (1868), 201; for South Kensington developments, *B*, xxvii (1869), 629.

7 The planning and equipment of the London house after the Georgian period has never been studied, partly because of the obvious difficulty of obtaining access to private houses. The building periodicals give few town-house plans.

8 For the various metamorphoses of the Office of Works, see *B*, xxxv (1877), 897. For early Victorian street improvements see 'A Quarter of a Century of London Street Improvements', *B*, xxiv (1866), 877, and J. W. Penfold, 'On Metropolitan Improvements', *B*, xxiii (1865), 427–8. The best sources for descriptions and illustrations of the new streets are the *Companion to the Almanac* and the *Illustrated London News*.

9 See T. C. Barker and Michael Robbins, *A History of London Transport* (1963), I; John Summerson, *Victorian Architecture: Four studies in evaluation* (New York, 1970); E. A. Course, *London Railways* (1962).

10 Alfred Blomfield, *A Memoir of C. J. Blomfield, Bishop of London* (1863), pp. 233–5.

11 T. F. Bumpus, *London Churches, Ancient and Modern* (2nd series: classical and modern) [1908]; B. F. L. Clarke, *The Building of the Eighteenth-Century Church* (1963); M. H. Port, *Six Hundred New Churches: A study of the Church Building Commission, 1818–56, and its building activities* (1961).

12 J. Summerson, 'An Early Modernist: James Wild and his Work', *Architects' Journal*, lxix (1929), 57–62.

13 Paul Thompson, 'All Saints, Margaret Street, Reconsidered', *Architectural History*, viii (1965), 73–94.

14 H.-R. Hitchcock, 'Brunel and Paddington', *Architectural Review*, cix (1951), 240–6.

15 The London and Westminster Bank, Lothbury (with William Tite), 1837–9, was demolished in 1928; the Sun Fire Office, Threadneedle Street, was demolished in 1970 but had previously been much altered. See A. E. Richardson, *Monumental Classic Architecture in Great Britain and Ireland during the Eighteenth and Nineteenth Centuries* (1914), p. 78 and plate xxxvii. Cockerell's employment in these instances was probably due to his position as architect to the Bank of England, where he succeeded Soane in 1833.

16 *Building News* (*BN*), iv (1858), 723; details, xii (1865), 447.

17 *BN*, xv (1868), 11, 29, 147. For critical comments on this and many other city buildings of the sixties see three leading articles in *B*, xxiv (1866), 641, 677, 792.

18 E. I'Anson, 'Some Notices of Office Buildings in the City of London', *Trans. Royal Institute of British Architects* (*R.I.B.A.*), xv (1864–5), 25–36.

19 *Illustrated London News*, vii (1845), 215–16. H.-R. Hitchcock, *Early Victorian Architecture*, II, plate xii, p. 2.

20 *BN*, iii (1857), 1125.

21 Exhibited R.A., 1860. See *B*, xviii (1860), 290.

22 *B*, xxix (1871), 187.

23 *BN*, xi (1864), 134–5. H.-R. Hitchcock, 'Victorian Monuments of Commerce', *Architectural Review*, cv (1949), 61–74.

24 A specially elegant example was Munt & Brown's warehouse, Wood Street.
    See *BN*, iii (1857), 68, 261, 285.

25 *B*, xxiv (1866), 851; *BN*, xiii (1866), 780.

26 *B*, xxvi (1868), 749.

27 G. G. Scott, *Personal and Professional Recollections*, ed. G. G. Scott, Jr (1879),
    p. 210.

28 The term is Robert Kerr's. Summerson, *Victorian Architecture*, pp. 8–9.

29 Destroyed by bombs: *B*, xxxi (1873), 358, 607, 632. Commenting on this building,
    shown at the R.A. in 1873, the *Builder* asked why Shaw should 'affect so unneces-
    sarily the manner of a bygone age . . . entirely contradicting the tone and feeling
    of his own day'. The aged Professor T. L. Donaldson could not 'conceive what
    motive could have induced [the architect] to rake up a type of the very lowest
    state of corrupt erection in the City of London, of a period that marks the
    senility of decaying taste.' R. Blomfield, *Richard Norman Shaw, R.A., Architect,
    1831–1912* (1940), p. 50, recalled that 'even ten years later . . . people were not
    quite sure whether they should regard the building as a freak or as a work of
    genius.'

30 The warehouse of Rylands & Sons by John Belcher: *BN*, xxxvi (1879), 17.

31 The premises of Cow, Hill & Co.: *BN*, xlii (1882), 25, 121.

32 The Submarine Telegraph Co.'s offices by John Norton: *B*, xxxix (1880), 617.

33 The London & Lancashire Assurance Office, by T. Chatfield Clarke, now called
    Yorkshire House: *B*, xli (1881), 174–5.

34 The early history of the street is summarized in J. Penfold, 'On Metropolitan
    Improvements', *B*, xxiii (1865), 427. See also *B*, xix (1861), 459.

35 Plan and details: *B*, xi (1853), 721–2. The flats, now let as offices, are entered from
    Nos 137, 147, 157, 167 Victoria Street.

36 *B*, xxv (1867), 121–3.

37 Priscilla Metcalf, 'The Rise of James Knowles, Victorian Architect and Editor'
    (unpublished Ph.D. thesis, University of London, 1971), pp. 359–61.

38 *B*, xxxiii (1875), 924. See also [Sylvain Mangeot], 'Queen Anne's Mansions',
    Arch. & Building News, 13 January 1939, 77–9.

39 Fully described by its architect, Andrew Moseley, in *B*, xx (1862), 165–7. The
    building still stands though with its mouldings shaved off and the walls rendered
    white. The staircase hall survives.

40 *B*, xix (1861), 570; xxi (1863), 490.

41 Percy J. Edwards, *History of London Street Improvements, 1855–97* (1898).

42 *BN*, xi (1864), 464–5.

43 *B*, xxii (1864), 901.

44 Southwark Street was largely destroyed by bombs in World War II. For the Hop
    Exchange, damaged but still (1972) standing, see *B*, xxv (1867), 731. For notes
    on the street, see *B*, xv (1857), 121; xx (1862), 870; xxv (1867), 348; 'Saunterings
    in Southwark Street', *BN*, xiv (1867), 707.

45 See Edwards, op. cit.

46 The first building in the street was I'Anson's British and Foreign Bible Society,
    still standing: see *B*, xxiv (1866), 447. Also still standing are the two remarkable
    office blocks designed by F. J. Ward for the developer, Major Wieland, standing

opposite each other at the eastern part of the street: Albert Buildings (see *B*, xxx (1872), 187) and Imperial Buildings (see *B*, xxxii (1874), 461).

47 By Davis & Emmanuel, 1880–2: *B*, xxxviii (1880), 600–5; xlii (1882), 495.

48 By Sir Arthur Blomfield, 1880–6: *B*, xxxviii (1880), 538, 541–2.

49 Now Incorporated Accountants Hall. By J. L. Pearson, 1895.

50 By John Dunn, 1889–94. Now (1972) almost entirely demolished.

51 Whitehall Court is by Archer & Green: *BN*, xlvii (1884), 90–1. The National Liberal Club, forming the eastern part of a nearly symmetrical river-front, is by Alfred Waterhouse: *BN*, xlviii (1885), 165, 174–5.

52 By J. Whichcord: *B*, xxxii (1874), 309.

53 *Architect*, 5 June 1891; *BN*, lviii (1890), 654.

54 By G. F. Bodley: *BN*, xxix (1875), 22.

55 *Book of the Hotel Cecil*. Publicity brochure with illustrations by J. Pennell, S. Reid and T. R. Davison [1895].

56 By John Gibson: *B*, xxxvii (1879), 1153.

57 The Northumberland Avenue Hotel, by Isaacs & Florence: *B*, lii (1886), 640, 642; liii (1886), 664 (sculpture). For Northumberland Avenue generally, see Edwards, op. cit.

58 *Survey of London*, XXXI, pp. 71–4.

59 Ibid., XXXIII, pp. 297–300.

60 H.-R. Hitchcock, 'London Coal Exchange', *Architectural Review*, i (1947, i), 185–6.

61 *B*, x (1852), 9.

62 *B*, xxiv (1866), 956–7; xxv (1867), 261.

63 *Companion to the Almanac*, 1855, p. 229.

64 *B*, xxvii (1869), 320–1; sections 321, 326.

65 *B*, xx (1862), 732–3.

66 Theo Crosby, *The Necessary Monument* (1970).

67 *BN*, xxxix (1880), 504. The house was greatly enlarged by Webb and subsequently much altered.

68 W. R. Lethaby, *Philip Webb and his Work* (1939), pp. 87–91, and plate opp. p. 20.

69 *BN*, xxvii (1874), 342, 351.

70 See R. Blomfield, *Richard Norman Shaw, R.A.* (1940).

71 Important for the beginnings of 'Queen Anne' are papers read by J. J. Stevenson at the Architectural Conference in 1874 (*B*, xxxii (1874), 537; *BN*, xxvi (1874), 689–92), and at the Architectural Association in 1875 (*B*, xxxiii (1875), 179–80).

72 *BN*, xliv (1883), 245.

73 E. R. Robson, *School Architecture* (2nd edn, 1877).

74 H. Percy Adams, 'English Hospital Planning', *Journal R.I.B.A.*, xxxvi (1929).

75 By Wilson, Son & Aldwinckle: *BN*, xlix (1885), 98.

76 By A. Hessell Tiltman: *BN*, lxxii (1897), 434.

77 By Spalding & Ould: *BN*, lii (1887), 78.

78 T. Greenwood, *Free Public Libraries* (1887).

79 *BN*, lvi (1889), 806–7.

80 H. S. Goodhart-Rendel, *English Architecture since the Regency* (1953), pp. 197–8.

81 Blomfield, pp. 39–41. See also *BN*, xli (1881), 526 ff.

82 See above, p. 319.

83 S. Perks, *Residential Flats of all Classes, including Artisans' Dwellings* (1905).

84 *B*, xxxvi (1878), 753.

85 Clifford Chambers, by T. H. Watson & F. H. Collins: *BN*, xxxiii (1877), 240.

86 *BN*, xxxii (1877), 90.

87 *B*, xl (1881), 126.

88 Nos 42, 44, 46 by Ernest George: *BN*, xlv (1883), 50; Nos 7, 9 by A. Payne & E. M. Elgood: lvii (1889), 152; No. 40 by Collcutt: lxi (1891), 10, 718.

89 Nos 126–9 by W. H. Powell: *BN*, liii (1886), 420. See also lvii (1889), 586; lxiii (1892), 805, 824; lxxii (1897), 91, 92.

90 *BN*, lx (1891), 229–30; lxx (1896), 563, 565.

91 *Companion to the Almanac*, 1853, p. 253; *Illustrated London News*, xxv (1854), 217.

92 See above, p. 318.

93 *B*, xviii (1860), 755; xix (1861), 375.

94 *Illustrated London News*, xliv (1864), 563–4.

95 *B*, xxiv (1866), 758.

96 *B*, xxi (1863), 533.

97 See Jack Simmons, *St Pancras Station* (1968).

98 By Isaacs & Florence: *B*, xxxii (1874), 212, 591.

99 Northumberland Avenue Hotel, by Isaacs & Florence: *BN*, xliv (1883), 254. The Grand and Metropole Hotels (*B*, xxxvii (1879), 344–5; *BN*, xliv (1883), 830) are both by F. & H. Francis.

100 *BN*, lxxvii (1899), 8, 9.

101 See note 54.

102 S. Hamp, 'Hotel Planning', *Journal R.I.B.A.*, xiv (1907), 405–7.

103 N. Taylor, 'Doll's Palace', *Architectural Review*, cxl (1966), 451–4.

104 *BN*, lx (1891), 80, 196.

105 *B*, xxviii (1870), 407.

106 *BN*, xxiv (1873), 270–1, 330.

107 All the architects named in this and the following paragraph are the subjects of biographical notices in the *Dictionary of National Biography*.

108 Summerson, *Victorian Architecture*, pp. 113–17.

109 See *BN*, xlvii (1884), 153; winning design, 168–9.

110 For the early development of the site, see *B*, x (1852), 677; xi (1853), 681; xiv (1856), 263; xv (1857), 45, 357; xvi (1858), 137–8; xvii (1859), 456–7; xviii (1860), 312, 836–7; xix (1861), 173, 213.

111 *B*, xix (1861), 497.

112 *B*, xxv (1867), 365, 368; xxviii (1870), 977, 986, 1046; xxix (1871), 249; *Architect* (1869), opp. p. 294.

113 *B*, xxviii (1870), 467.

114 *Fifty Years of Public Work of Sir Henry Cole* (1884), II, pp. 296, 305.

115 *B*, xxxi (1873), 10–11.

116 *BN*, lv (1887), 10, 12; unsuccessful designs, 92–110.

14 House upon House[*]
Estate development in London and Sheffield

Donald J. Olsen

'They were not so much towns as . . . the barracks of an industry,' wrote the Hammonds of the new industrial cities of the Midlands and the North. 'These towns reflected the violent enterprise of an hour, the single passion that had thrown street on street in a frantic monotony of disorder . . . these shapeless improvisations . . . represented nothing but the avarice of the jerry-builder catering for the avarice of the capitalist.'[1] 'Truly the state of London houses and London house-building, at this time,' exclaimed Carlyle in 1867; 'who shall express how detestable it is, how frightful!'[2]

However earnest our attempts to avoid imposing our own moral and aesthetic standards on the past, and to look at Victorian cities through Victorian eyes, it is hard not to think that they could have made a better job of it than they did. The pretentious gentility of the Victorian middle-class suburb is a denial of the urban values implicit in Bedford Square and Regent's Park; while the cramped, dark, unventilated, undrained hovels in which millions of the poor, deserving and undeserving alike, spent their lives were a standing reproach to the society that permitted their existence. Although we have reached the stage of being able genuinely to admire particular pieces of Victorian architecture, it is less easy to admire the Victorian townscape as an aesthetic whole—even the Victorians could rarely bring themselves to do that—still less to admire the quality of life imposed by the urban environment on the Victorians themselves.

* I wish to thank the John Simon Guggenheim Memorial Foundation for awarding me a fellowship for 1967–8 which enabled me to do the greater part of the research for this chapter.

Was the Victorian city perhaps a monstrous blunder, as remote from the nineteenth-century urban ideal as it is from ours? Whether or not the Victorians got the cities they deserved, did they get the cities they desired? The answer is to be sought in the mediocre, representative acres of middle-class villas and working-class back-to-back cottages as much as in their self-conscious aspirations towards urban art or magnificence: in the anonymous suburbs of North London and the grimy terraces of the West Riding as much as in Prince Albert's South Kensington or Cadbury's Bournville.

It is arguable that the Victorian building industry, whatever the aesthetic and sanitary defects of its products, on the whole responded well to the challenge of a population explosion, rapid urbanization, a revolution in transport, technological upheaval, and changing notions as to what the home and the city ought to be. Before attempting to account for some of the flaws in the Victorian city and its suburbs, it might be appropriate to suggest how it was that they were built as well as they were.

The nineteenth-century suburb clearly responded to some fundamental cultural need, for, however much aesthetes and planners may deplore it, it provided the model for the environment in which most English-speaking people choose to live even today. It is harder to praise Victorian housing for the working classes. Even the model dwellings seem almost as repellent as the speculative housing whose evils they were designed to alleviate. With respect to sanitation, the private producers of housing did little beyond cooperate reluctantly with the efforts of the public authorities. Nor can working-class housing be much admired for structural soundness, architectural excellence, or imaginative layout. Where the Victorian building industry did succeed was on the quantitative plane. With notable exceptions in places like central London, it managed for the most part to keep up with the massive growth in population and with the expectations of that population for rising standards of accommodation. It provided more middle-class housing than the middle classes could absorb, and a supply of working-class housing that, if of minimal standards of amenity, was in most cases adequate for the needs of the people, at a price that the great majority of the working classes could afford. The very poor and those forced to live near their employment in areas of abnormally high land values formed a special, if deplorable, case.[3]

Building-land on the outskirts of Victorian cities was plentiful, cheap, and not subject to significant fluctuations in price. In no town does there appear to have been a shortage of building-land, freehold or leasehold, once one left the central area: landowners consciously kept both freehold prices and ground rents low in order to attract purchasers and builders to their estates. The practice of charging peppercorn rents for the first years of a lease, or accepting payment in instalments meant that the speculator himself often paid little or nothing for the land.

Nor was there any shortage of speculative builders. Entry into the business required no specialized skills and little or no capital; the smallest of firms was able to coexist perfectly satisfactorily with the largest.[4]

To an abundance of landowners eager to participate in the unearned increment that urban growth offered them, and an abundance of builders ready to risk their all in covering their land with houses, there was added a complementary abundance of investors, virtually forcing their money on the builders and developers. The buoyant supply of capital for house-building matched the supply of land and labor. G. Calvert Holland attributed what he thought the over-production of houses in Sheffield to 'the petty capitalist . . . desirous of realizing a handsome per centage . . .' as much as to the landowner, 'naturally anxious to appropriate his land to building purposes,' and the 'pennyless speculative builder.'[5] John Nash had earlier charged 'attornies with monied clients [with] facilitating, and indeed putting in motion, the whole system . . .' by which London was artificially extended, 'by disposing of their clients money in premature mortgages, the sale of improved ground rents, and by numerous other devices.'[6] With opportunities for investment far more limited than today, the thrifty Victorian who wished a greater return than he could earn from Consols without undue risk was almost forced to invest in the housing industry.[7] 'The supply of capital for house-building certainly ebbed and flowed,' H. J. Dyos has concluded, 'but there is no clear evidence that it was ever checked in such a way as to impede development at all seriously; there is, on the contrary, rather more evidence of over-building in periods of easy money than of under-building when money was tight.'[8]

An examination of how two urban estates, the Eton College estate at Chalcots, in Hampstead, and the Norfolk estate in Sheffield, were developed for building-purposes suggests not only the variety of ways in which the Victorian city took shape, and that its history was not entirely one of lost opportunities and the complacent creation of the unsanitary and the ugly, but also what prevented the urban land-owner from doing very much to alter, for better or worse, the form that the new city took.

These estates exhibited vast differences but had two qualities in common: medio-crity and success. As to the first, there can be little argument. Neither Eton College nor the Duke of Norfolk ever did anything to startle the expectations or outrage the sensi-bilities of the builders or tenants on their estates. It is the unremarkable quality of the management and the indifferent nature of its results that give the estates their particular interest, just as second-rate books often have more to tell the intellectual historian than do masterpieces.

The success of the estates was clearly not an artistic one. No one would challenge Sir John Summerson's characterization of the architecture on Chalcots as 'catch-penny,' the result of a 'commonplace . . . chain of events . . . a process which comes as near as possible to complete anonymity in its results, for it can truthfully be said that not one solitary soul was ever really interested in what the physical visible results would be.'[9] Hugh C. Prince has described the houses of Samuel Cuming, the principal builder on the estate in the forties and fifties, as 'nondescript . . . inoffen-sive . . . only remotely classical yet no more than vaguely romantic. They were built to please respectable but undiscerning clients.'[10] (Plates 288 and 290 are elevations of Cuming's houses; Plates 289 and 291 are of residential and commercial property put up by other builders in the fifties.) Kate Simon has recently called the productions of William Willett, whose late Victorian and Edwardian houses were among the last to be built on the estate, 'dour, red-brick, lightless, airless, insane excrescences.'[11]

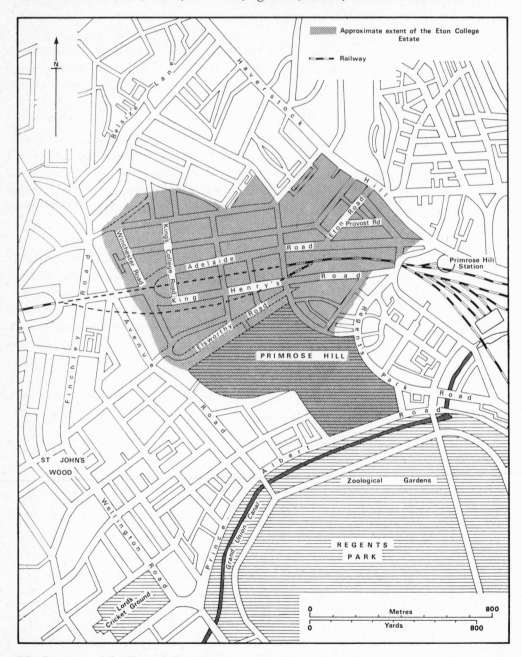

XI   Position of the Eton College Estate

Nor can Victorian Sheffield, either those parts owned by the Duke of Norfolk or elsewhere, be easily described as other than a blot on an otherwise magnificent landscape. 'We have surveyed Birmingham, Stafford, Wolverhampton, Newcastle-upon-Tyne, Hull, Shrewsbury, and other towns; but Sheffield, in all matters relating to sanitary appliances, is behind them all,' reported the *Builder* in 1861.[12] In 1848 James Haywood and William Lee described the leasehold houses on the Norfolk estate in Sheffield Park as 'very low, consisting of one or two stories, and . . . crowded together in the most irregular manner, forming angular yards of the most inconvenient description.'[13] The *Sheffield and Rotherham Independent* over twenty years later found 'the Park estate of the Duke of Norfolk almost unimproved . . . The buildings consist mostly of narrow rows of houses, along narrow streets north and south, at different elevations, forming a series of terraces. In many of these there have been no changes during the last fifty years, except that the houses have become dilapidated, and arrangements for light, air, and cleanliness seem never to have been thought of.'[14]

And yet Chalcots and Sheffield reflect as much of what was admirable about the Victorian city as of what was deplorable. In a period characterized by a chronic oversupply of middle-class housing, Chalcots attracted and continued to attract the kind of resident for whom it was designed. While the Bedford and Foundling Hospital estates were fighting their losing battles to keep their genteel tenants from deserting their elegant Georgian squares, the 'respectable but undiscerning clients' who constituted the bulk of the middle-class house-market moved into the anonymous Italianate villas of Chalcots and, as a class, remained there. Sir John Summerson has remarked on the unusual degree of social continuity in the neighborhood. After describing the inhabitants of 1851, according to the census records of that year, as 'a mixed lot—small manufacturers, solicitors, a Congregational minister, an architect, a painter or two, widows bringing up families on small incomes,' he pointed out that 'its character . . . remained much the same and so far as I can ascertain has always done so. Allowing for the changes which have taken place in the structure of society as a whole one can say that these houses are now inhabited by exactly the same type of people who lived in them a hundred years ago.'[15] There was a perceptible social decline by the early twentieth century. One resident, writing in 1918, observed that 'the character of the population has changed. This is no longer, to anything like the former extent, a neighbourhood wherein rising, or successful, professional and business men set up households and bring up families.'[16] Yet an examination of the *Post Office London Directory* shows the decline to have been far from catastrophic, certainly far less than occurred in Bloomsbury. What generations of architects, surveyors, solicitors, and stewards strove vainly to achieve in Bloomsbury, Eton College seems to have managed without really trying.

For the records of its estate show little evidence of serious planning, even of the landlord holding reluctant builders to higher standards of design, construction, or layout than they would themselves have wished. The history of the estate is one of mediocre management and mediocre builders proceeding according to an accepted pattern, a standard way of going about such things. If Bloomsbury is a magnificent failure, Chalcots is an undeserved success.

The Duke of Norfolk did even less to control or direct the building development on his estate. Michael Ellison, the agent from 1819 to 1860, intelligent, conscientious, energetic, and wholly devoted to what he saw as the best interests both of the Duke of Norfolk and the town of Sheffield, left most of the superintendence of the lease-hold development of the estate to the steward, Marcus Smith, a man of ordinary intelligence and limited attainments. London building-leases varied considerably in stringency, but none with which I am familiar left so much to the discretion of the tenant as did the standard Norfolk leases for nineteenth-century Sheffield. Yet in spite of this, both the quantity and quality of working-class housing in Sheffield compared favorably with that of most other English towns.

Given the level of wages and incomes for both the very poor and the industrious artisan in Victorian England, their chief requirement as to housing was that it be cheap and that it be densely enough built so that everyone could live within walking distance of his work. The landowners, investors, and speculative builders of London were unable to satisfy such requirements. The size and wealth of the metropolis made land values in the center—where most jobs were to be had—such that the construction and maintenance of working-class dwellings became increasingly uneconomical. The operations of the London Building Acts and the further requirements imposed by the landlords of leasehold estates raised the cost of building to a level higher than that of the provinces, while a variety of considerations encouraged both landowners and builders to concentrate disproportionately on middle-class housing. Speculative working-class housing on the cheaper land available in the suburbs did not, until perhaps the very end of the century, provide an adequate substitute, because of the insufficient service of workmen's trains, the casual nature of much employment, and a level of incomes too low to permit the very poor to pay the economic costs of decent housing anywhere.[17]

Sheffield, although it reached a population of 411,000 in 1901, remained physically compact. 'The population of Sheffield is, for so large a town, unique in its character,' Dr Frederick W. Barry reported in 1889, 'in fact it more closely resembles that of a village than of a town, for over wide areas each person appears to be acquainted with every other, and to be interested with that other's concerns.'[18] By the time it expanded beyond walking limits, cheap, municipally-owned electric trams brought the outer suburbs within the reach of the working classes.[19]

Despite the crowding of houses on the ground and the primitive state of sanitation for much of the century, most contemporaries were agreed that the Sheffield worker was comparatively well housed. John Parker, M.P., a member of the Select Committee on Public Walks, told his colleagues in 1833: 'Generally, in Sheffield, the average of the comfort of the lower classes is above that of most other places; we have not yet got into the abominable way of cellars, or of many families living in the same house.'[20] There was comparatively little overcrowding throughout the century: the average dwelling was the single-family three- to four-room cottage, and the average number of persons per house less than five.[21] Haywood and Lee, in their generally critical account of sanitary conditions in Sheffield, found housing as such perfectly adequate:[22]

> Notwithstanding all the evils we have seen during our inspection of the town, we do not hesitate to say, generally, that the *construction* of the houses occupied by the working classes in Sheffield is better, and the rental more moderate, than in almost any other town in the kingdom. The great amount of sickness, and the high rate of mortality here arises, so far as the dwellings are concerned, more from an inadequate supply of water and inefficient drainage, than from defective structural arrangements.

There were many attacks on the speculative builders of Victorian Sheffield, but no one suggested that they produced too few houses for the needs of the population. Rather, the complaint was that they built too many houses, of too flimsy a character.[23] 'Sheffield,' a local solicitor told the Select Committee on Town Holdings, 'is undoubtedly an over-built town.'[24]

'In building as in other things,' Marian Bowley reminds us, 'quality as well as quantity costs more. Anyone providing houses for the great mass of working-class families in the nineteenth century had to provide them at a price that they were willing or able to pay . . . The lower the income group to be served, the cheaper the buildings in terms of quality and quantity of materials, workmanship, fittings and amenities . . . Building which is frequently referred to as shoddy and nasty is not necessarily dishonest. It may be a thoroughly honest job for the price.'[25]

The ability of Chalcots to meet so precisely the wishes of its middle-class tenants, and of Sheffield to house, at whatever low standards of comfort, its vast artisan population may have come about not so much in spite of the passive policies of the ground landlords, as because of them. The Georgian tradition of town planning, the only one available to the Victorian landowner, was irrelevant to most of the needs of the nineteenth-century city.

What values underlay a 'good' eighteenth- or early nineteenth-century town plan—in Bath or Dublin or the New Town of Edinburgh? Coherence and uniformity: uniformity of facade, of design, of the social status of the occupants. This required segregation, with the garden squares and principal streets reserved for the better sort of resident, the back streets for the middling sort, and the courts and mews for the lower orders, decently screened from view. Georgian town planners were not able to achieve the single-class neighborhood that so distresses sociologists but so delights estate agents and building societies, but it was not from any belief in the virtues of social integration. There was less mixture of classes in eighteenth-century Bloomsbury than in seventeenth-century Covent Garden, more social uniformity in Belgravia in the 1830s than in Mayfair in the 1770s. Chalcots, though it discarded the outward appearance of Georgian urbanity, did achieve one of its principal aims in becoming an exclusively middle-class dormitory.

Along with social segregation went segregation of occupation. The ideal street to the Georgian planner was one of gentlemen's private residences, whose quiet and uniformity were undisturbed by trade, manufacture, or through-traffic. Shops, offices, and, above all, manufacture, were to be either hidden from sight or excluded altogether. Noise, smoke, and noxious odors were rigorously proscribed in all respectable leases. Such a policy swept the dust under the carpet, and helped members of the middle and upper classes to ignore the existence of poverty, filth, and even the necessary operations of the economy. Here again, Chalcots restricted shops to specified streets, and managed to hide even the London & Birmingham Railway in a tunnel. But the very nature of Sheffield's economy was such as to frustrate the most well-meaning ground landlord in this respect.

Chalcots succeeded without taking too much thought for success—in strict eighteenth-century terms. Its history suggests that, given sufficient size and a favorable location, a London estate planned and managed itself. The history of the Norfolk properties in Sheffield suggests that the techniques of town planning available to an eighteenth- or nineteenth-century landowner were of little use in the West Riding of Yorkshire.

'Irrespective of the sort of house adapted for the estate, and the area allowed to each,' advised the *Building News* in 1860, 'much depends on the "laying out": a greater income and more general success will occur from one form of planning roads, etc. . . than another.'[26] Even in Georgian London the extent of control that landlords exercised over builders had varied greatly. '. . . Some of the Proprietors,' wrote the architects to the Crown estate in 1811, 'have confined the Builders . . . to a certain Plan as to the general distribution of the intended Street, Squares, etc. without reference to the particular Class of Houses; others have gone further, stipulating the Class of Houses, and the numbers of them; others again have suffered the Builders . . . to distribute the Streets, and cover the Ground as they thought proper.'[27]

The instrument for putting such schemes into effect was the building agreement. The enforcement of restrictive covenants depended not only on the skill with which they were drawn up at the outset, but also on the perseverance of the ground landlord. He had every temptation not to employ his legal powers. J. Wornham Penfold remarked in 1858 that it was 'the builder's object and interest to build as cheaply as he possibly can,' while the landlord was reluctant to enforce the covenants, being 'oftentimes more anxious about what seems to be his present interest than about what is best for the future; and if too stringent conditions are placed on either design or construction, the estate will get a bad name among the speculators.'[28] The Select Committee on Town Holdings agreed: 'If the ground landlord makes it his first object to get the land covered with houses, and then secure to himself the commercial ground-rent . . . it is improbable that he will make the stipulations of the building agreement press too heavily upon the speculative builder.'[29]

In the latter years of the eighteenth century the 9th and 11th Dukes of Norfolk, and their agent Vincent Eyre, had attempted to astonish the North by adorning Sheffield with a succession of terraces whose architecture would not have been out of place in Bath or Dublin. They commissioned the architects James Paine and Thomas Atkinson to design the façades for new streets to be built on the former Alsop Fields, and the resulting elevations would have graced the capital of an enlightened despot of a German principality. The gridiron network of Norfolk, Arundel, Surrey, and Eyre Streets still stands out in contrast to the narrow, winding, and irregular pattern of both the older and newer parts of the town, and a fragment of one of Atkinson's designs can still be seen in Norfolk Street. But it is unlikely that any substantial portion of the planned buildings was ever erected: if it had been, some Man of Taste on a Picturesque Tour would have noticed it. For whatever reason, the 11th Duke sold the whole neighborhood in the early nineteenth century.

The disposal of the Alsop Fields development marked the abandonment by the estate of the Georgian approach to town planning. Regular street patterns, unified facades enforced by architectural controls written into the leases, and coherent neighborhoods in which street names, layout, and physical appearance expressed the wealth, taste, and public spirit of the landowner, however appropriate for a capital city or a fashionable watering place, evoked little enthusiasm from the independent cutlers of Sheffield.

Sheffield was a wealthy town, but not one whose wealth was of the sort to encourage good architecture or good urban design. The quality of life of a Sheffield artisan in his ugly back-to-back cottage may on balance have been preferable to that of the occupant of an exquisitely designed Georgian slum in Dublin. Certainly the principles and techniques of urban planning available to the Duke of Norfolk, however suitable to conditions in London, had nothing to contribute towards solving the problems of Sheffield. This is partly a question of social class, but more one of the realities of economic geography.

Sheffield never was, and probably never could have become, a place where people of wealth, leisure, and taste would willingly congregate. It was not a York, a Harrogate, or a Scarborough. Nor did its industries—at least until the great expansion of the steel industry in mid-century—produce the great concentrations of wealth that were to be found in Leeds or Manchester. Finally it was, to quote Horace Walpole, 'one of the foulest towns in England in the most charming situation.'[30]

Noisy, smoky, and loathsome, Sheffield was surrounded on all sides by some of the most enchanting countryside to be found on this planet. The flight to the suburbs and beyond was an early and understandable phenomenon for all who could afford the move. 'Within the past few years,' wrote G. Calvert Holland in 1841,[31]

> the town has extended widely in all directions . . . The same change presents itself in the picturesque sites of the immediate vicinity. There is no richly clothed hill or attractive valley but what is embellished by the tasteful decorations of art . . . All classes, save the artisan and the needy shopkeeper, are attracted by country comfort and retirement. The attorney,—the manufacturer,—the grocer,—the draper,—the shoemaker

and the tailor, fix their commanding residences on some beautiful site, and adorn them with the cultivated taste of the artist.

Segregation of function was a basic principle of Georgian planning. But the cutlery industry, on which Sheffield's prosperity was based, remained until the present century a matter of small workshops around which the cutlers and their employees lived. Later, the smoke and noise of the steel industry became at once Sheffield's greatest nuisance and the foundation of its greatness. 'A thick pulverous haze is spread over the city, which the sun even in the dog days is unable to penetrate, save by a lurid glare . . . and a buzz, softened down from the first clanging and clashing utterance of machinery, into a hum as of a swarm of bees, rises into the air and is distinctly audible,' reported the *Builder* in 1861, as much in admiration as in condemnation.[32] The Norfolk estate did from time to time send orders to tenants to abate the smoke nuisance, but, given the state of Victorian technology, to have abolished industrial nuisances would have been to abolish Sheffield.

The principal Norfolk holdings were to the east and north of the town. They were gradually covered with steel-mills along the valley of the Don, and with densely-built terraces of working-class cottages up the surrounding hills. Massive postwar slum clearances have obliterated most of what went up on the estate in the nineteenth century, but little that remains is calculated to excite admiration for the Duke's agents as town planners. Yet these terraces were no worse than what was going up elsewhere in Sheffield, and superior to much working-class property in other towns.

The building agreement, which in London was a lengthy and detailed document, precisely prescribing the nature and quality of the houses to be erected, setting forth the provisions of the leases to be granted when the houses were near completion, was in Sheffield no more than a verbal arrangement by which the future lessee agreed to put up buildings, and the landlord agreed to grant a lease at so much per square yard.[33] The leases required that the premises be kept in repair, but lacked the machinery for enforcement contained in the ordinary London lease. Instead of the provision, customary in London, that the premises not be used, without specific license from the freeholder, other than as a gentleman's private residence, there was merely a prohibition of any trade which the agent of the Duke of Norfolk might deem offensive. Such general covenants were notoriously hard to enforce.[34]

While the general tendency in London was for landlords to add more and more restrictive covenants to their leases as time went on, Sheffield leases granted in the nineteenth century were in some respects less stringent than those dating from the 1780s and 1790s. The printed form of lease in the time of Vincent Eyre and the 11th Duke included a specific list of offensive trades—soap-boiler, distiller, melting-tallow-chandler, and so on—unlike the later general covenant against nuisances. More important, it required that the lessee submit a plan and elevation to be approved by the Norfolk agent for any buildings 'at any Time hereafter to be erected and which shall front upon or adjoin to any public Street or Road in or near the said

Town of Sheffield.'[35] By 1800 such provisions had disappeared from most leases. Nothing, moreover, ever prevented the lessees from filling in the courts behind the houses with the meanest of erections, which was precisely what they proceeded to do.

Any attempts to introduce stricter controls brought immediate opposition. James Sorby wrote to Michael Ellison in 1835 to protest against a covenant that would have been taken for granted in any London lease:[36]

> A Draft of a Covenant which you propose to introduce into the Lease from the Duke of Norfolk to Mr. Alfred Sorby, has been handed to me for perusal. . . My Brother . . . certainly will not agree to so unexpected a clause, being inserted in the Lease, neither do I think that you can, in fairness expect him to agree to it, as it is a very novel idea, to restrict a Tenant from laying out Money upon the property of his Lessor, & occupying it to best advantage . . . it is . . . much out of the common way. My Brother has not any intention . . . of building either Workshops or Dwellinghouses upon the Land in question, but he naturally wishes to have it in the most marketable state, in case he should, (after expending so much Money upon the place,) be driven away by the nuisances, which surround him.
>
> I hope you will reconsider the matter, & grant a Lease, on the usual Terms.

The lease in question was for Park Grange, the mansion that Sorby was to build for himself south of the Farm, later the ducal residence. The houses that were erected on this part of the property in the thirties and forties were by far the most pretentious ever built on the estate. Yet even here, a 'gentleman's private residence' covenant such as would have been found in the leases in any genteel London street seemed an outrageous innovation.

William Fowler, of Birmingham, surveyed the operations of the Sheffield office in 1861. His penciled marginal comments on a 'Draft Proposed Form of Lease for 99 Years' indicates that an outside observer did not regard the degree of control permitted by the covenants as at all insufficient: if anything, he thought the leases erred on the side of severity. He wrote 'very stringent covenants,' beside the provisions against nuisances and assignments without license, and one stating that the lessee

> shall [not] use or exercise . . . upon the said premises any trade or manufacture which shall be declared by such Agent [of the ground-landlord] to be offensive or a nuisance to the neighbourhood without . . . consent in writing . . . Or [a provision for forefeiture] if the buildings erected . . . shall be suffered to be dilapidated or out of repair and the same shall not be repaired within one year after notice.

He commented on the provision permitting the agent to make a schedule of fixtures on the premises any time during the last five years of the lease, 'A power probably never exercised.'[37]

Building-leases remained in general loosely drawn on all estates in Sheffield throughout the century.[38] Such covenants as there were were rarely enforced. It would be fair to say that so long as the ground rent was regularly paid and no flagrant nuisance committed—and in Victorian Sheffield a nuisance would have to be flagrant indeed to be noticed—the landlord would not interfere with the leaseholder's interest. 'I have never heard of the Duke [of Norfolk] interfering at all with the property until it got to the end of the term,' the mayor of Sheffield told the Select Committee on Town Holdings.[39] His impression finds confirmation in penciled memoranda in the margin of the questionnaire sent by the Committee to the Norfolk estate office. Alongside question five, 'Is it your experience that ground landlords habitually abstain from enforcing the covenants to paint and otherwise keep in repair universally inserted in building leases?' is written, 'No [*sic*]—Ground Landlords only require Buildings to be maintained at a certain value & to be insured & do not notice painting or ordinary repairs.' In answer to question eight, 'Is it your experience that the system of building leases is conducive to bad building, to deterioration of property towards the close of the lease, and to a want of interest on the part of the occupier in the house he inhabits?' is the cautious opinion, 'Probably no worse than on freeholds.'[40]

The result was what one would have expected: building of the cheapest possible character densely crowded upon the ground; streets often left unpaved and undrained—in Sheffield (London varied somewhat), builders were not obliged to form roads and sewers at the same time as erecting the houses; property in a ruinous state at the expiration of the original lease. The preservation of the reversionary value of the leasehold property, on a London estate the continual preoccupation of the ground-landlord, rarely seemed a consideration in Sheffield.

It would be a mistake to blame Victorian Sheffield on apathy, or mismanagement in the Norfolk office. The surviving correspondence relating to Sheffield in the Arundel Castle MSS. is incomplete, but those years for which there is relatively full documentation—chiefly from the twenties to the fifties—bear witness to the consistent and well-informed interest taken in Sheffield affairs by both the Duke and his London agent. The Sheffield agents—in particular Michael Ellison and his son M. J. Ellison—displayed an obvious sense of responsibility both for the interests of the Norfolk estate and for the prosperity of Sheffield as a whole. Finally, the Duke of Norfolk as a London landowner—he possessed a considerable estate between the Strand and the Thames—seems to have behaved like any other enlightened metropolitan ground landlord at the same time that he was being so permissive in Sheffield.[41]

One explanation is found in a letter of 1840, which the Sheffield agent wrote to Edward Blount, then responsible for the management of all the Duke's properties, about the problem of determining policy with respect to the renewal of leases in Sheffield, particularly as to fines. 'The rule observed in such cases in London,' he argued, 'will not do for this place: the object there being for the Lessor, to exact the utmost amount, without reference to any other consideration. Here, we must take care not to destroy confidence, but on the contrary deal liberally with parties, and hold out encouragement to others, to embark capital in buildings on the Duke of Norfolk's Land.'[42] Whether or not one accept's Ellison's view of the principles governing estate management in London, it is significant to see the stress he placed on doing everything possible to encourage speculative building.[43] Actually anyone involved in the management of a London estate would have been equally convinced that his chief aim should be to make conditions attractive for the speculative builder. The difference lay in the builders and speculators in the two places: the builder in Sheffield was simply not in an economic position to bear the weight of the quality of building demanded in London.[44]

Land values, and hence ground rents, were not consistently lower on the outskirts of Sheffield than they were on the outskirts of London. What made Sheffield attractive to the builder of minimal or non-existent capital was that he could build as cheaply as the market permitted. Sheffield, like most provincial towns, had nothing comparable to the London Building Acts until 1867. Building agreements on well-managed metropolitan estates, by adding to the minimum standards of the Building Acts, necessarily increased costs. In Sheffield, the agreements did not even specify a minimum expenditure by the builder. The absence of any obligation to construct the streets brought costs even lower.

As a result, house-building proved irresistibly attractive to men of small capital —with whom Sheffield abounded—who built cheaply and in large quantities. Any attempt by the landowners to impose metropolitan notions of estate management would have reduced the quantity of working-class housing, not only by raising building costs, but also because a fundamental principle of Georgian town planning was to concentrate on building for the upper and middle classes. But nothing the Dukes of Norfolk could have done would have made central Sheffield attractive to the already suburbanized middle classes of the town. With the relative failure of the Alsop Fields development as a cautionary example, they did nothing because there was nothing to be done.

There was much more that could be done in London, at least in certain parts. The Select Committee on Town Holdings pointed out that it was 'easier to enforce salutary regulations . . . when there are special advantages attaching to a particular neighbourhood, and marking it off for the residence of a certain class.'[45] Chalcots had such advantages.

Its situation enabled Chalcots to absorb some of the prestige of Regent's Park to the south, St John's Wood to the west, and Hampstead to the north. The estate failed to develop a distinctive character of its own, and lacked even a name, for 'Chalcots' had meaning only for the antiquary.[46] The neighborhood was variously identified in whole or in part as Haverstock Hill, Primrose Hill, St John's Wood, and

South Hampstead, and its anonymity reflected the derivative nature of both its layout and its architecture.

In order to derive full advantage from its promising site, Eton College did no more than any other large, responsible London landlord did, and far less than some. It hired a succession of surveyors, who proposed, modified, and abandoned a succession of spacious but unoriginal street plans; it had its solicitors draw up versions of standard London building agreements and leases. It negotiated with a succession of developers and builders, who proceeded to erect detached and semi-detached villas in whatever style was currently in fashion. (See Plates 288, 290–1 for the fashions of the forties and fifties.) For amenities it encouraged the building of churches and an adequate number of respectably managed public houses. The houses were decently designed and substantially built, in accordance with the building agreements: not so much in consequence of their provisions, as because the builders and developers were accustomed to put up houses of that sort. One would imagine that the more respectable and better-established builders would be attracted to a sizeable, conservatively managed estate such as Chalcots. The dilatory behavior of the Provost and Fellows, and particularly the bursar and registrar, with respect to the management of their London property—leading especially to delays in the execution of leases—did nothing to encourage builders and, it might be argued, made it impossible for any but a builder of some standing and considerable capital resources to indulge in the luxury of an Eton College speculation.

Unlike many ground landlords, the college offered no financial assistance to builders in the form of loans, purchases of improved ground rents, or contributions towards the expense of roadways and sewers. The builders did not seem to find the controls and covenants in the agreements irksome, although they inevitably increased their costs. There were disagreements as to the rate of rent per acre, the amount of time during which the full rent would be replaced by a peppercorn and a 'grass' rent, and the time allowed for the houses to be built; but there is no evidence that the builders were either trying to scamp on the dimensions or quality of materials, or that they were trying to crowd more and smaller houses onto their plots than the agreements allowed—both recurring problems on the Bedford and Foundling estates.[47] From the point of view of the developers and builders, the situation called for precisely the large—but not too large—substantial houses on a spacious plan that the agreements called for. None of this is surprising, since there is every indication that most of the initiative for the layout and quality of construction came from the building developers themselves. The surviving estate plans that did originate with the landlords and their agents either proved impractical or were modified out of recognition in the negotiations with the developers.

The leasehold covenants served not so much as obstacles to bad building as encouragements to good, and an implied guarantee that the rest of the estate would be built to similar standards. What mattered was less the conscious policies of the ground landlord than the continuing existence of a market for the kind of houses being erected on Chalcots, the willingness of substantial builders to speculate on the estate, and the seemingly inexhaustible pool of capital available to support middle-class housing developments in London.

The earliest plan for Chalcots would have made it a northward extension of Regent's Park; the actual development began as an eastward extension of St John's Wood, and ended as a southern continuation of Hampstead. Perhaps its success derived from its ability to reflect the aesthetic and social character of all three.

The Crown architects had in 1811 suggested that what was to become the northern portion of Regent's Park, land adjacent to the Eton College estate at Primrose Hill, could be 'most advantageously disposed of for Villas, having each an allotment of from two to five, ten, or a greater number of Acres.'[48] John Nash similarly proposed that the whole of the Park 'be let in parcels of from four to twenty acres, for the purpose of building villas, and so planted that no villa should see any other, but each should appear to possess the whole of the park.'[49] The handful of villas actually built in the park is only a fragment of the original conception.[50]

The first plan for Chalcots, dated by Noel Blakiston 1822, proposed a similar layout. It argued that 'the Estate from its proximity to London and from its elevated situation is so well adapted for the erection of Villas with a small Quantity of Land attached thereto that it would be eagerly sought after by the wealthy Citizens of the Metropolis—and builders would readily speculate in taking the plots.' It proposed that the whole estate of about 230 acres, except for fourteen acres on Primrose Hill itself, be divided into seventy-seven building lots, all larger than half-an-acre.[51] Two years later John Jenkins produced a building plan (Plate 281). It divided the whole of Chalcots, including Primrose Hill, into seventy-five large plots, to be served by four new roads.[52] Primrose Hill was never developed, and was in 1842 granted to the Crown in exchange for property in Eton.[53]

By 1826, when the college obtained a private Act authorizing it to grant ninety-nine-year leases on Chalcots, the great building boom of the twenties had collapsed, and it was becoming evident that Regent's Park was not going to become a garden suburb for the very rich. More modest and realistic plans for Chalcots were thus called for, and the estate brought in the architect John Shaw (1776–1832), surveyor to Christ's Hospital and to the Eyre estate in St John's Wood, to supervise operations. In March 1827 he prepared a scheme for the small part of the estate immediately adjacent to Haverstock Hill (see Plate 282). It provided for thirty-four detached villas set in plots of at least half-an-acre. None of the villas was to face directly on Haverstock Hill, along which trees were to screen its traffic; instead three new roads were to be formed. Each house was to contain at least twelve 'squares' of building, i.e., 1,200 square feet, well above the minimum nine squares for first-rate houses specified by the London Building Act. Although a notable retreat from the grandiose intentions of the earlier plan, Shaw's scheme contemplated far larger houses than were ultimately built on the site.[54]

A later map, dated 1829, shows a less ambitious street plan and a smaller number of villas, fourteen in all, on either side of the new road paralleling Haverstock Hill (Plate 283). Later additions in pencil show two alternative routes for a projected road bisecting the estate and linking Chalk Farm with the Finchley Road, together with the line of the London & Birmingham Railway and the portal of the Primrose Hill tunnel.[55]

In the same year printed 'Proposals for Building,' with a colored plan on the back, were prepared (see Plate 284). They called the attention of builders to 'this very desirable Property, which is too well known to render necessary any description of its eligibility, in all respects, for Villas and respectable Residences, combining the advantages of Town and Country.' The college proposed to offer 'in the first instance . . . that part of the Estate adjoining the Hampstead Road at Haverstock Hill . . . containing about Fifteen Acres, in lots of not less than half an Acre, for the erection of single or double detached Villas.' The college would form the roads, which were intended, '(should the Buildings go on) to be continued and connected with other Roads, particularly with the new Turnpike Road from Mary-le-bone to Finchley, now in progress.' Even without such connections, 'the Roads at present proposed will afford very desirable Frontages for Buildings, having the advantage of adjoining the main Hampstead Road, and being at the same time secluded from its publicity.' There was no mention of the dimensions of the houses or their rate of building, except that they were to be 'substantial and respectable private Houses,' whose plans, elevations, and structural specifications would require the approval of Mr Shaw.[56]

The result must have been disappointing to all concerned. As Sir John Summerson puts it, 'some rather wretched pairs of villas sprang up on one side of the estate. Nothing more happened until 1842.'[57]

The younger John Shaw (1803–70) succeeded his father as surveyor in 1832, but it was 1840 before he presented the college with his own comprehensive plan of development. His proposals are interesting both as an expression of the ideas of suburban planning held by an experienced early-Victorian architect, and as an indication of how hard it was for any landowner rationally to direct the growth of London. For no portion of Shaw's plan was put into effect, since it proved to be as unacceptable to speculative builders as the plan of 1822 had been. For it was the builder, and behind the builder the investing public and their estimate of the market for houses, who ultimately determined the shape and character of the expanding English town. The landowner in London had greater power than landowners in most provincial towns, but he could exercise it only within the limits imposed by geography, fashion, the structure of the building industry, and the state of the money market.

Shaw was able to report that building on the portion of the estate fronting the Hampstead Road was virtually complete. 'Before making any further advance,' he wrote the bursar, 'it is highly important to consider . . . what will probably be the most beneficial mode of appropriating the Estate generally to the purposes of building, so that whatever may be done shall be upon a definite plan.' To that end he enclosed a plan containing a comprehensive pattern of streets and building lots (Plate 285). He surprisingly chose to locate a major roadway directly above the line of the railway tunnel. Negotiations were already in progress for the sale of Primrose Hill, but the plan showed that part of the estate marked out in building plots like the rest. So long as arrangements were made 'for definite and sufficient access into the Estate' from Regent's Park, Shaw thought the preservation of Primrose Hill as a public open space would 'materially benefit the Estate, while by securing the Roadways I have alluded to, it will not lead to any alteration in the design of the *residue* of the Estate.'

The plan represents an intermediate stage between the extremely spacious scheme of 1822 and the relatively compact layout that the building developers ultimately gave to the estate. In laying down the lines of roads, Shaw 'endeavoured to suggest the best Communications to the most important points, and to secure double frontages to each line as far as practicable.' He also provided for deep building lots, considering 200 feet the minimum that ought to be permitted. In fact, most plots turned out to be less than 150 feet deep. There were to be no more than three major east–west roads, compared with the five actually built, and two north–south roads, where there were eventually to be four. Apart from the comparatively narrow building plots for the houses already completed along Haverstock Hill, the plan provided for a total of no more than about 215 lots, nearly three times the number contemplated in 1822, but far fewer than there were eventually to be.[58] The accompanying map shows how Chalcots was actually to be developed.

The two indispensable amenities for any respectable housing estate were a church and a public house. William Wynn, the first substantial developer on the estate, gave it its first public house, the Adelaide Tavern—at the eastern end of Adelaide Road in 1842. In requesting the assistance of the college in his application for a license, Wynn pointed out that there was up to then 'not 1 public house [on the estate] . . . and taking the improvements altogether with the new park and Adelaide Road being a principal thoroughfare to the park the house will be an improvement to the estate.'[59] Three years later Shaw authorized Samuel Cuming to build a second 'Hotel or Tavern' in Adelaide Road, 500 yards distant from the Adelaide Tavern:

> its being restricted from being inferior to the *1st* Rate Class of Building
> will I think [Shaw wrote to the bursar] insure its respectability and Mr.
> Cuming who would be most interested in maintaining this respectability
> (considering his large Building Engagement) thinks such an house
> essentially necessary for the convenience of the large neighborhood which
> will be established: He is also desirous of ascertaining if the College would
> be willing to give a site for a Church on the new Line of Road . . . he tells
> me there is very great want of a place of worship and . . . he feels confident
> he could obtain the necessary funds for its erection.[60]

Shaw had given considerable thought to the need for a church in his 1840 report:[61]

> From frequent applications made by the Residents on the Property, and
> in the Neighborhood, I find that there is a general demand for a Chapel on
> the Estate, there being no place of worship within a very considerable

distance; Mr. Wynn the builder of many of the houses and other persons have led me to believe that it would be profitable even as a speculation to establish one, and that if the object could be entertained or promoted by the Provost and College such a subscription would be made by the neighborhood as would with their aid accomplish it.

Undoubtedly the existence of such a building on the Estate would most materially lead to the formation of a neighborhood around it . . . I have . . . in the Plan shown where a Church or Chapel might be advantageously placed, either at C or D.

The church that was finally erected, St Saviour's, was located at neither of the sites that Shaw suggested, but instead in the triangular enclosure, north of Adelaide Road, formed by Provost and Eton Roads and Eton Villas. Samuel Cuming was the largest of the original subscribers, pledging £200, and the college donated the site.[62] The church, in the Early English style, was completed in 1856, except for the tower and spire, which were added later.[63] In 1870 the college conveyed a freehold site at the junction of King Henry's and Elsworthy Roads to the Ecclesiastical Commissioners for the erection of another church, St Mary's, completed in 1873.[64]

Leases generally prohibited the use of houses as other than gentlemen's private residences, except in streets designed from the outset for shops, notably King's College and Winchester Roads, and England's Lane. Plate 289 is an elevation of four shops and a public house built along the east side of King's College Road by Robert Yeo; their lease was granted on 27 May 1858.[65] Yeo's lease for the terrace of six shops opposite the one illustrated prohibited the lessee from permitting 'any open or public shew of business . . . on that side of the house which abuts on the Adelaide Road,' or allowing 'the private door or entrance to be used for the purposes of any trade either for the reception or delivery of any goods and merchandize . . . nor [to] permit . . . any . . . of the said messuages or tenements to be converted into . . . a public house tavern or Beer shop nor in any way alter or add to the said six . . . buildings . . . nor destroy the uniformity of the said premises.'[66]

The initiative for setting out the actual pattern of streets lay with the building developers, notably Samuel Cuming. Cuming, who dominated the operations on the estate from the mid-forties through the fifties, continued to build until his death in 1870. Plate 286 shows how far the building had progressed by November 1849.[67] Plate 287 shows the houses, mostly along Adelaide Road, built by Cuming under his first five agreements.[68] Most of the houses shown in the earlier plan that are not in Plate 287 were built by Wynn or his subordinates, of whom Cuming was one, before he set out on his own.

The difference in the scale and density of construction between the plans of the ground landlord and the proposals of the building contractor reflected the customary conflict of interest between landlord and speculator, whereby the latter, with his better knowledge of the house market, would scale down the ambitious designs of the former.[69] Even so, the actual development carried out the surveyor's basic intention: that it consist of streets of villas, of the same order as those that were making the Eyre estate such a speculative and social success.

St John's Wood, 'resorted to by dissipated men of affluence for the indulgence of one of their worst vices,' already had a reputation for impropriety. Yet most of its inhabitants were 'opulent and industrious professional men and tradesmen,' and it set a pattern of suburban development that Chalcots wished to emulate. Whatever the 'dark, demoralizing scenes' that were supposed to take place in the 'handsome residences' behind the five-foot brick walls which were the 'peculiar characteristic' of the district, the estate found no difficulty in attracting residents of the utmost respectability.[70] Even Lady Amelia de Courcy, in *The Small House at Allington* (1864), was perfectly content to move to St John's Wood on her marriage, and her sister, Lady Alexandrina, would have been happy to do likewise had her husband not refused to live north of the New Road.

Shaw described the Eyre estate in 1845 as 'one of the most important and valuable Properties connected with the Metropolis, especially that part which adjoins Chalcots, the Roads being wide and the houses of a very superior Class.'[71] He therefore considered communications with the estate of the utmost importance, and laid great stress on pushing a road across Chalcots to join the Finchley Road. For this reason the central portion of the estate was developed several decades before either the northern or southern section.

The printed building-proposals of 1829 had promised through communications with St John's Wood. Ten years later negotiations were in progress with William Kingdom, 'a Gentleman . . . of great respectability, and considerable Property,' who had recently engaged in a speculation on Lord Holland's estate in Kensington, to construct the entire road and to build at its two ends, in 'a style of Building somewhat similar to the Terraces of the Regent's Park, or of the Oxford and Cambridge Terraces [Sussex Gardens, Paddington]; there can be little doubt of the new Road,' which would be called Eton Terrace, 'becoming a splendid addition to the projected improvements of the neighbourhood.' Shaw was willing to reduce Kingdom's ground rent from £35 an acre to as low as £20 if he would at his own expense build the road, 'intended to be 400 feet from the Center of the Railway and Tunnel and extending the whole length of the North side of it,' and from which 'branch roads may be formed . . . in many directions,' since it would 'so materially enhance the value of the Estate generally.'[72]

The negotiations with Kingdom fell through, but the following January Shaw was proposing to 'communicate with Colonel Eyre with reference to the access proposed to the St. Johns Wood Estate . . . which . . . will afford a mutual benefit to the *two* Estates.'[73] On 14 July 1845 Shaw reported that Adelaide Road had by then been formed 'to the extent of about 1500 feet,' one third of the way to the Finchley Road, and that arrangements had been made with Colonel Eyre for the junction of the two roads. He urged that the road and sewer 'be formed *at once*, & not progressively . . . and in this Condition Mr. Cuming acquiesces; indeed it is to his own interest with reference to his selling or letting the houses now building upon the Land he has taken, as there naturally exists a feeling in the Public, either that the Road may not be continued, or that many years may first elapse.'[74]

He wrote confidently the following January, 'when this new line is . . . opened I feel assured that the remaining frontages of the College Land will be advantageously disposed of, and the whole Estate greatly increased in value.'[75] He contemplated two more roads running west from the Hampstead Road north of Adelaide Road, but did not intend to extend the Private Road (later College Road) farther northward. There was also to be a road 'on the Chalcotts Estate running parallel with the Marylebone & Finchley Road at about the same distance from the boundary of the two Estates,' which became Winchester Road.[76]

The building agreements with Cuming, like those with later developers on the estate, while immensely more restrictive than a Sheffield builder would have tolerated, left him a fair amount of freedom to determine the details of his operations. For example, in his first agreement, he contracted to build 'not less than 8 single or double detached houses of not less than the 2d. rate on that part of the plan marked A,' with similarly loose specifications for the other four plots. 'Plans of each house and a general Specification of the same [were] to be submitted to, and to be subject to the approval of the Surveyor to the estate before it is commenced and no house [was] to be built inferior as respects materials and workmanship to those now building by Mr. Cuming [under an agreement made previously with William Wynn] on the estate.'[77] A standard covenant required that 'a space of at least 15 feet . . . be reserved between the main walls of each single or double detached House.'[78]

The surveyor found nothing to object to in Cuming's operations. In July 1845 he wrote to the bursar: '. . . I passed some hours yesterday in going over it [the Chalcots estate], and was very much pleased with the New line of Road which is now complete up to Mr. Cuming's last take, and with the houses he has built, & is building, which are of a superior description as he proceeds.'[79] Late in 1850 he reported that although 'there has been generally a cessation of building during the last two years . . . what has been done at Chalcot I am happy to say has been well done, and the Houses are of a respectable class & character.'[80]

Both the Chalcots estate and the Norfolk estate were developed on ninety-nine-year leases, but in every other way the policies and practices of the landlords and the developing builders on the two properties were totally different. Neither the Provost and Fellows of Eton College nor the Duke of Norfolk were consciously pursuing idiosyncratic methods of estate management, but they were instead responding to the wholly different sets of social and economic circumstances operating in North London and in a West Riding industrial center. Eton College developed Chalcots as an exclusively middle-class residential suburb; the Norfolk estate had an overwhelmingly working-class and industrial character. Eton College imposed strict regulations on its builders and tenants; the Norfolk estate exercised the mildest of

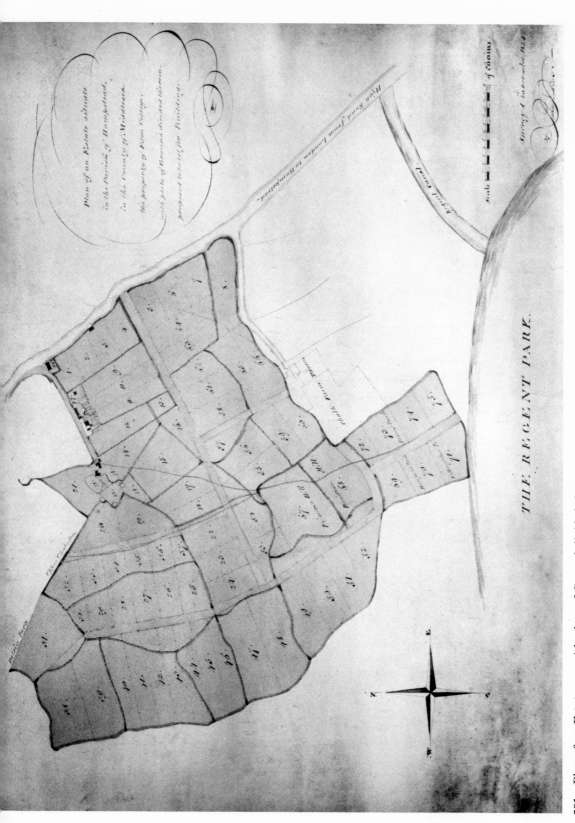

281 Plan of an Estate . . . with plots of Ground divided thereon proposed to be let for Building. Surveyed 20 December 1824, by John Jenkins. Eton College Records, vol. 51/13.
Photos: S. G. Parker-Ross
Eton College

282 Plan of part of the Estate of Eton College . . . showing a Design for building thereon, March 1827 [by John Shaw]. E.C.R. vol. 51/17. *Eton College*

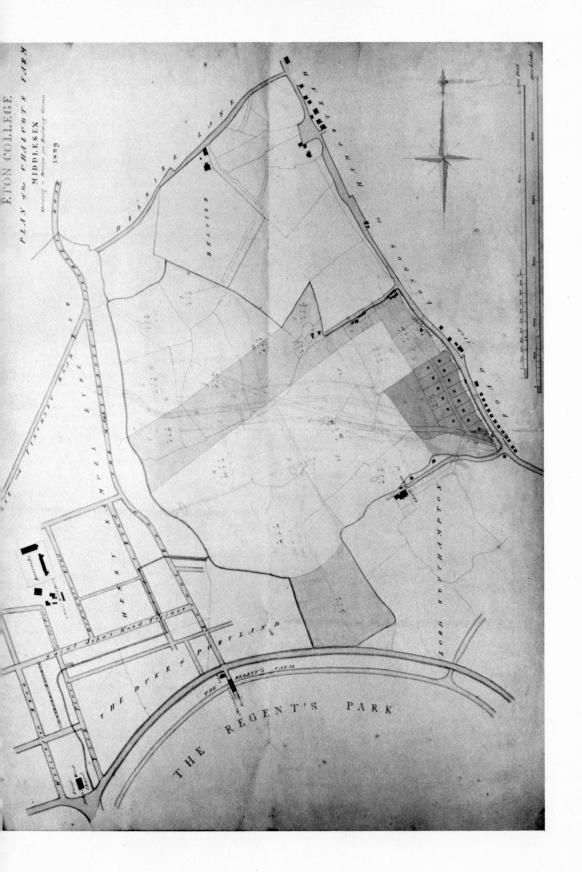

283 Plan of the Chalcots Farm . . . showing a Design for Building thereon, 1829. E.C.R. vol. 51/19.
Eton College

284 Eton College Estate, Chalcots, Hampstead. Proposals for Building, 1 May 1829. E.C.R. vol. 49/27. *Eton College*

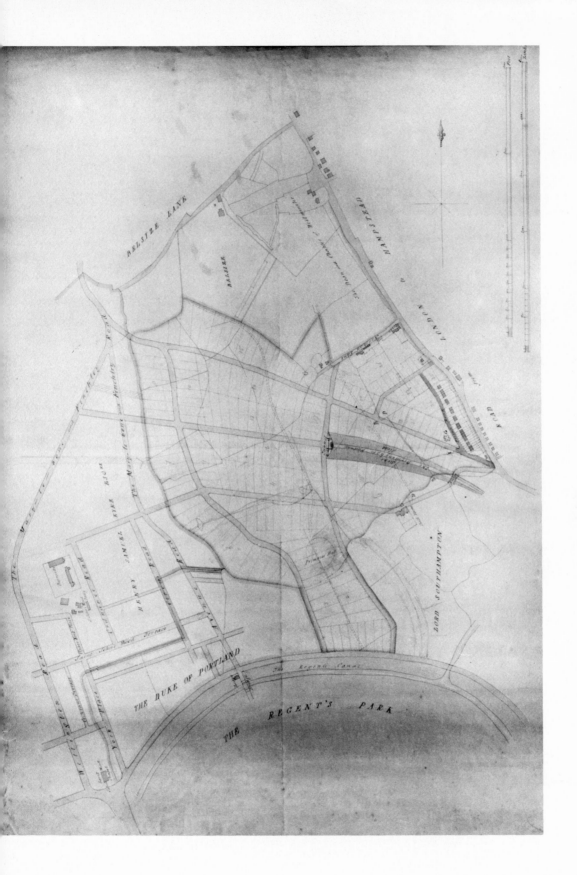

285 Chalcots estate [January 1840]. E.C.R. vol. 51/25.
Eton College

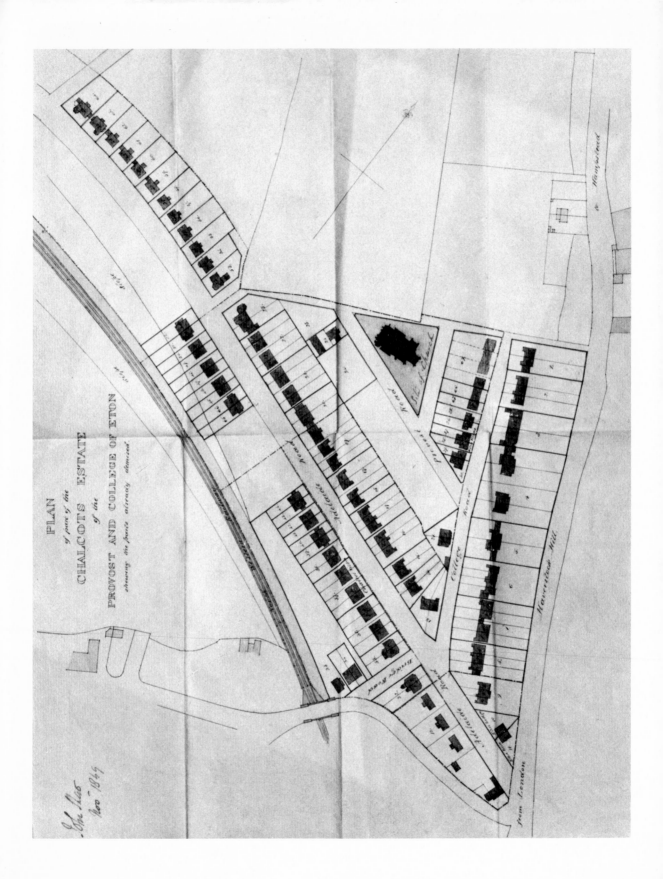

PLAN
of part of the
CHALCOTS ESTATE
of the
PROVOST AND COLLEGE OF ETON
shewing the parts already demised.

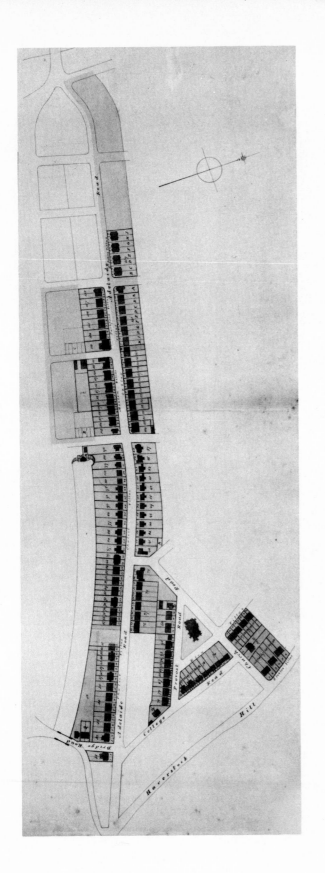

286 *above* Plan of Chalcots Estate showing the parts already demised. November 1849, John Shaw. E.C.R. vol. 49/131.
Eton College

287 *below* Plan of building on the estate to illustrate five building agreements . . . with Samuel Cuming, 4 January 1858. E.C.R. vol. 51/40.
Eton College

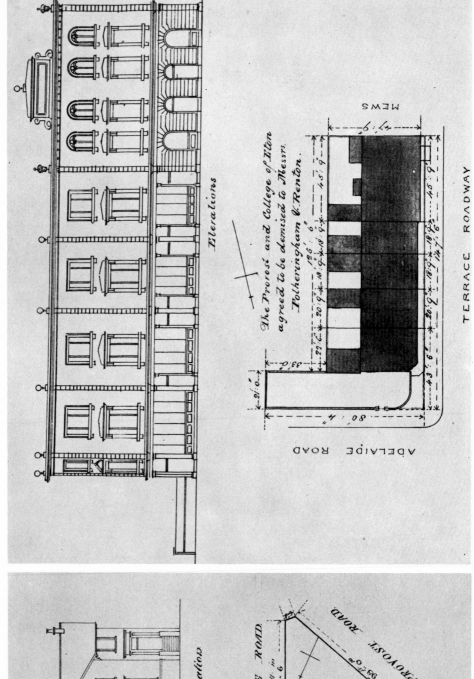

288 *left* Elevation for 1 Eton Villas, 28 March 1849, Chalcots Leases no. 1, fol. 56. *Eton College*

289 *right* Elevation, four shops and public house, Nos 1, 3, 5, 7, 9 King's College Road, 27 May 1858, Robert Yeo, Chalcots Estate. Leases, no. 1 (9 March 1836–26 September 1860), fol. 160. *Eton College*

290 *below* Elevations for 17–26 Oakley Villas, Adelaide Road, 2 May 1856, Samuel Cuming. Leases no. 1, fol. 151. *Eton College*

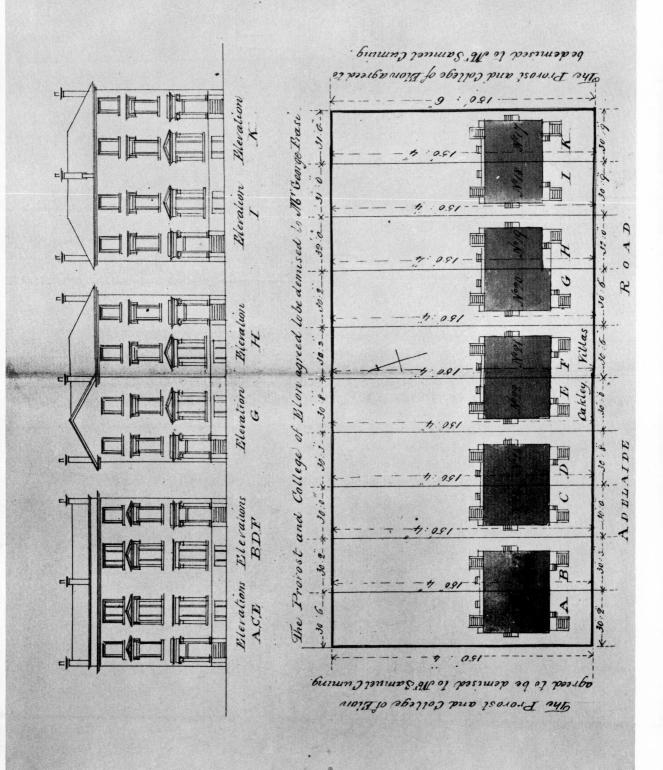

The Provost and College of Eton agreed to be demised to Mr Samuel Cuming

The Provost and College of Eton agreed to be demised to Mr George Frost

Oakley Villas

R O A D

A D E L A I D E

The Provost and College of Eton
agreed to be demised to Mr Samuel Cuming

Elevations Elevations
A.C.E   B.D.F.

Elevation
G

Elevation
H

Elevation
I

Elevation
K

291 Elevations for 1–4 Oxford Villas, Harley Road; and 1–6 Wykeham Villas, Winchester Road, 2 May 1856, Frank Clemow and Mary Anne

Angell, lessees. Leases no. 1, fol. 152.
Eton College

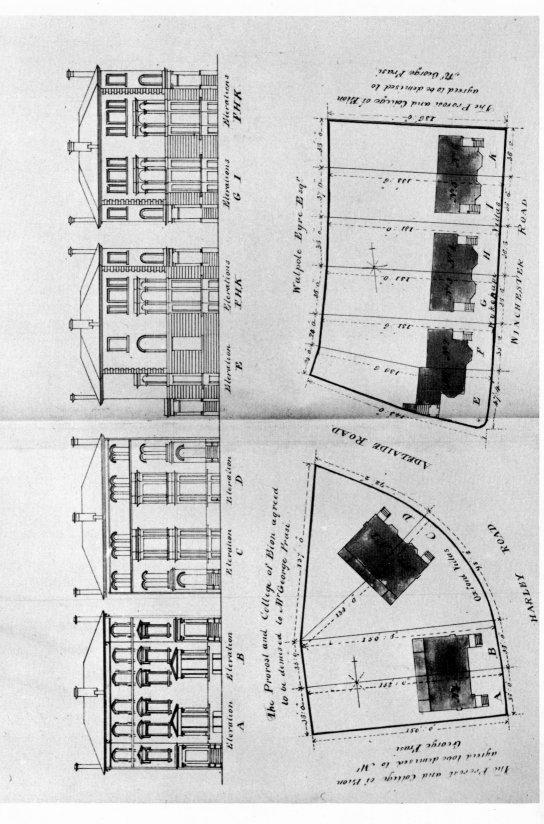

controls. Chalcots was a low-density neighborhood of detached and semi-detached villas; the Norfolk estate was a mixture of cutlers' workshops, steel mills, and low rows of cottages, back-to-back in the early Victorian years, fronting on narrow streets or courts. Chalcots was developed by comparatively large-scale builders and contractors; Sheffield by small speculators, with a minimum of capital. Speculators at Chalcots were themselves usually professional builders; speculators in Sheffield— at least until the 1850s—were more likely to be investors outside the building industry. In Chalcots, the responsibility for providing roads lay with the builder; in Sheffield, with the ground landlord. Before building could begin in Chalcots, carefully drafted articles of agreement had to be executed; in Sheffield, a verbal understanding was all that was required. For all its superior social aspirations, Chalcots is as much a denial of the basic principles of Georgian town planning as is Sheffield. As an exercise in urban design it pales in comparison with the near-contemporaneous development of the Bedford estate in northern Bloomsbury. Thomas Batcheldor and Samuel Cuming make a poor showing if set beside Christopher Haedy and Thomas Cubitt. Whatever the leafy charms of Eton Villas today or Adelaide Road until recently, they cannot compare in architectural excellence with Tavistock or even Gordon Square. Figs Mead, which was being developed in the forties and fifties at exactly the same time as Adelaide Road, and for a markedly lower class of intended resident, shows immensely greater imagination in layout.[81] Yet the same London & Birmingham Railway that frustrated the intentions of the Bedford Office to make Ampthill Square a center of gentility did no apparent damage to the houses in Adelaide and King Henry's Roads through whose back gardens it ran.[82]

Like the Norfolk estate in Sheffield, Chalcots is less a consciously imposed town plan than a rational response to a particular housing market. Sheffield demanded the maximum number of the cheapest possible cottages, crowded as closely together as possible around places of employment. The narrow streets and confined courts that hugged the slopes of Sheffield's hills did just that, reconciling the single-family house with a compact, high-density community. Chalcots demanded villas, separate and semi-detached, solid and respectable but not unduly costly, a church, trees, private gardens, seclusion; above all that the lower orders be kept at a distance. By cooperating with, rather than opposing, social and economic realities, the two ground landlords adopted unheroic roles for themselves. The real key to what happened lies with the builders, developers, and investors who embodied these realities.

Notes

1   J. L. and Barbara Hammond, *The Town Labourer 1760–1832* (1917), pp. 39–40.
2   Thomas Carlyle, 'Shooting Niagara: and After?' *Macmillan's Magazine*, xvi (1867), 332.
3   See A. S. Wohl, 'The Housing of the Artisans and Laborers in Nineteenth Century London, 1815–1914' (unpublished Ph.D. dissertation, Brown University, 1966);

'The Bitter Cry of Outcast London,' *International Review of Social History*, xiii (1968), Part 2, 189–245; and 'The Housing of the Working Classes in London, 1750–1914,' in Stanley Chapman, ed., *The History of Working Class Housing* (Newton Abbot, 1971).

4 H. J. Dyos, 'The Speculative Builders and Developers of Victorian London,' *Victorian Studies*, xi (1968), 641–90; Marian Bowley, *The British Building Industry* (Cambridge, 1966), pp. 337–40.

5 G. Calvert Holland, *Vital Statistics of Sheffield* (1843), p. 56.

6 John Nash in J. White, *Some Account of the Proposed Improvements of the Western Part of London* (2nd edn, 1815), Appendix, pp. xxvii–xxviii.

7 A. K. Cairncross, *Home and Foreign Investment 1870–1913* (Cambridge, 1953), p. 84.

8 Dyos, 'Speculative Builders,' p. 663. See also John R. Kellett, *The Impact of Railways on Victorian Cities* (1969), pp. 412–13.

9 Sir John Summerson, 'Urban Forms,' in Oscar Handlin and John Burchard, eds, *The Historian and the City* (Cambridge, Mass., 1963), p. 174.

10 Hugh C. Prince in J. T. Coppock and Hugh C. Prince, eds, *Greater London* (1964), p. 105.

11 Kate Simon, *London : Places and pleasures* (New York, 1968), p. 293.

12 *Builder* (*B*), xix (1861), 641.

13 James Haywood and William Lee, *Report on the Sanatory Condition of the Borough of Sheffield* (2nd edn, Sheffield, 1848), p. 10.

14 *Sheffield and Rotherham Independent*, 13 January 1872.

15 Sir John Summerson in Handlin and Burchard, op. cit., p. 175; and in 'The Beginnings of an Early Victorian London Suburb,' II, a lecture delivered at the London School of Economics, 27 February 1958, the MS. of which Sir John has kindly allowed me to read.

16 Reginald J. Fletcher, *St. Saviour's Church South Hampstead, A Retrospect* (1918), pp. 6–7.

17 See the works of A. S. Wohl cited in note 3.

18 *Parliamentary Papers* (*P.P.*), 1889, LXV, Report on an Epidemic of Small-Pox at Sheffield during 1887–88; by Dr Barry (C. 5645), p. 286.

19 Sidney Pollard, *History of Labour in Sheffield* (Liverpool, 1959), pp. 185–6.

20 *P.P.*, 1833, XV, Select Committee (S.C.) on Public Walks: Minutes of Evidence (448), Q. 899. See also ibid., 1833, VI, Select Committee on Manufactures, Commerce, and Shipping: Minutes of Evidence (690), Q. 2917.

21 Sidney Pollard, op. cit., pp. 100–1. See also G. Calvert Holland, op. cit., pp. 29, 46, 69; 'Plans generally adopted in the Town of Sheffield for Cottage Houses,' by William Flockton, in *P.P.*, 1845, XVIII, Royal Commission (R.C.) on the State of Large Towns and Populous Districts: 2nd Report, Part II, Appendix (610), p. 347.

22 James Haywood and William Lee, op. cit., p. 122. See also *P.P.* 1888, XXII, S.C. on Town Holdings: Minutes of Evidence (313), QQ. 859–62.

23 Ibid., Select Committee on Manufactures, Commerce, and Shipping (690), QQ. 2884–9; G. Calvert Holland, op. cit., pp. 56–8; *P.P.*, 1884–5, XXX, R.C. on the Housing of the Working Classes: Minutes of Evidence (Cd. 4402–I), Q. 10,795.

24   Ibid., 1888, XXII, S.C. on Town Holdings: Minutes of Evidence (313), Q. 720.

25   Marian Bowley, op. cit., p. 360.

26   *Building News*, vi (1860), 871. See also 'Report of Messrs Leverton & Chawner ...'
     in J. White, *Some Account of the Proposed Improvements*, Appendix, p. vi;
     Architectural Magazine, i (1834), 115; James Noble, *The Professional Practice of
     Architects* (1836), pp. 91–3; Donald J. Olsen, *Town Planning in London: The
     eighteenth and nineteenth centuries* (New Haven, 1964), pp. 14–20.

29   'Report of Messrs Leverton & Chawner,' pp. xi–xii.

28   B, xvi (1858), 177. See also Olsen, op. cit., pp. 34–5, 224–7.

29   *P.P.*, 1889, XV, S.C. on Town Holdings: Report (Cd. 251), p. 85.

30   Horace Walpole to George Montagu, 1 September 1760, in W. S. Lewis and Ralph
     S. Brown, Jr, eds, *Horace Walpole's Correspondence* (New Haven, 1941) IX, p. 295.

31   Holland, op. cit., pp. 50–1.

32   B, xix (1861), 641.

33   Sheffield City Libraries, 'Applications for Building Ground and Premises, 1824–
     1850 A,' passim, Arundel Castle MSS S384. All references to the Arundel Castle
     MSS in the Sheffield City Libraries are by the kind permission of His
     Grace, the Duke of Norfolk, E.M., K.G., and of the City Librarian, John
     Bebbington, F.L.A.

34   'Ratification by Henry, 15th Duke of Norfolk, of building leases in a schedule,'
     24 December 1868, Arundel Castle MSS–S.D. 546. Alfred Emden, *The Law Relating
     to Building, Building Leases, and Building Contracts* (2nd edn, 1885), pp. 79, 87,
     293–4.

35   Printed form of lease (dated 6 May 1788), Arundel Castle MSS–S.D. 868/184.

36   James Sorby to Michael Ellison, 12 September 1835, Arundel Castle MSS–S478
     (xiii).

37   Duke of Norfolk's Trust (Sheffield Estate), 'Draft Proposed Form of Lease for 99
     Years—As perused by Mr. Fowler, 1861,' pp. 3–6; Arundel Castle MSS–SP38.

38   *P.P.* 1888, XXII, S.C. on Town Holdings: Minutes of Evidence (313), QQ. 729–
     30.

39   Ibid., Q. 3517.

40   Marginal memoranda, *Queries Prepared with a View of Obtaining Evidence on the
     Matters Referred to the Committee*, S.C. on Town Holdings, 1886, Arundel Castle
     MSS–S439.

41   See Few & Co. to H. W. Beavan, 25 August 1836 (copy), Arundel Castle MSS
     S478 (xiv); for the policies on the London estate in the eighties, see *P.P.* 1887,
     XIII, S.C. on Town Holdings; Minutes of Evidence (260), QQ. 11,958–12,360.

42   Michael Ellison to Edward Blount, 20 April 1840, Arundel Castle MSS–S478
     (xviii).

43   In this connection, see also Henry Howard, Auditor, in 'Sheffield Order Book,'
     11 and 12 July 1815, Arundel Castle MSS–S391; Edward Blount to John Housman,
     10 August 1819, Arundel Castle MSS–S478 (ii); Michael Ellison, Diary, 26 April
     1853, Arundel Castle MSS–S523.

44   For the small resources and limited scale of operation of the Sheffield builders, see
     'Applications for Building Ground and Premises, 1824–1850 A,' Arundel Castle
     MSS–S384; 'Applications for Building Ground, and premises, From 29th September

1865 to 31st December 1867,' Arundel Castle MSS–SP38; Holland, op. cit., pp. 55–9, 66; *P.P.*, 1833, VI, S.C. Manufactures, Commerce, and Shipping (690), QQ. 2884–9; Ibid., 1884–5, XXX, R.C. on the Housing of the Working Classes: Minutes of Evidence (C. 4402–I), Q. 10,795; Pollard, op. cit., p. 101.

45 *P.P.*, 1889, XV, S.C. on Town Holdings: Report (251), p. 85.

46 *B*, xxxiii (1875), 274.

47 Olsen, op. cit., pp. 20, 33–4, 81–3, 224–7.

48 'Report of Messrs Leverton & Chawner,' p. xv.

49 John Nash, op. cit., pp. xxxiv–xxxv.

50 John Summerson, *Georgian London* (1945), p. 164.

51 'Proposed plan to divide the Land belonging to Eton College situate at Primrose Hill ... into plots of ground to be let for Building,' Eton College Records (hereafter cited as E.C.R.) vol. 51/12. All MS. references to material on Chalcots in the Eton College Library are by the kind permission of the Provost and Fellows of Eton College.

52 'Plan of an Estate ... with plots of Ground divided thereon proposed to be let for Building,' 20 December 1824, E.C.R. vol. 51/13. See also George Bethell, 'Observations heard at the meeting relative to the waste,' 1825, E.C.R. vol. 49/22.

53 *An Act for effecting an Exchange between Her Majesty and the Provost and College of Eton*, 5 & 6 Vict. cap. lxxviii.

54 'Plan of a part of the Estate of Eton College ... showing a design for building thereon,' March 1827, E.C.R. vol. 51/17.

55 'Plan of the Chalcots Farm ... Shewing a Design for Building thereon,' 1829, E.C.R. vol. 51/19.

56 Chalcots, Hampstead. Proposals for Building, 1 May 1829, E.C.R. vol. 49/27.

57 Summerson, 'Urban Forms,' p. 174.

58 'Chalcots estate plan' [January 1840], E.C.R. vol. 51/25; John Shaw to George Bethell, 14 January 1840, E.C.R. vol. 49/84.

59 William Wynn to Thomas Batcheldor, 12 December 1842, Chalcots, Box 1.

60 John Shaw to George Bethell, 8 January 1846, E.C.R. vol. 49/119.

61 Ibid., 14 January 1840, E.C.R. vol. 49/84.

62 Henry Bird to George Bethell, 7 September 1846, E.C.R. vol. 49/128; *Proposed District Church, Chalcott's Estate, Haverstock Hill, Hampstead Road*, 5 September 1846, E.C.R. vol. 49/128; Two plans 'of part of Fourteen Acres Field inserted in a conveyance from the Provost and College of Eton as a site for a Church ...' 17 December 1846, E.C.R. vol. 51/34; Tooke Son and Hallowes to the Provost of Eton, 10 July 1847, E.C.R. vol. 49/130; John Shaw to George Bethell, 21 November 1850, E.C.R. vol. 49/137.

63 *B*, xiv (1856), 390; Stephen Buckland, 'The Origin and Building of S. Saviour's Church,' *S. Saviour, Eton Road, Hampstead, Parish Paper*, October 1956.

64 'The Provost and College of Eton and The Revd. Chas. James Fuller and others, Agreement for Conveyance of Land ... for a Site for a Church,' 20 July 1870, Chalcots, Box 6.

65 'Chalcots Estate Leases No. 1 (9 March 1836–26 September 1860),' Lease no. 160.

66 Lease, Robert Yeo, 13 June 1859, 'Chalcots, Leases, January 1859–July 1865,' p. 59.

67 E.C.R. vol. 49/131.

68 'Plan of building on the estate to illustrate five building agreements . . . with Samuel Cuming,' 4 January 1858, E.C.R. vol. 51/40.

69 See, for instance, Olsen, op. cit., pp. 20, 35, 224–7.

70 Alfred Cox, *The Landlord's and Tenant's Guide* [1853], pp. 231–2.

71 John Shaw to George Bethell, 22 July 1845, E.C.R. vol. 49/116.

72 William Kingdom to John Shaw, 22 March 1839, E.C.R. vol. 49/81; John Shaw to George Bethell, 28 March 1839, E.C.R. vol. 49/82.

73 Ibid., 14 January 1840, E.C.R. vol. 49/84.

74 Ibid., 14 July 1845, E.C.R. vol. 49/114.

75 Ibid., 8 January 1846, E.C.R. vol. 49/119.

76 Ibid., 5 March 1846, E.C.R. vol. 49/123.

77 'Particulars of a proposed letting of part of the Chalcott's Estate to Mr. Saml. Cuming . . . Builder,' 5 August 1844, E.C.R. vol. 49/111.

78 'Particulars of a proposed letting . . . to Mr. Saml. Cuming . . . Builder,' 1 January 1845, E.C.R. vol. 49/112.

79 John Shaw to George Bethell, 22 July 1845, E.C.R. vol. 49/116.

80 Ibid., 16 November 1850, E.C.R. vol. 49/136. See also *Land and Building News*, ii (1856), 251.

81 Olsen, op. cit., pp. 63–73.

82 Ibid., pp. 150–1.

15   Slums and Suburbs

H. J. Dyos and D. A. Reeder

Victorian London was a land of fragments. Yet the immensity of its mass and the bewildering tissue of its human associations argue for something quite different. To all appearances, its streets abutted each other with a stumbling logic and the names of the neighbourhoods they enclosed unrolled with a continuous rhythm across the map. By day, the great improvised structure could be seen to heave into operation like a piece of fantastic machinery set going by an invisible hand. By night, its operatives could be seen submitting with equal discipline to a different spatial logic as they redistributed themselves for sleep. The impression created by this daily act is of a kind of social contract being discharged by a society held together by a common purpose and conscious to some degree of being a community. Such a symmetry was not a complete illusion even in Victorian London. People commonly congregate in cities because they look for mutual support and they accept unthinkingly the commercial ethos ruling there as the first organizing principle of their working lives. The rule of the market was the original and most natural means of settling rival claims to all things in short supply, not least to space, and the population reshuffled itself by day and by night in tacit acceptance of the prevailing values laid upon the land. Whatever space they occupied was everywhere contracted for in some terms, whether by duly attested indentures or merely a nod upon the stairs, and this great interlocking bargain came daily into play. It was a contract of a kind.

But the irrigations of commercial capital that sustained it even in the smallest channels were not capable of keeping a larger sense of community alive when it was in danger of being crushed by sheer force of numbers. Whatever sense of that kind could be said to have lingered within living memory at the start of the Victorian period had been fractured by just such growth, and the animus that was replacing it already looked more like an instinct for survival. London was too vast, and the consciousness of the crowd too immanent, to admit the intimacy of a single community for the whole. There was instead the beginnings of a fragmentation that has never been reversed. This was only partly geographical. It was also social and psychological. The characteristic tensions being produced were not so much, perhaps, between class and class as between the individual and the mass, and between the individual's inner life and his outward behaviour. The characteristic shapes which these produced on the ground—the realities composed from their images, then and now—were of suburbs and of slums.

In the crudest model of their development with which we might begin, it is here that urban society most visibly diverged. Centrifugal forces drew the rich into the airy suburbs; centripetal ones held the poor in the airless slums. But the compelling pressures of expansion caused ripples of obsolescence, which overtook places once dancing with buttercups and left them stale as cabbage stalks. Suburbs begat or became slums, rarely if ever the reverse, and the two never coalesced. Whole districts lost ordinary contact with their neighbours, and London became, in the most indulgent terms, an island of villages; in the most heartless, a geographical expression of increasing vagueness. Yet this disintegration was not a disconnected process. The fact of the suburb influenced the environment of the slum; the threat of the slum entered the consciousness of the suburb.

We want in this chapter to look at some of the ways in which their individual characteristics were mutually determined. It is confined to London because the relationship between these two ways of life was not exhibited so clearly anywhere else in Victorian Britain. We concern ourselves chiefly with the narrow focus of the economic forces which were at work simply because we believe that, apart from the multiplication of the population, these were the most fundamental. And we have not the space to go beyond them.

We can see this London quite literally, then, as a great commercial undertaking. Here, even in 1815, was a million-peopled city articulated by commerce into a single gigantic enterprise, the supreme money market of the trading world and the most commanding concentration by far of people, industry, and trade to be found anywhere. This commercial metropolis was presently made more impregnable still by the concentrative power of the railways at home and the gains of imperialism abroad, and its capacity to stimulate new demands within the national economy was enhanced by its indomitable leadership in wealth and fashion. It was an enterprise supported by a labour force that was docile, abundant, and cheap, and by a capital supply that seemed more and more mobile and less and less exhaustible. Here was a formula for inexorable growth—of numbers, output, distances, elevations, mass.

It was a headlong business. What mattered most to a commercial metropolis was commercial success, whether on some remote frontier where money mattered less than existence or on its own doorstep, where it sometimes mattered a good deal more. Building and extending its own plant were inseparable parts of the whole field of operations, and investment in the necessary urban equipment—in houses and domestic amenities no less than in the means of locomotion or places of work and the storage of goods—obeyed as it could the first rule of the market place: buy cheap, sell dear. The housing of the poor, as of the rich, was an item of real property, capable of providing titles to wealth for a whole series of property holders; it was expected to yield profits commensurate with whatever were regarded as the risks of investing in it; and it was held to be quite as much subject to the ordinary pressures of the market as any other commodity put up for sale. As the manipulators of capital, the middle classes helped to make possible the expansion of house-building in the suburbs, the parts of the city in which they were shaping their own environment, but in diverting resources for these purposes they also helped to determine the environment of those left behind in the city centre.

It must be remembered here that the distribution of personal incomes and social disabilities in any society helps to determine not only the way in which power is used at the top but also the way in which weaknesses are shared at the bottom. The condition of the housing of the poor was a step through the looking-glass of the rich— a reflex of the allocation of political power and economic resources in society at large. It was no accident that the worst slums were generally found in places where large houses were vacated by the middle classes in their trek to the further suburbs. Such property could only be occupied economically by lower classes by being turned into tenements, but the rent for a whole floor or even a whole room was often too much for those eventually in possession, and the sub-divisions of space that followed usually meant the maximum deterioration in living conditions. It must also be recognized that the resources which might have made such a transition less dramatic were being ploughed heavily back into the commercial machine instead of being distributed in higher wages. It was tacitly accepted that, if better houses had been built to house industrial workers during the nineteenth century, the higher wages paid out to make this possible would have raised the costs of exports and reduced the capital being sent abroad, which would in turn have held back the growth of exports. More sophisticated economic reasoning might suggest that, so long as there were few substitutes for British goods abroad, paying higher wages and charging higher prices would actually have increased these receipts, but it did not look that way at the time. More matter-of-fact logic demanded that labour costs be cut to the bone. The slums were part of this argument for the economy of low wages, and one of their practical functions was therefore to underpin Victorian prosperity. The truth of the matter now seems to be that they embodied some of the most burdensome and irreducible real costs of industrial growth that might have been imagined.[1] When Henry Jephson wrote his classic study, *The Sanitary Evolution of London* (1907), it was, he said, 'the all-powerful, the all-impelling motive and unceasing desire' for 'commercial prosperity and success' that provided London's motive power. 'That indisputable fact must constantly be borne in mind as one reviews the sanitary and social condition of the people of London . . .' (pp. 7–8).

London's appetite for people had always been immense, but its commercial aggrandizement made it even more voracious. From just under a million inhabitants at the beginning of the century, its requirements had grown, by its close, to about four and a half millions within its own administrative boundaries alone, and a further two millions were distributed, less congestedly but within easy daily reach, in an outer belt of the conurbation—known for statistical purposes after 1875 as Greater London. London grew by sucking in provincial migrants because jobs were either better paid there or thought to be so; it also offered a more liberal array of charities, richer rewards for crime, a more persuasive legend of opportunity than could be found anywhere in the country.[2] So the net migration into London during the 1840s resulted in the addition of about 250,000 inhabitants, or almost one-fifth of its mean population for the decade—a rate of intake which declined appreciably over the next two decades while its absolute level continued to climb, but which surged up again in the 1870s, when almost 500,000, or over fifteen percent, were added to the natural increase. By 1901 Greater London contained one-fifth of the entire population of England and Wales, and in the preceding decade it absorbed, one way or another, one-quarter of the net increase in population of the whole country.[3]

How this provincial tribute was gathered and where it was harboured we cannot tell for certain. The paths of migration into Victorian London have not been traced sufficiently systematically, and whole decades of coming and going, of movements by the million, have dropped completely from our view. The traditional place for the stranger, the poor, the unwanted—for any threatening presence—was at the city gates, and the motley colonies that had accreted there since the Middle Ages remained the receptacles for the sweepings of the city until the space available within the walls was exhausted by the growth of urban society proper in the sixteenth and seventeenth centuries. The suburbs were the slums. The process of accretion that was already in motion around London at the beginning of the nineteenth century was quite different from this. The colonization of London's nearby villages by merchants and men of affairs in the eighteenth century had pre-empted a new middle-class ring of suburbs which, as it spread, congealed in the nineteenth century into a great continent of petty villadom. The new suburb had leap-frogged the older slum.[4] Before 1861 or so the growth of these outer districts, though often dramatic topographically, was not the most rapid or most important. The central districts, which had always belonged to both rich and poor, remained the chief focus of growth. It was here that the main influx of newcomers congregated, and it was here too that the slum was first given its modern name.

It was originally a piece of slang which meant among other things a room of low repute—a term which Pierce Egan extended in his *Life in London* (1821) to 'back slums', defining it in one place as 'low, unfrequented parts of the town'.[5] Dickens used it so when he wrote a letter dated November 1841: 'I mean to take a great, London, back-slums kind of walk tonight.'[6] Presently it took the form of 'slums' and began to pass into everyday use, though it took another forty years for the inverted commas to disappear completely. It was perhaps always an outsider's word, the lack of which did not necessarily imply that the thing it named was too esoteric for ordinary speech, but one too readily accepted to require a general pejorative term. That did not come about before the 1880s—when the assumed place names of the suburbs were first swept aside by the collective gibe of suburbia—and the all-too-real housing 'problem' began to take shape as a public issue. Precisely what a slum ever meant on the ground has never been clear, partly because it has not developed that kind of technical meaning which definition in an Act of Parliament would have given it: indeed, it still lacks this kind of precision and tends to be defined even nowadays in terms of the number of obsolescent houses which a local authority can clear rather than the kind of houses involved. This vagueness has in practice been aggravated by the failure of parliament or the courts to define at all clearly the chief characteristic of a slum, namely its overcrowding, or the actual basis of the medical judgment that a house was 'unfit for human habitation'.[7]

The implication of this is that, like poverty itself, slums have always been relative things, both in terms of neighbouring affluence and in terms of what was tolerable by those living in or near them. Such a term has no fixity. It invokes comparison. What it felt like to live in a slum depended in some degree, for example, on what it might feel like to live in a suburb. Yet there was no simple polarity. There were degrees of slumminess just as there were degrees of suburban exclusiveness, and there were many irregularities in the declension between them. To Patrick Geddes the whole lamentable process of city-building in the nineteenth century was of a piece: 'slum, semi-slum and super slum,' he wrote, 'to this has come the Evolution of Cities.'[8] The old order of slum had certainly insinuated itself as readily into the central purlieus of wealth in St James's as the new order was doing in the suburban ones of Bayswater or Camberwell.[9] Slums as well as suburbs had their moving frontiers and to try to define either too concisely makes very little sense. In terms of human values, the slums of Victorian London were three-dimensional obscenities as replete as any ever put out of sight by civilized man; in terms of the urban economy, they were part of the infrastructure of a market for menial and casual labour; in terms of urban society, they were a lodging for criminal and vagrant communities; in terms of real property, they were the residue left on the market, the last bits and pieces to command a price; in terms of the dynamic of urban change, they were the final phase in a whole cycle of human occupation which could start up again only by the razing of the site. The making of these slums was a process that began far beyond the reach of the slummers who packed into them. It is important to recognize that the unfortunates who occupied the central slums, and those only slightly more fortunate, perhaps, who occupied the slums of the inner suburbs or the embryo slums of the outer districts, were more than anything else merely the residuary legatees of a kind of house-processing operation which was started by another social class with little or no idea or concern as to how it would end.

We cannot here explain in detail what one reviewer of Mayhew called 'this localicity of pauperization'.[10] The most general explanation for slum tendencies in particular places is that, without the kind of general control on the spatial development of the city that might have been given, say, by a rectilinear grid, there were bound to be innumerable dead-ends and backwaters in the street plan. A glance at Booth's maps shows how often these introspective places were seized by the 'criminal classes', whose professional requirements were isolation, an entrance that could be watched, and a back exit kept exclusively for the getaway. They were not difficult to fulfil in scores of places in every part of Victorian London. A more careful reading of Booth's maps would show how some additions to the street plan—a dock, say, or a canal, a railway line, or a new street—frequently reinforced these tendencies. What often made them more emphatic still was the incense of some foul factory, a gas-works, the debris of a street-market, or an open sewer. They all acted like tourniquets applied for too long, and below them a gangrene almost invariably set in. The actual age of houses seldom had much to do with it, and it was sometimes possible to run through the whole gamut from meadow to slum in a single generation, or even less. Animal husbandry survived, of course, in caricature in some of these places, where pigs, sheep, cows, and other livestock were still being slowly cleared in the 1870s from the slums they had helped to create. One man who had spent twenty years visiting the poor of a riverside parish could write as late as 1892 of the donkeys, goats, and chickens which had as free a run of some of the houses by night as they had of the streets by day.[11]

It is possible, too, to trace the origins of slumminess in buildings scamped, whether legally or not, on inadequately settled 'made ground' or by virtue of some builder's sanitary blunder. The history of building regulations is a tale of the regulators never quite catching up with the builders, and of the piecemeal enlarging of the statutory code so as to reduce risks from fire and to health. The machinery for approving street plans and drainage levels took time to evolve and an incorruptible corps of local government officers to administer it.[12] No one can say with real confidence that the many hands required in building and rebuilding slum-prone neighbourhoods were under full and proper control in the public interest before the last decade of the century. Whatever was physically substandard was inclined to become socially inferior, too: the slummers themselves, though often adding the penalty of their own personal habits to the descending scale, seldom *created* such slums as often as they confirmed the builders' and others' mistakes. When this social descent began it was seldom, if ever, reversed, but went inexorably on—respectability taking itself a little further off, the sheer durability of such houses visiting the sins of their builders on the third and fourth generations of those that occupied them.

The more fundamental explanation of the slums, as of the distribution of all urban space before the era of zonal controls, rests, however, on the more basic commercial concept of supply and demand—of housing itself and of the capital and land which were its vital elements. Take first the dominant influence, the supply of housing at the centre. Here, as compared with the outer districts, were much stricter economic limits to an increase in house-room at low rents, because the alternative uses of the land were capable of bearing a heavier charge for it. Economizing on land by building high was moreover inherently more costly per unit of space provided. Private capital was therefore shy of building flats on central sites for the working classes, and the working classes themselves had a horror of anything so undomesticated as a street standing on end. There was no real possibility of enlarging the housing capacity of the central districts. Indeed, it was impossible even to maintain it. The conversion of houses into offices and warehouses within the City alone began to force its total population down after 1861.[13] But the most draconian changes felt all over central London arose, as they had always done, in making way for a greater traffic in merchandise and fare-paying passengers, whether by sea, road, or rail; and the docks, street improvements, and railways being built in this period set off a whole series of detonations which could be felt not only on the spot but also in long chains of reactions which reached even to the suburbs.[14]

The connections between all this activity and the supply of living room became a commonplace among common people even though the scale of operations was never— nor perhaps ever can be—measured with real accuracy. In the history of the slums of Victorian London these 'improvements'—to use the generic term—had a special irony. They had always been hailed as the means of clearing the slums, though they had hardly ever failed to aggravate them, for their effect always was to reduce the supply of working-class housing, either absolutely or in terms of the kind of houses which those turned out of doors by their operations could afford or wish to occupy. 'Here was a continual pushing back, back, and down, down, of the poor', one slum clergyman told his lecture audience in 1862, 'till they were forced into the very places which were already reeking with corruption.'[15] This had been so, long before the Victorian period. It is possible to see, allied to the commercial zeal for wider streets and larger openings in the City since the eighteenth century, a restless opportunism for the demolition of the ugly, unhealthy, overcrowded—above all, commercially unjustifiable—bits of the ancient city.

Street improvement could even be justified on such grounds alone, for the 'perforation of every such nest', wrote one enthusiast for improvement in 1800, 'by carrying through the midst of it a free and open street with buildings suitable for the industrious and reputable orders of the people, would let in that *Eye* and observation which would effectually break up their combinations.'[16] Such a point of view was expressed literally over forty years later, when James Pennethorne pushed Victoria Street through the backstreets of Westminster along a line he chose solely for its effectiveness in puncturing Pye Street and its neighbouring slums, known locally as Devil's Acre. Not every pair of dividers that stepped across the map of London in this long age of street improvement between the 1780s and 1840s was guided solely by the topography of the slums: the Temple Bar improvers seem to have been practically oblivious of them; John Nash deliberately skirted them with his Regent Street; and to the arch-improver, James Elmes, the rightness of the line was settled primarily by reference to architectural principles. Yet by 1840 no stronger supporting claim for a scheme could be made than that it improved an unhealthy district; of marginally slighter importance only was the aim of the 'melioration of the moral conditions of the labouring classes closely congregated in such districts'.[17] Scarcely a scheme of street improvement in London failed to respond in some degree to this call of duty, or expediency, over the next sixty years. 'Courts, close, crooked, and ill-looking are in plenty; swarms of children . . . costermongers . . . the low night lodging-houses and ugly dens of Golden Lane,' was how one man saw such an opportunity as late as 1877. 'Let a good, broad, straight thoroughfare be cut through it from North to South: the whole district is at once opened up and plenty of elbow room given to the City.'[18] It was a deepening and pitiless irony that the 'moral condition' of those affected tended to deteriorate in processes like these.

London was being dug and re-dug with restless thoroughness by railway navvies, too, and would have been even more trenched by them, especially during the 1860s, if the struggle between the railway companies had not cancelled out some of the schemes. It was above all the railways' demand for land to carry their lines into or under the central districts that had the most direct effect on the dwindling supply of living room there, especially as they had, like the street improvers, every financial reason for choosing the poorest districts for their lines wherever they could. Until the 1870s or even the 1880s, their demolitions tended to evoke a mixture of barely modified censure and almost unstinted praise, except on the part of those directly affected, or their few champions. Scores of writers described what happened as the railways burrowed their way into the centre and swept aside whole neighbourhoods of densely packed houses: some were merely stupefied by engineering marvels or the new vandalism; some reflected on their unerring aim at working-class districts; some thankfully remarked on the supposed benefits of destroying slums so efficiently; some tried to tot up the real costs of operations which defied all normal accounting methods. Watching the trains come by became an almost routine assignment for journalists, ticking off the days 'to get out', picking their way over the rubble, counting the houses that had to come down, following in the footsteps of those turned out of doors to see where they had gone, estimating the further overcrowding of the already overcrowded. From the fifties to the seventies the press was full of this kind of thing.[19]

It is almost impossible to believe that the repercussions of all this random slum-clearance were not recognized at the time. 'Carts of refuse turn down one street and dirty families another,' explained one observer in the early 1860s in a book suggestively entitled *The Hovel and the Home*, 'the one to some chasm where rubbish may be shot, the others to some courts or fallen streets, making them worse than they were before.'[20] The notion that slummers turned out of doors could take flight for the suburbs, or that the shock of flattening acres of crowded houses could be absorbed by the surrounding areas without difficulty, was contradicted by brute facts so often, in every kind of newspaper, periodical, pamphlet, and public utterance, that one is driven to conclude that there was some deliberation in this kind of permissiveness. William Acton wrote: 'This packing of the lower classes is clearly not yet under control.'[21]

That is clear from the more or less bland acceptance, by select committees on railway bills and street improvement schemes before the late 1870s, of easy assurances by the promoters that no difficulty would be encountered by those displaced and of arguments which hinged on the facility of taking slum houses rather than factories or warehouses. At the back of this lay an over-tender but sharply legal regard for property compulsorily acquired, and a readiness of the courts to settle handsomely for property owners. Thus their lordships were told by the Metropolitan Board of Works' Superintending Architect, when examining the Bill for Southwark Street in 1857, that the course given to it enabled them to skirt several expensive properties (including Barclay Perkins's Brewery—'That was a property which it was desirable to avoid') and save £200,000, while displacing fourteen hundred people living in the slums of Christchurch and St Saviour's. 'No inconvenience is anticipated and the Bill does not contain any provisions,' ran the written statement. 'The surrounding district is much peopled with workmen engaged in the different factories and the Artizans are migratory and there is great accommodation for Artizans in the Borough—but the houses are dense and mostly too crowded for health, comfort and convenience.'[22]

Demolitions for docks, railways, and new streets added immeasurably to the slums that were spared, and exacerbated a problem they were powerless to solve without the most elaborate rehousing. The complete failure to do this was the prime reason why the West End Improvements—designed to carry Charing Cross Road and Shaftesbury Avenue, among other streets, through some of the worst slums at the centre—should nearly have been frustrated by a parliament which was coming to realize the need to rehouse those displaced. This was the first major scheme of its kind, outside the City, in which a proper attempt was made to prevent the multiplication of slums by the provision of alternative housing for those displaced, or at least for others who could afford the higher rents.[23] The failure even here to give permanent homes to the lowest grade of slummers displaced was also the major defect in the activities of the numerous charitable bodies which laboured to increase the supply of working-class housing in or near former slums. Their activities, puny as they were in relation to the problem, scarcely touched the principal classes involved.[24]

The other side to these market forces was the working man's inability to transform his need for living room at the centre into an effective demand for it. He could not outbid his employers in the rent they were prepared to pay for their premises where he went to work, nor could he follow them into the suburbs where they went to live. The reasons were almost entirely economic. Though we know far too little about family budgets, it is possible to relate slum or slum-prone housing to low and irregular incomes in a very general way. It is clear, for example, from a survey taken by the Registrar-General of about thirty thousand working men in different parts of London in March 1887,[25] that the scantiest living accommodation was occupied by the families of the lowest-paid and most irregularly-employed men and that the amount of living room increased roughly in step with money wages and security of employment: half the dock labourers, at one extreme, occupied a single room or part of one, while only 1 percent of policemen occupied less than two rooms. As the proportion of men who were married did not vary significantly between occupational groups— the mean was 82 percent—and the size of families appears to have been pretty constant, it seems reasonable to connect type of employment directly with room density. It is also fairly clear that, in general, the less a man earned the lower the rent he paid, the two sums bearing a rather surprisingly fixed relationship to each other, with rent coming out at around one-fifth of the income of the head of the family.[26] The picture is made still sharper by taking account of liability to unemployment in different groups. Very roughly, one may say that at one extreme (St George's-in-the-East) was a situation in which almost half the working men and their families in a whole parish occupied single rooms or less, with over a third out of work and over a quarter earning less than nineteen shillings a week; at the other extreme (Battersea) less than a fifth were unemployed, and around two-thirds occupied three rooms or more and earned over twenty-five shillings a week. This suggests that crowded living conditions were related to the general structure of the labour market.

So long as employment remained on a casual basis, with the number of available jobs fluctuating violently from day to day or hour to hour, not only for unskilled but also for some of the most skilled trades, working men were obliged to live within reasonably close walking distance of their work. The distance considered practicable varied between trades and might stretch to three or four miles, but there are many signs that working men often felt chained more closely to their workplaces than that.[27]

> I am a working man [explained[28] one factory worker, who had a regular job].
> I go to my factory every morning at six, and I leave it every night at the same
> hour. I require, on the average, eight hours' sleep, which leaves four hours for
> recreation and improvement. I have lived at many places in the outskirts,
> according as my work has shifted, but generally I find myself at Mile End.
> I always live near the factory where I work, and so do all my mates, no matter
> how small, dirty, and dear the houses may be . . . One or two of my
> uncles have tried the plan of living a few miles out, and walking to business
> in the morning, like the clerks do in the city. It don't do—I suppose because
> they have not been used to it from boys; perhaps, because walking
> exercises at five in the morning don't suit men who are hard at work with their
> bodies all day. As to railways and omnibuses, they cost money, and we
> don't understand them, except on holidays, when we have got our best
> clothes on.

The circle of knowledge of what work was going was in some trades a narrow one, and the prospect of making a journey for, rather than to, work shortened the commuting radius. Sometimes it was vital to be literally on call. In the docks or some of the East End trades, the connection between the worker's home and workplace sometimes had to be more intimate still, and it was in these circumstances of sweated labour and of insecure and poorly-paid employment that creeping congestion either made a district ready for the complete descent into slum or more indelibly confirmed a condition that had already been sketched in. 'A slum', in a word, 'represents the presence of a market for local, casual labour.'[29]

The circle that closed over so much of the labouring mass was a spring for the middle classes. The wealth that was created in the commercial metropolis benefited them first, and they used it quite literally to put a distance between themselves and the workers. Whatever proportion of their earnings remained in their hands, once the capital requirements of commercial enterprise itself were satisfied, was invested in the manufacture of the city itself. Augmented by a certain amount of capital drawn in from outside, these resources were committed to a kind of self-generating expansion, a re-investment—to use economists' language—in the social overhead capital that was needed not only for the conduct of the enterprise City of London Ltd, nor even for so many safe-as-houses additions to personal portfolios, but also for making available to themselves those suburban parts of the city in which it was now thought desirable to live. Here was one of the most beautiful parts of the metropolitan mechanism. There were the business openings themselves: turning fields into streets brought large speculative gains to nimble dealers in land; keeping the suburbs supplied with building materials, fuel, and provisions was full of promise for the railways and the new multiple stores; transporting the commuters lifted the ceiling for street transport as well; buying and selling the property was endlessly rewarding for solicitors, auctioneers, banks, and building societies. It was for many a bonanza. These things apart, the middle-class suburb was an ecological marvel. It gave access to the cheapest land in the city to those having most security of employment and leisure to afford the time and money spent travelling up and down; it offered an arena for the manipulation of social distinctions to those most conscious of their possibilities and most adept at turning them into shapes on the ground; it kept the threat of rapid social change beyond the horizon of those least able to accept its negative as well as its positive advantages.

Within the analysis we are offering here, these suburbs were above all the strategic component in the housing of the whole urban community. It was the pace of their development and the amount of capital resources they consumed which determined not only the general scale of provision that could be made for the housing of the working classes but also the actual dimensions of their houses. In this sense the slums were built in the suburbs, and some of them actually were. These financial and logistical influences required their own kind of infrastructure—a new social order capable of transmitting by imitation the habits and tastes of the middle classes through their intervening layers to the upper strata of the working classes so as to form a continuum—in a word, suburbia. This had become a geographical reality by the last quarter of the century and the economic and social processes that sustained it have never lost their momentum. We must recognize that beckoning the middle classes and their imitators in their flight to the suburbs were images of many kinds. We are not disposed to succumb to their siren calls here, but it is important to see how beguiling they were.[30] The 'suburban quality' they sought, according to Henry

James, was 'the mingling of density and rurality, the ivy-covered brick walls, the riverside holiday-making, the old royal seats at an easy drive, the little open-windowed inns, where the charm of rural seclusion seems to merge itself in that of proximity to the city market.'[31] For what filled their sails may well have been trade winds of irresistible reality, but what took hold of the helm were dreams of aspiration and even romance. It was the Englishman's practicality that found in the suburbs the solution to the essentially middle-class problem of escaping the snares of the city without losing control of it. It was his romantic idyll of pastoral bliss that wove in and out of all his plans for taking to the suburbs.

It was not merely that the central areas were becoming so clogged by commerce and infested by slums. These things assailed his sight, his touch, his smell. They undermined his health and his property. But what also became fixed in his mind was the realization that density itself spelt death and depravity on his own doorstep. The convulsions of the city became symbolic of evil tendencies in the best and in the worst writing of the day, while the serenity of the suburbs became a token of natural harmony. The undrained clay beneath the slums oozed with cesspits and sweated with fever; the gravelly heights of the suburbs were dotted with springs and bloomed with health. It did not greatly matter to the individual that neither the slum nor the suburb conformed in every case to its stereotype. What mattered to him was that here was his own way out of the urban mess, a protection for his family, a refreshment for his senses, a balmy oasis in which to build his castle on the ground.[32]

To return, however, to our own ground, we can see now that the middle-class suburb was both an invention for accentuating and even refining class distinctions, and a means of putting off for a generation or two the full realization of what was entailed in living in a slum. C. F. G. Masterman knew and shared these middle-class feelings, and his powerful imagery of the nether world across which the middle classes were carried daily on their railway viaducts towards the heart of the commercial metropolis conveys this well. The image of the working classes storming up the garden path was no more of a caricature to them than it had been, half a century before, to Ruskin, horrified at the cockneys tearing down the apple blossom and bawling at the cows.[33] To a society in which landed wealth, drawn though it increasingly was from urban revenues, was still underpinning great embankments of privilege and political leverage, as well as the smaller domains of parochial aristocracies, the slum people were like a sleeping giant. Reports of its size or its hideous appearance—even cautiously conducted inspections on foot—were as entertaining as a menagerie.[34] But when the thing stirred or broke loose it was as if those watching had seen a ghost. 'We are striving to readjust our stable ideas', wrote Masterman after one of these brief gestures of power by the multitude. 'But within there is a cloud on men's minds, a half stifled recognition of the presence of a new force hitherto unreckoned; the creeping into conscious existence of the quaint and innumerable populations bred in the Abyss.' That was written in 1902.[35] It was a premonition that the great days of the middle-class suburb were numbered. There were men in their fifties in certain suburbs who could not remember the time when workmen's tickets were not in use, and for twenty years this traffic had been planting new colonies of working-class commuters—at the behest of the Board of Trade if need be —around scores of suburban stations.[36] What had begun as a fugitive solution to the problem of rehousing slummers, turned out of doors where costs of new accommodation were prohibitive, was fast becoming by common consent the urban ethos of the twentieth century. It was now the turn of the suburbs to lose their immutability and for distance to lend less enchantment. To flight had been added pursuit.[37]

The means of making this mass exodus was a belated and perhaps dubious gift of the commercial system itself. Taine's native wits told him that the suburban trend of the 1860s implied 'large profits from quick turnover, an opulent free-spending middle class very different from our own'.[38] An earlier estimate had put commuters' incomes in 1837 at between £150 and £600 a year—'provided their business did not require their presence till 9 or 10 in the morning'.[39] What brought such giddy expectations nearer for the masses was not cut-price fares alone but advancing real incomes arising more than anything from the great fall in world commodity prices in the last quarter of the century, and by shorter working hours and securer jobs.[40] The employment of clerks, for example, rose geometrically in London after mid-century, and they went to live in their favoured inner suburbs—22,000 of them, one in eight of all London's clerks, were to be found in Camberwell, for instance, by 1901, when around 5 percent of London jobs were in offices of some kind.[41]

It should not be overlooked, of course, that neither these plebeian places nor their more patrician counterparts were inhabited solely by commuting workers. Once established, these suburbs put on natural growth—perhaps accounting for up to a third of their overall expansion in the second half of the century—and they created employment locally mainly in the service trades. The longer the lines of suburban communications were stretched the more transport and distributive workers were needed to keep them open. This may help to explain how it was that by the 1860s outer suburbs beyond the reach of buses were growing markedly more quickly than their railway commuting services.[42] We might also add that when this tendency began to be augmented at all substantially by a growing volume of visitors to London on business or pleasure—something plainly happening from the 1850s—it helped to create a disproportionately large number of relatively badly-paid jobs in London as a whole, and this reinforced the inherently depressing forces making the inner ring of places into potential slum.

It occasionally happened that this convoluted influence of the suburb on the structure of the city, and in particular on the slum, uncoiled itself as if to demonstrate beyond a doubt what was going on. Look for a moment at North Kensington, a district lying perhaps more off the line of fashionable progress beyond the West End than on it, but containing some of the more sublime as well as some of the more ridiculously ambitious suburban neighbourhoods to be found among the developments of the 1840s, 1850s and 1860s.[43] Among these were some where their builders had badly overreached themselves and raised reasonably prepossessing houses for single families that never came, and which had had instead to be sub-divided immediately into tenements. Worst of all, as one of Dickens's reporters explained to his readers in *Household Words* in 1850, 'in a neighbourhood studded with elegant villas . . . is a plague spot scarcely equalled for its insalubrity by any other in London: it is called the Potteries.'[44] Here was a custom-built slum of seven or eight acres, nurtured by expediency, occupied by people made homeless by improvements in the West End or in the process of shifting in or out of London altogether, and sustained by a kind of bilateral trade with its affluent neighbours.[45] Its topography included a septic lake covering an acre, open sewers and stagnant ditches galore, a puzzle of cul-de-sacs and impenetrable settlement (especially on its most fashionable quarter), and a heap of hovels numbering under two hundred by mid-century. It was exceptionally low-lying, but made more of a gully for surface water from the surrounding district by having been extensively dug for brick-clay for the mansions round about, and left unpaved and unmetalled. In 1851 the population was returned as 1,177; pigs out-numbered people three to one. It was a nauseous place, but from it came a substantial supply of good quality bacon raised on middle-class swill, a profitable flow of rents for middle-class landlords, and a large pool of adult and juvenile labour for middle-class households—domestic servants, cleaners, wet-nurses, prostitutes, laundry-women, needlewomen, gardeners, night-soil men, chimney-sweeps, odd-job men, and builders. The return flow had to be reckoned not only in wages and charitable coppers but in things pilfered or pockets pinched. It was an impressive trade. Nor was it an isolated one. Agar Town in St Pancras and Sultan Street in Camberwell are similarly documented, and it is hard to believe that this uneven enterprise between suburb and slum was not being carried on in some degree in places barely known to historians even by name.

We have been speaking so far as if these migratory movements into the suburbs and the slums were taking place within closed frontiers, but it is clear that they were not. London, we noted earlier, was drawing off people from the rest of the country as well as redistributing them itself. The question naturally arises, where did these provincial migrants to London go? Were the inhabitants of the slums provincial in origin, drawn in perhaps at different times from overmanned farms or from under-developed or technologically obsolescent industrial towns? The evidence for the 1870s—to take a decade of high growth—does not suggest this. It is not possible to discover, by looking merely at the numbers enumerated at a particular census, which of those born elsewhere had arrived in the last ten years, nor is it possible to discover how many came and went. However, what the birthplaces of those enumerated on census night in April 1881 suggest is that, at a time when not much over one-third of London's population had been born elsewhere, the movement into London was producing in the most rapidly expanding suburbs a larger proportion of provincials than were to be found in districts nearer the centre. Mayfair was an exception in drawing practically 60 percent of its population from outside London. Bethnal Green, by contrast, which had been three parts slum when Hector Gavin had rambled over it in the late 1840s,[46] and was by now one of the most extensive congeries of slum in London, contained little more than 12 percent who had been born outside London, and the whole area of Whitechapel and St George's-in-the-East surrounding it did not raise the figure above 20 percent; Seven Dials itself, plumb centre, had less than half as many inhabitants born outside London as had the most affluent parts of the same West End.[47]

This general pattern corresponds very closely with that prevailing in the Notting Dale Potteries as compared with the surrounding parts of Kensington. If we look simply at the birthplaces of heads of households in 1861, we see that just over half of them were born in London, whereas less than one-quarter of those in the entire district were—a disparity that appears to have increased as the area was being settled in the course of the preceding decade. Similarly, if we look simply at servant-keeping households for the same date in two long-developed districts of Bayswater—a very affluent quarter—we find the corresponding figures are 28 percent and 35 percent; whereas if we do the same for a district of quite new and less affluent settlement—to be quite precise, having exactly half the servant-keeping establishments (1·9 domestic servants per household as compared with 3·6 in Bayswater)—what we see is that the proportion of London-born was just over half.[48] By this date the proportion of London-born in London as a whole was dwindling below the half-and-half division of 1851. Charles Booth's calculations for the 1890s suggest that there was here an inverse ratio between the proportion of provincial immigrants and the poverty of a district, and if we look finally at the proportions of cockneys to provincials in what he regarded as one of the vilest slums he knew in London—Sultan Street in Camberwell—we can see just how true this is.

The birthplaces of the heads of the 104 households and their wives enumerated there in 1871, when the whole area had just started its social descent, divided in the proportion of six Londoners to four provincials and Irish, a ratio which widened considerably over the next three censuses: in 1881, 36 percent of heads and wives were born outside London; by 1901 the figure had fallen as low as 26 percent. Interestingly enough, the ratio of London-born in Sultan Street increased very markedly during this period as compared with that in Camberwell as a whole, even though by 1901 this larger community was showing signs of deterioration in social class and, along with this, an increase in the proportion of Londoners to the rest. That only 8 percent of the children enumerated in Sultan Street in 1871 should have been born outside London (and less than 2 percent in 1901) supports the evidence of the more general statistics that the slums of Victorian London were mostly occupied by second or later generation Londoners, and that the suburbs were the ultimate destinations of the incoming provincials. The slums of Victorian London are therefore more properly thought of as settlement tanks for submerged Londoners than as settlement areas for provincial immigrants to the city.[49]

We get here another glimpse of that centripetal and downward movement in the development of Victorian London that needs to be set in relation to the more familiar one of the centrifugal deployment of another instalment of population into the suburbs. Here were two social gradients that sometimes intersected and sometimes even changed direction for a time—it all depends, as it commonly does, on where one is standing and how far one can see, and especially on when one is looking. In as general terms as we dare use, what we see is one such slope leading upwards and outwards, and the other leading downwards, if not inwards. The cultural slopes of Victorian London, which must be mapped one day more carefully than anyone has yet attempted, made no doubt an undulating plain of dull mediocrity—which is perhaps the natural condition of human society—relieved only occasionally by peaks or precipices of dramatic dimensions.[50] Moving up and down these slopes was always an exertion of some kind, whether to cut a better figure or to tap fresh credit, to escape the rent-collector, or even the police. How it all happened on the way up we know well enough: Wilkie Collins, Chesterton, Galsworthy, the Grossmiths, Thackeray, Trollope, Wells, describe some of the traverses and ascents; and Keble Howard, Pett Ridge, Shan Bullock, and unsung authors like Mrs Braddon and William Black, whose tedious novels were set in the suburbs because they were designed to be read there, echo some of the chatter that took place on the way.[51] Fewer people— Arthur Morrison, Israel Zangwill, Walter Besant, Gissing, and Kipling certainly among them—have told how it was on the way down or at the bottom.[52] Before we take a last look in a moment at the suburbs and the commercial ascendancy to be found there, it is worth measuring as dispassionately as we can the human ingredients of a slum as its slumminess intensified.

We must return to Sultan Street. Here was a street of around seventy six-roomed stock brick houses arranged on three floors, which had been virtually completed between 1868 and 1871. It was built, with an adjoining street, on a small plot of cow-pasture which for forty years had been completely enclosed by a heap of clap-board cottages on two sides, a row of modest villas on another, and by the long back-gardens of a decent Georgian terrace on the fourth. What gave to this ineligible building land still greater insularity was a railway viaduct, pierced by two bridges. The Herne Hill & City Branch of the London Chatham & Dover Railway was taken clear across the back-gardens of the terrace between 1860 and 1864 as part of the larger strategy that that company was using to get the better of its rival, the South-Eastern Railway, in its drive for the Continental traffic to Dover. The building of Sultan Street was therefore specially speculative, as nothing makes plainer than the speed with which the improved ground-rents were passed from hand to hand. The local influences at work on this place correspond closely with what was said earlier. Cowsheds and piggeries squeezed up with the surrounding houses, and a glue factory, a linoleum factory, a brewery, haddock-smokers, tallow-melters, costermongers keeping their good stuff indoors with them while leaving rotting cabbage-stalks, bad oranges, and the like on the street, created between them an atmosphere which, mingled with household odours, kept all but the locals at bay.[53]

Sultan Street was *not* badly built, but some of its houses became slums almost at once and the rest followed inexorably. By 1871 these seventy or so houses were packed out by 661 persons and almost a quarter of them were being made to hold between thirteen and eighteen occupants each, or more than two to a room. However, just over half of all the houses contained, in 1871, between seven and twelve occupants apiece, a situation which could not be described as one of overcrowding. In ten years the whole spectrum had shifted. The total number living in the street had grown by more than half as much again (57·4 percent) to 1,038, over half of whom were now to be found thirteen to eighteen per house, while a further 14 percent were living nineteen or more per house; only one-third of the inhabitants of the street were living, on the average, less than two to a room. The net effect of what had happened was that another forty-three families (197 persons) had come in and lifted the mean figure of persons per house from about nine in 1871 to fifteen in 1881. How many families had come and gone in the interval there is no way of telling precisely, but it seems clear enough from a statistical analysis of age-patterns at successive censuses that there was a big turnover in inhabitants, a process that produced by the 1890s a community that was distinctly older than it would have been if the younger people who had gone there at the start had stayed: the tendency was for older people to move in as the houses themselves aged.

As this was happening, the structure of households was changing appreciably. One noticeable feature was that relatives and lodgers were disappearing from the street. That lodgers should be declining is probably more revealing than that relatives should be growing scarcer, because families too poor to put up a nephew or a parent might be supposed to have taken in a lodger, provided room could be found: few indexes of poverty and overcrowding could conceivably be more significant than the inability to sub-let even sleeping-room. In 1871 the proportion of households with lodgers, almost 15 percent, had been practically the same as the average for Camberwell as a whole, but by 1881 it had fallen to just over 4 percent. By this date the whole pattern of Sultan Street society was beginning to diverge with statistical significance from that of the surrounding population in Camberwell as a whole. Three features make this plain: the marital status of the heads of households; the size of families; the occupational and industrial distribution of wage-earners. In all three respects Sultan Street society had in 1871 corresponded quite closely with that of Camberwell as a whole. By 1881, and still more markedly by 1891, there were signs that it was tending to become more matriarchal: relatively more widows, more married women whose husbands were 'away', and more single women as heads of households. So far as the size of both the household and the family are concerned, there was again virtually no difference between Sultan Street and Camberwell in 1871. By 1881, the average size of household had begun to diverge appreciably and before long the same was true of the size of families: both were larger in Sultan Street. Rather interestingly, although there seem to have been no significant differences in the number of children to be found in families of the different social groups in Sultan Street or outside it, in 1871, both skilled and unskilled workers in Sultan Street in 1901 had appreciably more children than the average for their class in Camberwell as a whole. The street seemed to be somewhat deficient in fathers and abundant in children, a situation which was liable to be open to only one interpretation. So far as jobs were concerned, the Sultan Street community already had many more labourers and domestic servants in 1871 than were to be found in Camberwell as a whole

(80 percent against 44 percent), though the distribution between skilled and un-skilled scarcely varied. It was this distribution which now proceeded to vary: the proportion of skilled to all labourers in Camberwell fell only slightly (62 percent to 54 percent between 1871–1901), but in Sultan Street it was halved in these thirty years (62 percent, 46 percent, 29 percent, 32 percent); actually, the disparity was at its greatest between 1881 and 1891, for Sultan Street was slightly redeemed in the nineties, whereas Camberwell at large deteriorated a little more rapidly than it had become accustomed to do. There were by now enough other slums in it to offset the effect of its middle-class residents in keeping its average status high. Across the northern reaches of Camberwell, at least, the menace of more general social decline was beginning to show. The suburb that had at the beginning of the nineteenth century contained 'few poor inhabitants and not many overgrown fortunes'[54] contained too few fortunes of any size and too many poor by its end. For it, as for other suburbs on the original frontier of London's expansion, the tide of middle-class settlement had rolled on. The erstwhile suburb had to take increasing care not to become a slum.

The dynamics of urban growth by suburban accretion had just such an irresistible momentum. The spread of the built-up area gave every appearance on its leading edge of an unstoppable lava flow; the encrustations that eventually cooled behind it seemed to take on the dull unworkability of pumice. The inhabitants of large cities begin to accept as part of the ground of their being the obduracy of these forces and see them almost as urban nature's way. And when we look at the suburban flux in the full heat of its making, there do seem to be relentless pressures demanding a release. It was there that money not only talked but also lived and moved almost under its own compulsion. The supply of middle-class housing in the suburbs was not simply a reflex of the demand for somewhere to live. It was the active quest for its own outlets that kept the supply of capital on the move. This was not the operation of some anonymous, inscrutable financial wizard who knew some special incantations. Anyone with a bit to spare could open sesame. Lending on mortgage was the passive 5-percent way of taking part; going into the land market, getting some suburban land ripe for development, making it go, was the active, speculative, all-or-nothing way of doing so.[55] 'The formation of ground rents', one auctioneer's notice blandly proclaimed in 1856, 'has been the study and occupation of many of the most intelligent men of the day, and is accomplished by the purchase of freehold land, to be let on building leases.'[56] To this should be added innumerable supporting enterprises which were also creating their own demand, adding their weight to the engine of suburban economic growth: drainage schemes, gas and water undertakings, shops, schools, pubs, music-halls, parks, bus and jobmaster concerns, tramway and railway companies—the whole intricate web of agencies without which a suburb would have been a castle in the air.

The opportunities for this speculative enterprise were too numerous and too diverse, and their interpenetrations too tangled, to be described in any detail here. Nor can we draw up a balance sheet which would show their debit and credit sides. What mattered most was the *expectation* of gain. The tide ran too fast for the experience of loss to impede the flow. In fact, many were disappointed. Main-line railway companies in particular, compelled by their shareholders to get a share of the suburban market, had many regrets over their passenger accounts when they understood the economics of the rush-hour better.[57] Most of the money to be made out of suburban enterprise went to the men who dealt in land, who were first on the scene, who leased or bought before the rise, who developed or sold it on the very top of the tide. What evidence we have about land values in the Victorian city suggests that land prices in the outer suburban districts appreciated by ten- to twenty-fold in the thirty years after 1840.[58] In this the railway played the role of inflating land values *en route* and offering windfalls to those quick or knowing enough to pick them up while still ripe. The Engineer of the Acton & Hammersmith Railway remarked in 1874: 'The moment a line is deposited and there appears a chance of carrying on, the speculative builders of London all rush to the ground to cover it with houses. Many cases have arisen where the Act has not gone through one committee before the builders were on the spot and commencing to sell.'[59] Those who courted ruin either moved in too soon or arrived too late, and occupied some salient easily outflanked by more desirably placed estates. These were the men who committed themselves to unsound schemes in the belief that they would share what others were known to have reaped, who kept doggedly on when their returns failed to rise, or tried to bolster the market by taking shares in railway companies when all their capital was locked up in bricks and mortar.[60]

Such men did not lose their nerve; nor did they normally run out of capital. By failing to sell their houses they fell short on the payment of interest on their loans and their creditors foreclosed on their security—the houses that had dragged their mortgagees down. There were too many undertakings, and too much was expected of them individually in the short run. In terms somewhat alien to the times, such investments looked too much for growth and too little for income. In the long run they made collectively very handsome holdings indeed, but the whole atmosphere in which they were created was charged with speculation and the operations themselves were hobbled by their scale. The supply of capital was never seriously depleted by other demands being made upon it—partly because the money market was more specialized than is often supposed—and even the counter-attractions of overseas investment merely had the effect of making funds more readily available when they were not going abroad, not of restricting them when they did.[61] The most palpable consequence of this in the suburbs was the sight from time to time of new untenanted streets of houses, a temporary fall in house prices, and an increase in bankruptcies among builders. The long-term trends in population growth and the supply of houses in London as a whole, on the contrary, scarcely wavered or diverged. All that these marginal alternations in the supply of capital did in the suburbs was to fix the reckoning day and to award the prizes. The estates that suited the tastes and the pockets of their middle-class adjudicators went on; those that did not were put on one side for more vulgar approval later on; and the housing industry re-formed its battalions for another campaign.[62]

The bowler-hatted field-marshals commanding these operations were the speculative builders—if by this term is meant not only those directly involved in erecting houses but also anyone capable of remaining solvent long enough to raise the carcass of a house and to find a tenant or a buyer for it. These were functions as readily discharged by men totally inexperienced in building as by men that were. The Forsytes' fortunes were based reputably enough on the success of a mason from Dorset, but there were speculative builders who had been tailors, shopkeepers, domestic servants, publicans: one District Surveyor complained in 1877 of a clergyman-cum-speculative builder whom he remembered only too well because he had built several hundred houses and left the district without paying him his fees.[63] The big men were veritable entrepreneurs as much at home among the scaffolding as in the chambers of money-lending solicitors, men who were not only scrupulous businessmen but discreet vulgarizers of the fine arts, whose work was the stuff of dreams that would not fade, and whose plumbing was impregnable. But there were also others, not necessarily dishonest or incompetent men, whose business methods precluded such attention to detail or a guarantee of the best materials being used—men more skilled very often in raising money than raising houses. In any rapidly growing suburb of size there would be scores of such builders rubbing along on precarious credit from timber-merchants or brickmakers (something harder to obtain, incidentally, from the 1850s), mortgaging their houses floor by floor or pair by pair or terrace by terrace to a building society, a solicitor, or even to a bank. If they were lucky they would survive with virtually no stock-in-trade nor capital of their own, and skip from one take to another by finding buyers for their houses at the eleventh hour and transferring to their clients the mortgage they had raised on the house when the roof went on, in time to finance the first stages in the next operation. There were in this category some speculative builders who were little more than hirelings of the ground-landlord or the developer who had first laid out the estate, and who came almost inevitably and often very quickly into financial servitude to more powerful men. There were also builders' merchants and building societies which had to step in to complete a job on which they had been forced to foreclose. It was the kind of enterprise which tempted many men, not least the long-established family concerns of jobbing builders—father and son, brothers and brothers-in-law—who, when new houses did not seem to hang on the market above a week or two, could be seen measuring the leap into full-scale speculative building, and taking it.

These suburban outlets for capital were like a delta of a great river system, made fertile by deposits collected in distant places and carried along irreversibly by superior force. Landowners of London estates made advances in cash and kind—the prevailing leasehold system itself was but the means of transferring capital assets on credit—and were doubtless as ready to tap the resources of their country estates as to return them the proceeds of their urban ones. Cash left on trust in the country made its way into solicitors' hands in London, and professional men in particular knew such channels well. The intermediaries themselves also became the principals, and the legal system—despite its obscurity in the annals of economic history—became the axis for many of these movements of capital, especially after 1872, when advances to speculative builders by building societies began to flag. Thus the savings of the farmers and retired gentlefolk of Chippenham were channelled during the 1880s into the making of a seedy suburb in Paddington, and in 1874 some of Mr Speaker's money was combined in Lincoln's Inn with that of a reverend gentleman in Southampton to finance the building of a terrace in Walworth.[64] The most conservative of City institutions, the Royal Exchange Assurance, and several other insurance companies, along with two leading London banks, engaged in this disposal of loanable funds too, doing so in such a way as to accentuate the uncertainties of speculative building and, arguably, to make the employment of this capital more wasteful.[65] The standard instrument for all these transfers was the mortgage deed, the main outlet for surplus funds in the nineteenth century, but it was used to special effect by the building societies. Whether as channels for funds for occupying owners or for speculative builders, these highly parochial institutions performed the prime function of releasing the capital resources of one suburb for the development of a neighbouring one, just as the Church building societies were the means of transforming that wealth into places for prayer apart.[66] The crucial role of all these institutions was to convert the savings of the suburban communities into funds for re-investment in their own structure, into a hoopsnake of incomes and satisfactions that recycled what was earned in the tangible means of enjoying it.

But what of the slums? The mechanism that activated and populated the suburbs did not function for them in the same way. In the suburbs, a correspondent to the *Builder* was commenting as early as 1848, it was[67]

> as though one-half of the world were on the lookout for investments, and the other half continually in search of eligible family residences . . . There is a leaven of aristocracy in the parlour with folding-doors . . . The villa mania is everywhere most obtrusive . . . But the poor want dwelling-places. Whilst we are exhausting our ingenuity to supply our villas with 'every possible convenience,' we are leaving our working-classes to the enjoyment of every possible inconvenience, in wretched stalls to which men of substance would not consign their beasts of burden.

It is indeed an interesting question whether the flow of private capital into suburban house-building has not always tended to be at the expense of investment in lower-grade housing, unless moderated by public subsidies for working-class housing. The whole ethos of the 5-percent philanthropy idea which was developed in the 1850s and 1860s to get private capital for this type of investment really evolved from a situation in which the returns on suburban house-building were not only setting the pace but also making the *idea* of securing comparable returns on housing the lower working classes, as distinct from the 'aristocracy', largely nugatory.[68]

Worse than this, it cannot be taken as an open question whether the people of the slums were not actually contributing to the environment of the suburbs. The lubrications of the money economy had made even these rusty parts revolve. 'There are courts and alleys innumerable called by the significant name of RENTS,' explained one sociologist, in all but name, of the 1840s. '. . . they are not human habitations . . . They are merely so many man-traps to catch the paying animal in; they are machines for manufacturing rent.'[69] It was profoundly true. The urban landlord already appeared to have become a kind of dinosaur across the water who took his tribute in flesh and blood. Whereas in the old pre-urban days, when the rent-receiver was often visible as employer or social better within a tolerable frame, and when the rent-night gathering might sometimes almost be said to have been celebrated 'as if the thing, money, had not brought it there',[70] the relations between landlord and tenant in the city were characteristically impersonal, conducted through agents called rent-collectors, and the rent itself seldom bore any demonstrable connection with the human container itself. The money that passed was the sum necessary to deny the space on the ground to some other use, and it soon bore, in the central districts, little relationship to the amenities available in the shape enclosing it. One enthusiast for garden suburbs for the masses, long ahead of his time, calculated in 1846 that a four-roomed cottage could be provided for half the rent of six shillings a week paid by working men for two rooms in town.[71] Little wonder, perhaps, that these extractions were so painful. 'Absentee-landlordism, subleases, rack-rents,' wrote Henry Lazarus in a diatribe hurled at the landlords of London in 1892, 'here is the trinity of England's land curse.'[72] Between tenant and landlord often stretched a whole chain of shadowy intermediaries, held in their contracted order by a series of subleases which divided responsibilities for the upkeep of the property and inflated the rents paid for it.

The direction in which these financial obligations led could scarcely fail to be outwards towards the suburbs. And when George Bernard Shaw first tried his hand as a playwright it was to these calculated connections between slums and suburbs that he turned. 'In *Widowers' Houses*', he explained after it was put on in 1892, 'I have shewn middle class respectability and younger son gentility fattening on the poverty of the slum as flies fatten on filth.'[73] The rent-collector describes his client's business:

LICKCHEESE. . . . I dont say he's the worst landlord in London: he couldnt be worse than some; but he's no better than the worst I ever had to do with. And, though I say it, Im better than the best collector he ever done business with. Ive screwed more and spent less on his properties than anyone would believe that knows what such properties are. I know my merits, Dr. Trench, and will speak for myself if no one else will.

COKANE. What description of properties? Houses?

LICKCHEESE. Tenement houses, let from week to week by the room or half room— aye, or quarter room. It pays when you know how to work it, sir.

Nothing like it. It's been calculated on the cubic foot of space, sir, that you can get higher rents letting by the room than you can for a mansion in Park Lane.

TRENCH. I hope Mr. Sartorious hasnt much of that sort of property, however it may pay.

LICKCHEESE. He has nothing else, sir; and he shews his sense in it, too. Every few hundred pounds he could scrape together he bought old houses with—houses that you wouldnt hardly look at without holding your nose. He has em in St. Giles's: he has em in Marylebone: he has em in Bethnal Green. Just look how he lives himself, and youll see the good of it to him. He likes a low death-rate and a gravel soil for himself, he does. You come down with me to Robbins's Row; and I'll shew you a soil and a death-rate, so I will! And, mind you, it's me that makes it pay him so well. Catch him going down to collect his own rents! Not likely!

TRENCH. Do you mean to say that all his property—all his means—come from this sort of thing?

LICKCHEESE. Every penny of it, sir.

That scene was enacted in 'the library of a handsomely appointed villa at Surbiton'. It conveys, as the most meticulous property ledger perhaps never will, the underlying logic of what another earlier Victorian commentator described as the 'terrible physiology' of the map of London.[74] The movements of capital in the making of the metropolis determined the social space available to its different users, and hence the relative wealth or poverty of its different districts. This is not to say that the living conditions which were produced by these commercial discriminations were necessarily inferior to, or their limits more extreme than, what had gone before. What was different was the geographical scale and the fact that with virtually no curbs placed on the way in which capital was allowed to spend itself—beyond the rather narrow limits set by legislation for the public health—the poor were quite literally starved of such finance. The curse of these poor was no greater than the poverty of any other, but it produced more visible ironies. The wealthiest parishes of London had the lowest municipal rates.[75] It was difficult at first to reverse the capital flows we have been describing within the boundaries of any one of them. Kensington, the wealthiest of them all, for example, reacted to efforts to do so on behalf of the Potteries as a healthy body does to some foreign matter embedded in it—by trying to evict it.[76] The effort to redress such unbalances, to equalize the rates, to steer capital where it would not normally go, was what the municipal socialism that found its voice with the establishment of a single government for London in 1889 was all about.[77] It was about the need, among other things, to make transfer-payments between suburbs and slums, to give the community a conscience, to put together again the fragments into which it had been shattered by the impact of its own growth. It was the start of a road that would never end.

Notes

1 This argument was originally advanced in a paper from which some of the material for this chapter has been drawn: see H. J. Dyos, 'The Slums of Victorian London', *Victorian Studies*, xi (1967–8), 5–40. It has benefited since from the comments of Professor Lionel Needleman, to whom we are grateful. His own work, *The Economics of Housing* (1965), deals more theoretically with the subject, especially in regard to the supply and demand factors influencing housing.

2 For a discussion of the relations between London and the rest of the country, see H. J. Dyos, 'Greater and Greater London: Notes on Metropolis and Provinces in the 19th and 20th Centuries', in *Britain and the Netherlands. IV: Metropolis, Dominion and Province*, eds J. S. Bromley and E. H. Kossmann (The Hague, 1972), pp. 89–112.

3 H. A. Shannon, 'Migration and the Growth of London, 1841–91', *Economic History Review*, v (1935), 79–86. These and other estimates of population growth given in this chapter have been calculated from the census returns.

4 For an account of this, see H. J. Dyos, 'The Growth of a Pre-Victorian Suburb: South London, 1580–1836', *Town Planning Review*, xxv (1954), 67–78.

5 Pierce Egan, *Life in London* (1821), pp. 274, 288, 343, 345–6.

6 To Daniel Maclise, 20 November 1840. For other contemporary definitions of the slum, see J. H. Vaux, *Flash Dictionary* (1812); Jon Bee, *A Dictionary of the Turf* (1823), p. 161; Henry Mayhew, *The Great World of London* (1856), p. 46; J. S. Farmer and W. E. Henley, *Slang and Its Analogues* (1890–1904), see 'slum'; *The Times*, 17 January 1845.

7 'It may be one house', wrote Robert Williams in *London Rookeries and Colliers' Slums* (1893), p. 13, 'but it generally is a cluster of houses, or of blocks of dwellings, not necessarily dilapidated, or badly drained, or old, but usually all this and small-roomed, and, further, so hemmed in by other houses, so wanting in light and air, and therefore cleanliness, as to be wholly unfit for human habitation.'

8 Quoted by Lewis Mumford, *The City in History* (1961), p. 433.

9 See, for example, Rev. Thomas Beames, *The Rookeries of London: Past, present, and prospective* (1851); Cardinal Wiseman, *An Appeal to the Reason and Good Feeling of the English People on the Subject of the Catholic Hierarchy* (1850), p. 30. Bayswater and Camberwell are dealt with below.

10 'Ragged London', *Meliora*, iv (1862), 300. There is a large bibliography of contemporary writings on the slums in Dyos, 'Slums of Victorian London'.

11 [Thomas Wright], *The Pinch of Poverty* (1892), p. 187.

12 The only available history of building regulations in London during this period is C. C. Knowles, 'A History of the London Building Acts, the District Surveyors, and their Association', an unpublished MS. dated 1947 in the Members' Library, Greater London Council, County Hall, Westminster Bridge.

13 Corporation of London, *The City of London: A record of destruction and survival* (1951), p. 165 ff.

14 The large displacements in the vicinity of the new Waterloo station in 1858–9 for the Charing Cross Railway were augmented by the actions of landowners seizing the opportunity of re-shuffling their tenantry in the vicinity. The only step-by-step

reconstruction of such a process is H. C. Binford, 'Residential Displacement by Railway Construction in North Lambeth, 1858–61' (unpublished M.A. thesis, University of Sussex, 1967).

15 Rev. G. W. M'Cree, *Day and Night in St. Giles* (Bishop Auckland, 1862), p. 6.

16 [C. G. Stonestreet], *Domestic Union, or London as it Should Be!!* (1800).

17 For a more extended account, see H. J. Dyos, 'Urban Transformation: the objects of street improvement in Regency and early Victorian London', *International Review of Social History (I.R.S.H.)*, ii (1957), 259–65.

18 Henry Chevassus, *Overcrowding in the City of London* (1877), p. 10.

19 See the references in H. J. Dyos, 'Railways and Housing in Victorian London', *Journal of Transport History*, ii (1955), 11–21, 90–100.

20 Ebenezer Clarke, Jr, *The Hovel and the Home; or, Improved dwellings for the labouring classes, and how to obtain them* (1863), p. 31.

21 William Acton, *Prostitution . . . in London and Other Large Cities* (1857), p. 180.

22 Quoted from the Demolition Statement submitted with its Bill by the M.B.W. under the provisions of a House of Lords Standing Order adopted in 1853 (House of Lords Record Office).

23 See Dyos, 'Urban Transformation', *I.R.S.H.*, 261.

24 See the references in J. N. Tarn, 'Housing in Urban Areas, 1890–1914' (unpublished Ph.D. thesis, University of Cambridge, 1961); C. J. Stewart, ed., *The Housing Question in London, 1855–1900* (1900); E. R. Dewsnup, *The Housing Problem in England: Its statistics, legislation and policy* (Manchester, 1907); J. S. Nettlefold, *Practical Housing* (Letchworth, 1908).

25 *Parliamentary Papers*, 1887, XV, Tabulation of the Statements made by Men living in Certain Selected Districts of London in March 1887 (C. 5228). The areas covered were the registration sub-districts of St George's-in-the-East, Battersea, Hackney, and Deptford. Despite the warning given that the details of the returns were 'of very small statistical value', there is a very general pattern discernible in them.

26 For a discussion of house rents in London in relation to the problems of housing the working classes, see A. S. Wohl, 'The Housing of the Working Classes in London, 1815–1914', in *The History of Working-Class Housing* (1971), ed. Stanley D. Chapman, pp. 15–54.

27 See E. J. Hobsbawm, 'The Nineteenth-Century London Labour Market', in *London: Aspects of change* (1964), Report No. 3, edited by the Centre for Urban Studies [University College, London], pp. 3–28.

28 John Hollingshead, *Today: Essays and miscellanies* (1865), II, p. 306.

29 B. F. C. Costelloe, 'The Housing Problem', *Transactions of the Manchester Statistical Society*, 1898–9, 48. The economic forces at work here have been brilliantly analysed by Gareth Stedman Jones, *Outcast London: A study of the relationships between classes in Victorian society* (Oxford, 1971), especially in part I.

30 These images can be discerned best from the numerous guides to the politer parts of the metropolis and the advertisements accompanying the 'well-advertised' building estates. See, for example, the Homeland Reference Books, *Where to Live Round London (Northern Side)*, ed. Freeman Bunting (1897, 1908).

31 Henry James, 'The Suburbs of London', *Galaxy*, xxiv (1877), 778.

32 For an explanation of these generalized statements, see H. J. Dyos, *Victorian Suburb: A study of the growth of Camberwell* (Leicester, 1961), especially pp. 20–33.

33 C. F. G. Masterman, *The Condition of England* (1909), p. 72; John Ruskin, *Praeterita* (Orpington, 1886), I, p. 70.

34 See Dyos, 'Slums of Victorian London', 11–24.

35 [C. F. G. Masterman], *From the Abyss* [1902], p. 4.

36 The background will be found in H. J. Dyos, 'Workmen's Fares in South London, 1860–1914', *Journal of Transport History*, i (1953), 3–19.

37 For some discussion of the dynamics of suburban change in Victorian London, see D. A. Reeder, 'A Theatre of Suburbs: Some patterns of development in West London, 1801–1911', in *The Study of Urban History* (1968), ed. H. J. Dyos, pp. 253–71; and for an outline account of the rise and decline of a suburban district, see his description of Fulham in P. D. Whitting, ed., *A History of Fulham* (1970), pp. 150–64, 275–90.

38 H. Taine, *Notes on England* [1868–70], translated by Edward Hyams (1957), p. 14.

39 *Penny Magazine*, 31 March 1837, quoted in T. C. Barker and Michael Robbins, *A History of London Transport* (1963), I, p. 36.

40 William Ashworth, *The Genesis of Modern British Town Planning* (1954), ch. 6.

41 Dyos, *Victorian Suburb*, p. 62.

42 For a discussion of the relationships between suburban rail-travel and suburban development in Victorian London, see John R. Kellett, *The Impact of Railways on Victorian Cities* (1969), especially pp. 365–87, 405–19. Some account has been taken of the growth of low-paid jobs in the service industries by Mary Waugh, 'Suburban Growth in North-west Kent: 1861–1961' (unpublished Ph.D. thesis, University of London, 1968).

43 Reeder, 'Theatre of Suburbs', pp. 255–6, 264.

44 *Household Words*, i (1850), 463.

45 We are grateful to a former student for permission to use her work on this suburban slum. See Patricia E. Malcolmson, 'The Potteries of Kensington: a study of slum development in Victorian London' (unpublished M.Phil. thesis, University of Leicester, 1970).

46 Hector Gavin, *Sanitary Ramblings: being sketches and illustrations, of Bethnal Green. A type of the condition of the metropolis* (1848). See also R. J. Roberts, 'Sanitary Ramblings . . . by H. Gavin', *East London Papers*, viii (1965), 110–118.

47 Stedman Jones, op. cit., ch. 6, deals more extensively with distribution of provincial immigrants in Victorian London.

48 These few calculations are derived from a larger study being undertaken by D. A. Reeder due to be published under the title *Genesis of Suburbia* by Edward Arnold in 1974.

49 These figures are also taken from a larger piece of work on the social organization of Victorian Camberwell, by H. J. Dyos. For a discussion of the methods being used to calculate these data, see H. J. Dyos and A. B. M. Baker, 'The Possibilities of Computerising Census Data', in *The Study of Urban History*, ed. Dyos, pp. 87–112.

50 For an attempt to work out some of the broad contours of this map for the mid-nineteenth century, see F. Bédarida, 'Croissance urbaine et image de la ville en Angleterre au xixe siècle', *Bulletin de la Société d'Histoire Moderne*, third series, No. 1 (1965), 10–14; also by the same author, 'Londres au milieu du xixe siècle: une analyse de structure sociale', *Annales*, March–April 1968, 268–95. Interesting work has also been done on the internal movements of particular and easily identifiable ethnic

groups. For example, Lynn Lees, 'Patterns of Lower-Class Life: Irish slum communities in nineteenth-century London', in *Nineteenth-Century Cities*, ed. Stephan Thernstrom and Richard Sennett (1969), pp. 359–85. See, too, Vivian D. Lipman, 'The Rise of Jewish Suburbia', *Transactions of the Jewish Historical Society of England*, xxi (1968), 78–103.

51 For example, W. M. Thackeray, *Vanity Fair* (1848); Anthony Trollope, *The Three Clerks* (1858); Wilkie Collins, *Hide and Seek* (1861); George and Weedon Grossmith, *The Diary of a Nobody* (Bristol, 1892); G. K. Chesterton, *The Napoleon of Notting Hill* (1904); W. Pett Ridge, *Mrs Galer's Business* (1905); Keble Howard, *The Smiths of Surbiton* (1906); Shan Bullock, *The Story of a London Clerk* (1907); H. G. Wells, *Ann Veronica* (1909).

52 See P. J. Keating, *The Working Classes in Victorian Fiction* (1971).

53 Dyos, *Victorian Suburb*, pp. 109–13.

54 J. C. Lettsom, *Village Society* (1800), p. 5.

55 For more extended accounts of these business operations and of the financial interests involved, see H. J. Dyos, 'The Speculative Builders and Developers of Victorian London', *Victorian Studies*, xi (1968), 641–90; D. A. Reeder, 'Capital Investment in the Western Suburbs of Victorian London' (unpublished Ph.D. thesis, University of Leicester, 1965).

56 From the notice of sale of the Gunter Estate including building land in Chelsea and Fulham (G.L.C.R.O.), 1856.

57 The economics of railway operations in Victorian London and other cities are discussed in: Barker and Robbins, op. cit., pp. 208–40; Kellett, op. cit., pp. 60–99, 388–405; H. J. Dyos and D. H. Aldcroft, *British Transport: An economic survey from the seventeenth century to the twentieth* (Leicester, 1971), pp. 215–19, 147–75.

58 Reeder, 'Capital Investment', pp. 104–9.

59 Minutes of Evidence, House of Lords Committee, Acton & Hammersmith Railway Bill, 1874, p. 208. For a discussion of the timing of estate development in outer west London after mid-century and for some examples of how development prospects were frequently over-estimated, see M. A. Jahn, 'Railways and Suburban Development: outer West London, 1850–1900' (unpublished M.Phil. thesis, University of London, 1970).

60 There was, for instance, the case of Charles Henry Blake, a retired Indian civil servant, who put savings of £116,000 into building thirty-six houses on the Kensington Park estate in the 1850s, lent heavily to unreliable builders, and plunged into railway speculation, before being hauled back from ruin by his solicitors in time to catch a boom that brought financial success. His large collection of papers are in G.L.C.R.O.: Ladbroke Estate.

61 The most comprehensive statements on investment in house-building in the nineteenth century are: H. J. Habakkuk, 'Fluctuations in House-Building in Britain and the United States in the Nineteenth Century', *Journal of Economic History*, xxii (1962), 198–230, and J. Parry Lewis, *Building Cycles and Britain's Growth* (1965). Among other writers whose work is indicated in Professor Parry Lewis's book, E. W. Cooney was the first to discuss building fluctuations in London and S. B. Saul offers an explanation nearest to the interpretation offered by us. See, respectively, 'Long Waves in Building in the British Economy of the Nineteenth

Century', *Economic History Review*, xiii (1960), 257–69; 'House Building in England, 1890–1914', *Economic History Review*, xv (1962), 119–37.

62 From the 1840s to the 1870s, 80 percent of house-builders undertook six houses or fewer per annum, and very few built more than fifty. Following the boom that peaked in 1880–1, relatively depressed conditions forced the industry to rationalize somewhat, and at the next peak in 1899 a mere seventeen firms (3 percent of the total) were building over 40 percent of new houses in London; even so, 60 percent of all builders were still undertaking six houses or fewer in a year, and they accounted between them for about one-fifth of all new houses (G.L.C.R.O., Monthly Returns of the District Surveyors, 1872–99).

63 *Builder*, xxxv (1877), 42.

64 Details of the Paddington estate loans are contained in the St Peter's Park estate records of the ground-landlords, the Dean and Chapter of Westminster, now the Church Commissioners; details of the Walworth transactions are contained in the property ledgers of Edward Yates, a speculative builder in South London, the only such business records known to us to have survived as historical records.

65 See P. G. M. Dickson, *The Sun Insurance Office, 1710–1960* (1960); T. E. Gregory, *The Westminster Bank through a Century* (1936); Barry Supple, *The Royal Exchange Assurance. A history of British insurance, 1720–1970* (1970).

66 The operations we are describing here have not been sufficiently researched as yet but we are confident from the two most helpful collections of building society records that we have examined—those relating to the Temperance Permanent and the West London Permanent Building Societies—that there is much more to be done by way of detailed investigations in this field. The best available general histories of the building society movement in the nineteenth century are: Sir Harold Bellman, *Bricks and Mortals* (1949); J. Seymour Price, *Building Societies, their Origins and History* (1958); E. J. Cleary, *The Building Society Movement* (1965).

67 'The Building Mania', *Builder*, vi (1848), 500–1, quoting the *Morning Herald*.

68 See David Owen, *English Philanthropy, 1660–1960* (1964), pp. 372–93.

69 William Howitt, 'Holidays for the People. Michaelmas', *People's Journal*, ii (1846), 171.

70 Ibid., 170.

71 Andrew Winter, 'Country Houses for the Working Classes', *People's Journal*, ii (1846), 135.

72 Henry Lazarus, *Landlordism: An illustration of the rise and spread of slumland* (1892), p. 46. For the rise of urban land-reform movements at this time, see D. A. Reeder, 'The Politics of Urban Leaseholds in Late Victorian England', *I.R.S.H.*, vi (1961), 1–18.

73 *Plays Unpleasant* (1926 edn), p. xxv. The following excerpt comes from Act II (pp. 33–4).

74 Winter, op. cit., p. 134.

75 For 'rates made' see the annual volumes of *London Statistics* from 1890 onwards.

76 Malcolmson, op. cit., ch. 4. For the law on this, see G. St Leger Daniels, *A Handbook of the Law of Ejectment* (1900), which was designed to be 'specially useful to those landlords and their agents who often find the "getting rid of tenants" an unpleasant necessity'.

77 J. F. B. Firth, 'London Government, and How to Reform It', in *Local Government and Taxation in the United Kingdom*, ed. J. W. Probyn (1882), pp. 147–269; S. and B. Webb, *The London Programme* (Fabian Society Tract, 1891).

IV   A Change of Accent

16   Another Part of the Island
Some Scottish perspectives

G. F. A. Best

One of the things that must strike anyone reading this book thus far is how much of what we know about the Victorian city is subject to illusion. We see it for the most part on a darkened stage in which pools of light are cunningly thrown by the illusionist. But like any small boy at a production of this kind we suspect that there is much more to be seen. That is a revelation not easily granted. If we were to be allowed behind the scenes we might find a wholly different paraphernalia of stage furniture and backcloths stored away—the scenery for another part of the magic island. But out front the view we have of the stage itself is governed to an unsuspected degree by our own optical and psychological readiness to see what is not there.

It is possible, for example, to be so stunned by a sense of the speed of physical change in the twentieth-century city that one may slip into thinking of this or that Victorian city as a relatively fixed, solid thing, that emerged, dingily, from some Georgian chrysalis and only changed to become the less fixed twentieth-century thing we know. This illusion is perhaps promoted by the masters of the British topographical illustration school, who left such attractive, clean, clear-cut vistas (no doubt somewhat idealized) of the later-Georgian and very early-Victorian city and who had no immediate successors, until photography for popular commercial purposes brought the sight of the Victorian city back to us most vividly in its very late-Victorian form. This shortage of visual information helps to produce the erroneous impression that the Victorian city was more fixed than the twentieth-century one. The fact is that prosperous cities of that time experienced physical flux no less than those of our own. The railways and the new roads wrought great changes on the face of the Victorian city. 'Improvements', as they were almost always called, were going on from the very early nineteenth century, and the ones we have heard most about cannot have been more than a fraction of the whole. The clearance of old city-centre inconvenience and squalor to make way for handsome business buildings, which achieved such flattering publicity when Chamberlain did it in Birmingham, was going on as best it could in every city where business boomed and local pride surged. Everyone knows about the city centres' characteristic loss of resident populations as their concerns became dominantly civic and mercantile, but it is less easy to bear in mind the physical change that accompanied this demographic and functional one. Birmingham men returning after fifteen years' absence in 1890 and 1970 respectively might be equally perplexed to find their way from New Street station. In the most prestigious streets of the City, façades may well have changed several times in the course of the century. Mayfair's rebuilding as the ground-leases fell in during the eighties and nineties totally changed its appearance from the Mayfair which Palmerston knew.

Another illusion of the Victorian city tends to be its size. Here was the most urbanized country in the world, with the biggest city in the world and far and away the biggest cluster of large-sized cities to support it; with, moreover, continual complaint all through the century from administrators and magistrates about the unmanageability of cities of these sizes and from spokesmen of the labouring classes about the difficulty of ever getting out of them. The paradox is that these allegedly unmanageable and prison-like cities were not all that large by the genuinely unmanageable and prison-like standards of our own day. London was indeed a monster by 1870 and no description of the green suburban belt will persuade anyone that mid-Victorian London did not present a problem to get out of for those who did not have several hours to spend, together with the energy to sustain them. But even so, it cannot have taken a Westminster pedestrian more than two hours to get well into the fields beyond Fulham or Hammersmith, or for one from Shoreditch to get into the countryside beyond Clapton and Leytonstone. These are not prohibitive times and distances. Proportionately still less so are the distances between the hearts of provincial towns and their green hinterlands. At the beginning of Victoria's reign Manchester and Leeds were physically as easy to walk out of as Winchester or Stirling are now. So far, then, as the Victorian city was difficult to get out of, or likely to inspire feelings of enclosure and imprisonment, the cause was not sheer physical immensity. Perhaps the 'countryside' was made unwelcoming by gamekeepers, guard-dogs, policemen, railings, fences, and intimidatory notices to keep the gentle traveller in mind of the abundance of laws for the defence of property. Whatever the reason for that constantly alleged divorce of townee from countryside, it cannot have lain in the factor of mere size.

Then there are the dangers of 'London fixation': of interpreting provincial matters in metropolitan terms. Henry James's remark that 'all England is in a suburban relation' to London[1] was less true in the nineteenth century than it has become in the twentieth. The bright lights of London are dangerous. The world city, the city where the wealth and display of Britain were gathered, the city where contrasts were most startling and thought-provoking, the city which so many different kinds of writer liked to explore and write about is such an attractive and absorbing subject that the historian is in real danger of judging provincial urban matters by London standards. London's differences went beyond the sufficiently obvious ones of being the world city and a socialite one. Wages did not go nearly so far in London as they did in Glasgow or Middlesbrough. There was in London a spectacular mass of destitution and pauperism which called into existence the most elaborate philanthropic apparatus that we can trace in the world in the nineteenth century, and yet defied that philanthropic apparatus to abolish or much diminish it. London had an 'entertainment' quarter so notorious that one is forced to conclude that London was the seedy vice capital of the western world. In these and many other respects London was a different kettle of fish entirely from the other cities of the land, and yet historians, I think, often slip into the trick of describing this or that attribute of nineteenth-century urban society in terms of the London society that is easiest to find out about, and that we know the most about, and perhaps (because of the literary quality of the evidence) most enjoy finding out about.

And, last of these preliminary points, there is the probability that the Victorian city is less of a type than would be the Victorian city of this or that region. I know of no attempt as yet to determine what these provincial patterns were and how far they spread. The regions to study would be of course the standard ones: Tees–Tyne, West Riding, Lancashire–Cheshire, Black Country, South Wales; and—call it regional or national—Scotland. So to the main business of this essay: to investigate some of the aspects of the Victorian city as it developed in Scotland.[2]

The big cities of Scotland at the 1901 Census were a small group, in this order of size:[3]

Glasgow (excluding Govan, Partick, and Pollockshaws)	762,000
Edinburgh (excluding Leith)	317,000
Dundee	161,000
Aberdeen	154,000
Paisley	79,000
Leith	77,000
Govan	77,000
Greenock	68,000

Glasgow's pre-eminence had been undisputed since quite early in the century. Edinburgh (I am now perforce including Leith, as, in respect of Glasgow, I shall include Govan, etc.) had actually been larger by 6,000 in 1801, by 2,000 in 1811. Thereafter Glasgow leapt ahead. By 1851 only Dublin was larger in the U.K.; by 1871 Glasgow was next after London; Liverpool, Manchester, and Birmingham were above Dublin, in that order.

The first trap awaiting the incautious historian who lumps them in with the English cities for common study is that the statutory framework which controlled the Scottish cities (so far as any statutory framework did control Victorian cities, which was not greatly, before the 1870s) was not coincident with that controlling the English ones. The quantity of statutes clearly labelled 'Scotland' indeed strongly suggests this, but they do not tell quite the whole story. For one thing, many public and general statutes right through the century were supposed, at the time of their passing, to work on both sides of the border. Some indeed were able to do so, but others were not. The Board of Supervision (Scotland's central health and local government authority, such as it was) complained to the Lord Advocate in November 1866 that it had tried and failed to work the Nuisance Removal (Scotland) Act of 1856, Lindsay's Burgh Police Act of 1862, the 1865 Sewage Utilization Act, and the 1866 Sanitary Act; besides being largely irreconcilable with one another, the two last-named Acts simply did not fit Scottish law and circumstances.[4] The same hard truth was, about the same time, being discovered independently in Whitehall. Certain leading inhabitants of Uddingston, Lanarkshire, took up the 1866 Act's suggestion that the Home Secretary should be memorialized to put pressure on their laggardly local authority. The official endorsements of the Uddingston memorial tell their own story: '[Tom] Taylor to inquire S.H.W. [Spencer Walpole]'; 'Does the Act apply to Scotland?'; 'I do not find any provision to the contrary but ask Mr. Thring.' Henry Thring, the Home Office Counsel, soon came to the lame conclusion that the Act (Part I of it, anyway) was apparently meant to be applicable to Scotland, but that it was no use applying it there because the ultimate means of enforcement was the exclusively English court of Queen's Bench.[5]

The series of statutes designed to assist good-quality working-class housing, known after their promoters as the Torrens and Cross Acts, are another case in point. The Torrens Acts (1868, 1879, and 1882) were said to be 'practically a dead letter' north of the border;[6] Cross's Acts, however, *were* applied, presumably because Cross had the sense to get a special version tailor-made to suit Scottish conditions.[7] A generation earlier, a similar tailoring had done the same for the Lands Clauses Act of 1845, which cheapened and simplified the compulsory acquisition of property by public authorities.[8] But public and general statutes did not absolutely have to adopt Scottish costume in order to survive north of the border. The 1890 Housing of the Working Classes Act and its lineal successors functioned everywhere, as apparently did the Small Dwellings Acquisition Act of 1899 and the Housing and Town Planning Act of 1909.

The preliminary difficulty, however, is not yet fully exposed. It goes beyond the facts that some general Acts did, and others did not, work in Scotland, and there is no cut-and-dried means of telling which is which. There is the further difficulty that in some of its branches the course of Scottish social legislation ran much nearer to the English than it did in others. This fact will not upset a purely Scottish historian, to whom the course of purely English legislation is of no interest. But it can upset the historian who seeks to bring shared English and Scottish concerns within a single

'British' view. He will (quite rightly) be on his guard, for instance, about such matters as education, for there the differences between the two nations are celebrated and obvious. In the cases of legislation about primary local authorities and the Poor Law the historian will also know from the start that he is dealing with two perfectly independent sets of institutions, and he will not be surprised, therefore, if their legislative histories are out of phase with one another.

In respect of public health, however, the case is surely rather different. Here was a nineteenth-century innovation, a brand-new problem demanding legislative intervention to cope with problems much the same wherever they cropped up. One might expect the English and Scottish legislative and administrative histories of public health to be coincident and concurrent. But they actually appear more different, both in content and chronology, than any of those three parallel cases already mentioned. And they are the more confused and confusing, because it seems to have taken some years before the inapplicability to Scotland of English-framed general public health legislation was clearly realized. Only in the 1860s did the general government of Scotland attain, in respect of public health, the state which England had been in since 1848, and only in the 1890s did the Scottish laws of public health really catch up with the English.

The Scottish equivalents of the 1848 Public Health Act and its lineal successors were Lindsay's Burgh Police Act of 1862 and the Public Health (Scotland) Act of 1867. Lindsay's Act enabled communities which chose to adopt it to make the sort of building and sanitary by-laws which were the very foundations of early-Victorian public health; the 1867 Act established a Scottish equivalent to the central sanitary office which had been functioning in England (under changing titles) since 1848, and (ominously foreshadowing the English development of 1871) lumped it in with the central poor-law authority, the Board of Supervision. It was no more than a pale copy of the English office already established. As one of its more intelligent critics, the Sheriff-Substitute of Lanarkshire, W. C. Spens, pointed out ten years later: 'that the duties under the Act were not supposed to be very onerous may be gathered from the fact that the remuneration which was proposed to be allowed to the legal members of the Board [i.e. the three Sheriffs] ... was £50 a year.' None of that Board's honorary members regularly attended. The Chairman, W. S. Walker of Bowland (he had been Secretary from 1852 to 1868), was, Spens conceded, active and capable; but he said, 'although I always am prepared to stand up for my profession, I certainly am not prepared to hold that the supervision of public health matters in Scotland should be entrusted to a committee of advocates.' The Board had no medical member, and only one medically-qualified officer—and he a part-timer, Dr H. D. Littlejohn, the Edinburgh Medical Officer of Health, who was prevailed upon to accept 'the huge salary of £200 per annum ... upon the understanding that for that salary he shall undertake all investigations within ... a day's journey of Edinburgh'.[9]

Nor was this feeble Board's powers *vis-à-vis* the local sanitary authorities at all adequate to the situation.[10] It had only three full-time Inspectors for Poor Law and Public Health functions combined, and their salaries—'fixed by the Treasury'—

393

were a good deal lower than those of their English and Irish counterparts. Its English counterpart—in the sixties the Local Government Act Office—drew some of its large and ever-growing measure of control and influence over local boards of health from its powers to approve sets of by-laws and to issue time- and money-saving Provisional Orders. The Board of Supervision had no such powers.[11] Most burghs that thought fit to make by-laws under Lindsay's Act did not even need to get the approval of that Pooh-Bah of Scottish local administration, the Sheriff. It was nobody's official business, until the nineties, to make sure either that the by-laws which were needed were made, or that, having been made, they were enforced. Regulations made under the Scottish Public Health Act came under the Board's purview, but, again, the Board had no power to see that they were made. These provisions for urban public health were not impressive even at the dates of their introduction, and they remained substantially unchanged for over twenty years.[12]

They were not unchanged because nobody saw their failings. Repeated attempts at improving them foundered, it seems, on rocks painfully familiar to the well-intentioned Scottish legislator: shortage of parliamentary time; lack of interest or lack of intelligence in Lords Advocates and, after 1885, Scottish Secretaries; selfish and stupid opposition from the very local authorities in Scotland whose performance most needed improvement. And when, at last, in the nineties, substantial improvements were made, there was not, in the Burgh Police (Scotland) Act of 1892 which replaced Lindsay's Act of thirty years before, that clear and helpful distinction of health from police and building functions which the reformers desiderated. The Public Health (Scotland) Act of 1897 extensively reorganized its administration. From that time on, Scottish and English public health law marched more in step, but Scotland was, by then, a long way behind. It was not in every respect so far behind in the big cities, which had been steadily looking after themselves under their own local Acts for anything up to a hundred years. 'The truth is', said Chairman Walker to the Dilke Commission,[13] 'that we have no great anxiety about the large towns. We are aware that their staff is ample . . . and they are intelligent and active in the executing of the [Public Health] Act'; but it was lamentably behind in the smaller urban areas and in the country towns and villages, where the cause of public health, lacking the steady pressure of a vigilant and sufficient central authority, seemed still at the turn of the twentieth century to be in its infancy, and where only the closer proximity of the countryside sometimes made insanitary horrors less horrific.

We turn back from the unlovely spectacle of late-Victorian Coatbridge, Motherwell, Blantyre, and Port Glasgow to the major cities, where urbanization was being experienced at its most intense. These big six—Glasgow, Edinburgh, Leith, Aberdeen, Dundee, and Greenock—preferred to keep themselves to themselves and to work under their own local 'Police Acts', as did some of the greater English cities. On both sides of the border, motives of local pride and independence often urged municipalities to shape and pay for their own statutes. Manchester men firmly believed (reasonably or not) that its 1844 Improvement Act was Lord Morpeth's main model for his 1848 Public Health Act, and Glasgow men believed that R. A. Cross got the idea for his first, 1875, Artizans' and Labourers' Dwellings Improvement Act, from its own pioneer Improvement Act of 1866. Provincial citizens argued that they had to be left free to attend to particular local needs, which were bound to vary from place to place. This may well have been true; yet the mainspring of their action was surely the determination not to admit central authorities to any share in the management of their local affairs. Such a measure of local pride, independence, and, perhaps, obstinacy, was one of the many shared characteristics of English and Scottish Victorian cities, itself neither surprising nor discreditable, but worth attention because it appears that its Scottish form was rooted in a civic tradition and an urban outlook so different in one important particular that it merits closer examination.

Scottish cities in general were accustomed to a civic government much firmer and more positive, in some respects, than were English cities. Evidence of many varieties suggests that Scottish city government was in the last century in some ways tougher, and in others more enterprising, than English. Consider, first, Edinburgh, in its golden age. Was it absolutely by chance, or was it partly because it was set in a Scottish tradition of civic authoritarianism, that Edinburgh was in fact the only city in eighteenth- or early-nineteenth-century Britain officially to develop itself to such a remarkable extent, and that, as A. J. Youngson points out,[14] 'all Scottish towns of any consequence undertook building programmes in these decades'? John Nash's metropolitan magnificence was a special case: the beautification of the imperial capital under the passionate stimulus of the monarch and with a good deal of Crown property in hand to start with. Dublin's great array of public buildings was an even more special case: Dublin was the Georgian New Delhi. The splendour of Georgian Bath was entirely the creation of a family of gifted property developers; the municipal contributions to the amenities of Bath were consequent upon the initiatives of the Woods. Early Victorian Newcastle, for a tragically short while Britain's most handsome industrial city, was principally the achievement of a gifted property developer, though Robert Grainger was certainly much helped by his friendship with the Town Clerk. Beyond Newcastle there is nothing to match the City of Edinburgh's conception and development of its New Town. All the rest—Bloomsbury, Belgravia, Brighton, Bournemouth, Birkenhead, *et hoc genus omne*—were so much the creations of private landowners and/or speculators, that the role of the public authority was in comparison quite negligible.

The episode of Edinburgh's New Town may the more plausibly be set into a context of civic authoritarianism because several nineteenth-century Scotsmen thought this existed, and there is some evidence to suggest that they were right. For instance, the Edinburgh lawyer John Hill Burton—whose summary of *The State of the Law as regards the Abatement of Nuisances and the Protection of the Public Health in Scotland* for the benefit of Edwin Chadwick's famous Sanitary Inquiry is one of the clearest pictures we have of this side of 'the condition of Scotland question'—said in 1840 that 'formerly any public regulations or restrictions which the courts of law approved of were very arbitrarily enforced, without much respect to individual rights'. Perhaps too much could be made of this reference to a strict regime which had, on Burton's own plentiful evidence, shrunk from its earlier grandeur; but only fifteen years later allegations of civic authoritarianism were made by another citizen of Edinburgh, one Robert Mason of Meadowbank. Complaining to the Home Secretary about the proposed amalgamation of the southern suburbs with the City, he concluded by denouncing the Council for already possessing a bigger empire than they could efficiently handle. 'Our present Lord Provost [Sir John Melville, Writer to the Signet] is a great admirer of the abilities and management of the Emperor of the French; and although he may possess much unheard-of wisdom, he is not appointed to be hereditary Provost of Edinburgh.'[15] It is interesting that, whereas English Mayors held office for a year at a time, Scottish Provosts served for three years at a stretch.

Though, perhaps, no ratepayer of an English city in the fifties would have felt moved to express himself thus strongly about his mayor, it is very doubtful whether any English city was yet doing anything spectacular or expensive enough to provoke such passionate reactions. Similar things were probably being said in Birmingham about Mayor Chamberlain in the later seventies, and in the County of London about Chairman, the Earl of Rosebery, in the nineties. Each presided over a regime which showed three unmistakable marks of the collectivist beast: willingness to spend ratepayers' money for the common good; positive anxiety to spend it for the benefit of those who were too poor to pay rates; and a Germanic idea of civic magnificence and subsidized culture. Birmingham and the London County Council regularly appear in the accounts as shining lights of later-Victorian civic enterprise, and Liverpool's record seems to have been extraordinarily impressive, though its full measure has not yet been taken. But a fourth British city ought to be put beside them: a city which may well not have needed to acquire notions of civic enterprise, because they were already in its national tradition—Glasgow.

Glasgow certainly took over from Edinburgh as the show-city of Scotland in the second half of the nineteenth century, and, long before it became controlled by the Labour party, its collectivist enterprise was provoking unsympathetic observers to the same sort of alarm and disapprobation that it now provokes as a model of socialist civic planning. A commentator in normally sober legal circles angrily called Glasgow 'the oppressor of the West'.[16] Anger and fear informed his whole piece, which was printed in 1905, when Glasgow had been in the van of municipal enterprise for at least fifty years. By 1888 Glasgow's Medical Officer of Health, the great Dr J. B. Russell, was already complaining that 'The public of Glasgow trust too much to authorities and officials for the solution of their social difficulties—more, I think, than any other community'. Proud of Glasgow's sanitary and housing work, he regretted the city's relative backwardness in the ' "Open Spaces and Playgrounds' Associations"... "Artizans' Dwellings Companies" and the like, which unite the business capacity and Christian sympathy of the citizens of so many other cities in successful labour for the common good.' Why, he concluded, 'have we not an Octavia Hill in Scot-

292 An intersection in the St Leonard's district
of Edinburgh (St Leonard's Hill—Dumbiedykes
Road—Carnegie Street—Heriot Mount) at the
time of demolition, *c*.1960. This crossing was
complete, in this shape, by 1867. At exactly what
dates through the preceding fifty years each
separate block was erected, I cannot judge.
Scotsman Publications Ltd

293 *above* Amphion Place, Calton Road. Built about 1825. The photograph (1958) shows the railway into Waverley from the east tunnelling under the Calton Hill. From a photograph in the Local History Collection.
Edinburgh Central Public Library

294 *right* Lower Viewcraig Row, in the Dumbiedykes district, 1957; the terraces are on a hillside descending to the valley between Holyrood Palace and Salisbury Crags.
Photo: Adam H. Malcolm

295 Tweeddale Court, off the High Street.
Undated, but *c.*1950, showing a characteristic
scene in the Old Town as it was inhabited
through the nineteenth and into the early
twentieth century.
Edinburgh Central Public Library

land?'[17] Dr Russell's complaint about a certain lack of *voluntary* citizens' enterprise towards better urban life was echoed by others; by, for instance, the Edwardian Royal Commissioners on the Poor Law, who, finding it remarkable that there were in the big Scottish cities no medical Provident Dispensaries of the kind by then quite common in English cities, said they thought it 'regrettable that so many persons in the large centres of population in Scotland appear to be willing to accept charitable medical relief instead of adopting some form of providence or thrift in order to provide themselves with medical attendance', and urged the Scots to 'vindicate the national character' and establish some.[18]

Glasgow was not a 'model' city in all respects. The extent of its municipal enterprise was not unlimited. But it was, by Victorian standards, both extensive and early; and Glasgow's record seems more impressive than—at any rate—Birmingham's, and deserves to be much better known. It shows that Glasgow was at least as active as the other early enterprising English municipality, Liverpool—at least according to one American through whose eyes, as yet undazzled by Brummagem glitter, we might look at the Glasgow of 1889.[19]

The Municipality of Glasgow 'transformed the Clyde from a mere rivulet with mud banks into an artificial channel for navigation by the largest vessels'. The Loch Katrine water scheme, completed in 1859, was, with the possible exception of Liverpool's, the first of the great municipal long-distance water projects, and the only cities in the United Kingdom that got their water more cheaply were Dublin and Edinburgh. The city bought out the two existing private gas companies in 1869, and in 1893 was supplying a higher candle-power gas than any other city except Liverpool, at a price cheaper than most. With Dundee, it pioneered the public lighting of private courts and common stairs. On its own it led the way in the municipal leasing and hire-purchase of gas-stoves and fires. When tramways suddenly became the rage, Glasgow took a course in the early seventies which London and other less collectivist-minded cities soon came to regret not having taken: it built the tramlines itself and leased them to private companies to work; thus it retained control of the amenities of the highways and of the development of the system, and was the more easily able to municipalize them later on. It was not the Council's fault that the obstinate long refusal of the circumambient little burghs (all by nature parts of 'greater Glasgow') to come within the municipal boundary, reduced the efficiency of the tramway system's suburban services, just as they impeded the efficiency and growth of other municipal services. Glasgow owned and managed all its markets and slaughter-houses—nothing exceptional about that—and owned what the American observer called 'a magnificent system of public baths and wash-houses'.

But the most impressive of Glasgow's early municipal enterprises was in something much bigger and more basic than abattoirs and laundries: it was in housing and town-planning. The three big Scottish cities led the way in slum-clearance. Their own Improvement Acts gave to Dundee in 1871, Edinburgh in 1867, and Glasgow in 1866 the powers to purchase, clear, and redevelop central slum areas which the Cross Acts, from 1875 onwards, made generally available. These pioneer improvements are obviously of great interest, and one student has summarized the Glasgow property development in terms of 'municipal socialism' thus: 'By 1902 the Corporation owned, among other things, 2,488 houses, 78 lodging-houses, 372 shops, 86 warehouses and workshops, 12 halls, 2 churches [and] a bakehouse.'[20]

This venture into 'council-housing' was quite remarkable but too much should not be made of it: first, because the city only went into it *faute de mieux*, after failing to find private speculators to put up the much-needed houses; second, because there is no adequate material for comparing it with the municipal housing achievements of other cities; and third, because after all the significant thing was not that some quantity of housing was municipally erected and leased but that it was the biggest Scottish city that undertook 'the first massive municipal intervention [in Britain] to sweep away the most insanitary and dilapidated and archaic central urban areas and to replan them on a modern basis'; it was Glasgow that first recognized 'that a free market, and private philanthropy and public health regulations could not provide an adequate solution to these problems: that the City Fathers must at least supervise and plan redevelopment';[21] and it was Dundee and Edinburgh, not Birmingham or anywhere else, that quickly followed suit.

Now why were the Scottish cities the pioneers in this business of slum clearance? It is not enough to say simply that they happened to have worse slums than anywhere else. Probably their slums were the very worst—at least, equal with the very worst—in Britain; but surely history and contemporary experience alike suggest, however unhappily, that social remedial measures are not necessarily taken most decisively by the cities that most need them. Perhaps there was something in the Scottish local government tradition which encouraged an in some ways tougher handling of the problems of poverty.

Dr H. T. Hunter—one of Dr John Simon's brilliant band of investigators in the sixties—whose *Report on the Housing of the Poorer Parts of the Population in Towns*[22] is among the most important social enquiries of that inquisitive decade, included the memorable fact that 'At Glasgow the question of over-crowded houses has attained such magnitude of importance as to compel the abandonment of all prejudice, and the peremptory defence of society against individual aggression, by the enforcement of a fixed ratio of capacity and inhabitation.' This was the origin, in the sixties, of the famous Glasgow system of 'Ticketed Houses':[23] registration and labelling, by tin-plate 'tickets' firmly fixed on the outer wall, of private houses of three or fewer rooms in which the aggregate volume of air-space (not including lobbies and recesses) did not exceed two thousand cubic feet. The 'ticket' stated the cubic content and the number of occupants allowed at the low rate of three hundred cubic feet for each adult. But this was not all. The police as well as the sanitary inspectors had the power to enter and inspect 'ticketed houses' at any time of day or night—and it was almost invariably at night that they did enter, since it was only then that the over-crowders could be caught at it.

This was indeed a 'peremptory defence of society against individual aggression'! There was nothing like it in England at that date (the registration and inspection of common lodging-houses was quite a different thing), nor anything else yet in Scotland. But in the course of the next fifty years it became known in all the big Scottish cities, and it was made generally available by the 1903 Burgh Police Act. The only English cities in which anything like it could be discovered by the 1917 Royal Commission on Housing in Scotland were Bradford, Birmingham (where a stricter sense of propriety confined inspections to Sunday mornings), and Liverpool, where it was worked with full Glaswegian vigour.[24]

The fact of its flourishing in Liverpool so much more than anywhere else south of the border rather suggests that by 'individual aggression' Dr Hunter may actually have meant 'Irish pauperism'. The extreme nastiness of the slums inhabited by Irish immigrants was a constant theme with Victorian social and sanitary reformers, and close investigation would very probably discover public authorities and police to have become tougher, and more emphatic in their use (or abuse) of discretionary powers, when they were dealing with the 'paddies'. Glasgow and Liverpool of course were worse hit by Irish immigrants than anywhere else: T. H. S. Escott observed in 1879, without a flicker of surprise, that 'the repressive measures enforced by the Liverpool magistrates are exceptionally severe, and that the police often apprehend upon charges which would be deemed trivial elsewhere'.[25] Glasgow's statistician, James Cleland, thought there were about 35,500 Irish natives in Glasgow in 1831, nearly 18 percent of the total population, and all of it crowded into the worst slums. J. H. Clapham wryly comments that 'the West Scottish towns [were not] hospitable to the newcomers', and that by some unspecified ' "moral compulsion" . . . 1,517 Irish were shipped from Paisley in 1827', and even more from Glasgow.[26] Again, it may have been because the denizens of the fearful Sandgate slums were largely Irish that the two police inspectors in charge of Newcastle's common lodging-houses (under Shaftesbury's Act of 1851) went beyond their legal brief and in practice inspected, between ten and two at night, 'all houses let in single-room' dwellings, as well as common lodging-houses proper. Dr Hunter was rather astonished at their audacity, but reported that the sanitary and moral results had been excellent, and, 'such [was] the tact of the officers, that no anger or resistance seems to have been produced'.[27]

The foreign character of the slum-dwellers of the Scottish cities may have contributed to bringing out strong authoritarian streaks in public officials. But it does seem likely that some national characteristic in the authorities governing those cities was also operating. The Poor Law Commission of 1909 discovered that some Scottish poorhouse authorities had gone a long way beyond what was legally permissible in their liberty-restricting rules and regulations. They also reported that 'It has long been the practice in Scotland to remove children from vicious parents'. In Glasgow, they said, the Parish Council retained a special officer for prosecuting the parents of deserted or 'separated' children.[28] And John Naismith startled the National Association for the Promotion of Social Science in 1874 with his account of the ways in which Glasgow magistrates, Justices of the Peace, procurators-fiscal (i.e. public prosecutors), and police between them so operated the local Police Acts as to perpetrate petty injustices without possibility of appeal.[29] One of his instances was of a prosecution, under the Police Act, of a workman for loitering in and obstructing the street.

> Not only was the offence not proved, but it was directly negatived by the police officers called to prove it. The sitting bailie, however, convicted the accused, but dismissed him with an admonition. The worthy magistrate afterwards explained to me that he did so because there had been grievous complaints from the shopkeepers in the neighbourhood of the annoyance caused to themselves and their customers by the workmen loitering about at meal times, and that it was necessary that the practice should be put a stop to.

The practical operation of these Scottish City Police Acts invites scrutiny. Mayhew printed on the wrappers of his weekly issues of *London Labour and the London Poor* in early 1851 a number of letters from Edinburgh correspondents reporting a regular crusade against or, from the opposite angle, persecution of, street-sellers, asserting that one magistrate had announced his refusal to go along with his colleagues in thus enforcing the City Police Bill. One gets a strong impression that Scottish towns were 'better' policed, earlier, than English towns. Did Scottish municipal authorities enjoy under their Police Acts larger powers of interference in citizens' lives than normally did English ones? That they did so is suggested by Sheriff James Watson's address to the Social Science Association in 1877. He said that the Police Acts and magistrates' 'provisional orders' (by-laws?) had raised 'a vast number of frivolous acts . . . into criminal offences punishable by a caution to keep the peace, a small fine, or a few days' imprisonment'.[30] Did magistrates friendly with shopkeepers, on no matter which side of the border, connive with police to keep the lower classes a-moving along respectable pavements? Perhaps; and yet I should like to close this section of my argument with a quotation from an embattled Glasgow pawnbroker, Mr William McKay of 99 Cowcaddens Street, who complained of police oppression (under the local Police Act) in a letter to the *Glasgow Herald* of 15 November 1860. In England, he alleged, referring to a Commons debate on 4 July 1860, such police powers were not tolerated. But in Glasgow, the police enjoyed and freely used power to enter and inspect his premises at any hour of day or night—'up out of your bed, away from drill, or from any other evening engagement, to accommodate a tyrannical set who, if they got us under their heel, would oppress us like the worst Bomba that ever swayed a sceptre'.

There is then some circumstantial evidence to suggest that the Scottish municipal approach to the manifold problems of industrial urbanization may have been essentially different from the English one. As to the problems themselves, which of them took on, north of the border, a distinctive shape and colour?

It is difficult to avoid the impression that Scottish city slums had, as indeed they still seem to have, some peculiar nastiness about them. Whether or not they were absolutely 'the worst' in Britain, they did appal observers.[31] And that their constant major characteristic was the density of their overcrowding, there can be no doubt.

Professor W. P. Alison, whom Professor Flinn allows to have occupied 'a similar position in Scotland . . . to that held by Chadwick in England',[32] dwelt significantly on a description of life in old Glasgow's wynds given to the 1839 Handloom Weavers Inquiry.[33] It was from Alison's writings, apparently, that Thomas Carlyle drew both his warning parable of 'the poor Irish widow'—conceivably the germ of that theme of providential retribution soon afterwards exploited by Kingsley in *Cheap Clothes and Nasty* and by Dickens regularly from *Dombey and Son* (ch. 47) onwards—and his summary of the Scottish wynds as 'scenes of woe and destitution and desolation, such as, one may hope, the sun never saw before'.[34] Edwin Chadwick appeared to be equally shocked. 'The most wretched account of the stationary population of which I have been able to obtain any account, or that I have ever seen, was that which I saw in company with Dr. Arnott, and others, in the wynds of Edinburgh and Glasgow.' And again, his summary: 'It might admit of dispute, but, on the whole, it appeared to us that both the structural arrangements and the condition of the population in Glasgow was the worst of any we had seen in any part of Great Britain.'[35]

This bad eminence of the Scottish slums continues to be proclaimed throughout the nineteenth century and into our own. Dr Hunter indeed neglected to mention any Scottish city when he deliberately described 'life in parts of London and Newcastle [as] infernal', but his colleague Dr George Buchanan, whom Simon had set to investigating the epidemic typhus of Greenock, found its population almost as densely crowded as Liverpool's (the densest in England) 'and considerably denser than in the poorest parts of London'. 'In Greenock', he said, 'no less than 2,747 persons . . . are living under conditions which would not be permitted in the worst parts of London.' About five hundred souls were living or partly living in a manner 'to which', he thought, 'there can be but few parallels and which represents people living day and night in a space about the size of a street cab apiece.'[36]

Ten years later Chadwick, in jolly mood, told the Social Science Association that if he had to construct a city sacred to Siva the Destroyer, with a guaranteed death-rate of over forty per thousand, he would 'copy literally and closely the old parts of Whitehaven, those of Newcastle-upon-Tyne, and the wynds of Glasgow and Edinburgh'.[37] Chadwick was going, as he had always gone, by mortality figures, which had always been worst in the cities. The sanitary reformers' campaigns had therefore been directed mainly at the cities, with the gratifying result that, by the turn of the century, the killing powers of the cities were much diminished. This was true of the Scottish cities as well as of the English ones.[38] Their overall death-rate figures of course concealed sharp variations between the better and the worst localities; thus in Glasgow about 1900, the overall death-rate of 20·7 per thousand concealed the gap between Kelvinhaugh's 15 and Brownfield's 36;[39] but the improvement in the general urban death-rates during the past thirty years was undeniable, and a comparable and quicker improvement in the urban infant death-rates was about to begin. Sanitarians' attention began to turn from the cities proper, where the battle seemed to have been won, to the rough frontier-towns of industrialism—above all, the mining communities of Glamorgan, the Midlands, County Durham, Lanarkshire, and Fife. In such forlorn industrial districts the infant death-rate could be nearly as bad—over a larger population, and without a fraction of the administrative excuse—as it still was in the worst quarters of Glasgow,[40] and it was to those hitherto neglected places that the national battle for public health now moved. But to one feature of big city life the attention of sanitary and social reformers alike remained riveted—a lingering and loathsome feature, for which the Scottish cities held and hold an unenviable palm: overcrowding.

It was for the peculiar character of their overcrowding that the Scottish cities were notorious. They had always been so to some degree, but they became increasingly so as Victoria's reign wore on, because there were elements in the nature of Scottish overcrowding which prevented its amelioration during years which witnessed its diminution elsewhere. So, always absolutely worse, it seemed relatively much worse, too, as time went by. Density of population had always meant public ill-health and the reformers had been quite clear about this since Alison's and Chadwick's heyday: but the mid-Victorian public health experts had learnt to distinguish between one sort of density and another, and had come to appreciate that some sorts of density were more dangerous than others. Dr J. B. Russell of Glasgow, faced with density problems equalled only by those of Liverpool, conclusively demonstrated that the most lethal sort was that measured (and it required more sensitive instruments to measure it), not in persons per acre, but in persons per room.[41] More people lived in one- and two-room houses in Scotland than anywhere else in Britain: in 1911, 47·9 percent, as against England's 7·5 percent.[42] These one- and two-room houses, moreover, if they were in cities (and most, though not all of them were), were almost always in tall, deep tenements which presented reformers with other special problems.

The origins of the Scottish urban tenement and the one- or two-room home (which together gave the Scottish Victorian city much of its distinction) were often discussed, as reformers tried to accustom their inhabitants to higher standards of comfort and space. Earlier in Victoria's reign, reformers supposed that, once three- or four-room 'houses' or independent two- or three-room 'cottages' were available, the poor one- and two-room families would voluntarily and gladly move into them. Such 'houses' and 'cottages' did become available from the sixties onwards. The poor did not rush into them. Sympathetic reformers attributed this to the fear which the uncertainly-employed poor had of getting into a home the higher rent (or mortgage repayment) of which they could not afford in times of slack trade or family misfortune; unsympathetic reformers attributed it to the slum-dwellers' debased preference for dirt and drink. But by the early years of our present century it was clear that the complete explanation of the persistence of one- and two-roomed housing had to include some recognition of the ghastly fact that experience of it had made it seem a natural thing to the third and fourth generations. It was, for many of them, a way of life.[43]

When and how came about the urban Scot's induration to the overcrowded life of the tenement? Russell's predecessor, the first Glasgow Medical Officer of Health, Professor William Tennent Gairdner, fancifully supposed (as from time to time have others) that the tenement plan came to Scotland from France, a disagreeable by-product of the Auld Alliance.[44] Clapham comes much nearer the mark when he strikingly says, 'The Scottish way of living had been got by ancient country habit out of ancient town necessity, and it was a one- or two-room way, very tough and indestructible, as were the eighteen-inch or two-foot stone walls of the houses which encased it.'[45] The plentiful supply of stone must have had something to do with it, and the example of Edinburgh, for so long the biggest Scottish city besides being the capital, must have had some influence, too. The tenements of its Old Town remained into the nineteenth century the national archetypes of one of the two main species of low-class housing: the nearly indestructible vast old tenement, never undercrowded even in the better days which it had usually known, now utterly gone to seed and divided and sub-divided again and again—'made down' was the expressive technical term—until it had become a warren of one- and two-room dwellings. London had its equivalents in the 'rookeries' of old Westminster, Holborn, Jacob's Island, and other places well known to Dickens. One hears less often of similar places in Liverpool, Nottingham, and Newcastle. But whereas even in London they were regarded (and feared) as exceptional, in Edinburgh and Glasgow they were the hearts of the cities: the wynds which trickled narrowly down each side of the Royal Mile in Old Edinburgh, which sneaked at right-angles off the main grid thoroughfares of Old Glasgow. 'End-on to the building line of these streets', explained Dr Russell,

> we see long narrow strips, extending in what was the natural direction of the growth of a house placed endwise to the street—*backwards*, looking on the maps like sections of geological stratification, with cracks or flaws in between . . . parallel intervals left between tenements simply for convenience of access, only wide enough to permit two persons to pass, or perhaps a barrow or a cart. Each proprietor was bent on covering every inch of his grounds with his building, and the only function exercised by the Dean of Guild Court was that expressed in the phrase, which is still in use, 'to grant a lining'—that is, to see that if he built *up to*, he should not *build over* the line of his building.

The end-result of decades of 'making-down' in such places was house-addresses like 'Bridegate, No. 29, back land, stair first left, 3 up, right lobby, door facing'.[46]

Such were the typical pre-nineteenth-century tenements with which the ancient Scottish cities were burdened. More modern tenements, however, were not necessarily better. They began to appear in Glasgow late in the eighteenth century, as that city's pent-up prospering population, like Edinburgh's at much the same time, burst its seams and sought better-style housing in the then suburbs: Hutchesontown, Tradeston, Cowcaddens, Laurieston, Gorbals. Some of it was in villas or terraces of the common English style, but most of it was in three- or four-storey common-staired blocks, rectangularly lining the gridded streets beloved of the Georgian estate developer. From these initially not unsavoury blocks of flats there soon—sometimes very soon[47]—came unmistakable evidence of social decline. The speculation had gone sour; the more moneyed citizens were not moving in as briskly as they should; some neighbouring development—some factory, canal, or wagon-way, perhaps— had drastically damaged the amenities. In financial desperation or as a calculated switch from a respectable to a disreputable means of making a profit, the ground-owner filled the hollows behind the first façades with other tenement buildings, of meaner cast. The streets and stairs became noisy with a lower class of more numerous residents than had been originally foreseen; the hammer and chisel of the 'maker-down' sounded in these newish tenements as they had long done in the old, and the second main species of low-class Scottish Victorian housing had arrived. Its style was, from whatever causes, hypnotic. Later tenement blocks, of similar external appearance and basic common-stair design, needed no 'making-down', for they were of one- and two-room dwellings from the start; though it should be observed that the one- and two-room dwellings newly built as such would usually be of quite large rooms, and equipped with sleeping-closets and storage-space in plenty. Of the 26,794 dwellings built in Glasgow between 1866 and 1874, half were of two rooms and a quarter of only one;[48] in 1911, 20 percent of Glasgow's families were still living in one room, 46·3 percent in two rooms; of those one-room families, 57 percent were living three or more to the room—not counting lodgers.[49] Glasgow and Dundee were respectively about one-half and one-quarter as bad again, in percentages of population living more than two to a room, as the *worst* London boroughs, Bethnal Green, Stepney, Shoreditch, and Finsbury—the populations of which were, of course, nothing like so large. On the other hand it may reasonably be suspected that a Scottish family in a *new* 'single-end' was likely to be immeasurably better off than any English family in a made-down single room.

It remains only to answer two obvious questions about this tenement-type housing which was characteristic of the poorer parts of the Scottish Victorian city. Why did it, with all its evident nastiness, become characteristic? And—keeping a constant eye on the English comparison—was it in practice even more difficult a staple form of slum for Scottish municipalities to deal with than any which English ones faced?

To the presumed causes already suggested for this slum style's virtual universality in nineteenth-century Scotland must be added the workings of the feuing system. The independence of Scottish from English common law no doubt made innumerable practical differences to the business of local government and property ownership—differences which might well repay detailed investigation. The biggest and basic difference, however, was the Scottish landowner's normal method of developing his estates not (as in England) either by outright sale of the 'freehold' or by a lease of the ground for a stated term of years, but by a sort of compromise between these two normal English modes—a sale of the piece of land in perpetuity on condition of a perpetual payment of a 'feu-duty' in respect of it. Like the English landowner who issued a ground-lease, the Scottish could, if he were so minded (and if his bargaining power were strong enough), stipulate certain conditions for the ground's development; unlike the English, he (or rather his successors in the title) would never be able to resume absolute control of it. All owners of property in Scotland own it absolutely, in the sense that their right to it is inextinguishable except by their own voluntary cession of it; but no Scottish property owners, except the inheritors of property so ancient and secure as never to have been itself feued, are free from some obligation to pay a feu-duty on it; and that includes the owners of flats above the ground. Some feu-duty was bound to have become attached to each flat or, in Scottish parlance, 'house' that anybody owned, with the extremely complicated result that modern processes of sub-infeudation could give to each owner of each 'house' in a many-staired four-storey tenement block an absolute right to a proportionate interest in the piece of ground above which his 'house' stood. John Hill Burton did his best to explain this 'peculiar' tenure, as he called it, in his 1840 report for the benefit of Chadwick: 'should the tenement be destroyed, [the "house" owners] retain their right, though it can have no physical representative, till the proprietors who held beneath them have, by rebuilding, made as it were a pedestal for the real property to be erected on.'

The obstacles that such properties could put in the way of authorities seeking substantially to improve or to demolish them can be easily imagined, and constituted a weighty item in the list of Scottish city singularities. The feuing system made such transactions even more complicated than they were bound to be anyway. But—to revert to the question of Scottish slum origins—how far was the feuing system itself to blame for the staple Scottish slums being there at all? The extent of its responsibility can be exaggerated. For instance, the 1917 Royal Commission on Housing in Scotland, after carefully describing it, concluded that it had 'in many cases hampered the free development of land for building purposes' and encouraged landowners to feu land for beetling tenements, rather than for pleasanter, lower-level buildings, because they could thus get a higher aggregate of feu-duties.[50] No doubt this happened.[51] But the Scottish feuing system cannot have been much more to blame than the general British systems of private landownership and, through most of the nineteenth century at any rate, feeble or non-existent public controls of land-use and housing standards. Property owners south of the border also knew the greater financial returns to be gained, where demand was insistent enough, by similarly intensive exploitation of the housing needs of the poorer classes, who, no less in Glasgow than in Liverpool and London, absolutely had to live close to their places of (potential) employment, and hence on land the value of which was likely to be enhanced by its alternative suitability for industrial or commercial uses. If it is argued that, nevertheless, the Scottish estate developer did in his tenements generally crowd more persons on to an acre than did his English counterpart in his back-to-backs, it is also arguable that regional building and mortgaging customs were partly responsible, and English speculators, if they had known about tenements and understood how to build them, would certainly have done so. But in one respect, certainly, the feuing system did tend to encourage this tenemented exploitation of the land. The Scottish proprietor, or, to use the legal term, 'superior', parting with his land, knew that he would never recover it for redevelopment as would the Englishman developing it by building-leases. For the Englishman, especially if he was (as in the older cities he often was) of a hereditary land-owning family, accustomed to 'think big' and over a long term, immediate gains were not everything. An estate that was relatively lightly built on for the present was often thought to have a better chance of retaining its amenities within the growing city and of guaranteeing richer rewards when the ninety-nine-years leases expired, than one which was from the start exploited to its uttermost. The English suburban landowner was likely to have more of a choice; if he cared for his descendants' prospects, he would keep his development classy, and unconcernedly accept a financially lower return than was offered by immediate intensive develop-ment. The Scottish suburban landowner had no such choice. His national system compelled him, willy-nilly, to get the most he could, straight away. So up went the blocks; into them moved the house-owners or tenants; into the superior's coffers flowed the feu-duties; and, unless the district was one which exceptionally retained a high initial social rating, into the municipal offices sooner or later came intimations of social and sanitary nastiness.

In two respects this nastiness was different in kind from any that could bother an English municipality. First, it might have to do with that Scottish peculiarity, the common stair and the 'lobby' leading to it, which, being everybody's business to keep clean, became in effect nobody's. Its nastiness—'an upright street, constantly dark and dirty'—was specially mentioned in the famous *Proposals* of 1752, the blue-print for the making of classical Edinburgh. Both of Glasgow's Victorian Medical Officers of Health specified the common stairs of the tenements as one of their worst features. W. T. Gairdner remarked that in England there was always some ultimate owner of a tenement who was responsible for the stairway, and could be compelled to clean it; in Scotland it was simply an untended 'receptacle for foul air'.[52] J. B. Russell thus memorably summarized it:[53]

> The common stair of a Scotch flatted tenement is the analogue of the
> English court, not only as the means of access to the houses, but
> especially in the old buildings, in respect that it contains the common
> jawbox—the representative of the English gully-hole—and the common
> water-tap . . .; and in modern buildings in respect that it contains the
> common water-closet, the representative of the privy or trough water-closet,
> which stands at the head of the English court. Yet with all this
> similarity of function, the English court is at the worst a box open above to
> the free air, while the Scotch common stair is *at best* a longer, narrow box,
> fully open only at the lower end, with or without certain mockeries of
> ventilators at the upper end, and with windows at intervals, which may admit
> light, but are never opened, and serve no useful purpose for ventilation
> until by a providential accident, or a merciful exhibition of malice, the

panes of glass are smashed. In their *worst* form it is hard to say what the
Scotch common stair is but a dark noisome tunnel buried in the centre of the
tenement, and impervious both to light and air, excepting the fetid air
which is continuous and undiluted from the house along the lobbies and
down to the close, from which you start on your perilous and tedious
ascent.

The second respect in which the social and sanitary problems of the Scottish
slum were characteristically different from those of the English one had to do with
the practice of 'making-down'. Victorian legislators, local and national alike, were
(understandably enough) slower to authorize public interference with the insides
than with the outsides of private dwellings, and the early public-health reformers
were only able to get at insanitary interiors during cholera emergencies, which by
general agreement justified exceptional powers. During the forties and the fifties
building regulations began to be enforced by the better English local authorities—
there were prescriptions of minimum volume, lighting, solidity, sanitation, and so on
—but such regulations applied only to *new* buildings, and left the interior conditions
of already existing ones subject merely to such limited interferences as could be
justified under the Nuisance Removal Acts (1855 and 1858) and the 1848 Public
Health Act.[54] In Scotland the situation was even less satisfactory, partly because the
jealously guarded ancient jurisdiction of the Dean of Guild Courts—which, intelli-
gently extended, might have been the Scottish slums' salvation—was, until very late
in the century, concerned only with structural strength and *external* amenity (thus,
for instance, Dr Littlejohn was once obliged to complain, that the city officials had
no power to prevent the installation of defective drains, or the ventilation of internal
water-closets into bedrooms; they could do nothing until, a building being furnished
and occupied, its occupants formally complained):[55] and partly because that wholly
internal 'making-down', which was so much more a Scottish problem than an English,
produced slums in exactly the way which was most difficult for the Victorian legislator to envisage tackling. Edinburgh—ahead, for once, of Glasgow in a housing
context—seems to have got these powers for itself in its Police Act of 1879;[56]
Glasgow and the rest of Scotland had to wait until after 1890.[57]

The chief impression we are bound to take back from this limited though outlandish
excursion to the most northerly Victorian cities is one of contrast and variety. The
Scottish cities themselves plainly differed from one another in the ways in which
they met or did not meet the challenges that peculiar combinations of urban circumstances threw up in one place or another. These were differences of response, as
palpable in their way as the differences of accent, to which long force of social
circumstance had given rise in every place. There could on the face of it be no justifica-
tion for a Scottish stereotype of the Victorian city. Yet the more one looks the more
one feels justified in identifying a very general type of Scottish Victorian city, characteristically unlike the English one. To discover the whole extent of its singularity

would naturally require a far more searching expedition than the one I have been conducting. It would have to be a full-scale undertaking, concerned not only with superficial differences of urban form or the means of civic identification but also with a whole range of matters—beginning perhaps with climate and geology, crossing the whole terrain of the arts and sciences, and ending with Calvinism and the national character. None of these considerations need—or should—obliterate the particular characteristics of the individual case, for cities are human aggregates and cannot conceal their human inclinations. Whenever Englishmen think of Scotland they think, as often as not, of 'Caledonia stern and wild'. They never lose sight of the contrasts between their own landscape and that of the Scots. The point of this essay is to suggest that the contrasts of townscape, if not of the urban lives they shaped, were as great.

Notes

1 'London', in *English Hours* (1905), p. 34 [first published in *Century Magazine* in 1888].

2 What follows is an amended version of my paper, 'The Scottish Victorian City', *Victorian Studies*, xi (1968), 329–58.

3 *Parliamentary Papers* (*P.P.*), 1902, CXXIX, Eleventh Decennial Census of the Population of Scotland: Appendix VII, 'Municipal and Police Burghs' (Cd. 1257), pp. 937ff.

4 Public Record Office (P.R.O.), Home Office Papers (H.O.), 45/7940. The Board's complaint led to the appointment of George Munro, the Sheriff of Linlithgow, to draft the bill which became the Public Health (Scotland) Act of 1867.

5 P.R.O., H.O., 45/7933/22–4.

6 The only attempt to apply this legislation was in Leith. See *P.P.*, 1884–5, XXXI, Royal Commission (R.C.) on the Housing of the Working Classes: Scotland [Dilke Commission] Minutes of Evidence (C. 4409), QQ. 18,470–1, 19,923–8.

7 Cross's English Acts were 38 & 39 Vict. cap. xxxvi [1875], 42 & 43 Vict. cap. lxiii [1870]; the Scottish one was 38 & 39 Vict. cap. xlix [1875].

8 The Lands Clauses Consolidation (Scotland) Act, 1845: 8 & 9 Vict. cap. xix.

9 W. C. Spens, 'On the Necessity of a General Measure of Legislation for Scotland with regard to Public Health', *Proceedings of the Philosophical Society of Glasgow*, xi (1877–9), 129–43.

10 See Dilke Commission, Q. 18,371.

11 See Royston Lambert, 'Central and Local Relations in Mid-Victorian England: The Local Government Act Office, 1858–71', *Victorian Studies*, vi (1962), 121–50.

12 Various piddling amendments to the Public Health (Scotland) Act were passed in 1871, 1879, 1882, and 1891. They are conveniently summarized by a complacent lawyer, T. G. Nasmyth, 'The Public Health (Scotland) Act, 1897', *Juridical Review*, x (1898), 12–24.

13 Q. 18,363.

14 *The Making of Classical Edinburgh 1750–1840* (Edinburgh, 1966), pp. 50–1.

15 Letter of 12 May 1856, P.R.O., H.O., 45/6365.

16 *Scottish Law Review*, xii (1905), 223–30.

17 'On the "Ticketed Houses" of Glasgow, with an Interrogation of the Facts for Guidance towards the Amelioration of the Lives of the Occupants', *Proc. Phil. Soc. Glasgow*, xx (1888–9), 1–24; the article also appears in a memorial volume of his writings edited by his successor, A. K. Chalmers, *Public Health Administration in Glasgow* (Glasgow, 1905).

18 *P.P.*, 1909, XXXVIII, R.C. on the Poor Law: Report on Scotland (Cd. 4922), p. 263.

19 Albert Shaw, 'Municipal Socialism in Scotland', *Juridical Review*, i (1889), 33–53. I have added some information given by William Smart, 'The Municipal Industries of Glasgow', *Proc. Phil. Soc. Glasgow*, xxvi (1894–5), 36–53.

20 C. M. Allan, 'The Genesis of British Urban Redevelopment with special reference to Glasgow', *Economic History Review*, new ser., xviii (1965), 608.

21 Ibid., 613.

22 *P.P.*, 1866, XXXIII, Eighth Report of the Medical Officer of the Privy Council: Appendix No. 2 (3645), pp. 421ff.

23 25 & 26 Vict. cap. cciv [1862]. 'Ticketing' is mistakenly dated from 1866 in *P.P.*, 1917–18, XIV, R.C. on the Housing of the Industrial Population of Scotland, Rural and Urban: Report (Cd. 8731), p. 345, para. 794.

24 Ibid., paras 790–3. It was introduced into Liverpool in 1866. By 1888, 18,967 'houses' were under inspection. (Glasgow had 23,288.) See E. W. Hope, *Health at the Gateway* (Cambridge, 1931), pp. 150–2. Somewhat similar powers were given to metropolitan local authorities by section 35 of the 1866 Sanitary Act, but only two of them, Chelsea and Hackney, seriously sought to use them. See C. J. Stewart, ed., *The Housing Question in London 1855–1900* (1900), p. 71.

25 *England: Its People, Policy and Pursuits* (1879), I, p. 153.

26 *An Economic History of Modern Britain* (Cambridge, 1930), I, pp. 61–2.

27 Hunter, *Report on the Housing of the Poorer Parts of the Population in Towns*, pp. 145–6. On pp. 150–7, he lists the names of one-room dwelling proprietors who were found to be keeping lodgers. Most of them certainly sound Irish.

28 R.C. on the Poor Law, 1909, pp. 199, 201, 230, 231.

29 'Suggestions with regard to the Summary Jurisdiction of Magistrates in Scotland', *Transactions of the National Association for the Promotion of Social Science* (*T.N.A.P.S.S.*), 1874 [Glasgow meeting], pp. 230–3.

30 'Crime in Scotland', *T.N.A.P.S.S.*, 1877 [Aberdeen meeting], pp. 312ff.

31 See Edwin Muir, *Scottish Journey* (1935), p. 116.

32 See his introduction to his edition of Edwin Chadwick's *Report on the Sanitary Condition of the Labouring Population of Great Britain* (Edinburgh, 1965), p. xxiii. The judicious William Smart described Alison as 'neither a sentimentalist nor a doctrinaire'. See Smart's impressive 'Memorandum on the History of the Scots Poor Laws prior to 1845', appended to the Report on Scotland (p. 313) of the R.C. on the Poor Law, 1909.

33 *P.P.*, 1839, XLII, Reports from Assistant Hand-Loom Weavers' Commissioners (159), pp. 565–6. Alison concludes: 'It is my firm belief that penury, dirt, misery, drunkenness, disease and crime culminate in Glasgow to a pitch unparalleled in Great Britain.'

34 *Past and Present* (1843), Bk III, ch. 2; Bk I, ch. 1.

35 Flinn, op. cit., pp. 97–9.

36 Appendices to Eighth Report of the Medical Officer of the Privy Council, 1866, pp. 62, 213.

37 'Address on Health', *T.N.A.P.S.S.*, 1877 [Glasgow meeting], p. 100. He added 'some edifices in Paris and Berlin, and some tenement-houses and crowded slums reported of in New York and Boston'.

38 Clapham, op. cit., III, pp. 451–5.

39 A. K. Chalmers, *The Health of Glasgow* (Glasgow, 1930), opposite p. 76.

40 Cf. the figures given by Chalmers, op. cit., p. 193, with those in Clapham, op. cit., III, p. 455.

41 See especially the following papers: 'On the Ticketed Houses of Glasgow' (no. 17); and 'The House in Relation to Public Health', *Trans. Glasgow Insurance and Actuarial Society* (1877), series 2, no. 5 (repr. Chalmers, ed., *Public Health Administration in Glasgow*, pp. 170–89). He also gave, in *Life in One Room* (Glasgow, 1888), an unforgettable impression of its accumulated nastiness (originally a lecture delivered to the Park Parish Literary Institute, Glasgow, 27 February 1888; repr. Chalmers, pp. 189–206).

42 Clapham, op. cit., III, p. 462.

43 This conclusion is based partly on my reading of the evidence given to the R.C. on Housing (Scotland), 1917–18, pp. 345ff. Clapham (III, p. 463) seems to say the same.

44 See his paper, 'Defects of House Construction in Glasgow', *Proc. Phil. Soc. Glasgow*, vii (1870–1), 245ff. He may have been wrong about this, but he was ahead of his time in the clarity of his recognition of the force of habit and custom.

45 Clapham, op. cit., II, p. 495.

46 'On the Immediate Results of the Operations of the Glasgow Improvement Trust at May 1874, as Regards the Inhabitants Displaced, with Remarks on the Question of Preventing the Recurrence of the Evils which the Trust seeks to Remedy', *Proc. Phil. Soc. Glasgow*, ix (1873–5), 214.

47 See John R. Kellett, 'Property Speculators and the Building of Glasgow, 1780–1830', *Scottish Journal of Political Economy*, viii (1961), 211–32.

48 Russell, 'On the . . . Operations of the Glasgow Improvement Trust', *Proc. Phil. Soc. Glasgow*, ix (1873–5), 225.

49 Tables 69 and 73 in *Glasgow* ('Third Statistical Account of Scotland'); Clapham, op. cit. III, p. 460; R.C. on Housing (Scotland), 1917–18, pp. 345ff., paras 724–51.

50 *Report*, para. 1511.

51 Kellett, op. cit., p. 212.

52 See note 44.

53 'On the . . . Operations of the Glasgow Improvement Trust', *Proc. Phil. Soc. Glasgow*, ix (1873–5), 217.

54 Dr Hunter gives a detailed description of how this was done in his report, already referred to in note 22. On p. 58 he sums up thus: 'The administration of [these Acts] by the local authorities varies in efficiency in various places with the strength of the bye-laws, the skill, industry and independence of the officers, and lastly with the presence or want of a M.O. in places where such an appointment is desirable.'

55 In his *Report on the Sanitary Condition of the City of Edinburgh* (Edinburgh, 1865), pp. 118–19.

56   See Russell, ed. Chalmers, *Public Health Administration in Glasgow*, pp. 224–5; evidence of James Gowans (Edinburgh's Dean of Guild Courts) to Dilke Commission, QQ. 18,848–50; and, in general, Dr Littlejohn's evidence to the same, Q. 18,939ff.

57   See G. W. Barras, 'The Glasgow Buildings Regulations Act (1892)', *Proc. Phil. Soc. Glasgow*, xxv (1893–4), 158–9. The relevant legislation was the Glasgow Police (Amendment) Act of 1890, and the Glasgow Buildings Regulations Act of 1892; respectively, 53 & 54 Vict. cap. cci (Local) and 55 & 56 Vict. cap. ccxxxix (Local).

17 Metropolitan Types
London and Paris compared

Lynn Lees

How can we reconstruct the Victorian city? Pictures, newspapers, and reminiscences tangibly recreate the 'light and shade'[1] of the Victorian environment and thus present the historian with indelible images of a vanished urban world. Visual and personal links to the nineteenth century are indeed indispensable, but a note of caution must be sounded. The human memory is selective, and artists and journalists are involuntarily drawn to the picturesque, to the different. We should not neglect those sources which describe the typical as well as the unique. We should turn more often to the work of those bureaucrats and amateur statisticians who tried through their reports to keep pace with the urban world exploding around them. Although these men were sometimes too close to their subjects to do more than record and classify, the historian can return to their voluminous tabulations and turn them to his own purposes. That is, he can go beyond the numbers to discover the half-hidden structure of the nineteenth-century city.

The search for the Victorian city will be both simplified and enriched if the historian turns not only to the English past but also to the foreign analogues of his chosen subject. International comparisons of urban structures can help to establish the distinctively English qualities of Victorian cities. Moreover, they force the historian to refine his vocabulary and his analytical approach. To use the term, 'Victorian city,' is to suggest that national differences, rather than functional ones, provide the most useful way of classifying cities in the modern period. But the evidence for this assumption has not been adequately examined. If our use of the Victorian label is to have anything more than sentimental significance, we must be prepared to justify its application to English towns and to specify how and why these cities in the nineteenth century differed from hundreds of others located abroad. The search for variations on an English type should not deflect historians from the task of defining the place of English cities generally in the international urban spectrum.

Before proceeding any further with this design for research and analysis, I should add that this chapter will not attempt either of these projects with reference to 'the Victorian city,' but instead will compare two specific cities—London and Paris —during the nineteenth century. The aim of the comparison will be to illustrate certain similarities and differences of structure and of function between these capitals. Finally, I hope to justify the use of the category 'metropolis' as an urban type and to specify ways in which the English variant was unique. Whatever national characteristics link Victorian cities, it is a mistake to neglect international uniformities that can help to explain the structure of cities and the consequences of urbanization at specific points in time.

Cities such as London and Paris had a special identity in the minds of contemporaries. Cobbett's description of London as 'the Great Wen' was only one of many that marked the metropolis off from other English cities. Calling the capital 'Babylon' or simply marking it off from 'the provinces'—as was also done in France—indicates an awareness that these cities were extraordinary. They were, in fact, viewed in a highly ambivalent manner, as if they possessed both the best and the worst that the nineteenth-century city had to offer. Part of their symbolic value as prototypes of urban good and evil came from their attraction for outsiders and from their unique sizes. Indeed, their extraordinary growth, which set them apart from many other cities, was one of the primary determinants of those changes in urban geography that marked their evolution during the Victorian period. Between 1801 and 1851, Paris doubled while London almost tripled in size as a result of growth rates that ranged from 10 percent to over 25 percent per decade. Consequently, the Victorian metropolis passed the million mark by 1811, and Paris did the same thirty-five years later. By 1891, over 4,000,000 people lived in London and 2,500,000 in Paris.[2] Growing far faster than its national population, each reinforced its long-established dominance as the country's major city over the very weak claims of rivals who lacked the political and cultural importance of a capital.

In societies not accustomed to the galloping expansion of 'megalopolis,' the immense size of these cities seemed extraordinary, particularly in France where far more of the population lived in rural areas. Even in the much more urban English society, the size of London was clearly atypical. As was the case with many large English cities at the time, migration into it was a flood rather than a slowly moving stream; during the 1840s, over 300,000 people settled in the metropolis, and during the 1870s, an equivalent number moved into Greater London. Even if London's rate of expansion was slow when compared with that of northern industrial cities, its growth remained largest in absolute terms. Across the Channel, the preponderance of Paris was equally marked, and the element of imbalance even more striking, although both the rate of increase and the absolute level of migration into the French capital remained far lower than in London. (For example, about one-third as many people moved into Paris during the 1840s as settled in the English capital.) Parisian growth, nevertheless, has been called 'monstrous' and 'aberrant'; during the years between 1831 and 1851, when the French population grew only by 9 percent, Paris grew by 55 percent.[3] Not only did the capital expand enormously at a time when the national rate of population increase was slowly declining, but also it regularly attracted more newcomers, both relatively and absolutely, than the manufacturing and commercial cities which were directly affected by industrialization.

In addition to this internal expansion, both capitals induced intensive migration into nearby areas—into Greater London and the remainder of the Seine Department —producing a fringe of urban districts. During the second half of the nineteenth century, these areas grew at faster rates than did the center cities and quickly became part of the gargantuan urban regions which today dominate England and France. Already in 1851, 13 percent of the population of England and Wales lived in metropolitan London, but at that time the northern industrial region provided a second center that attracted men, money, and attention. Since 1900, however, when the economic expansion of the northern textile and metal industries slowed, London has had little competition which could redirect migrants elsewhere. Movement into the south-east intensified, producing by 1961 a metropolitan region of 722 square miles and over 8,000,000 people, itself dwarfed by the London planning region that extends roughly forty miles in all directions from Charing Cross. In France, the attraction of Paris has been even more consistently unchallenged, with the result that the expanding ring of industrial suburbs around the city proper spread throughout the Seine during the nineteenth century and beyond the department by 1918. Again, planners and administrators have been forced to redirect their attention from city to region, to an area of several thousand square miles where 18·5 percent of the French population lives.[4] The distinction between city and country no longer applies because the metropolis has constantly expanded beyond the formal limits set by its governors.

Even before suburban London and Paris engulfed the nearby countryside their links with neighboring counties and departments were close. Arthur Redford has described the 'drift' of new settlers from farm to village to metropolis that characterized migration in England during the early nineteenth century. Subsequent studies of the birthplaces of Londoners show that about half of the migrants to the capital during the Victorian period came from bordering counties and other areas of the east, south-east, and south Midlands. The Scots and the Irish were the only exceptions to the rule that movement into London decreased rapidly as the distance to travel increased. Over 50,000 Celts (one migrant in six) arrived and stayed in the city during the 1840s, although the number dropped to 25,000 during the next decade. Paris, too, recruited most of its migrants from bordering departments and the north-east part of France. Except for a stream of men coming from the Massif

Central, a legacy from a time of heavier seasonal migration, Paris in 1850 held far less attraction for those who had a long distance to travel.[5]

Although the growth of both capitals depended to a large extent upon regional migration, it should be noted that the reliance of Paris upon outsiders was much more extensive. A comparison of the birthplaces of Londoners and Parisians makes this quite clear. (See Table 17.1.) Approximately 40 percent of all Londoners during the mid-nineteenth century were born elsewhere. In Paris, migrants made up an even larger share—50 percent to 60 percent—of the capital's population. Indeed, Adna Weber has calculated that only 15 percent of the city's expansion between 1821 and 1890 resulted from natural increase. In contrast, London's growth during the second half of the century depended very heavily upon an excess of births, despite

Table 17.1   *Birthplaces of inhabitants, London, 1841–91 and Paris, 1833–96*

London	1841	1861	1891	Paris	1833	1861	1896
		(percent)				(percent)	
London born	64·9	62·1	65·0	Paris born	50·0	36·1	36·8
				banlieue	—	—	3·0
Other counties—							
England & Wales	28·9	30·4	29·4	Other departments	43·0	58·7	50·1
Scotland	1·3	1·3	1·1	Alsace-Lorraine	—	—	3·7
Ireland	7·6	3·8	1·1	Abroad	4·0	5·2	6·4
Abroad	1·8	2·4	3·4	Unknown	3·0	—	—

Sources: H. A. Shannon, 'Migration and the Growth of London, 1841–1891,' *Economic History Review*, v (1935). L. Chevalier, *La formation de la population parisienne au xixe siècle* (Paris, 1950), p. 46.

Table 17.2   *Mortality and fertility in London and Paris, 1821–81*

	London		Paris	
	Births per 1,000	Deaths per 1,000	Births per 1,000	Deaths per 1,000
1821–30	—	—	37·4	32·6
1841–50	30·0*	26·1*	31·2	29·3
1861–70	35·4	24·4	30·5	26·4
1881–90	33·2	20·4	26·3	23·7

* 1838–41 only.

Sources: Jacques Bertillon, *Des recensements de la population de la nuptialité, de la natalité, et de la mortalité* (Paris, 1907), pp. 17–18. *Annual Reports of the Registrar-General* (1841–81).

the high level of migration. Weber attributed this difference between the two capitals simply to the difference between their birth- and death-rates. (See Table 17.2.) Mortality in Paris was substantially higher, and the birth-rate lower, than in the English metropolis. To some extent, these cities were merely reflecting national demographic patterns which produced a much slower rate of population growth in France than in England at this time, but the specific effects of extreme overcrowding, poverty, and inattention to sanitation, problems which seem to have been relatively more acute in Paris, should not be overlooked.[6]

Differences in the capacity of these two capitals to house their thousands of new citizens adequately can help to account for the more dismal Parisian demographic situation. London had one substantial advantage, that of space. Although Paris remained surrounded by the *octroi* wall of Louis XVI until 1861 and by the fortifications of Louis Philippe until the First World War, London had spilled over its Roman wall centuries earlier, gradually absorbing the small settlements in the area. When reached by speculative builders and the transportation network, outlying parishes became part of London's suburban sprawl and joined the metropolitan district for all practical purposes. Thus shaped by the availability of transportation to the center and by the entrepreneurial expertise and interest of large landowners rather than by administrative fiat, London continued its haphazard development throughout the Victorian period.[7] Because its physical area was almost ten times the size of Paris, the city avoided, for the most part, those extremes of concentration that transformed blocks of gracious *hôtels* into rabbit warrens. While most of London's outside ring of districts contained fewer than twenty-five persons per acre in 1851, the lowest density in a Parisian *arrondissement* at this time was three times that level. (See Maps XII and XIII.) Although a few of the more notorious workers' quarters in central London sheltered over 300 persons per acre, these areas were very small in comparison with the large sections of the center city that were much less densely populated. Moreover, the average density per dwelling in the most tightly-packed parishes did not exceed fifteen persons per house, and rarely did it rise over a rate of ten. On the other hand, in central Paris virtually all of the central *arrondissements* north of the river sheltered more than 200 persons per acre, and fewer parks and open spaces existed to relieve overcrowded areas. As early as 1826, the IIIe *arrondissement* had an average density of thirty-five persons per house. Paris was a concentrated city whose growth both upward and outward was confined by government regulations limiting the heights of buildings and preserving the eighteenth-century boundary of the commune. Only in 1861 were adjoining suburbs annexed, and even then the area of the city was little more than doubled. This style of growth contrasts directly with the London pattern.[8]

The urban landscapes of London and Paris were, nevertheless, evolving in the same direction. By mid-century, rapid migration into the historic cores of both cities had slowed decisively. Although newcomers still settled in the center cities, their arrival was balanced by the regular exodus of others. The City of London's population, which had remained stable for the first half of the nineteenth century, declined rapidly thereafter in size. Adjoining areas in both the east and the west

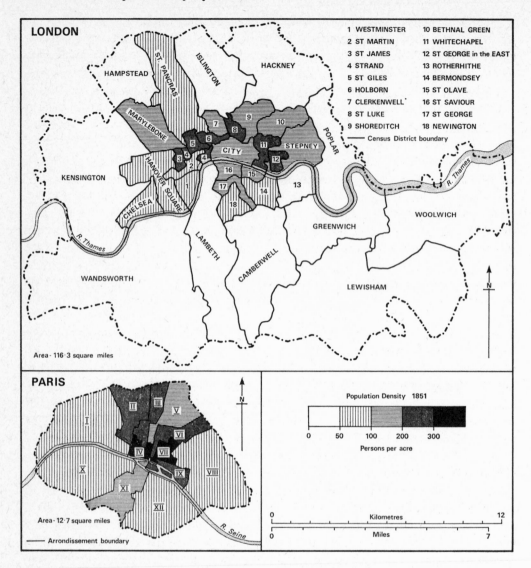

XII and **XIII**   Population densities: London and Paris, 1851

underwent a similar change around 1851: net migration into St Giles, the Strand, parts of Holborn, and Whitechapel virtually stopped, while movement into the outer ring of districts intensified. Similarly, the growth of the central *arrondissements* in Paris declined and sometimes stopped during the 1830s and 1840s in periods when the city was expanding less rapidly. After 1861 the central ring lost population regularly to the area beyond the boulevards under the impact of Haussmann's razing and an accentuated tendency to move out of the overcrowded core to areas of lower rents and lower density.[9] In both capitals, this centrifugal movement intensified the separation of social classes in residential areas which, in London, was already well advanced.

The cost of transport into the city effectively insulated the outer ring of suburbs from most working-class residents until the 1870s, and thereafter the availability of cheap trains directed them into certain areas. Meanwhile, many in the London middle class had deserted the center of town for the villas and wide streets of Kensington or Camberwell, and the Parisian bourgeoisie marked out for its own the expanding quarters that flanked the Seine in the west. The much-lauded Parisian system of mixed housing, where class divisions operated in vertical rather than horizontal space, broke down during the July Monarchy and the Second Empire. The whirlwind of renewal that changed the city geographically also changed it socially, destroying the older pattern of settlement along with the houses that had maintained it. As in London, areas in the east became much more exclusively inhabited by workers, while the middle and upper classes settled in the west. The communes of the soon-to-be-annexed Parisian *banlieue*, classic examples of the industrial suburb, became and have remained working-class areas.[10]

These currents of internal migration helped not only to differentiate areas from each other socially, but also to accelerate changes in the capitals' economic geography. As pre-industrial patterns of production broke down and fewer and fewer households lived, made goods, and sold them in the same building, these activities separated into different streets and parts of the city. Particularly in the case of capitals like London and Paris, which performed complex economic functions for the entire country, the specialization of their economic geography by region was inevitable. Each was its country's largest center of manufacturing and distribution; each provided a multitude of services and products obtainable elsewhere only with difficulty. In addition, London served as the chief port and international entrepôt for England's commercial empire. As these activities expanded, much of the manufacturing that had taken place in the centers of the capitals became unprofitable and was displaced. The watchmaker of Clerkenwell and the masons of the Place de Grève had to move elsewhere in order to make room for new banks, department stores, and offices.[11]

By the middle of the nineteenth century this transition was under way, but by no means complete. Although the secondary and tertiary sectors provided a growing share of the jobs available, industry still employed the largest share by far of the labor forces. (See Table 17.3.) London and Paris were advancing at different rates, however, in this transformation of their economies. At first glance, their industrial structures in 1850 look surprisingly similar; a variety of artisanal trades and light industries were located in both capitals, and several of these trades employed almost the same proportion of the male labor force.

Yet the more advanced state of the English economy can be seen in the greater development of several important sectors. The existence in London of substantial service and transport industries, as well as the higher proportion employed in commerce and finance, testifies to the more complex and diversified economic development of the English metropolis.[12] In Paris, each of these activities occupied a smaller percentage of the work force, in part because the city did not provide as favorable a physical or financial climate for international trade and business transactions. By

Table 17.3 *Occupations of inhabitants, London and Paris, 1851–4*

	London, 1851		Paris, 1854	
	Males	*Females*	*Males*	*Females*
	(percent)		(percent)	
Agriculture	2·1	0·1	0·2	0·1
Industry	35·3	12·2	50·1	30·0
Transport	8·1	1·0	3·0	0·1
Service	3·6	17·0	6·1	13·7
General labor and unclassified occupations	6·0	2·4	5·1	3·9
Commerce and finance	4·2	0·5	2·7	0·8
Professions, administration, education	6·4	1·1	10·1	5·3
Outside labor market	34·3	66·4	23·4	47·5

Sources: *Census of Great Britain, 1851*, 'Occupations of the People, London.'
Seine, *Recherches statistiques sur la ville de Paris et le département de la Seine*, VI (Paris, 1860).

1850, French merchant bankers had not yet diverted large amounts of energy into the joint stock investment companies that would soon export French capital and entrepreneurial skills to Central and Eastern Europe, and their methods of financing trade were more stringent than those of the English. The heyday of the French Bourse and bond market that drew foreign governments in need of cash into Paris, like pins to a magnet, lay in the second half of the century.[13] But even apart from differences in banking systems, Paris simply could not handle the volume of foreign trade that regularly passed through the Victorian metropolis. The French shipping industry was no match for the English; the *quais* along the meandering Seine bore little resemblance to the giant wet docks of the Thames, built to hold ocean-going ships. As a result, Paris was less involved with international commerce.

Yet when all parts of these urban economies are taken into account, it is clear that we are dealing with basically similar industrial landscapes. Both London and Paris were centers of artisanal production before the Industrial Revolution and remained so long afterward. Despite the general shift to a machine-dominated technology, the transition to factory production was a slow process in both cities. But each was an important center of craft production. The size of the cities meant that a local mass-market for simple necessities existed, and their status as national capitals with comparatively large, resident upper classes also provided important markets for handmade luxury goods. 'Cheap and nasty' versions of the same items could be easily produced for those who would emulate the style of the rich without their incomes. In both places, the tradition of skilled handlabor remained strong. Therefore, artisans and journeymen—tailors, shoemakers, printers, butchers, and bakers— served both the rich and the poor; they, rather than proletarians, formed the major part of the urban working class in London and Paris before 1850. In both cities, the small workshop dominated the process of production. In 1851, only 21 percent of all industrial establishments in London employed over four workers, and a mere 14 percent had ten or more employees. In Paris at mid-century, 18 percent of industrial firms employed ten workers or more. While there were many small factories in both cities, which combined work by skilled laborers and simple machinery driven by steam power, large establishments were concentrated in a few trades. The capitals could boast large building and engineering firms, and also a few big gas-works, metallurgical plants, and refineries. A small but growing number of wage laborers worked in these trades and in the transport sector, particularly on the docks or on the railroads.[14]

The English example of this artisanal-city-in-transition was, paradoxically enough, less directly affected by industrialization than its French counterpart. Initially, rather than stimulating the growth of either the textile or metal trades in London, the Industrial Revolution dampened their progress. Except for a few residues of the silk industry, textile production virtually ceased in the metropolis by 1850, and the amount of heavy industry was quite limited. London specialized in other things, in the manufacturing and finishing of many items of clothing, machinery, consumer goods, and in trades where large-scale factory production emerged only gradually. Its vast and constantly expanding home market meant that local demand for food, clothes, and housing was exceptionally strong and that other industries which had been solidly established in the eighteenth century remained in the capital. Despite pressures to lower costs and to expand the supply of goods, the London labor force maintained its primacy in many areas. Large contingents of highly skilled residents produced the finest jewelry and surgical instruments in the country, and an unceasing supply of cheap low-skilled workers were recruited into the sweated clothing trade and into jobs such as the making of boxes or matches. Many types of manufacturing, therefore, continued in the metropolitan area in spite of competition from other cities.[15]

Paris, on the other hand, had much more heavy industry. Several large metallurgical and engineering firms were solidly based in Paris, and the suburban areas that were annexed in 1860 had become by that time minor industrial areas sheltering railroad yards, chemical plants, and a variety of small factories. Although many of these plants had been driven out of the city by high rents and high wages, the pressures of decentralization drove them no further than the city wall. Yet the economic growth of Paris, which encouraged these establishments, undermined them at the same time. The strength of Parisian industry lay in the high quality of its techniques and in the abundance of skilled labor available locally. But costs of production were comparatively high. As soon as firms began to produce for a mass-market and to mechanize, they found it more profitable to move elsewhere. By the 1830s, the Parisian textile industry had become increasingly decentralized and had turned from cotton spinning to the more specialized, luxury branches of the trade—to silk, cashmere, and fine wools. Firms which needed a great deal of space moved into the suburbs or the provinces; even luxury workshops decentralized their production, allowing the routine stages of work to be done outside the city and leaving only the difficult tasks to Paris artisans. Operations which required highly skilled labor could still flourish in the capital, but industrial progress elsewhere in France contributed to the relative economic decline of the city. Over the long run, Paris, like London, would turn more and more to the provision of services.[16]

If we turn away from the economic structures of these capital cities to the structure of their labor forces, we can explore the operation of two urban societies, translating their economic functions into human terms. The first point to be made is that, during the middle of the nineteenth century, most adults considered that they had an occupation, and indicated this to the census-taker when he enquired. Whether or not they were currently employed, the vast majority of men in both capitals and a sizeable percentage of women identified themselves with one specific trade. The proportion of both men and women in the labor force, however, differed significantly between the two capitals. (See Table 17.3.) Comparatively more Londoners were supported by their families and did not work themselves. The difference in the position of women is especially marked: only one-third of London women had an occupation, while in Paris the proportion was one-half. In this case, however, the statistics are deceptive, for they do not take into account the substantially different demographic profile of the two cities. Part of this difference between the two proportions of employed women results from differences in the age structures of the two populations. In London in 1851, 32 percent of the residents were under the age of fifteen, while the corresponding figure for Paris was only 20 percent. In as much as there were substantially fewer children in the French capital, average Parisian fam;.ies in 1851 were small relative to those in London. (Compare a range of 2·01 to 2·87 persons per family in the French capital with mean family sizes between 3·5 and 4·5 persons found in London.) Death and estate records for the year 1847 in Paris indicate that only one-third of the workers' or servants' families had more than one surviving child. While bourgeois families in Paris tended to be larger, only in a few occupations did the proportion with more than one child rise over 50 percent. Local studies of London working-class families show, however, that most had between two and three children.[17]

Part of the difference, therefore, between the proportions of people in the London and the Parisian labor markets resulted from the simple fact that there were fewer children in the French capital. But two other factors, the availability of education and the frequency of child labor, also affected the rate. In England, children had a greater opportunity to attend school. One child in three under the age of fifteen living in the metropolis was listed in the 1851 census as 'scholar.' Enrollments in Paris in 1846, however, were limited to one child in five under the age of fourteen. There is also evidence to indicate that the level of child employment was higher in the French capital around 1850. If information contained in the English census is used as evidence of participation in the labor market, 10 percent of residents under the age of fifteen claimed to have had an occupation; at the same time, 11·4 percent of Parisian children of fifteen and under were employed in the primarily skilled jobs surveyed by the Chamber of Commerce. Although various kinds of factory jobs were included, many of the unskilled, casual jobs that children would have held were not covered by the enquiry. The most plausible conclusion, therefore, is that comparatively more children had jobs in the French capital.[18]

Even though demographic factors help to account for differences in these metropolitan labor forces, other pressures helped to produce this outcome. A comparison of social structures will clarify some of these forces. Statistics on the social structures of London and Paris can be obtained indirectly from the censuses of 1851 and 1854. I have reclassified information on employed residents by placing each occupational category into one of the five status groups outlined by the English Registrar-General in 1950. Comparisons between the two capitals are possible because of the degree of specificity in the occupational listings of both censuses. The report for Paris in 1854 is more general than the English tally but many of the categories used correspond exactly. In addition, distinctions made in the French census between *patrons, employés* or *ouvriers,* and *domestiques,* separate the Parisian labor force automatically into social groups. This tripartite scheme does not permit the division of French workers into detailed categories according to the nature of their jobs, but the lines of demarcation between the middle class and workers are clearly drawn. Although detailed problems of classification abound and certain trades are suspiciously hard to find among the supposedly exhaustive published lists, the French categories can be compressed into the English ones.[19]

Both London and Paris around 1850 can be described as hierarchical societies which consisted of comparatively small upper and middle classes completely outnumbered by a working class of artisans, laborers, and domestic servants. The proportion in each capital that should be counted as working class falls between 75 percent and 80 percent. The remainder of the people can be divided between two categories that include upper- and middle-class occupations (*grande* and *moyenne bourgeoisie, petite bourgeoisie*). (See Table 17.4.) In both countries, the elite composed of professionals, bankers, large employers, and administrators was quite small. Yet the top category of Parisian society appears to have been significantly larger than its London counterpart. This disproportion results primarily from the position of two groups, the bureaucrats and the *rentiers.* For example, over 46,000 persons were classified as *rentiers* or *propriétaires* in Paris; they constituted over half of category I. The figure for London's men and women of independent means and house or land proprietors was only 14,920. Even if part of this disproportion arose from different official definitions, the nature of social values and of social reality was responsible for much of it. Many English property owners also had occupations and listed them in the census, thus placing themselves in other categories; in France, a generalized bourgeois prejudice against commerce and industry probably produced the opposite effect. It also led families to retire and live on unearned income in greater proportion than in England at this time, thereby swelling the ranks of group I in Paris. This difference in the position of the *rentier* illustrates two dissimilar standards of social

Table 17.4   *Social structure of London and Paris, 1850*

Social groups	Percentage of employed population	
	London	Paris
I. Capitalists, professionals, administrators, *rentiers*	4·3	10·4
II. Lower ranking professionals and administrators, *patrons* and small employers, shopkeepers	16·6	13·0
III–V. Working Class—all levels	79·1	76·1
Skilled labor	39·7	—
Domestic service	17·9	11·0
Other semi-skilled labor	6·6	—
Clerks	2·0	—
Unskilled labor	10·6	—
Unclassified	2·3	—

Sources: *Census of Great Britain, 1851*, 'Occupations of the People, London.'
Seine, *Recherches statistiques sur la ville de Paris et le département de la Seine*, VI (Paris, 1860).

behavior and patterns of behavior. Another obvious difference in French and English social structure can be seen in the larger size of the French bureaucracy. Approximately 19,000 Parisians were employed in *administrations publiques*; an equal number worked in local and national government posts in London. (These figures include the civil service as well as the police, customs, judiciary, and local administration of the capitals.) Since Paris was half the size of London in 1850, the group in government employ in France was proportionately twice the size of the one in London. But the representation of other occupations, such as doctors and lawyers, was relatively stronger in the English metropolis. When both categories I and II are added together, therefore, the upper and middle classes of the capitals seem to have been equivalent in size, even though not identical in structure.[20]

At the opposite end of the social spectrum were the workers, who can be divided into several groups according to the level of skill and security of their jobs. Craftsmen and other skilled workers made up the largest share. Some of these men can be called the 'aristocracy of labor,' a group which Eric Hobsbawm estimates to be no more than 15 percent of the working class although it varied from trade to trade, but others were far less favored. As might have been expected as a result of London's industrial structure, the skilled—whether well or badly paid—far outnumbered those employed in semi-skilled or unskilled jobs (the proportion of men with unspecified casual jobs having been 5 percent of the working class). This division into three categories is also useful for analyzing the Parisian working class. Unfortunately, neither the Paris Chamber of Commerce nor the census divided those employed within certain industries by the nature of the job that each man did. Until other sources are discovered, a statistical comparison of the structure of the Parisian working class with that of London will not be possible. The only group that can be isolated with some assurance is the domestic servant. The number employed in this trade in the English capital was proportionately much larger than in Paris. (See Table 17.4.)[21]

Some persons were better fitted than others to rise within this hierarchical structure. The lack of access to training and to education clearly blocked many from joining the favored few in the 'aristocracy of labor' or in the ranks of the middle class. The London Irish illustrate an extreme case of a group that clustered at the bottom of the society.

About half of the employed Irish-born males living in five London parishes of heavy Irish settlement in 1851 were either employed as general laborers or had similar jobs in the transport industry, principally on the docks. Many of the rest earned their livings as construction workers, street hawkers, tailors, or shoemakers. Fewer than 2 percent could be called 'middle class,' and under 10 percent had skilled jobs of any sort; moreover, half of this latter group worked in the worst of the sweated trades and can scarcely be counted among the 'aristocrats' of labor. Charles Booth's data on the position of migrants in a wide range of London trades clearly show that most of the jobs demanding skilled labor were dominated by the London-born. Except for some branches of the building, clothing, and engineering trades which were common in the provinces and, therefore, recruited heavily from them, the list of jobs held primarily by working-class migrants is weighted towards semi-skilled and low-skilled occupations. Where the rewards were low, so were the barriers to entry. Respectable branches of artisanal trades as well as the better paid jobs on the docks, where men were protected somewhat from the vagaries of fortune and economic changes by trade unions or friendly societies, could easily take on the character of closed shops, where entry was limited to a specific number of trained apprentices, often the relatives of those already in the trade. The power to exclude outsiders could offer protection in precarious times, and newcomers tended to be those excluded.[22]

Similarly in Paris, migrants were concentrated in the lowest ranks of the working class. A survey based upon the city's death-records in 1833 shows that of the migrants from twenty-six departments (73 percent of whose occupations could be traced), 16 percent were professionals, *propriétaires*, or *rentiers*, while 77 percent worked in industry or had a salaried position. Of this latter group, over half were porters, domestic servants, unskilled laborers, tailors, shoemakers, or laundresses. Almost certainly migrants were overrepresented in these trades. In addition, Adeline Daumard has shown that the Parisian bourgeoisie, with the exception of government employees, were more likely to have been born in Paris or to have resided there for over twenty years than were men employed as domestic servants or laborers, jobs which recruited much more heavily from the provinces. Despite the fact that migrants formed the majority of the Parisian population, the bourgeoisie was dominated by

425

native Parisians or long-time residents. Booth's data on London middle-class occupations indicate that in the English capital migrants dominated education, the civil service, the ministry, and literature. Yet without information on length of residence in London of the men surveyed, it cannot be determined whether this result is incompatible with Daumard's findings.[23] Very little is known about social mobility among migrants; until more specific studies are made, it is premature to make a definite pronouncement upon their place in urban societies of the nineteenth century. The most plausible conclusion appears to be, however, that more of them entered and probably remained on the bottom levels of the society than their numbers warranted. This tendency was particularly strong in the case of identifiable ethnic groups like the Irish.

Up to this point in the analysis the structural similarities of London and Paris have outweighed the differences between them. Both capitals expanded enormously during the nineteenth century under the impact of heavy migration, each becoming the center of a vast metropolitan region. At the same time the geography of both cities underwent similar transformations, which were closely linked to wider changes of economic structure triggered by the Industrial Revolution and by their position as national capitals. Each acquired a variety of national and international economic functions which entailed the development of complex links with the provinces and with other parts of the world. On another level, the social structures of these urban societies resembled each other closely. Both were composed of similar groups with almost identical proportions in the middle class and the working class.

But a detailed comparison of the two capitals has also revealed important differences between them. The composition of the middle class, for example, differed substantially. In Paris, the elite was dominated by those claiming to live on unearned income and by men in the employ of the government, while the representation of several independent professions and of commercial occupations was much stronger in London. In keeping with England's economic supremacy, her upper and middle class was much more deeply involved in business and in other kinds of productive employment. The evidence presented in this essay indicates the presence of greater wealth and probably a more even income distribution in the English capital around 1850. Not only did proportionately more Londoners have domestic servants but also there were fewer people in the labor force and more children in school. To be sure, relative poverty within the working class is hard to measure. But the fact that Londoners had more children and lived longer than their Parisian counterparts offers circumstantial evidence that Londoners had a higher standard of living.

The most obvious difference between London and Paris, of course, lay in the realm of political structures. Paris was closely controlled by the central government, through the Prefect of the Seine and the Prefect of Police. The city was thought to be too dangerous to rule itself, and every new outbreak of revolutionary violence has reconfirmed this feeling. Even its Municipal Council had very limited powers: during the Second Empire, it was appointed from above. London parishes, on the other hand, possessed the right of self-government almost up to the point of urban anarchy:

no effective government beyond that of the City of London was installed until 1889 when the London County Council came into being. In neither case were these arrangements typical. The capitals' political structures were sharply differentiated from those of other cities. The English and the French alternatives, however, pointed in different directions. London was administratively ill-equipped to handle the day-to-day crises of metropolitan growth and change. Paris had a strong authority with easily expandable rights and powers that could, in theory at least, cope with urban problems. Yet with the exception of Baron Haussmann's concerted attack on Paris during the Second Empire, both cities moved only slowly and often ineffectively to improve the conditions of urban life. To borrow the words of one historian, 'Street improvements appeared to be a panacea for every urban problem.'[24] In fact, the status of London and Paris as capitals worked against any opportunities for constructive change and adaptation. So immense, expensive, and difficult to solve were their problems that even the halting steps toward reform taken in other cities were often denied them. As urban giants they could not be given the tools of mortal men.

The position of London and Paris as capitals decisively shaped the institutional framework within which their economic and social functions could operate. Without further research and statistical comparisons it is impossible to say whether each was structurally more like its international rival or its provincial siblings, but the special conditions under which each developed placed Paris and London in a category by themselves. The metropolis was distinct not only in size and splendor from the ordinary city but also in its institutions and its opportunities for development. Although the Victorian metropolis was unique in several ways, it should be seen as a national example of an international urban type.

Notes

1 Gustave Doré and Blanchard Jerrold, *London. A Pilgrimage* (1872), p. 2.

2 Adna F. Weber, *The Growth of Cities in the Nineteenth Century* (New York, 1899), pp. 46, 73.

3 H. A. Shannon, 'Migration and the Growth of London, 1841–1891,' *Economic History Review*, v (1935), 81; Charles Booth, *Life and Labour of the People in London*, first series: *Poverty* (1902), III, p. 124; Charles H. Pouthas, *La population française pendant la première moitié du xixe siècle* (Paris, 1956), p. 174.

4 Peter Hall, *The World Cities* (1966), pp. 30–1, 59, 68–9; Weber, op. cit., p. 47; Donald Read, *The English Provinces, 1769–1960. A study in influence* (1964), pp. 271–3.

5 Arthur Redford, *Labour Migration in England, 1800–1850* (Manchester, 2nd edn, 1964), pp. 62–6; Shannon, op. cit., 80–1; Louis Chevalier, *La formation de la population parisienne au xixe siècle* (Paris, 1950), pp. 162–7.

6 Shannon, op. cit., 80–2; Chevalier, op. cit., p. 45; Weber, op. cit., p. 240; Seine (département), *Recherches statistiques sur la ville de Paris et le département de la Seine*, V (Paris, 1840), Tables 118, 119.

7 Steen Eiler Rasmussen, *London: The unique city* (1937), pp. 23–4.

8 H. Price-Williams, 'The Population of London, 1801–1881,' *Journal of the Royal*

Statistical Society, xlviii (1885), 401–13; Louis Chevalier, *Classes laborieuses et classes dangereuses* (Paris, 1958), p. 218; Pouthas, op. cit., pp. 158–64.

9   Price-Williams, op. cit., 389–99.

10   Chevalier, op. cit., pp. 240–1; Harold Pollins, 'Transport Lines and Social Divisions,' in Centre for Urban Studies, *London: Aspects of change* (1964), pp. 41–6.

11   Booth, op. cit., second series, V, pp. 59–60.

12   François Bédarida has calculated that in 1851 the tertiary sector employed over 50 percent of the active population. See 'Londres au milieu du xixᵉ siècle: une analyse de structure sociale,' *Annales: Économies, Sociétés, Civilisations*, xxiii (1968), 278.

13   Rondo Cameron, *France and the Economic Development of Europe, 1800–1914* (Chicago, 2nd edn, 1961), passim.

14   George Dodd, *Days at the Factories; or, The manufacturing industry of Great Britain described. Series I-London* (1843); *Parliamentary Papers* (*P.P.*) 1852–3, LXXXVIII, *Census of Great Britain, 1851:* Pt I, pp. 28–9; Chambre de Commerce de Paris, *Statistique de l'industrie à Paris* (Paris, 1851), pp. 38–48; Chevalier, op. cit., pp. 107–11.

15   Booth, op. cit., second series, V, pp. 86–95.

16   Maurice Levy-Leboyer, *Les banques européennes et l'industrialization internationale* (Paris, 1964), pp. 116–18, 345–7; Chevalier, op. cit., pp. 108–17.

17   *Census of Great Britain, 1851*, Pt I, pp. 10–15; Chevalier, op. cit., p. 264; Adeline Daumard, *La bourgeoisie parisienne de 1815 à 1848* (Paris, 1963), pp. 9, 337; Lynn H. Lees, 'Social Change and Social Stability among the London Irish, 1839–1870' (unpublished Ph.D. thesis, Harvard University, 1969), pp. 94–5, 188–9; *P.P.* 1863, LIII, *Census of Great Britain, 1861*, Pt I, p. 11; R. W. Rawson, 'Results of some Inquiries into the Condition and Education of the Poorer Classes in the Parish of Marylebone in 1838,' *Journal of the Statistical Society of London*, vi (1843), 44.

18   *Census of Great Britain, 1851*, Pt I, pp. 10–15; Chambre de Commerce de Paris, p. 48; M. Gréard, *L'instruction primaire à Paris et dans les communes du département de la Seine en 1875* (Paris, 1876), p. 33.

19   More specific discussions of problems arising from the classification of occupations listed in the English census can be found in Bédarida, op. cit.; H. J. Dyos and A. B. M. Baker, 'The Possibilities of Computerising Census Data,' in H. J. Dyos, ed., *The Study of Urban History* (1968), pp. 87–112, and W. A. Armstrong, 'Social Structure from the Early Census Returns,' in E. A. Wrigley, ed., *An Introduction to English Historical Demography* (1966), pp. 209–37. Many of the same cautionary notes apply to the procedure of fitting French occupations into English categories.

20   Seine, *Recherches statistiques*, VI, pp. 626–51; *Census of Great Britain, 1851*, Pt I, pp. 10–15; David S. Landes, 'French Entrepreneurship and Industrial Growth in the Nineteenth Century,' *Journal of Economic History*, ix (1949).

21   E. J. Hobsbawm, *Labouring Men* (1967), pp. 328–36; Lees, op. cit., p. 160.

22   Booth, op. cit., second series, V, pp. 29, 131; Lees, op. cit., p. 152; J. C. Lovell, 'Trade Unionism in the Port of London, 1870–1914' (unpublished Ph.D. thesis, Cambridge University), pp. 97, 119–20, 127–31.

23   Daumard, op. cit., p. 9; Seine, *Recherches statistiques*, V, Tables 118–19; Booth, op. cit., second series, V, p. 29.

24   Anthony Sutcliffe, *The Autumn of Central Paris* (1970), p. 27.

Index

Figures in italic type indicate illustrations; those in bold type indicate principal entries. Superior figures refer to notes.